Praise for Jeffrey Toobin's

AMERICAN HEIRESS

"[R]iveting. . . . *American Heiress* is a page-turner certainly, but Toobin, a gifted writer, infuses it with much more. . . . Even if he ridicules the ideas and condemns the violent deeds of this ragtag group of revolutionary wannabes, they emerge not as cardboard villains but flesh and blood protagonists."   —*The Boston Globe*

"Mr. Toobin has used the . . . winning formula of delving deeply into an American crime story that had tremendous notoriety in its day and retelling it with new resonance. . . . [I]n an age of terrorism, the chronicle of how a sedate heiress named Patricia morphed into a gun-toting, invective-spouting revolutionary calling herself Tania holds a definite fascination."   —Janet Maslin, *The New York Times*

"Offer[s] fresh insights into this truly mythic tale. . . . [C]onnects the forces of the counterculture, Hearst's amorphous public identity, and alienation that not even Hearst's own account (published as *Every Secret Thing* in 1981) could offer."   —*Smithsonian*

"Riveting, stranger-than-fiction. . . . [A] spellbinding retelling. . . . Everything about this book feels right: the structure, the style and the tone, which is *The New Yorker* meets Raymond Chandler. As always with great writing, it comes down to a strong, distinctive narrative voice spiced with the judicious use of juicy details."

—*LA Weekly*

"[A] terrific new book out about another lurid crime story with its own toxic mix of race, class, celebrity and sex." —Associated Press

"A remarkable story, skillfully and engrossingly told . . . by the brilliant and prolific Jeffrey Toobin in his new book, *American Heiress*. . . . Even for those readers who've long since forgotten the Patty Hearst saga, or who grew up long after it ended, this account is well worth the time and attention." —*Pittsburgh Post-Gazette*

"Compelling. . . . Intriguing. . . . [*American Heiress*] capitalizes on [Toobin's] powerful storytelling ability, his expertise at identifying and explaining legal strategies and missteps, and a precise use of the language." —*St. Louis Post-Dispatch*

"Engaging. . . . Breezily written. . . . A terrifically detailed recounting of the Hearst case and its aftermath. But *American Heiress* is more than that. In telling this story, Toobin also opens a window on the surrealism of the '70s in a way that makes it all of a piece— and, in some instances, a harbinger of the future."

—*Milwaukee Journal Sentinel*

"A brilliant evocation of an era and a stunning example of reporting. Toobin tells Hearst's story—a tragedy with farcical elements— with aplomb, placing it firmly in its era."

—*Richmond Times-Dispatch*

Jeffrey Toobin

AMERICAN HEIRESS

Jeffrey Toobin is the bestselling author of *The Nine*, for which he won the J. Anthony Lukas Book Prize, *The Oath*, *Too Close to Call*, *A Vast Conspiracy*, and *The Run of His Life*, which was made into the critically acclaimed FX series *The People v. O. J. Simpson: American Crime Story*. He is a staff writer at *The New Yorker* and the senior legal analyst at CNN.

www.jeffreytoobin.com

ALSO BY JEFFREY TOOBIN

AMERICAN HEIRESS

AMERICAN HEIRESS

*The Wild Saga of the Kidnapping, Crimes
and Trial of Patty Hearst*

Jeffrey Toobin

ANCHOR BOOKS
A Division of Penguin Random House LLC
New York

FIRST ANCHOR BOOKS EDITION, APRIL 2017

Copyright © 2016 by Jeffrey Toobin

All rights reserved. Published in the United States by Anchor Books, a division
of Penguin Random House LLC, New York, and distributed in Canada by
Random House of Canada, a division of Penguin Random House Canada
Limited, Toronto. Originally published in hardcover in the United States by
Doubleday, a division of Penguin Random House LLC, New York, in 2016.

Anchor Books and colophon are registered trademarks of
Penguin Random House LLC.

Frontispiece: Courtesy of Polaris

The Library of Congress has cataloged the Doubleday edition as follows:
Names: Toobin, Jeffrey, author.
Title: American heiress : the wild saga of the kidnapping, crimes and trial of
Patty Hearst / Jeffrey Toobin.
Description: New York : Doubleday, a division of Penguin Random House, 2016.
| Includes bibliographical references and index.
Identifiers: LCCN 2016016625 (print) | LCCN 2016018859 (ebook)
Subjects: LCSH: Hearst, Patricia, 1954– | Hearst, Patricia, 1954—Trials,
litigation, etc. | Symbionese Liberation Army. | Trials (Robbery)—United States.
Classification: LCC F866.4.H42 T66 2016 (print) | LCC F866.4.H42 (ebook) |
DDC 322.4/2092 [B]—dc23
LC record available at https://lccn.loc.gov/2016016625

Anchor Books Trade Paperback ISBN: 978-0-345-80315-3
eBook ISBN: 978-0-385-53672-1

Author photograph © Robert Ascroft
Book design by Michael Collica

www.anchorbooks.com

Printed in the United States of America
10   9   8   7   6   5   4   3   2   1

To Phyllis Grann

CONTENTS

AMERICAN
HEIRESS

PROLOGUE

The doorbell rang at 9:17 on the evening of February 4, 1974. From their perch on the sofa in the living room, Patricia Hearst and Steven Weed looked at each other and shrugged. No one was expected. But it was Berkeley, so who knew?

Still, visitors were unlikely. Their cozy duplex was one of four apartments at 2603 Benvenue Avenue, a sturdy, well-made structure covered in the chocolate-brown shingles that were a signature of the neighborhood around the University of California, where both Patricia and Steve were students. The apartment offered an unusual degree of privacy. There was no door to the street, only a pair of garage doors, which were open. To enter, one had to walk up an outside stairway along the side and then find the entrance to apartment 4 on an interior walkway. Few did.

With some trepidation, Patricia and Steve walked to the front hall. Weed pulled open the door a crack and saw a woman he did not recognize. Her clothes appeared slightly disheveled.

"I'm sorry but I think I backed into your car," the woman said. "I'm sorry. Can I come in and use the phone?" Patricia turned away in disgust, thinking that the visitor had damaged her beloved MG roadster. Then, as she headed back toward the living room, she heard a crash.

Three people, all bearing weapons, burst into the apartment. The woman at the door was named Angela Atwood, and she had not had a car accident. She was acting, and she was, as it happened, an actress who had recently played a leading role in a local production of Henrik Ibsen's *Hedda Gabler*. On this night, however, she was using her talents to initiate a kidnapping.

Two men rushed in behind Atwood. Later, Weed would insist that both were black, but only one was—Donald DeFreeze, who had recently applied a political filigree to a lifetime of petty and not-so-petty crime. The other man was Bill Harris, an agitated, compulsive talker, also a theater person at one time as well as a Vietnam veteran, and currently a revolutionary. DeFreeze knocked Weed to the floor, and Patricia fled toward the kitchen, in the back of the apartment.

"Where's the safe? Where's the safe?" DeFreeze demanded. He had an almost quaint conception that rich people kept their money at home in safes. Steve and Patricia did no such thing, and Steve protested that there was no safe. "Take my wallet," Weed said. "It's all the money I have. Take anything you want!" DeFreeze, unhappy with this answer, belted Steve across the head with a homemade sap—a leather-covered piece of lead. The pain knocked Weed almost unconscious.

Atwood chased Patricia into the kitchen and put a black automatic pistol in her face. "Be quiet and nobody'll get hurt," she said. Harris ran after Patricia as well and then dragged her back toward the front door, where he placed her facedown on the floor. Atwood began tying Patricia up. She fought back—Patricia was stronger than her delicate, barely five-foot frame suggested—but Atwood managed to get some nylon cord wrapped around her arms and legs. She also tried to put a gag (actually a racquetball) into Patricia's mouth and a blindfold over her eyes, but her fierce resistance left both restraints hanging loosely around her head. Still, with Weed semiconscious and Hearst trussed, there was a brief moment of silence, which was broken by the arrival of a new face at the door.

Steve Suenaga, also a Cal student, lived in one of the apartments across the walkway. He was heading out to see his girlfriend, when he noticed some unusual activity inside apartment 4 and poked his nose in the door.

DeFreeze grabbed Suenaga and told him to get on the floor, facedown. Atwood tied him up, too. Suenaga heard Hearst whimpering, "Please leave us alone . . ."

"Quiet!" Harris said to her. "Or we'll have to knock you out."

Atwood said to DeFreeze, who seemed to be in charge, "They've seen us, we've got to kill them."

Suenaga raised his head, and DeFreeze struck him on the head three times with his weapon—an M1 carbine converted into a machine gun.

A moment later, Weed was able to rise from his stupor. He made a wild rush at Harris, who blocked his advance with the sawed-off automatic he was carrying and slammed Weed to the ground. Weed then bolted for the back door. He pushed through the screen, busting it off its base, fled into the tiny yard, ran past his marijuana plants, vaulted the fence, and disappeared into the night. Two hostages—Hearst and Suenaga—remained tied up on the floor by the door.

Lying facedown, Patricia began to realize that she was confronting more than a robbery. These people had demanded a safe but didn't look for one. They didn't even take Steve's money. What did they want? Why would mere thieves take the trouble to tie her up?

She soon found out that her fears were justified. Atwood left first for the getaway car, a 1964 Chevrolet Impala convertible that the kidnappers had carjacked earlier in the evening. (In the backseat of the car, tied up and dazed from a pistol-whipping from Atwood, was Peter Benenson, the owner of the vehicle, covered by a blanket. He had been accosted after leaving a nearby market in Berkeley.) Camilla Hall, a poet as well as a terrorist, was at the wheel of Benenson's car, which she had backed into the driveway of 2603. The trunk was ajar, awaiting human cargo.

The commotion had started to draw attention. In the house next door, a Berkeley student named Sandy Golden and three classmates were studying for a bacteriology exam in his apartment. When they heard a woman scream, they ran onto a small porch that faced 2603.

For a moment, they stared eye to eye with DeFreeze, who lifted his weapon and fired two quick bursts at the students. He missed. Atwood jumped in the passenger seat.

Harris, meanwhile, was half dragging, half carrying Patricia down the stairs along the side of the building toward the waiting car. She was kicking, screaming, and wearing nothing but a bathrobe, a pair of panties, and fuzzy blue slippers. Harris raised the trunk with one hand, but it bounced up and slammed shut. He groaned in frustration. He now had to put Patricia down and retrieve the key from Camilla Hall, in the driver's seat. While Harris went for the key, Hearst . . . disappeared. The kidnap victim had wiggled free from her bonds, for Atwood's training for the stage had yielded few insights about knot tying. After a few panicked seconds, Harris located Hearst, who had scampered into the garage, near her own MG. Harris again lifted her up and this time managed to deposit her in the trunk and close the lid on top of her.

Then, for Patricia Hearst, chaos yielded quickly to darkness and silence.

And cold. The temperature in Berkeley had dropped into the forties, and she had only her bathrobe for warmth in the trunk. A trunk? What was she doing there? What did they want? Why was this happening?

In a way, she already knew: it was because of her name. It is difficult, at a remove of several decades, to conjure what the name Hearst still meant in 1974. Fame, wealth, and power on a grand scale. Her grandfather William Randolph Hearst (who died several years before Patricia was born in 1954) was a newspaper publisher, but that barely captures the scope of his renown. The Chief, as he was known, built the grandest private residence in the United States, San Simeon, and his life inspired perhaps the greatest American film, *Citizen Kane*.

Patricia was just nineteen, restless and unformed, the product of a lonely childhood in a big wealthy family. She was the middle child of five daughters, the rambunctious one, the one the governess (that was the term the family used) disciplined with a hairbrush. She was sent off to boarding school when she was only ten and was in and out of five schools before she graduated from high school. She was never exactly expelled—Hearsts were not expelled—but it was suggested that she would be happier elsewhere, especially by the nuns who ran the Catholic institutions chosen by her mother. Mrs. Hearst was displeased, often.

Catherine Campbell Hearst was a regal presence, as austere as the limestone mansion in Hillsborough where she and Randolph Apperson Hearst presided. In temperament, she differed greatly from her husband. Catherine was tightly wound, a stickler for proprieties, a Georgia beauty who persuaded Randy to make a kind of halfhearted conversion to Catholicism. In contrast, Randy liked nothing so much as a long day in a duck blind followed by a big meal fueled by scotch and red wine. He was a businessman of sorts, the publisher of the family's flagship newspaper, the *San Francisco Examiner,* but his role there was mostly that of a figurehead. Still, Randy possessed a kind of journalistic curiosity about how the rest of the world lived. Patty was his favorite; he related to her spunk and moxie as well as to her aversion to formal education. And she, in turn, loved her dad and allowed him to call her Patty without complaint. For others, she preferred Patricia. As for the Hearst name or her family's history, Patricia had little interest. She made a point of never seeing *Citizen Kane.*

Her final high school had been the Crystal Springs School for Girls, in Hillsborough, which aspired to be a finishing school in the mode of Madeira or Miss Porter's, where the daughters of the San Francisco elite would prepare graduates for a women's college and, more important, for marriage. But by the early 1970s, the turmoil of the era had penetrated the manicured hedges of Crystal Springs, and the girls there began wanting something more than the lives of their mothers. Some wanted careers. Patricia wanted Steve. After graduating from Princeton, Steve Weed took a job teaching math at Crystal Springs, and his shaggy good looks generated more than academic interest among the girls in his classes. Patricia began driving her MG to his apartment for, she said, extra help with her geometry homework.

They began sleeping together right around her seventeenth birthday. Steve was twenty-three.

Patricia accumulated enough credits during her peripatetic education to graduate from Crystal Springs after the eleventh grade. A year at a local junior college followed. When she told her parents she was staying with girlfriends, she was actually spending most of her nights at Steve's. Upon her return from a long trip to Europe, she announced to Randy and Catherine that she would be moving in with Steve. Her mother wanted Patricia to enroll at Stanford, which was more socially prominent, but Patricia preferred the University of California at Berkeley, where Steve had started graduate school in philosophy.

There, abruptly, the fun stopped for Patricia, even if few people knew the depth of her despair. In those days, as always, she spoke in a kind of lock-jawed monotone that gave away little of what she was feeling. That fall, in their first days together in the apartment, Patricia pinned her hope for happiness on an actual marriage, or at least an engagement, and she hinted that she expected a ring. (In the manner of most unmarried couples who lived together in those days, they felt compelled to sign the lease as "Mr. and Mrs. Steven Weed.") In time, Patricia got a ring—sort of. For Christmas, in 1973, Steve gave her a pair of moccasins and a piece of paper with the word "ring" written on it, as a kind of promissory note. Hardly a romantic gesture. Steve thought Patricia was sarcastic. Patricia thought Steve was condescending. (Both were right.) Patricia enrolled as a sophomore at the university, and when she told Steve she was thinking of becoming a veterinarian, he informed her that she could never master the math and science requirements. She chose art history instead.

Reluctantly, Patricia lapsed into the life of a proto-housewife. She bought furniture and crammed every surface with knickknacks—little vases, ceramic shoes and bunnies, glass jars with stoppers, tiny sculptures. Tasteful prints, mostly Impressionist, lined the walls. (Patricia's mother, in a forlorn nod to Catholicism for a daughter living in sin, gave the couple a sixteenth-century stations of the cross bas-relief.) Above their bed, on the second floor, in an oval frame, was the photograph of the couple that had run in the newspaper to announce their engagement. The decor matched their lifestyle—middle-aged. (Still, in a couple of ways, their tastes did reflect those of their generation. By the front door, there was a rack of their favorite wine, called Romance, which retailed for ninety-nine cents a bottle, and they always maintained a generous stash of pot, which Steve also tried to grow in the garage as well as in the backyard.)

Patricia cooked and cleaned; Steve did neither. They did everything, including have sex, on his schedule, not hers. Patricia made the beds or left them unmade, as she did on February 4. Their evening together on that occasion was typical. Dinner was chicken soup with tuna fish sandwiches, followed by *Mission: Impossible* on television, then schoolwork in silence on the downstairs sofa. Bathrobe and slippers had become her home uniform. At nineteen, *this* was her life? On the eve of her kidnapping, Patricia later acknowledged, she was "mildly suicidal."

Now, incredibly, those fuzzy slippers were evidence of her struggle to escape from Bill Harris. Police photographers would note the presence of one on the stairway and the other on the driveway. And where was Steve, the man of the house? Her fiancé? Her protector? He had run away. "Take anything you want!" Steve had told the kidnappers, and indeed they had. They had taken Patricia Campbell Hearst, and now she was locked in the trunk of a car.

The kidnappers brought three vehicles to 2603 Benvenue that night. There was the stolen convertible with Hall at the wheel, along with the kidnap team of Atwood, Harris, and DeFreeze; one hostage, Benenson, was in the backseat, and the other, Hearst, was in the trunk. Emily Harris (Bill's wife) and Nancy Ling Perry parked a stolen station wagon parallel to the front of Hearst's apartment. A sometime sex worker turned terrorist, Ling (as she was known) was volatile even by the standards of her colleagues; when she saw DeFreeze firing at the students on the porch next door, Ling stuck her automatic weapon out the window of her car and shot two quick bursts at them as well. She also missed. Waiting on the other side of Benvenue, facing 2603, was a blue Volkswagen Beetle driven by Willy Wolfe, the youngest in the group and the least experienced criminal. He was joined by Patricia Soltysik, known to all as Mizmoon, the name given to her by her occasional lover the poet Camilla Hall. The plan was for Wolfe to lead a three-car caravan away from the scene, followed by Hall driving the kidnap vehicle and Emily Harris and Nancy Ling Perry in the rear.

The plan nearly failed at the outset. Wolfe made a left onto Parker Street, with the two other cars following close behind. Suddenly a Berkeley police cruiser appeared from nowhere and flashed its lights at the Volkswagen. The officer walked slowly to the driver's side to talk to Wolfe.

Were they caught? The kidnapping itself was over quickly, but the gunfire prompted several calls to the police.

DeFreeze and Harris, with automatic weapons splayed across their laps in the Chevy, faced a moment of decision. With eyebrows more than words, they asked each other, could we waste a cop? If the officer was questioning Wolfe about the kidnapping, it was only a matter of minutes until the whole plan unraveled. The only way to protect their mission—their "action," in the military argot they favored—was to kill the cop right now. DeFreeze was a killer, as he had proven just a few weeks earlier. But Harris was bigger on talk than violence; in Vietnam, he'd never even removed the rifle from beneath his bunk. But that was then. In unspoken accord, DeFreeze and Harris prepared to open their doors and turn their guns on the officer who was questioning their comrade.

Just then, DeFreeze and Harris saw the police officer walk away from Wolfe's window, return to his vehicle, and drive away. Later, they learned that the officer had only stopped the Volkswagen to tell Wolfe to turn on his lights.

And so the three cars headed off into a future that was nearly as mysterious to the captors as to their captive. There were just eight of them—Donald DeFreeze, Bill and Emily Harris, Angela Atwood, Camilla Hall, Nancy Ling Perry, Mizmoon Soltysik, and Willy Wolfe—but they called themselves an army, the Symbionese Liberation Army. As they drove off into the California night, with Patricia Hearst as their unwilling passenger, their unofficial motto might well have been "What now?"

PART ONE

NERVOUS BREAKDOWN NATION

The kidnapping of Patricia Hearst is very much a story of America in the 1970s, not the 1960s. From the vantage point of nearly half a century, the two decades sometimes merge in historical memory as a seamless epoch of idealism and change. Generalizations about eras are necessarily imperfect, of course, but these two decades actually look very different in retrospect. The 1960s were hopeful, the 1970s sour; the 1960s were about success, the 1970s about failure; the 1960s were sporadically violent, the 1970s pervasively violent.

There were assassinations and riots in the 1960s, but the vast majority of protests were peaceful and even, occasionally, successful. After an extraordinary public outpouring from African Americans and their allies, official racial segregation, which had plagued the United States since its inception, faded in the 1960s. Men walked on the moon. The economy boomed. Much of the discontent in the 1960s emerged from a sense of possibility—that blacks and whites could live in harmony, that the Vietnam War could end, that there could be a better future for all. Those hopes, for the most part, were dashed by the 1970s. Richard Nixon became president in 1969 and did not end the war. An oil embargo in 1973 led to gas lines. The economy stagnated. The stock market lost almost half its value between 1973 and 1974. Inflation hit 12 percent a year. Watergate confirmed every cynical expectation about American politics.

The nature of protests changed, too. Nixon might not have brought the Vietnam War to a close, but he did end the draft. Freed from the threat of conscription, many thousands of otherwise apolitical young people drifted away from the antiwar movement. The marches against the war became considerably smaller. But as the protests shrank in size, they built in intensity. Frustration, especially at Nixon's reelection in 1972, convinced many that the era of peaceful demonstrations had passed. To a degree that can scarcely be imagined today, the bomb became a common mode of American political expression. In 1972, there were 1,962 actual and attempted bombings in the United States, with twenty-five people killed; in 1973, 1,955 bombings, with twenty-two killed; in 1974, 2,044 bombings, with twenty-four killed. The movement was small, but those who remained were the violent core. Membership in the Weathermen, the most notorious bombers in the counterculture, shrank from four hundred in the late 1960s to just fifty in the early 1970s, but their bombings continued.

No region symbolized the rapture of the 1960s or the venom of the 1970s more than the San Francisco Bay Area. The Summer of Love, a carnival of music, drugs, and sex in 1967, established the city as the center of the American counterculture. This largely spontaneous festival drew about a hundred thousand young people to the Haight-Ashbury neighborhood and brought the word "hippie" into broad circulation. In a similar vein, the Free Speech Movement, at Berkeley, also began in the mid-1960s. At the time, speakers on campus were allowed to advocate only on behalf of the Democratic or Republican Party, and an earnest young cadre of students began conducting demonstrations arguing for a greater range of expression. In short order, the movement defined Cal as the epicenter of American student activism. These events became magnets drawing young people to the Bay Area—for adventure, for politics, for some fantasy of what the country might become. Yet by the 1970s, both San Francisco and Berkeley were wilting under the weight of so many new arrivals. Politics and music yielded, in significant measure, to drugs and violence.

And then, in an especially sinister confluence of events, a series of unspeakable crimes beset San Francisco almost simultaneously. A serial killer—who portrayed himself as a kind of macabre inversion of a counterculture figure—taunted police for several years in the late 1960s and early 1970s. He killed at least five and perhaps as many as thirty-seven people and then bragged about the killings in a series of letters to Paul Avery, a crime reporter at the *San Francisco Chronicle*. The letters contained mysterious codes and symbols that gave rise to the killer's nickname—Zodiac. He spoke in a kind of hippie argot with its ersatz Eastern mysticism (and poor spelling), but his message could scarcely have been darker. "I LIKE KILLING PEOPLE BECAUSE IT IS SO MUCH FUN IT IS MORE FUN THAN KILL-ING WILD GAME IN THE FORREST BECAUSE MAN IS THE MOST DANGEROUE ANAMAL OF ALL."

As 1974 began, Zodiac contacted Avery again with a single, chill-ing message: he was back. Not surprisingly, in a kind of cosmic refuta-tion of the Summer of Love, San Francisco became synonymous with crime in the 1970s. Clint Eastwood's Dirty Harry, a San Francisco detective, wreaked vigilante justice on the outlaws who afflicted the city. Karl Malden and Michael Douglas played television detectives fighting the same kind of mayhem in *The Streets of San Francisco*.

But fictional criminals represented only a minor threat to the city compared with the nest of genuine psychopaths who appeared in late 1973. In October of that year, a group of black Muslims who called themselves the Death Angels began a concerted campaign to kill white people in a series of random, senseless, vicious murders—simply because they were white. They became known as the Zebra killers, after the code name for the radio frequency that the San Fran-cisco police assigned to the investigation, and they probably spread more terror than any set of criminals in modern American history. As with the Zodiac killer, the Zebra marauders represented an evil parody of the world that many had hoped to create in the 1960s. They met at the Black Self-Help Moving and Storage company, which was affiliated with the Nation of Islam, and they cruised for victims in one of its vans. The spree began on October 19, 1973, when a young couple, Richard and Quita Hague, were accosted on Telegraph Hill, where they were taking a walk after dinner. Forced into a van, they were driven to a remote location in the city, where Quita was hacked to death with a machete. Richard was mutilated too, but he somehow survived. Then the killings accelerated. A future mayor, Art Agnos, was shot on the street after a community meeting. Another victim was taken to a warehouse and tortured to death—his hands, feet, and genitals cut off one at a time. In all, there would be fifteen murders and eight attempted murders. "The eruptions of unspeakable violence made this most beloved of cities seem like hostile territory," the San Francisco historian David Talbot wrote, adding that the "lovely jeweled city became strange and ominous—the way one's house feels after it's been broken into and ransacked. Whites saw blood in the eye of every able-bodied black male, and every black man saw fear and rage in white faces. . . . The city's very identity began to dissolve." Two more men were killed on December 22, 1973. Another was killed on Christmas Eve.

The Zebra crisis reached its apogee on the night of Muhammad Ali's second heavyweight fight with Joe Frazier, which took place in New York's Madison Square Garden. Ali was a hero to the Death Angels, and after watching his victory in a theater on a closed-circuit feed, they decided to celebrate with a vengeance. On a single night, they shot five people, a random assortment of white San Franciscans going about their business, including a sixty-nine-year-old man celebrating his birthday by buying donuts; a homeless man; a woman on her way to a fabric store; a woman doing her laundry. (She was the only white person among a dozen black people in the Laundromat.) Four of the five died, and the city neared a collective nervous breakdown. The headlines the next day read "Madmen Slay Four on City Streets," "SF Killing Spree—5 Shot on Streets."

These stories appeared on Tuesday, January 29, 1974. Patricia Hearst was kidnapped on the following Monday.

American movies during World War II usually portrayed combat units as paragons of regional and ethnic diversity; they might consist, for example, of an Italian American from Boston, a Jewish soldier from Brooklyn, and a slow-talking sharpshooter from Texas. The Symbionese Liberation Army represented a kind of devil's inversion of these celebratory archetypes, updated for a new and very different world. With one exception, they all came from somewhere else and represented part of the great youthful migration to the Bay Area. As it happened, though, they filled distinct niches in the ecosystem of the counterculture. There was a radical black man (Donald DeFreeze) and a crazed Vietnam vet (Joe Remiro). The SLA consisted mostly of women, and they too fit well-known profiles. The group included a militant lesbian (Patricia Soltysik), a scary vixen (Nancy Ling Perry), and an otherworldly poet (Camilla Hall), as well as an empty-headed actress (Angela Atwood). Finally, there was an idealistic young boy (Willy Wolfe). Like all human beings, the members of the SLA were more complex than any stereotype, yet it is still possible, through them, to see how different tribes on the coast formed and related to one another.

During the brief life of the SLA, its members issued thousands of words in proclamations, communiqués, and interviews. But verbosity did not mean coherence. For the most part, the SLA spoke in a kind of pidgin leftist dialect, with phrases borrowed from the fashionable sources of the era. These included Pan-Africanist solidarity movements; Cuban and South American Marxism, especially the Tupamaros of Uruguay; and samplings from China (Mao Zedong), Germany (the Baader-Meinhof gang), and Italy (the Red Brigades). In truth, the rhetoric meant little. The words were scarcely understood by the SLA members who uttered them and totally ignored by the public who heard them. The infantile spirit of the SLA's public expression is best captured by the phrase with which the group closed its communiqués: "Death to the fascist insect that preys upon the life of the people."

But if the SLA did not have a coherent ideology, it did have a spirit—an anarchic intensity drawn from the chaos of the time and place. Criminals, by and large, avoid attention, but the SLA sought it out, including for its most appalling crimes. Several of the key figures in the group were trained as actors, and there was an unmistakable element of guerrilla theater in their operations. For the SLA, performance was not a means to a goal but often the goal itself.

The legacy of the SLA itself may be nonexistent, but its story provided a kind of trailer for the modern world. The kidnapping of Patricia Hearst foretold much that would happen to American society in a diverse number of fields. The story illuminated the future of the media—especially television and book publishing—the culture of celebrity, criminal justice, and even sports. The Hearst kidnapping itself had an effect on the politics of the 1970s, including on the career of the governor of California, Ronald Reagan. In other words, even though the kidnapping was an anomalous event, it provided hints of what America would become.

Above all, though, the story of the kidnapping is the story of a single young woman. Few people in American history have been subjected to as dramatic a transformation of circumstances as Patricia Hearst. In an instant, her life of ease and privilege vanished, replaced by an ordeal of pure terror. And then—most remarkably of all—she responded to this extraordinary trauma by becoming a member of the very group that took her freedom away.

Or did she?

FROM INSIDE THE TRUNK

The three-car caravan, with Patricia Hearst in the trunk of the middle car, inched through the darkened streets of Berkeley. The group maintained a cautious speed, well under the limit, to avoid any further attention from the police. Disoriented, frightened, cold, and alone, Patricia had no idea where they were going or why. Still, it was in her nature to resist. A more timid teenager might have remained frozen in terror, but Patricia, while still in the dark of the trunk, shucked off her restraints and blindfold. As Bill Harris learned when she howled for help and nearly escaped in her driveway, this woman was a fighter.

Patricia was still just learning the neighborhood. She had the status of a sophomore, but that was because she received a year's credit for her time at junior college. Then she had spent the fall as a clerk at a department store. She'd been a student at Cal for only a few weeks. In that period, her life was circumscribed by the fifteen-minute walks to and from her classes. Still, she had explored enough of the storied campus to recognize that her family had practically built it.

One Hearst in particular. Everyone passing by the Cal campus drove by the grand Beaux Arts pile of the Hearst Memorial Gymnasium. The facility contained several gyms and three pools, including a famous one on the roof, which is surrounded by urns and statuary. The building's main office included an incongruous feature for an athletic facility—a large oil portrait of a woman dressed in fashionable attire for the turn of the previous century: Phoebe Apperson Hearst.

Then, as now, it is a Cal tradition for university staff and faculty who pass through the gym office to acknowledge Mrs. Hearst's portrait and thank her out loud for her largesse to the university.

With her slim build and diffident smile, Phoebe resembled her great-granddaughter Patricia. And though Phoebe is less well-known than many in her family, she established a template for Hearst women. Phoebe never graduated from college or held a full-time job as such, but she set her own goals, pursued them intently, and saw a remarkable number through to conclusion. She was not easily deterred. She had a soft voice and a fierce will.

Born in Missouri in 1842, Phoebe and her parents moved to California in the gold rush era. Though instructed only briefly in a one-room schoolhouse, Phoebe always placed a high value on education and possessed a firm sense of the rights of women, including their right to vote. When she was just twenty, in the midst of the Civil War, she married a rough-hewn mining prospector named George Hearst, who was two decades her senior. George made and lost several fortunes in quartz mines and other ventures, and his peripatetic life kept them separated for much of their marriage. (He even served briefly as a U.S. senator from California.) George loved to buy land, and through good times and bad he held on to one special parcel, forty thousand acres near San Simeon Bay in the Santa Lucia Mountains, about two hundred miles south of San Francisco.

On April 29, 1863, Phoebe gave birth to the couple's only child—William Randolph Hearst. Phoebe devoted herself to her son with singular intensity, toting him with her on trips around the world and trying to direct the boy's relentless energy into productive pursuits. Her success was mixed—Will was expelled from Harvard for neglecting his studies—but the young man soon discovered he had a talent for the newspaper business. George Hearst had purchased the *San Francisco Examiner* in 1880, mostly as a vehicle for his political ambitions, but his son saw the paper as the means to his own ascendancy. By the turn of the century, the young publisher had parlayed the *Examiner* into an empire—a chain of newspapers, a major political voice in the country, and the beginnings of a vast fortune. William Randolph Hearst was known ever after as the Chief.

His mother, during this time, began a project of her own. California had boomed in the nineteenth century, but the state's flagship university remained a backwater. Phoebe made it her mission to turn Berkeley into a university worthy of the nation's biggest state. She demonstrated her commitment by financing a master plan for the campus, which was known as the Phoebe Hearst Architectural Plan and adopted by the regents in 1900. Then, to a remarkable degree, Phoebe set out to build the buildings laid out in her plan. In some cases, she financed the construction out of the funds that George left to her, and in others her son honored her by paying for the construction himself.

For all of Phoebe's accomplishments, she was not a celebrity. Her son, William Randolph Hearst, was famous and notorious.

There has never been an American publisher who wielded power with such zest and swagger. After taking over the *Examiner* in 1887, Hearst bought the *New York Journal* eight years later (with Phoebe's help) and established a ferocious rivalry with Joseph Pulitzer's New York *World*. Their papers introduced the phrase "yellow journalism" into public discourse, and Hearst, it is often claimed, led the nation into the Spanish-American War as a circulation-building stunt. (In *Citizen Kane,* Orson Welles as Charles Foster Kane instructs a reporter on the ground in Cuba, "You provide the prose poems, I'll provide the war!")

Hearst's politics began in a populist mode, and he won two terms as a Democratic congressman from New York. His journalistic and political ascendancy was such that he sought his party's presidential nomination in 1904. And though his political ambitions were never fully realized, he kept buying up newspapers around the country, eventually accumulating more than two dozen. Still, the Chief's journalistic heyday was relatively brief, lasting only until the Depression, when changing tastes, as well as economic conditions, thwarted his plans to expand further. By World War II, the Hearst papers, like the Chief himself, had shed their populist spirit and settled into a hard-core conservatism. In any event, by that point Hearst was at least as well-known for his scandalous personal life as for his newspapers.

In 1897, Hearst, then thirty-four, became infatuated with a teen-age vaudeville dancer named Millicent Willson. He courted her for six years, and they married in 1903. She bore him five sons over the next decade, including in 1915 the twins David and Randy, Patricia's father. Shortly after their birth, the Chief met an eighteen-year-old Broadway chorus girl named Marion Davies, and he began pursu-ing her with the same kind of ardor he brought to his journalistic crusades. Hearst used his newspapers' columns to promote Davies's show business career, and they soon commenced a public romance that would endure for the remainder of their lives. Millicent refused to give Hearst a divorce, and Hearst refused to leave Davies. The standoff lasted for decades.

The five Hearst boys grew up amid the icy feud between their parents. For the most part, they lived in their mother's apartment in Manhattan, though their real homes were the boarding schools to which they were all shipped at early ages. The boys also visited their father and Davies in California, first in their mansion in Beverly Hills and then in the vast castle the Chief built on his mother's land at San Simeon. Hearst (and Phoebe) ultimately quadrupled his landowner-ship, to about 270,000 acres, and hired the architect Julia Morgan to design more than a dozen buildings on the property. The castle itself, with 127 rooms, soars above the California coastline, and its twin tow-ers are international landmarks. (Among other features, Hearst also built the world's largest private zoo at San Simeon.) Perhaps most remarkably, San Simeon might not even have been the Chief's favor-ite residence. Near the Oregon border, Hearst lavished attention on another remarkable estate called Wyntoon. This Bavarian-themed hunting and fishing resort was every bit as lavish as San Simeon and a great deal more private.

The Chief did his best to promote Davies as a movie star, which her talents failed to justify, and the couple became known for the lavish parties on their estates. Perhaps not surprisingly, the Hearst boys grew up rich in financial resources but otherwise impoverished. None of them flourished. All five did poorly in school, and not one graduated from college. The Chief and Davies were serious alcoholics, and all five sons were problem drinkers, of varying severity. Randy emulated his father by attending Harvard without graduating. As the Chief's biographer David Nasaw wrote, "The boys, following in their father's footsteps, continually ran into debt and called on their parents to bail them out. This they did, as had Phoebe before them, but never without complaining."

After Randy's ignominious departure from Harvard, the Chief gave him a sinecure as an assistant to the publisher of the Hearst paper in Atlanta. There Randy fell for the most socially prominent debutante in the city—Catherine Campbell, the nineteen-year-old daughter of a telephone company executive. They married in 1938, in what was described as Atlanta's wedding of the year, which included nine bridesmaids and fifteen groomsmen. The ceremony was Catholic, and Randy, who had been a nonobservant Presbyterian, became a nonobservant Catholic in deference to his bride.

Trauma visited the young couple almost immediately. Catherine became pregnant soon after the wedding and gave birth to a daughter, also named Catherine, in 1939. Much later, the elder Catherine would describe her daughter's medical issues in veiled terms. In Patricia's criminal trial, Catherine testified that her eldest daughter "has a shortage of hemoglobin" and was subject to ear infections. This might have been true, but it obscured the larger truth that young Catherine was mentally disabled, a matter of some shame in that less enlightened era. The tragedy turned the child's mother ever more deeply to her Catholic faith. It also led to a ten-year gap between Catherine and the next child, Virginia, born in 1949. Another significant gap followed, until she had three more daughters in quick succession: Patricia Campbell Hearst, on February 20, 1954, followed by Anne in 1956, and Victoria in 1957.

After a few years in Los Angeles, Randy and Catherine Hearst and their five daughters settled into a château-style mansion in Hillsborough, the toniest of the San Francisco suburbs. The Chief, who died in 1951, despaired about the business acumen of his sons, so he took steps to make sure that they would enjoy comfortable livings while preventing them from tampering with his beloved newspapers. According to the terms of the trust that established the management structure of the Hearst Corporation, the five sons and their heirs could never control more than five of the thirteen seats on the Hearst board. In 1965, Randy was named chairman of the executive committee of the Hearst Corporation, and in the early 1970s he was also designated the publisher of the *San Francisco Examiner*. Neither title meant much. Professional managers ran the corporation and the newspapers.

Randy Hearst dedicated his life to leisure—shooting deer near San Simeon, trolling for sailfish off Mexico, duck hunting anywhere fowl might be found. Closer to home, he played tennis and swam at the Burlingame Country Club. He spoke in a plummy diction that seemed old-fashioned even at the time. (A loose woman was a "Sally Roundheels," and he was forever freshening drinks with "just a splash" of one spirit or another.) Like many sons of volatile fathers, Randy erred on the side of emotional restraint. There was a formality about him, but a decency, too. He lived surrounded by retainers—from newspaper reporters to domestic servants—and he might not have regarded them precisely as equals, but he treated everyone well and inspired a kind of loyalty.

His wife, Catherine Hearst, was another matter altogether. In fairness, Randy left to Catherine (and a succession of governesses) the real work of raising five daughters, and Catherine struggled more than most with what was called, in her era, the generation gap. Her rules—no blue jeans on visits to San Francisco!—drew eye rolls from her daughters. Catherine's Catholic faith was deep and real and shared by no one else in the household. She sent all five daughters to Catholic schools, which they all fled, sooner rather than later. She insisted on the completion of academic work and met resistance from her daughters from their earliest school days. (Academic distinction did not run in the family. As noted above, none of the five sons of William Randolph Hearst graduated from college, and only one of the five daughters of Randy and Catherine Hearst, Virginia, graduated from college.)

The Chief had become a thoroughgoing reactionary by the time he died, but Randy inherited none of the hard edges of his father's politics. He was a Republican, to be sure, but his passions ran more to sport than to the ballot box. Randy's charitable obligations were conventional but numerous and heartfelt; indeed, on the night Patricia was kidnapped, he and Catherine were in Washington at a function for a foundation, which Randy chaired, to bring high school students to visit the U.S. Senate. Catherine, on the other hand, had harsher political views and a perfect outlet for them, too. In 1956, Governor Goodwin J. Knight, a Republican, appointed Catherine to the Board of Regents of the University of California. It was a measure of the Hearsts' influence, and Phoebe Hearst's legacy, that Catherine was chosen, because she had neither attended school in California nor graduated from any college at all. But as the student protests began at Berkeley and elsewhere, Catherine became known as a fierce hard-liner and a strong ally of Governor Ronald Reagan's. (As Patricia later observed, "My father is a registered Republican who always votes Democrat. My mother is a registered Democrat who always votes Republican.") In her family and on campus, Catherine's mission was the same: impose discipline.

Her most notable failure on that score was with her middle daughter. By the standards of the day, Patricia Hearst's teenage rebellions were modest, but they were real. She was not her mother's daughter.

Of all the Hearst daughters, Patricia rejected Catholic school, and the Catholic faith, the fastest. She was sent away to Convent of the Sacred Heart when she was just ten, and the lesson she learned best there was how to provoke the nuns. As Patricia later recalled, one nun had a practice of leaning over students and yelling directly in their faces. "When she did this to me one day, the idea flashed in my mind that I could make her stop by shocking her," she recalled. "So when she paused for breath, I very deliberately said, 'Oh, go to hell!' It worked, stopped her cold." Patricia started high school at Santa Catalina School, another Catholic boarding school about a hundred miles south of Hillsborough, and she loathed it there as well.

Patricia lived for summers, when she could revel in the joys of San Simeon and Wyntoon and in the company of her father and their three dogs, Whiskey, Pablo, and Mike. Patricia was an athletic kid, and the vast play spaces of her many homes (and country club) appealed to her. At twelve, she was the only daughter who took up Randy's invitation to learn to shoot. They went duck hunting together, and the education proved useful in a way that surely neither could have imagined at the time.

Patricia took an early interest in boys, which was distressing to her mother but typical for the times. She had her first real boyfriend at fifteen, and when she moved to Crystal Springs the following year, she made a determined play for a hot young teacher named Steven Weed. "He was everything a high school girl could want: a college graduate, an older man, so mature, so experienced, so sophisticated," she said later. "I suppose I threw myself at him, but I hope not in any obvious way."

Weed took her attention as his due, for he had an imperious style for a man in his early twenties. He was determined to prove that he would not be intimidated by the Hearsts, even as he nearly became a member of the family. For example, as his relationship with Patricia ripened, Weed flunked Vicki Hearst in his math class, even though she was a borderline student. He enjoyed his role as Patricia's tutor in life, and for a time anyway she reveled in the attention of an older man. Of course, the attraction itself was a form of rebellion for Patricia—in light of the differences in their ages and status and the forbidden nature of student-teacher contact. Considering the basis of their relationship—which would be seen as outrageous, if not unlawful, at a later time—the Hearsts were tolerant of Steve. (They couldn't stand his mustache, however, and their first gift to him was a razor.) Still, in light of the Hearst family tradition of older men courting teenage girls, they were hardly in a position to complain.

As Patricia moved toward her college years, her relationship with her mother deteriorated. Catherine wanted Patricia to be a debutante; Patricia refused. Catherine wanted Patricia to break it off with Steve; Patricia moved in with him instead. Catherine wanted Patricia to go to Stanford; Patricia decided to follow Steve to Berkeley. With time to kill before she started classes at Cal, Patricia even took a job as a clerk at Capwell's, an Oakland department store, in a brief foray to see how the other half lived. There, she had a modest political awakening as she saw how the store made many of her colleagues work off the clock, keeping their hours down, so they would not be eligible for benefits.

Patricia and Steve Weed lived modestly on Steve's $650-per-month teaching stipend and Patricia's $300-per-month allowance. Steve had enjoyed long weekends at the family compounds at San Simeon and Wyntoon, but during the school year he preferred to stay closer to home. Those festive outings yielded to somber evenings with his fellow graduate students, which bored Patricia to tears, sometimes literally. One rare dinner where Patricia actually showed some interest in the conversation involved Errol Morris, another graduate student in Steve's program, who was also starting to display the eclectic interests that would later make him a celebrated documentarian. As it happened, shortly before this dinner, Morris had gone to Wisconsin to interview Ed Gein, a notorious serial killer and grave robber. This story of life's dark side interested Patricia a great deal more than the dreary academic politics that her boyfriend preferred to discuss.

Some of Weed's friends called him Mr. Spock, after the *Star Trek* character, because of his austere, highly logical personality. (He was a teaching assistant in a logic class at the university.) Reflecting later on Patricia's personality, he expressed himself more like a professor than the boyfriend of a nineteen-year-old: "She judged things as they arose in the concrete, not along any systematic lines of principle." In short order, this side of his personality began to grate on Patricia. Once, during a dispute at the dinner table, he picked Patricia up and deposited her outside their front door, until he decided she had cooled off enough to be readmitted to their home. During another fight in the car, he pulled over to the side of the road and said, "If you don't like it, you can get out and walk home." Patricia almost did, until she realized it was her car.

Still, their relationship moved forward on a kind of automatic pilot. They became engaged through a sort of osmosis rather than an actual proposal. They notified Patricia's parents without ceremony. One night at dinner with Randy and Catherine, Patricia mentioned their plan to marry while Steve was in the bathroom. Catherine was from the old school when it came to publicity for the family; she believed that a woman's name should be mentioned in the newspaper three times: when she is born, when she dies, and when she gets married. But she made an exception and decided that the engagement (and the looming end to their sinful living arrangements) should be announced posthaste. This quaint society tradition would have unexpected consequences.

Randy summoned an *Examiner* photographer to the estate in Hillsborough, and Patricia and Steve (sporting a fresh haircut and his only blazer) posed in front of the fireplace. Patricia smiled; Steve barely grinned. Hearsts were always big news in California, so the story ran not only in the *Examiner* but also in the rival *San Francisco Chronicle*. On December 19, 1973, under the headline "Patricia Hearst to

Marry," the *Chronicle* story began, "Mr. and Mrs. Randolph A. Hearst of Hillsborough have announced the engagement of their daughter Patricia Campbell Hearst to Steven Andrew Weed." The next three paragraphs summarized the pedigrees of the betrothed, and then the story concluded,

> Patricia graduated from Crystal Springs School, studied at Menlo College, and is a junior in art history at UC-Berkeley.
>
> The young people plan to be married early next summer.

The wedding was set, very tentatively, for June 29, 1974.

On the night of February 4, as the vintage convertible crawled through the darkened streets near campus, Patricia could only reflect bitterly on her fiancé. *Take anything you want,* he had said. They sure had. They had taken her. And Steve, who was supposed to be her protector, had run away.

Then, after a few minutes, and less than a mile of driving, the traffic disappeared, and the caravan slowed to a halt at a clearing on a quiet street called Tanglewood. Someone popped the trunk, and Patricia, with some help, extricated herself. The residential street was only a little brighter than the interior of the trunk. Patricia saw some hedges and wondered if she could make a break for it. But she was surrounded by eight people; she couldn't outrun them all. It was clear that a diminutive black man was in charge, for he was the one who said, "How the fuck did she get untied?" His subordinates shrugged. Patricia pleaded to be let go. Within a moment, a blanket was tossed over her head, and she was bundled into the back of the station wagon. (Benenson was left on the floor of his convertible and told not to call the police.)

"Shut your mouth, bitch," the black man said to Patricia, "or I'm going to blow your fucking head off."

Within seconds, they were moving again, but for Patricia, being in the back of the station wagon was better than being in the trunk of the convertible. Now she could hear what they all were saying, including how the others addressed their leader as Sin. *Sin?* He actually called himself *Sin?* These people, she thought, were really evil incarnate.

THE SLA

Before the night was out, Patricia learned that the leader's name was not *Sin* but *Cin*. That was short for his adopted name of Cinque M'tume, a combination of the Swahili words for "prophet" and the number five, which was the assigned name of the African chief who led the slave revolt aboard the ship *Amistad* in 1839. Patricia also learned that Cin had taken a title too: general field marshal in the United Federated Forces of the Symbionese Liberation Army. Still later, Patricia would discover that he was born Donald DeFreeze and that the grandeur of his pretensions existed in inverse proportion to the shabby realities of his actual existence.

DeFreeze was thirty and the oldest of Patricia's captors. Born in Cleveland, the first among eight children, he was apparently loathed from birth by his father. Cin later said that his father broke his arms, as punishments, on three occasions. He dropped out of school at fourteen and escaped his father by fleeing to Buffalo. There DeFreeze was promptly arrested several times, including for car theft, and before he was eighteen, he endured about two and a half years in a state reform school.

DeFreeze spent the 1960s in a nomadic journey around North America—Buffalo, Newark, back to Cleveland, Canada—until ultimately he made his way to Los Angeles. When he was eighteen, DeFreeze met Gloria Thomas, who was twenty-three and already the mother of three, and the couple soon married. Their union was fraught. They had three children together, though DeFreeze later said he thought only two of them were his. Their separations were frequent and lengthy; their reunions, tempestuous. DeFreeze worked occasionally as a housepainter. His most enduring attachment was to the Akadama brand of plum wine, which he drank incessantly.

Guns and bombs were his obsession and his downfall. DeFreeze was almost the opposite of a master criminal; he was most inventive in finding ways to get caught. In New Jersey, he tried to kidnap the black caretaker of a synagogue in hopes (he thought) of obtaining a ransom from the rabbi; in Cleveland, he was arrested coming out of a bank with two guns and a bomb; in Los Angeles, he was stopped carrying a pair of bombs on a bicycle; he paid a prostitute $10 for sex, then pulled a gun on her to get the money back. Remarkably, in light of this long series of crimes during the 1960s, DeFreeze never received much more than probation. After one arrest, in 1968, a court-appointed psychiatrist wrote that DeFreeze was an "emotionally confused and conflicted young man with deep-rooted feelings of inadequacy. . . . His disorganization and impaired social adjustment seem to suggest a strong schizophrenic potential. . . . His fascination with firearms and explosives makes him dangerous."

DeFreeze's run of luck in sentencing finally ran out in 1969 after he pistol-whipped a Hawaiian tourist in Los Angeles and stole a check from her purse. He was caught when he tried to cash it two days later. At his trial, DeFreeze rejected the aid of a lawyer and represented himself, with predictably disastrous results. His defense was built around a rambling and largely incomprehensible explanation of how the victim's check came to be in his possession. After his conviction, DeFreeze was given an indeterminate sentence: five years to life in prison. He was sent, fatefully, to a prison called Vacaville.

Vacaville was the original link that connected the eight kidnappers. They were all part of what was known, loosely, as the prison movement, and it was through this work that the SLA emerged most clearly as a case of metastasized good intentions. Vacaville was the closest prison to Berkeley, about fifty miles away, and as such it attracted the students and other activists who wanted to commune with inmates. About three dozen people from Berkeley and the surrounding areas made regular pilgrimages to Vacaville to tutor inmates and to learn from them. Several of these tutors and other visitors were young women; and prisoners, notably DeFreeze, welcomed the opportunity for contact with the opposite sex. In the relatively unstructured environment of Vacaville, there were chances for intimate exchanges between inmates and visitors; the frisson of forbidden encounters, especially those interracial in nature, gave these meetings an undeniable charge.

It was true, too, that California prisoners confronted appalling injustices, starting with the system of indeterminate sentencing, under which convicts were sent to prison not for specified periods but rather for broad ranges of years. (DeFreeze's sentence of five to life was typical.) A parole board, basically an arm of law enforcement, determined release dates. Inmates suffered the worst of all worlds—living in a punitive environment, free from rehabilitative services, while depending for their release on a quixotic process designed to determine whether they had been rehabilitated. Anger among prisoners simmered, then exploded.

The prison movement had a superstar—George Jackson. Born in 1941, Jackson was nineteen when he received the classic indeterminate sentence of one year to life in prison. He never again saw the outside of prison walls. By the late 1960s, Jackson had become a leader among the inmates. Both handsome and powerful—he did a thousand fingertip push-ups a day—Jackson had affiliations with the Black Panther Party and founded his own gang, the Black Guerrilla Family. Revered by his fellow prisoners and loathed by his guards, Jackson became embroiled in the most notorious series of violent events in California prison history. On January 13, 1970, a prison fight at Soledad was silenced when a guard shot and killed three black inmates. Three days later, after the announcement that the guard had been cleared in the shootings, a different guard was killed in apparent retaliation. Jackson and two other inmates were charged with first-degree murder, and these defendants came to be known as the Soledad Brothers. Their case became a cause célèbre for the Left.

During this period, Jackson became a voracious reader and loquacious letter writer. He steeped himself in the liturgy of the New Left: Marx, Lenin, Mao, and perhaps most notably Régis Debray, a young French philosopher whose work with Fidel Castro and Che Guevara led him to develop the "foco" theory. The idea behind foco was that revolutionary change could be led by small bands of "vanguard groups" that would inspire the broader population to rebel. Jackson began exploring these ideas, and meditating on prison life, in letters to his lawyer, Fay Stender, and others. As Jackson was awaiting trial for the murder of the guard, Stender arranged for publication of a collection of those letters under the title *Soledad Brother*. Jackson's letters combined autobiography with a blazing indictment of American racism, which he wrote was "stamped unalterably into the present nature of Amerikan sociopolitical and economic life." The book came garlanded with a rapturous introduction by the French intellectual Jean Genet, achieved best-seller status in both the United States and France, and marked Jackson as the rugged philosopher-king of the prison movement.

California prisons shuddered with violence in this era. In 1970–71, nine guards and twenty-four inmates were killed inside prison walls, and George Jackson's own story came to its perhaps inevitable conclusion as well. On August 21, 1971, someone smuggled a gun to Jackson in San Quentin. He freed several of his allies from solitary confinement, and then his group took six guards and two white inmates as hostages. Five of these men, three guards and the two inmates, were later found dead in Jackson's cell, with their throats slit. Scores of heavily armed law enforcement officials converged on the prison. "It's me they want," Jackson told a comrade, and then he walked into the prison courtyard, where he was killed instantly by a marksman's bullet. Two thousand people attended his funeral. (In a characteristic gesture, the Weather Underground set off bombs at a pair of California Department of Corrections offices to commemorate Jackson's death.)

A year later, Jackson's final book, *Blood in My Eye,* was published posthumously. It became the bible of the Symbionese Liberation Army.

A tall, awkward twenty-year-old Berkeley student named Willy Wolfe provided the link between the black Vacaville prisoners and the white student radicals. At the time, Wolfe knew little about politics and nothing about prisons. Yet this young man—little more than an overgrown boy, really—served during his time in Vacaville as the catalyst for the creation of the SLA. Wolfe also became a central figure in the life of Patricia Hearst.

After his first year at Berkeley, Wolfe moved into a rambling, broken-down old house at 5939 Chabot Road, in a rough neighborhood of Oakland. The house operated as a kind of commune, with a shifting roster of politically attuned residents. The owner's girlfriend ran a food cart called Peking House, which was usually stationed near the Cal campus, so the house itself came to be called by the same name. Wolfe went to Vacaville for the first time in March 1972, to write a term paper for a class in African American studies. He stayed on to become a tutor, and he brought his friends and roommates along with him. Wolfe's fellow Vacaville tutors, who came to include Russ Little, Joe Remiro, Nancy Ling Perry, and Mizmoon Soltysik, went on to form the core of the SLA.

The white visitors congregated at the prison's Black Cultural Association, which was a self-improvement club of sorts that offered classes on African American history and culture, among other subjects. In this respect, the BCA was a fairly typical establishment response to the black power movement—an attempt by prison authorities to allow black inmates to express ethnic pride in a productive, nonthreatening manner. Its meetings had a Pan-Africanist flavor. They opened with a clenched-fist salute to the flag of the Republic of New Africa and a chant in Swahili. As in the outside world, many black inmates at the time changed their "slave names" to those that reflected an African or Muslim affinity. Here, in that spirit, Donald DeFreeze became Cinque M'tume.

It wasn't long, though, before it became apparent that the visitors were not doing tutoring in any conventional sense but rather clandestine political organizing. They smuggled in banned books, like *Blood in My Eye,* and talked about revolution with the prisoners. They all gravitated toward DeFreeze—now known as Cinque, or Cin—who reigned over them with a Delphic near silence. "Follow black leadership" was a well-known phrase in the counterculture at this time, so Cinque's white visitors paid him considerable deference.

They also grafted their fantasies about Jackson onto the less deserving DeFreeze. In prison, Cin began working his way through the same reading list as Jackson did a few years earlier, and there were other parallels between their lives. Both were African American men, of similar age, who spent most of their lives enmeshed in the criminal justice system, and both viewed themselves as self-taught intellectuals and revolutionary leaders. But DeFreeze amounted to a junior varsity Jackson. In almost every respect, DeFreeze was a lesser man—not as intelligent, not as good-looking, not as strong, not as charismatic, not as competent. To paraphrase Marx, if George Jackson was tragedy, then Donald DeFreeze, as Cin, was farce.

On December 11, 1972, Cin was transferred from Vacaville to Soledad prison. There his positive disciplinary record earned him an assignment working at a training facility for guards, off the main prison campus. Alone on duty, on March 5, 1973, DeFreeze walked through an open door, scaled a six-foot chain fence, and vanished. He headed for the Bay Area, about 130 miles north of the prison.

Hitchhiking and walking, DeFreeze made his way to the one place he knew he would be welcome: Peking House, in Oakland. Given his friendship with the residents, it was an obvious destination for him but not, apparently, to the authorities. Prison officials noted DeFreeze's escape but made virtually no effort to find him. Over the next few months, DeFreeze would take steps to avoid his nonexistent pursuers, but he was, essentially, a free man.

Still, he was worried that he'd be caught in Peking House, so he asked Russ Little to help find him a new place to live. Little steered his friend to another activist who had been an occasional visitor at Vacaville—Patricia "Mizmoon" Soltysik. Within a few weeks, DeFreeze had moved in with Soltysik in Berkeley, and the pair were soon lovers as well as co-conspirators. (Mizmoon, who was bisexual, had just broken off a relationship with Camilla Hall, who was devoted to her.) A few months later, Nancy Ling moved in too, and Cin became romantically involved with her as well.

Patricia was to learn much later that the union of DeFreeze, Soltysik, and Ling marked a peculiar turning point for the inchoate SLA. The future members had met through Willy Wolfe's efforts to teach and organize at Vacaville prison. But once the half a dozen or so protagonists assembled in the Bay Area in early 1973, their relationships became personal as much as political. They were, in short, a veritable counterculture Updike novel, their romantic attachments a bewildering roundelay. Everyone slept with everyone—except for Wolfe. This was in keeping with the broader cultural moment, which was the decade or so after the ascendancy of the birth control pill and before the advent of AIDS. But the polymorphous intimacy of the SLA was both a reflection of its brief, fierce intensity and a reason for its downfall.

Inside Vacaville, the future comrades had spun their revolutionary fantasies insulated from the realities of life on the outside. But now

DeFreeze, though nominally free, disappeared into a well of rage and paranoia. Closeted with Mizmoon, who worked in the Berkeley Public Library, and Ling, who alternated waitressing with sex work in San Francisco, he imagined himself the leader of an actual movement. He even gave it a name. He envisaged a fruitful alliance of different ideas and people—a symbiosis. He turned this noun into an adjective: "Symbionese." Their goal would be freedom—thus, "Liberation." And he would wage war against the status quo with an army. For a symbol, DeFreeze adopted a seven-headed cobra, with each head representing one of seven principles of African heritage—unity, self-determination, collective work, cooperation, purpose, creativity, and faith. Cin had learned these concepts in his studies with the BCA, in Vacaville, and they are a perversion of the same ideas that underlie Kwanzaa, the African American holiday that takes place around Christmas. Nancy Ling, the in-house propagandist for the SLA, even drew up a constitution, dated August 21, 1973. "The Symbionese Liberation Army has selected the Seven-Headed Cobra as our emblem because we realize that an army is a mass that needs unity in order to become a fighting force," Ling wrote. "It is a revolutionary unity of all people against a common oppressor." She went on, using a phrase that would recur in all SLA communications, "And with the venom of our seven heads we will destroy the fascist insect who preys upon the life of the people."

The fanaticism of DeFreeze, Mizmoon, and Ling meant little without the help of people who were willing to put their revolutionary ideas, however half-baked, into action. That was where Russ Little and Joe Remiro came in. Both boasted of proletarian roots. Little, a Floridian, called himself "a white Southern cracker" and claimed that he received his first shotgun at the age of seven. But Little overstated his backwoods origins for effect. His background was middle class—his father was a civilian electronics mechanic at Naval Air Station Pensacola—and Russ grew up with the paradigmatic ambition for all-American boys of his generation: he wanted to be an astronaut. Russ graduated near the top of his high school class, won a scholarship to the University of Florida, and majored in engineering.

But like so many of his generational peers, Little experienced a personal transformation at college. He took a philosophy class, taught by a Marxist graduate student, and changed his major to philosophy. He started writing for an underground paper. He was appalled by the killings of the student protesters at Kent State in 1970. Still, even then, Little only managed to rouse himself to wander the West Coast with a girlfriend, Robyn Steiner, surviving off food stolen from grocery stores. They slipped into Peking House out of lethargy more than commitment, and Little turned to prison work out of guilt that he was doing so little for the revolution. He was, in short, always more hippie than killer.

Remiro, on the other hand, was more of a killer. Unlike his friend Russ Little, Joe Remiro was a true proletarian, a son of pre-gentrification San Francisco. His father emigrated from Mexico and drove a laundry truck for a living; his mother horrified her Italian parents by marrying a Mexican. They lived in the Sunset District, then heavily conservative and Catholic, and turned their son over to the nuns for his education. Joe took to the discipline, if not the book learning; he barely graduated from high school. One day, Remiro walked by an early anti–Vietnam War protest at the City College of San Francisco, and he taunted the demonstrators. They taunted him back and dared him to enlist, which he did the next day. "I was gung-ho, man," he said later. "I wanted to kill a commie for Christ in those days."

He frequently had the chance to kill. In Vietnam, Remiro was assigned to a long-range reconnaissance patrol, which meant that he was sent on lengthy forays deep into enemy territory. He described his duties this way: "They go through an area and they kill everything living—dogs, cats, women, children, anything. When they're through, there's not supposed to be anything alive behind them." When he completed his first tour of combat duty, he signed up for another, and he wound up serving through the most intense period of the war, from 1966 to 1968. When Remiro returned to the States, he was diagnosed with what was then called PVS—post-Vietnam syndrome. A later generation would call the malady post-traumatic stress disorder. "I lost my way somewhere in Vietnam," Remiro said much later, "and lost my empathy for other human beings."

Back home in San Francisco, Remiro self-medicated with whatever he could buy from dope dealers. He worked odd jobs. Girlfriends came and went. His political views hardened. He was neither a Democrat nor a democrat but rather a combatant. "The revolution don't have nothin' unless they have an organized military," Remiro said. "Unless you have military tactics and strategy and trained theoreticians—military theoreticians. Discipline is a necessary evil." He believed the coming cataclysm would leave many casualties. The "revolution is horrible to look forward to—years and years of urban guerrilla civil war in America—horrible to so clearly see it coming and know how many fine people will be killed."

Military service had left Remiro with one useful skill, especially for a self-professed revolutionary. He became an expert in all matters relating to guns: how to build, modify, dismantle, and fire virtually any kind of firearm and to train others to do the same. For this reason, Remiro became the unofficial paramilitary trainer for the counterculture in the Bay Area. He often took trainees to the Chabot Gun Club, in the hills above Berkeley. One day, a Cal law student and a friend happened also to be on the club's range. "That afternoon I noticed a group of three or four men shooting at the far left of the range, dressed in camos and shooting what I thought was an M-1 carbine," he recalled. "Sometime while my attention was on my own target, I heard someone to my left let loose a three-shot burst that sounded like a fully automatic weapon, something illegal in California at the time." The law student and his friend "looked at each other and we each mouthed the words, 'Auto ?!?!'" In light of the dangerous and unlawful firepower nearby, the pair decided to depart the premises posthaste. The man with the machine gun was Joe Remiro, and the student was Lance Ito, who later became the judge in the criminal trial of O. J. Simpson.

DeFreeze fancied himself a leader of the African American people, even though the Symbionese Liberation Army never had a single black member, except for himself. He disdained conventional politics, even during the spring of 1973, when a genuine African American political crusade was taking place in front of him. Bobby Seale, of the Black Panthers, who could scarcely be accused of moderation, was running a serious campaign for mayor of Oakland. (He came in second but lost the runoff to the incumbent.) Unwilling to share the tiny spotlight of Ling and Soltysik's attention, DeFreeze ignored Seale's campaign in favor of his own self-indulgent, and doomed, crusade.

The events leading directly to the kidnapping of Patricia Hearst in February 1974 began the previous fall, when DeFreeze fixated on a different perceived rival in Oakland—Marcus Foster, the city's superintendent of schools. Foster had no idea who Donald DeFreeze even was, but Cinque imagined that they were in a death struggle for control of the destiny of the city. In his messianic way, DeFreeze vowed that only one of them would survive.

Marcus Foster's life once looked as if it were heading in the same direction as Donald DeFreeze's. Born in 1923 and raised in the ghettos of Philadelphia, he drank wine as a boy, fought more than he read, and hung out with peers who were destined for the penitentiary. But steeled by the example of his mother, who named him after the Roman emperor Marcus Aurelius, he developed an unyielding belief in the value of education. He graduated near the top of his high school class and went on to the only nearby institution of higher education that would welcome a striving but poor African American, the all-black Cheyney State Teachers College. He graduated near the top of his class in 1947 and much later went on to obtain a Ph.D. in education from the University of Pennsylvania.

During his two decades in the Philadelphia public school system,

Foster offered students both an example and a lesson. His own life story showed that anyone, including an African American, could achieve success. As a principal, he turned around an elementary school, then the city's main school for children with disciplinary problems. As an administrator, he steered a middle course between the city's right-wing mayor, Frank Rizzo, and the ascendant black power movement. In the words of Foster's biographer John Spencer, "Above all, Foster wanted his students to fit into and excel in the mainstream—not to vindicate themselves to disapproving whites, but to claim a birthright."

Once, at a meeting of top school officials about gang violence, ten actual black gang members burst into the room and began firing guns. "Hey, what are you doing?" one shouted. "Talking about gangs? We'll show you what a real gang is!" After the intruders were pushed from the room, Foster admitted that he had set up the demonstration. (The guns fired blanks.) Foster told his colleagues he wanted to show them "how you might feel if you were a kid and you didn't know when or where something like this would happen to you." Marcus Foster was an unusual man. Later in 1970, he was named Oakland's school superintendent.

In the fall of 1973, the SLA had a constitution and exactly three members: DeFreeze, Soltysik, and Ling. Still, the trio had a group of friends who had the potential to be converted into more active supporters. Willy Wolfe had moved out of Peking House and into an apartment with Joe Remiro. Angela Atwood, an aspiring actress from Indiana, had split with her husband and started a romance with Russ Little, before she moved on to an even more torrid affair with Remiro. Thero Wheeler, an eccentric BCA member at Vacaville, escaped over the summer and spent time with DeFreeze and the two women. But the SLA as an entity had done exactly nothing, nor had it given any sign that it would do anything in the future.

DeFreeze and his roommates followed the news obsessively, and Mizmoon Soltysik used her time at the library to provide DeFreeze and Ling with research material to craft the SLA polemics. They all clipped newspapers, including the thriving underground press, and filed stories, indexing each by name and subject matter. They were political pack rats, and even though DeFreeze rarely left the apartment, much less participated in the life of his community, he always let his acolytes know what he thought about the outside world. In 1973, Marcus Foster was much in the news. Through Mizmoon, Cinque closely followed, and passed judgment upon, the superintendent.

Oakland had a third as many students as Philadelphia but perhaps twice as many problems, as well as perhaps the most divisive municipal politics in the nation, which whipsawed Foster and his deputy Robert Blackburn (also from Philadelphia) as soon as they arrived. On the one hand, Foster had to appease the conservative governor of California, Ronald Reagan, and his local ally William Knowland, the publisher of the *Oakland Tribune,* who stood for low homeowner taxes and tough discipline in the schools. On the other, Foster was confronted by a militant and growing black power structure, led by Bobby Seale and others in the Black Panthers, which was based in Oakland.

The issue of school violence underscored the dilemmas Foster faced. A grand jury report in July 1973 showed that there had been forty-two assaults and one murder on school property in the past year, as well as almost $1 million in property damage. Foster responded by ordering the placement of armed security guards (but not police officers) in the schools. Republicans denounced him for coddling criminals; the Panthers said Foster was a tool of the oppressors (and volunteered to be hired to handle school security themselves). Foster tried to walk the line between demands for more security and calls for more community control. In the summer, he said he was studying a plan, funded by the federal Law Enforcement Assistance Administration, to make the schools safer. It was a routine request for federal help from a superintendent in a big city school system, and while Foster received criticism from both sides, he nevertheless became a popular figure in the city. In 1973, Oakland renewed his contract for four years, which was cause for celebration, because it was widely known that other cities were looking to poach him.

Still, in one small apartment, fury against Foster grew. DeFreeze assigned Ling to draft an indictment against Foster and Blackburn, drawing on the fringe underground publications that Soltysik had gathered from the library. The core accusation involved the use of federal funds to pay for security guards in the Oakland schools. The document charged the two men with "the forming and implementation of a Political Police Force operating within the Schools of the People." It said that they were compiling "Bio-Dossiers through the Forced Youth Identification Program" to build files for the "Internal Warfare Identification System."

The language was incoherent, but the underlying rage was real. Thero Wheeler remembered a discussion at the apartment that fall. "We were sitting around at the house one day drinking wine," he recalled for Vin McLellan and Paul Avery, the authors of *The Voices of Guns,* "and somebody started talking about this dude Foster. At the time there was a lot of feeling against him in the community. Bobby Seale was raising hell about him and all. All of a sudden DeFreeze sits up and says, 'Man, we are going to waste that nigger!'"

November 6, 1973, was a typical, exhausting day for Foster and Blackburn. They had become close friends, despite the differences in their background. Blackburn was white, an idealistic former Peace Corps member from a middle-class background. There were signs, at that moment, that they had turned things around in Oakland. The school security crisis had eased, and the two men had just finished a negotiation with the teachers' union over a new contract. "I tell you, Bob, the Lord's in this thing," Foster had once teased his less religious friend as they bounded cheerfully from one meeting to another, and Blackburn replied, "Yeah, he's saving us for some really indescribable misadventures."

At a city council meeting that afternoon, Foster urged the members to restore funding to keep school gyms open for after-school activities. From the council chamber, the pair raced back to the administration building for an uneventful school board meeting. Shortly after 7:00 p.m., the two men gathered their belongings and headed to the parking lot, in an alleyway behind the building. The sun had set, and the asphalt was slick from recent rain. Blackburn noticed three people waiting there, and he quickened his pace to reach his Chevy Vega so he could drive Foster, and then himself, home.

Nancy Ling fired first, with two flashes coming from the muzzle of her handgun, a Walther PP .380 automatic. She missed with the first and hit Foster's leg with the second. Donald DeFreeze stepped forward next and fired two blasts from a 12-gauge Remington shotgun. The pellets raked Blackburn's back, and he spun and staggered but remained upright. (He had twenty-three entry and exit wounds and might have been saved by a leather appointment book in his breast pocket.) Then Mizmoon Soltysik walked calmly toward Foster, who was lunging for the car door. In her hand was a .38 Special Rossi revolver. She fired as she walked closer, hitting Foster repeatedly. After he fell to the ground, facedown, Soltysik stood over his unmoving body and fired a final shot into the back of his neck, severing his spinal column. He was dead before the ambulance arrived. Blackburn survived.

DeFreeze, Ling, and Soltysik raced two blocks to a getaway car, where Remiro and Little were waiting to drive them to safety. The "action," as the SLA called the assassination, was completed. The next day, a document written by Nancy Ling arrived at Berkeley radio station KPFA.

SYMBIONESE LIBERATION ARMY
WESTERN REGIONAL YOUTH UNIT

Communique No. 1.	Warrant order
Subject: The Board of Education,	Execution by
Implementation of Internal Warfare	Cyanide bullets
Identification Computer System	

Date: November 6, 1973

Warrant Issued By:
The Court of the
People . . .

On the afore stated date, elements of The United Federated forces of The S.L.A. did attack the Fascist Board of Education, Oakland, California, through the person of Dr. Marcus A. Foster, Superintendent of Schools, and Robert Blackburn, Deputy Superintendent.

Written in the radical cant that would become familiar in the months ahead, the document explained the Foster assassination as a protest against the practices of "Amerikan financed puppet governments in Vietnam, The Phillipines [*sic*], Chile and South Africa." It went on, "The Black, Chicano, Asian and conscious White youth in our communities recognize the importance of the Oakland-Berkeley area to the liberation struggle of all oppressed people." The communiqué also made specific references to the federal funding of Oakland school security as a justification for the assassination. After several more paragraphs of similar harangue, the document concluded,

DEATH TO THE FASCIST INSECT
THAT PREYS UPON THE LIFE
OF THE PEOPLE

S.L.A.

Three months later, when Patricia was wrenched from her apartment by DeFreeze, Bill Harris, and Angela Atwood, she had no idea about their motives. As she lay in silence in the back of the station wagon on February 4, the shock began to wear off and her adrenaline rush receded. In the course of the kidnapping, she had been hit in the cheek with a gun butt, and the concrete steps scraped her legs. Her wounds oozed and throbbed as she lay under the blanket. Still dressed only in her bathrobe and underwear, her slippers now gone, she was somehow both cold and hot. Her injuries burned, but she shivered. She murmured a question about what happened to Steve Weed, and DeFreeze growled at her to shut up.

Later, she heard DeFreeze say the words for the first time—that she had been taken by the Symbionese Liberation Army. At first, Patricia couldn't place the name. What? Who? Then it hit her. These were the people who killed Marcus Foster. These people were not just kidnappers; they were killers. Her fears redoubled.

4

THE POINT OF NO RETURN

Beneath the blanket in the back of the station wagon, Patricia had no idea where they were going. Their destination was an SLA safe house in Daly City, a blue-collar suburb of San Francisco. Under normal circumstances, the trip from Berkeley took about forty minutes. But in planning for the action, the SLA thought that the authorities might be checking the traffic coming off the Bay Bridge, which is the most common route out of Berkeley. So the kidnappers took a long detour south to the less traveled San Mateo Bridge and then drove north to Daly City. The trip dragged on for more than an hour.

On the way, DeFreeze's group referred to each other only by code names, and Cinque—DeFreeze—took the lead in establishing discipline. "Shut up or we'll kill you!" he shouted from the front passenger seat as soon as they took off. Bill Harris, on the other hand, was impressed with Patricia's composure, especially compared with the panicked reaction of her fiancé, and he wanted to comfort her. Bill was in the backseat, with Patricia curled up and silent behind him. As Cinque bellowed, Bill Harris—Teko—reached under the blanket and held Patricia Hearst's hand. She was threatened and reassured at the same time.

The unplanned juxtaposition of terror and kindness in the station wagon would prove typical of Patricia's time in captivity. The SLA comrades lacked the skills, or even the inclination, to attempt anything as ambitious as a brainwashing. Their schizophrenic treatment of Patricia reflected the muddled thinking within the SLA. Literally and figuratively, the comrades didn't know what they were doing. But this non-strategy turned out to be a strategy itself, and so the body and the mind of their captive were whipsawed accordingly.

In the assassination of Marcus Foster, the SLA did deliver on the most bizarre claim in its communiqué—"execution by Cyanide bullets." Allan McNie, the pathologist who conducted Foster's autopsy, confirmed it. One of the bullets had passed through Foster's body and come to rest inside his front shirt pocket. McNie removed the bullet and brought it toward his nose. Then he invited two other people, his assistant and an Oakland police sergeant, to sniff the bullet as well. They shrugged, detecting no odor. But McNie had a genetic disposition that allowed him to recognize the smell of cyanide, which resembles burned almonds.* The other two men lacked that inherited gift. But McNie was certain: the bullet was spiked with cyanide.

The assassination of Marcus Foster had been the first attempt by the SLA to put Régis Debray's foco theory into action. The idea was that an action by a small vanguard group would set off a larger rebellion by the masses. The opposite occurred. All of Oakland mourned. Thousands of people, black and white, filled memorial services. The Black Panthers, which had a rocky relationship with Foster, denounced his murder and demanded that the police capture his killers.

Shortly before they killed Foster, DeFreeze, Ling, and Soltysik had moved out of their latest apartment in Berkeley. The core trio (plus Remiro and Little) wanted a place well removed from the heat that would be coming down after Foster's murder. So they selected a location far from the neighborhoods in Berkeley and Oakland where radicals congregated. Instead, Little and Ling, using the names George and Nancy DeVoto, signed the lease on an ordinary three-bedroom

---

* About 10 percent of the population cannot detect the smell of cyanide.

house at 1560 Sutherland Court, in a subdivision in the middle-class San Francisco suburb of Concord. The sleepy town was more than twenty miles and a world away from the tumult of Berkeley.

Freed from the confines of small, urban apartments, the SLA comrades could indulge their pack-rat tendencies and build up their arsenal. They collected maps—topographical maps of the Rockies, abandoned silver mines in the Sierras. They rehearsed violent encounters in the closed space of the house. Remiro set up the drills: "For stakeout at restaurant and parking lot: Cin's room is our base—there are three of us there. Zoya's [Mizmoon's] room is Camilla's pad in Oakland. Osceola's [Russ Little's] room is the 24 hr. café," one document read. Thanks largely to Mizmoon's obsessive research skills, and her thefts from the library where she worked, there were many boxes full of documents. They also stored thousands of rounds of ammunition. In a closet, there were cyanide-tipped bullets. They were inveterate list makers, too, and Nancy Ling Perry's to-do compilation reflected her surreal constellation of interests:

- the Communique
- all these papers
- the filing cabinet
- memorize addresses
- make a dress
- Molotov cocktails
- Wood cutting
- Buy bolts of material

The group saved DeFreeze's empty bottles of plum wine for use in making Molotov cocktails.

Stung by the negative reaction to Foster's assassination, DeFreeze decided to dial back the violence a little—by planning kidnappings as opposed to murders. This idea had its roots in the international radical movement that the SLA fancied itself joining. The Tupamaros of Uruguay were the model. The Sutherland Court house had a well-thumbed set of interviews with their leaders, where they explained how the group used kidnapping as a political tool. All the SLA members had also seen the film *State of Siege,* which focused on the Tupamaros. In the course of their brief heyday, the Tupamaros kidnapped a score of prominent local figures, including bankers, judges, the British ambassador to Uruguay, and the president of the Uruguayan House of Representatives. They held their prisoners in what they called the People's Jail and used their captives both for propaganda and for financial gain. In particular, the Tupamaros described, and the SLA members underlined, the story of how the group kidnapped Homero Fariña, the editor of a right-wing newspaper. Their aim in kidnapping Fariña, the Tupamaros said, was to "warn a certain class of newspapers that it was part of the repressive apparatus. We wanted to make clear the role played by the media at the time." Kidnapping as opposed to murder—this was what passed for moderation in the SLA.

Who would be their victim? The SLA made lists. There were almost two dozen names—mostly local bankers and corporate executives but also Raymond Procunier, the director of the California Department of Corrections. For some putative victims, the SLA drafted communiqués, in the style of the one sent to media outlets about Foster. One was headed "Kidnap and ransom and/or execution for failure to meet," and it listed the target as E. F. Trefethen Jr., an executive at the Kaiser Corporation. Another referred to Charles W. Comer, of the T. A. White Candy Company, with a note stating, "kidnap and ransom and/ or failure to meet." As ever, the SLA documents pretended the group was bigger than it was. All the draft communiqués were headed, like the one following the Foster operation, "Western Regional Unit 10"— as if the SLA had additional regions and other units.

One evening in early December, Bill and Emily Harris were blindfolded and driven to the house at Sutherland Court for a sort of audition. Bill had met Joe Remiro at an Oakland supermarket, where Bill was registering voters for Bobby Seale's campaign for mayor and Joe was handing out leaflets in support of farmworkers. Both had been loosely affiliated with Venceremos, one of the many radical groups in

the Bay Area. They became friends, and Joe felt Bill out on joining the
SLA. After DeFreeze approved them, Bill and Emily quit their jobs
and joined the comrades.

If one could pinpoint a nadir for the American spirit in the 1970s,
that moment in late 1973 might represent a fair choice. The nation
watched in astonishment all summer as the Senate Watergate Committee, led by North Carolina's Sam Ervin, revealed the depth of Richard
Nixon's corruption. The economy was cratering, thanks to an energy
crisis. After Egypt and Syria attacked Israel on October 6, starting the
Yom Kippur War, motorists had to wait in long gas lines to pay prices
that had quadrupled. On October 10, Vice President Spiro Agnew
resigned in a separate scandal. On October 20, Nixon led the Saturday
Night Massacre, when his own attorney general, Elliot Richardson,
and the deputy attorney general, William Ruckelshaus, quit rather
than follow the president's order to fire Archibald Cox, the Watergate
special prosecutor. In San Francisco, three thousand gas stations closed
for three days to protest rising prices from their suppliers. America
at this moment combined international turmoil, economic collapse,
and high-level depravity. The historian Rick Perlstein wrote of this
period, "America suffered more wounds to its ideal of itself than at
just about any other time in its history."

The union of the Harrises with the rest of the SLA reflected the
sour spirit of the time. Though they had read their Debray and could
articulate the notion of a revolutionary vanguard, none of them had
any realistic expectation that their actions would set off a broader
rebellion. They were shaking things up, stirring the pot, proving to
the world that the counterculture was still active. They wanted to
shock the system and the people who lived by its rules. Beyond that,
they had no goals, no agenda.

So the question remained of what exactly the SLA would do next.
DeFreeze wanted a kidnapping but had no target and no plan. Harris

had a different idea that reflected his roots in guerrilla theater. (Harris had studied theater as an undergraduate.) Christmas was coming. Why not hijack an eighteen-wheeler full of turkeys and give them to the poor? Why be the Tupamaros when you could be Robin Hood? That would give people a different impression of the SLA. It was a typically zany idea from Harris—completely impossible to accomplish. Where to find the right truck? Who would stop it? And then how to distribute the turkeys? The whole plan made no sense.

Then, on December 19, 1973, the *San Francisco Examiner* announced the engagement of Randolph Hearst's middle daughter. The article began,

> This is a week of special family significance for the Randolph Apperson Hearsts of Hillsborough.
>
> Today they are announcing the engagement of their daughter Patricia Campbell Hearst to Steven Andrew Weed.
>
> And on Friday, another daughter, Anne, will be presented at the annual debutante Cotillion at the Sheraton Palace Hotel.

Displaying his usual rapacious appetite for news, Bill Harris read both local papers' stories about the engagement. He noticed that the *Chronicle* included a detail that was omitted in the *Examiner:*

> Patricia graduated from Crystal Springs School, studied at Menlo College, and is a junior in art history at UC-Berkeley.

The last part caught Harris's eye: *a junior at Berkeley.* (She was actually a sophomore, but no matter.) A student and a *Hearst!* What a splash that would make! The Tupamaros had kidnapped a mere editor, but this was the most famous name in American journalism!

Bill knew that there was a directory of students' home addresses, available to the public, in the university administration building. Harris found his way to a secluded nook where an ancient-looking ledger book, with handwritten entries, held the information he sought:

Patricia Campbell Hearst, 2603 Benvenue, Apartment 4, Berkeley.

This was promising. Harris reported back to his cell and then to DeFreeze. They agreed to start surveillance of the apartment, to see if they could identify Hearst's regular movements and determine when best to grab her. In her notebook, Nancy Ling added her name to the list of possible kidnap victims. "At UC," she wrote, "1) That daughter of Hearst." Elsewhere, she wrote out the full name, as noted in the engagement announcement: "Patricia Campbell Hearst." The plan was set in motion.

Then, shortly before the SLA could conduct the kidnapping, disaster struck. In the early morning hours of January 10, 1974, David Duge, an alert local cop in Concord, noticed a car out of place on the quiet residential streets. Thinking the vehicle might be tied to some local burglaries, Duge pulled it over. Russ Little, the driver, gave him a license in the name of Robert Scalise. Duge also asked the passenger, Joe Remiro, for identification, and Remiro gave the officer his own license. Duge noticed that the back of the van was surrounded by black curtains, making it impossible to see what was inside. He asked "Scalise" what he was doing in the area at that hour. The driver said that he was looking for the home of a friend named DeVoto, who lived on Sutherland Court. (In a way, this was true. Little was trying to find the safe house that he and Nancy Ling had rented in that name, but he had gotten lost.) Duge retreated to his car and ran a quick check of the names.

Finding nothing, but his suspicions still aroused, Duge walked back to the car, tapped on the glass, and asked Remiro to get out of the car. "Do you have any guns or knives on you?" the officer asked. "I'm going to frisk you." Duge reached toward Remiro, who took a quick step back and pulled open his jacket, revealing a bulge near his waist. Recognizing the outline of an automatic pistol, Duge raced back toward his car and crouched behind it, just as Remiro fired off two blasts. Duge fired back twice; Remiro shot two more times. The flashes from their guns lit the pitch-dark. Little, meanwhile, restarted the van and took off. Remiro bolted on foot.

"Concord eleven-ninety-nine," Duge shouted into his radio, "officer in trouble! I've been shot at!" But by the time Duge's backup arrived, the scene was quiet.

Then, all of a sudden, the van with "Scalise" at the wheel came barreling back. Little had become disoriented in the tangle of streets and wound up where he started. Duge's backup swung his vehicle in front of the van, which the driver brought to a screeching stop. The backup cop inside pointed a shotgun at the driver. "Police!" he said. "Come out with your hands up!"

The officers ordered "Scalise" to lie on the ground and found his pockets stuffed with .38-caliber bullets—fourteen in one pocket, thirteen in the other. He had no weapon, but an empty pistol holster was on his waist. "Where's the gun?" the officers asked, and Little gestured toward the driver's seat, where there was a .38 Colt as well as a rifle. As they were pulling "Scalise" to his feet, they noticed he was bleeding. He had been grazed on the right shoulder by Duge in the initial exchange.

The officers pushed the curtains in the back aside and found a stack of hundreds of newly printed leaflets bearing the SLA's seven-headed cobra. For more than two months, police in the area had been searching for any clues to the murder of Marcus Foster. Now they had a major break in the case, but the passenger in the van, the one who fired on Duge, was gone. (The van itself was registered to Nancy Ling, but it contained an engine that had been removed from a different van that had been hijacked by Joe Remiro.)

Police from Concord and other departments in the area swarmed into the neighborhood, looking for the gunman who had fled on foot. Hours passed—nothing. Then, at 5:31 a.m., just before dawn, more than four hours after the initial confrontation, a patrol officer saw a figure dart between two nearby houses. After the officer loaded his shotgun, he heard a voice saying, "I've had it. . . . I give up. . . . I'm coming out." Joe Remiro emerged from the half-light and lifted his hands to be frisked. "It's in my right pants pocket," he said. The officer reached in and found a Walther PP .380 automatic—one of the guns used to kill Marcus Foster.

The SLA safe house—1560 Sutherland Court—was about two blocks from the site of the initial confrontation and the place where Remiro was arrested. During the course of the morning, word reached the house that the two men had been busted. Remiro himself had actually drawn up plans for responding to a possible confrontation there. It called for the SLA members to station themselves in the crawl space beneath the house or behind barricades of bundled newspapers upstairs. The plan continued as follows:

—Keep your hand gun with you at all times.
—Keep your amo and rifles, etc. together and ready to carry out immediately.
—Always know where your shoes are.
—Always know where your Molotov cocktails are.

But Remiro and Little were gone, and the remaining people in the house—Nancy, Mizmoon, and DeFreeze—had no stomach for a last stand against the police. They decided to flee. Still, they knew that they had to get rid of the incriminating evidence in the house. But how? They could burn the paper in the fireplace. Or pack everything into the car and take it away.

But Nancy Ling—twisted with demented passion—had a different idea. She decided to burn 1560 Sutherland Court to the ground.

Nancy and Mizmoon worked through the afternoon, buying gasoline and spreading gunpowder throughout the rooms. DeFreeze, as always, left the real work to others. They set a six-inch fuse leading to a puddle of gasoline and streaks of fuel that were meant to spread the fire throughout the house. This, they thought, was sure to destroy both the house and its contents. Mizmoon and DeFreeze left first. Ling then lit the fuse and bolted in a 1967 Oldsmobile that Willy Wolfe had left behind. The fire started with a great bang but extinguished itself almost immediately. Ling had forgotten to open the windows, starving the fire of oxygen. The trove of evidence in the safe house was scarcely singed.

In short order, the police had it all. Unused to processing major crime scenes, the Concord authorities failed to secure the premises, allowing journalists and curiosity seekers to rummage through the partially burned interior. The investigation of the SLA would include many such failures by law enforcement. When Marilyn Baker, a local television reporter, arrived on the scene, the residence had taken on a carnival-like atmosphere; "as kids and neighbors paraded by clutching their Symbionese trophies, I kept pulling more papers from under the pile on the bed." Paul Avery of the *San Francisco Chronicle* described some of what was inside:

> The house was furnished in crash-pad modern: mattresses on the floor and wooden crates. There were several typewriters, a mimeograph machine, and boxes and handfuls of bullets all around—.30 caliber, 9 millimeter, .38 special caliber, .45 caliber, .30-06 caliber, and 12-gauge shotgun shells. The walls were covered with posters, Mao and Stalin, and pinned with photos of police officers and slogans signed "Cin." Taped to three walls were well over 100 newspaper and magazine clippings about the exploits of foreign guerrillas and revolutionaries. There were gas masks, bandoliers, stacks of gun and ammo catalogues, stolen license plates, and three BB guns.

There were also .38-caliber rounds with hollow points filled with cyanide, a drill, and a plastic container marked "CYANIDE WATER."

Nor was that all. There were books—*Who's Who in American Industry* and the *California International Business Directory*—as well as the usual radical tracts. There were ammonium nitrate and other bomb-making ingredients. There were boxes and boxes of documents and notebooks, mostly written by Nancy Ling and Joe Remiro. And there were the lists of potential kidnapping targets, mostly local corporate executives but also Patricia Campbell Hearst. The police never warned any of them.

DeFreeze summoned the remaining comrades to an emergency meeting in San Francisco's Castro neighborhood, far from their blown suburban hideout. Because Bill and Emily Harris were less seriously compromised than the rest of the SLA members, DeFreeze designated them as "runners"—intermediaries with the outside world. In this capacity, Emily and Mizmoon found the next SLA safe house, at 514 Winchester Street, in the suburb of Daly City, on the other side of the bay from Concord. But when the landlord made clear that he would keep his own key to the house, the SLA crew decided to move out after just a couple of days. Next, on January 20, Emily and Mizmoon, posing as TWA flight attendants, rented a three-bedroom stucco house at 37 Northridge Drive for $265 a month, plus a $50 cleaning fee. The landlord thought that for a pair of flight attendants, his tenants were unusually concerned about security. They installed a heavy-duty bolt-type lock on the front door (to which the landlord did not have a key) and something even more peculiar. In the walk-in closet in the master bedroom, the new tenants changed the knobs so that the door could not be opened from the inside.

The full SLA reassembled in the house on Northridge Drive. DeFreeze, Mizmoon, and Nancy were joined by Bill and Emily Harris as well as Angela Atwood as they spread their sleeping bags on the floor and awaited a final decision about what to do next. At DeFreeze's direction, Harris had summoned Willy Wolfe back from a visit to his father in Pennsylvania. Camilla Hall had returned, too. One thing was sure. They had reached the point of no return. All of their names were easily determined from the contents of the house in Concord; their fingerprints were all over the place. The evidence tying the house and the van to the Foster murder was overwhelming, and that was potentially a death penalty case. Before January 10, all the SLA members (except DeFreeze) had been able to work in regular jobs and circulate more or less freely throughout the Bay Area. Now, suddenly, they would be completely cut off from society—until they were arrested or killed.

The crisis, following the arrests of Remiro and Little, prompted DeFreeze to assume a more military-style form of leadership. In addition to directing Harris to fetch Wolfe, he decreed that the group would henceforth address each other only by their code names. All of them already had aliases but had rarely used them. Some of the names had meanings; others did not. But now they would be used exclusively:

DeFreeze—Cinque, or Cin

Mizmoon—Zoya (a Russian name meaning "life")

Nancy Ling Perry—Fahizah (one who is victorious)

Russ Little—Osceola (a white man who became a leader of the
    Seminole tribe in Florida), also called Osi

Joe Remiro—Bo

Emily Harris—Yolanda

Bill Harris—Teko (Bill wanted Camilo, after a Cuban
    revolutionary, but DeFreeze insisted on Teko)

Angela Atwood—General Gelina

Willy Wolfe—Cujo, or Kahjoh (a Central American Indian
    word for "unconquerable")

Camilla Hall—Gabi

DeFreeze also recognized that it was time to commit to the next SLA action. He felt the arrests of Little and Remiro forced his hand. They had to prove that they were still a force, still an army. He had earlier suggested that they kidnap two corporate executives, but the SLA, with its diminished resources, lacked the ability to track wealthy adults who lived protected lives. That left Patricia Hearst as the lone viable target.

Bill Harris was a skeptic—a role he would persist in for the remain-

der of the SLA's strange odyssey. It wasn't that he questioned the revolutionary goals of the SLA (such as they were), but he saw himself as
the in-house pessimist about their tactics, the Eeyore of the SLA. Bill
understood the appeal of kidnapping a Hearst. After all, he was the
one who came up with the idea and then located her home address.
Like DeFreeze, Bill loved publicity, and he recognized that snatching
a newspaper heiress would be a blockbuster story. But now that the
kidnapping might actually take place, Bill had questions: What did
they hope to accomplish? What were their ransom demands? Would
they ever be met? Sure, it would be great to kidnap a Hearst, but what
would they *do* with her?

DeFreeze dismissed Harris's concerns. The goal of the kidnapping
would be to free Osceola and Bo—Little and Remiro. But how? The
SLA would trade Hearst for the two men. But what if the government
didn't want to trade? When had it ever traded murder defendants for
anyone? Well, if the government wouldn't trade Little and Remiro,
the SLA would tell the authorities to give them safe passage to Cuba.
Really? Harris asked. *Really,* DeFreeze said. Harris relented and joined
in the planning.

The SLA made meticulous preparations for its actions. They surveyed Hearst's apartment. They knew that she lived with her fiancé,
Steven Weed, and that they seldom went out at night, especially on
a Monday. They knew that the four-unit apartment complex on Benvenue had no security; they could simply walk up to the door of apartment 4; and they knew there was little traffic in this residential area.

At last, the night for the action was selected: February 4, 1974.
If the larger goals of the SLA were vague, and even if the purpose of
the kidnapping was opaque, the plan itself was straightforward and
refined. They would arrive at 2603 Benvenue shortly after sunset,
which was at 6:37 p.m. Camilla Hall would back into the driveway
with the entry team of DeFreeze, Bill Harris, and Angela Atwood and
wait for Hearst to be placed in the trunk of their car. Willy Wolfe and
Mizmoon Soltysik would park in the VW Bug, on the far side of Ben-

venue, to lead the caravan away from the kidnap scene. Emily Harris would wait in a station wagon in front of the apartment, with Nancy Ling Perry riding (literally) shotgun.

There was just one problem. They needed three cars, and they had only two.

PART TWO

PRISONER OF WAR

They weren't sure how to find another car. Remiro knew how to hot-wire a car, but he was locked up. No one else had a clue how to do it. So how else did you steal a car? They'd have to carjack someone—just steal the car out from under him. After all, how hard could that be?

The eight members of the SLA team got off to a late start leaving Daly City on February 4, and the sun had already set by the time they crossed the Bay Bridge. Wolfe and Mizmoon, leading off in the blue Volkswagen, went straight to their position across the street from 2603 Benvenue. Their initial assignment was to keep an eye on the building to see if Hearst and Weed went out. If they did, of course, the kidnapping would have to be postponed. The other six piled into the green-and-white 1964 Chevrolet station wagon, and they headed for Shattuck Avenue, the main shopping street in Hearst's part of Berkeley. That's where they were going to steal a car.

But by the time the SLA station wagon arrived, most of the stores, in that pre-gentrification era, had already closed. They pulled to a stop near a wreck of a 1964 Chevy convertible, but they agreed that they could do better than this "junker."

What followed, though, was a comedy of errors. They could not find a car to steal. There was little traffic, and most drivers simply didn't stop in the area. The SLA followed several pedestrians, hoping they would get into a car, but their targets kept walking. Bill Harris was steps away from one man when he turned and walked up the stairs to his house. The owners of the cars parked nearby simply didn't show up. The whole point of their plan was to knock on Hearst's door in the early evening, when they wouldn't call a lot of attention to themselves. But evening was turning to night. Harris prowled the empty sidewalks, muttering to himself that he was right all along to disparage the plan. The six SLA soldiers on Shattuck, all wired for action, seethed in helpless frustration. Meanwhile, Wolfe and Mizmoon parked for hours on Benvenue. Bewildered by the delay, they started to draw quizzical stares from Hearst's neighbors. They couldn't sit in the Beetle all night.

Finally, around 9:00 p.m., a local resident named Peter Benenson walked toward the junker, carrying two bags of groceries. After quick consultations, DeFreeze gave the word that this car would have to do. Angela Atwood approached Benenson as he arrived at the door to his car. "Give me the keys," she said. "We want your car, not you." When Benenson, stunned, hesitated, Angela and Emily and Bill Harris pounced on him, tied him up, shoved him on the floor of the backseat, and covered him with a blanket. They told him to keep quiet and left the trunk empty.

At last, the SLA had assembled a full complement of vehicles, and the station wagon and the convertible made the short drive to 2603 Benvenue. After confirming that all three cars were in place, DeFreeze, Harris, and Atwood approached the door to apartment 4.

The kidnapping itself took four minutes. DeFreeze left a sinister calling card on the floor of the apartment—a box of cyanide-filled .38-caliber bullets, just so there would be no doubt that the SLA conducted the attack. The kidnappers also remembered to take Patricia Hearst's purse with them on the way out; her credit cards and other forms of identification would prove useful in demonstrating that the SLA actually held the heiress. That night the SLA was lucky in certain ways. They were fortunate that the wild gunfire from DeFreeze and Nancy Ling hit no one, and it was providential for all concerned that the police officer who stopped Willy Wolfe's Volkswagen only wanted him to turn on his lights. In addition, Steve Suenaga, the neighbor who blundered into the kidnapping, had been subdued without suffering permanent injuries. No one, fortunately, had been killed.

The three SLA cars stopped half a mile from the apartment, and Patricia was quickly transferred from the trunk of the convertible to the back of the station wagon. They left the convertible behind, with Benenson still trussed on the floor of the backseat. Nancy Ling told him he'd be killed if he went to the police. Benenson freed himself almost as soon as his captors departed, but he was too traumatized to report the attack until the following morning.

After the long ride from Berkeley to Daly City, the station wagon pulled into the garage attached to 37 Northridge Drive. Scared as she was, Patricia managed to think clearly. She viewed it as a positive sign that the kidnappers were so concerned that she might see their faces and be able to identify them. That meant that she was likely to be released someday. After making sure her blindfold was in place, Harris guided her from the car into the house. A door opened, and Patricia inhaled an earthy smell that produced her first moment of true panic. Her mind flashed back to a recent story about a woman who had been kidnapped and buried alive. She thought the same thing was about to happen to her. She screamed and kicked to get away.

"It's a closet," Bill Harris said. "Relax, it's just a closet."

The enclosed space was six feet seven inches long, a little more than two feet wide, and eight feet high. A dirty foam mattress (the source of the smell) had been cut to fit the space. After Harris deposited her inside, she heard the door lock from the outside. Even behind her blindfold, she could tell it was pitch-black.

It might have been "just a closet," but Patricia faced an extraordinarily terrifying situation. She had been kidnapped in a country where high-profile kidnappings had all but disappeared; no one with a famous name had been kidnapped in the United States since Charles Lindbergh Jr. was seized and murdered in 1932. Despite Harris's calming words, the threat of death hung over Patricia. Even though she was only a teenager, she faced her situation with courage and intelligence. She didn't panic or collapse; she listened to her captors and quickly recognized that there were considerable differences, in personality and temperament, among them. Her judgments about their characters, and about her own predicament, were sound.

The first person to open the door to the closet put a radio inside and told Patricia to be quiet. Then DeFreeze informed her that she was in the custody of the Symbionese Liberation Army. Even in that desperate moment, Patricia was able to think strategically. She knew that the SLA had claimed responsibility for the murder of Marcus Foster, but she figured it would be safer if she feigned ignorance about the group. That way, she wouldn't be forced to take a position on their actions or to debate the man she knew as Cinque. In a sign of DeFreeze's real priorities, he was offended by Patricia's apparent unfamiliarity with his army—"how could you not know the SLA?" He boasted of the success of the Foster action, noting with pride that the deed had been accomplished with cyanide bullets.

DeFreeze said she had been arrested, not kidnapped, by a "combat unit" of the SLA because her father was "a corporate enemy of the people." He tried to interrogate Patricia about her father's business activities, including his income and stock holdings. But Patricia had been well sheltered from the family's finances (and shown little curiosity about them), so she replied with unfeigned ignorance. She knew a few random facts—the family had received a gift of rugs from the shah of Iran—but she didn't know much more.

"You are a prisoner of war of the Symbionese Liberation Army," DeFreeze told her. "You will be held in protective custody and you will be treated according to the Geneva Convention governing prisoners of war."

In the midst of this monologue, Cinque injected a bizarre question.

"Do you have any watches, jewels or religious medals on you?" he asked.

Religious medals? Was this man insane? Because she was still wearing just the bathrobe and underwear, it was obvious that she did not.

"Under the Geneva Convention, you are entitled to keep religious medals, but everything else will have to be in our custody." Reflecting the strangely obsessive nature of SLA research, DeFreeze accurately characterized the rights of prisoners of war. The references to war and to the conventions also fit with the grandiosity of DeFreeze's conception of his undertaking. This was no mere kidnapping but an act of war, like the Tupamaros' seizures of their enemies. And as in Uruguay, the point was to reeducate and reform prisoners of war, not to harm them. DeFreeze told Patricia she would probably be released soon, based on the outcome of negotiations with her family. In the meantime, she would be kept as comfortable as circumstances allowed. The only danger to her, DeFreeze said, in a theme that he would frequently repeat, was if the fascist police tried to rescue her.

DeFreeze explained that Patricia's "arrest" had been part of a series of actions by the SLA and its affiliates across the state of California. There had been five or six other "arrests," and the SLA was in the process of coordinating combat, intelligence, medical, and support teams. (This was a fantasy, of course. There were no other actions, and the entire unincarcerated roster of the SLA was contained in that single grubby house.) In addition, Cin went on, the SLA was linked with revolutionary "people's movements" around the globe.

DeFreeze insisted that the people must understand the need for revolution, the power of the SLA, the reason for the "arrest" of Hearst, and he knew that he was the prophet to spread the word. His megalomania was the engine driving the SLA, which was, in many respects, his cult. This was an era of quasi-political cults, like those of Charles Manson and the Reverend Jim Jones. The leaders shared a hunger for public recognition of their unique genius. As DeFreeze continued his initial lecture to Patricia, what was clearest was his need for attention. They were speaking on the morning of February 5, and Cinque was seething because the newspapers had not yet reported that Patricia had been kidnapped. Where was the press coverage? This obsession with outside perceptions—with public relations—would remain a touchstone of the SLA.

In time, during the course of his meandering monologue, Cinque explained the specific reason they kidnapped Patricia. "Our two comrades are being held in a pig's prison, and that's why we took you," he said. "You're going to be treated exactly as they are. Your condition here will duplicate their situation. If their condition changes for the worse, then your condition will change—in exactly the same way." This was how she learned that her fate was tied to that of Little and Remiro—Osceola and Bo.

Finally, Cinque wound down.

"When will I go home?" Patricia asked.

"What, do you want to go home for your birthday?" Cinque sneered. Patricia would turn twenty on February 20. This was, perhaps, the most unnerving thing that Cinque had said to her. He knew her *birthday*. It underlined that this was no random attack. They had been researching her life, which was chilling.

The first call to the police probably came from the students who were roused from their study session in the house next door to 2603 Benvenue. In light of the gunfire from DeFreeze and Ling, other calls soon followed. After bolting from his apartment with his head bloodied, Steven Weed ran through his yard, turned left in an alley, and rushed to Parker Street, where he screamed for someone in a darkened house to call the police. Hearing no response, he staggered back to Benvenue and struggled up the steps to his apartment, where a crowd was already starting to gather.

"Where's Patty?" he asked. "Where's Patty?"

"They took her," he was told. "She's gone."

Neighbors had just found Steve Suenaga, still tied up inside the apartment. Soon after, ambulances came for both of them.

Reporters picked up the story, and the Berkeley police asked them to hold off reporting anything for the time being. A brief embargo was common for a breaking crime story, at least in those days, and the deadlines for Tuesday's newspaper soon passed. Patricia's sister Virginia lived with her husband a few blocks away from Benvenue, and police went to inform and warn her. She told them that their parents were at an event in Washington. The second-youngest daughter, Anne, who was at home in Hillsborough, roused her parents at the Mayflower Hotel with the bad news. Randy Hearst took the news calmly and called the *Examiner*. He learned that a team of reporters was already on the story, but the *Examiner* was honoring the embargo. "Be careful," Randy said. "Don't do anything that could get Patty hurt." Then he made reservations for the first flight back to San Francisco on Tuesday morning.

By the time Randy and Catherine returned to their home in Hillsborough on Tuesday afternoon, they had the answer to the first question that was torturing them. Who had done this? Police had found Cinque's cyanide-tipped calling cards in the apartment. The bullets served their purpose of informing the authorities that the kidnappers were the SLA, the people who murdered Marcus Foster. At that point, the crime even made a perverse kind of sense. Little and Remiro had been arrested, and now the SLA was looking for something, or someone, to trade for their freedom. At least, that was the theory, but no one knew for sure, because the first twenty-four hours passed without a word from the kidnappers.

DeFreeze was still grousing about the lack of immediate press attention when he instructed Nancy Ling to draft a communiqué about the kidnapping. They sent it to KPFA on Tuesday, but it didn't arrive until Thursday, February 7, forcing the Hearst family to endure almost three full days of silence from their daughter's kidnappers. (It came in an envelope that also included Patricia's Mobil Oil credit card, which, in an appropriate touch, was in her father's name.) Even by the standards of the SLA, the communiqué was a strange document.

SYMBIONESE LIBERATION ARMY
WESTERN REGIONAL ADULT UNIT

Communique #3   February 4, 1974
Subject: Prisoners of War   Warrant Order:
                                         Arrest and protective
Target: Patricia Campbell Hearst   custody, and if
Daughter of Randolph A.   resistance execution
Hearst, corporate enemy
of the people

Warrant Issued By:
The Court of the People

On the afore stated date, combat elements of the United Federated Forces of The Symbionese Liberation Army armed with cyanide loaded weapons served an arrest warrant upon Patricia Campbell Hearst.

It is the order of this court that the subject be arrested by combat units and moved to a protective area of safety. . . .

It is the directive of this court that during this action ONLY, no civilian elements will be harmed if possible, and that warning shots be given. However, if any citizens attempt to aid the authorities or interfere with the implementation of this order, they shall be executed immediately.

This court hereby notifies the public and directs all combat units in the future to shoot to kill any civilian who attempts to witness or interfere with any operation conducted by the people's forces against the fascist state.

Should any attempt be made by authorities to rescue the prisoner, or to arrest or harm any S.L.A. elements, the prisoner is to be executed.

The prisoner is to be maintained in adequate physical and mental condition, and unharmed as long as these conditions are adhered to. . . .

All communications from this court MUST be published in full, in all newspapers, and all other forms of the media. Failure to do so will endanger the safety of the prisoner.

Further communications will follow.

S.L.A.
DEATH TO THE FASCIST INSECT THAT PREYS UPON THE LIFE OF THE PEOPLE.

The most peculiar thing about the communiqué was that it was a ransom demand without a demand for ransom. There was no reference to money, no mention of freedom for Little and Remiro, no condition stated for Patricia's release. The message threatened her with harm, but only if efforts were made to free her. Otherwise, it more or less guaranteed her safety. The most important part of the communiqué was not obvious at first glance. This was the demand that the communiqué "MUST be published in full" and "in all newspapers, and all other forms of the media." The document was a macabre press release, aimed more at garnering attention than at starting negotiations. The real question was whether Hearst and his newspaper would comply.

Charles Bates, the special agent in charge of the FBI office in San Francisco, also happened to be in Washington when Patricia was kidnapped. Like Randy and Catherine, he took an early flight west the following morning. He went to the Hearsts' Hillsborough mansion. Ordinary crime victims went to the FBI; the FBI went to the Hearsts.

It was a peculiar moment in the history of the bureau as well as in Bates's life. J. Edgar Hoover, the FBI's longtime director, had died in 1972. President Nixon then installed as acting director one of his loyalists, L. Patrick Gray, but he was caught up in Watergate and forced out in 1973. Gray was replaced by Clarence Kelley, the chief of police in Kansas City, but the bureau in 1974 remained an institution in crisis. It had become clear that Hoover used his position to nurse his personal and political grievances, especially against Communists, both real and imagined, with the result that he neglected vast swaths of criminality in America. The bureau operated without regard for civil liberties, and its declining fortunes reflected the fall of many once-great American institutions in the Watergate era.

But Charlie Bates thrived in Hoover's FBI and dodged the fallout from the director's departure. As chief of the FBI's Criminal Investigative Division, Bates had actually been placed in charge of the Watergate investigation in its first days. When assigned the case, he wrote a memo that said "that the FBI's reputation was at stake, and that the investigation should be completely impartial, thorough and complete." But Gray had betrayed Bates, destroying documents and allowing the Nixon White House to subvert the inquiry. Bates was not implicated in Gray's misdeeds, but he felt compelled to seek a change of scenery. When the job of special agent in charge of the San Francisco office opened up, Bates grabbed it. He was still new to the post when he reported to Hillsborough. He brought with him his deputy, a veteran agent named Monte Hall, who would be in charge of the day-to-day investigation.

Although the murder of Marcus Foster was considered a state crime, the FBI had still opened what was known as a passive file on the Symbionese Liberation Army. The file didn't amount to much more than newspaper clippings. Kidnapping, though, was long regarded as a federal offense, so the Hearst case belonged to the FBI from the beginning. The bureau gave the investigation the code name HER-NAP. Bates directed an agent to move into the mansion, to provide security and to monitor for ransom demands. But the truth was, after searching the scene of the kidnapping for clues, the FBI had very little idea how to proceed. At this point, the bureau was populated almost entirely by white male agents who wore white shirts and black shoes and had crew cuts; they knew little about the radical underground and had no chance of infiltrating those circles. Who were the SLA? Where were they? Who were their friends and allies? The FBI had no idea and few ways of finding out.

Still, there was an immediate question to be addressed. The one demand in the communiqué was for newspapers to print it in its entirety. Other publications would almost certainly follow the lead of Hearst's own *Examiner*, so the issue was really up to Randy to decide. One could argue that to print the communiqué was to give in to terroristic demands; one could say, further, that giving kidnappers this sort of forum created a bad precedent and a perverse incentive for future politically motivated criminals. Randy Hearst had no interest in those arguments. He wanted his daughter safe back home, and the way to achieve that result appeared to start with printing the communiqué. It ran in the *Examiner* the next day.

Back in the safe house, DeFreeze displayed no evident satisfaction that his words had been published around the world. In a pattern that would recur, his attention wandered, and he retreated in silence to his bedroom and plum wine. For Patricia, day two in the closet resembled day one. But then a new figure opened the door. She called herself Gelina, but her real name was Angela De Angelis Atwood, and she would turn out to be another critical figure in Patricia's captivity. If DeFreeze was the bad cop, Angela was the good one.

When Jane Pauley, the future newscaster, arrived on the campus of Indiana University in Bloomington as a freshman in 1968, her sister Ann was already a junior math major at the school. One day, while the sisters were drinking sodas in the Student Union, a beautiful young woman walked by, followed by every eye in the room. Ann didn't know the woman personally, but she knew her name. "That's Angela De Angelis," Ann told Jane. On a campus of thirty thousand students, Angela—exotic, theatrical, charismatic—had made herself a celebrity.

Her name meant Angel of the Angels, which pretty well summed up her upbringing. Raised in a suburb of Newark, New Jersey, she was the first and favorite of three daughters. Her mother was a home-maker, and her father was business manager of Local 999 of the Teamsters union. A devout Catholic and attentive student, Angela was a prototypical good girl (and head cheerleader). When her mother died when she was fourteen, Angela took over the parenting duties for her younger sisters. Small wonder that her father called her Angel. She went to study acting in Indiana, where her dark-haired good looks stood out among the blondes in the corn belt. In Bloomington, she stumbled on a *Life* magazine feature on the Mafia. Many of her father's friends were featured, and Angel started to realize that the world was a more complicated place than she had imagined.

At Indiana, Angela had an awakening common to students in the late 1960s, but her transformation was a gradual one. Angel, as she was still known, belonged to the Kappa Pickers, the singing group affiliated with the elite Kappa Kappa Gamma sorority that performed on Arthur Godfrey's television show, where they sang "I'll Never Fall in Love Again." But Angel was not long for such middle-of-the-road fare. The theater world had taken on a political cast at Indiana, where students began performing on street corners and in prisons. The leader of the avant-garde scene was a student named Kevin Kline, and Angela became his assistant, running a guerrilla theater group based in a local coffeehouse. Still, even as Angel embraced a harder-edged politics, there was always a sweetness about her. One weekend, she brought some friends from New Jersey to town, and she fixed one of them up with Jane Pauley for the day. At a party that evening, Pauley's date had maneuvered her into a bedroom. Sensing her naive young friend was in danger, Angel swooped into the bedroom and freed Pauley from her date's advances.

While still an undergraduate, Angel married another Indiana actor, Gary Atwood. (Atwood beat out Kline for the lead in a university production of *Hamlet*.) At that time, Angel and Gary cared more for drugs, especially LSD, than politics, but then Bill Harris, a Vietnam vet who was back at Indiana for a second tour as a student, joined the theater program. He and his girlfriend, Emily Montague, and Angel and Gary Atwood became neighbors and friends. Then the Atwoods, followed by the Harrises, moved out to Berkeley.

Angel (who now preferred to be called Angela) was still trying to make it as an actress, and she won a leading role in a community theater production of Ibsen's *Hedda Gabler*. But community theater didn't pay the bills, especially after Gary split and went back east. Now single, Angela made ends meet by working as a cocktail waitress at a restaurant called the Great Electric Underground, in the basement of San Francisco's Transamerica building. She also found a job at the restaurant for her friend Kathy Soliah, who had the title role in *Hedda Gabler*. The two aspiring actresses became inseparable and even wrote a one-act play to perform together. In *Edward the Dyke,* Kathy played a lesbian and Angela a psychiatrist who tried and failed to convince her that sex with men would be her salvation. The two also took an adult education class together on radical feminism, which became a touchstone of their own lives and, indeed, the core SLA experience. The names of Angela's four cats—Lalenya, Abraxas, Chagall, and Vagina—also provided clues about her interests and character.

After Gary Atwood's departure, the remaining three refugees from

Indiana—Angela, Bill, and Emily—lived together, and they quickly found their way into the radical underground. On the rebound from her husband, Angela fell for Russ Little and then, more seriously, for Joe Remiro.

Angela was, in short, an unlikely revolutionary and kidnapper—as Patricia quickly came to learn. On Patricia's second day, Angela offered Patricia a meal, which she declined. How about some tea or water? She could tell that Patricia feared being poisoned, so Atwood made her an offer. "I'll bring it here, and I'll drink half of it, so you know it's OK," she said. Patricia took a sip of water.

Atwood, improbably enough, tried to be Patricia's best girlfriend. She left the door to the closet open and gabbed in girlish monologues, mostly about her love for Joe Remiro. Like an adolescent mooning about a crush, she talked about how handsome Joe was, what a kind person he was . . . Atwood (as Gelina) just wanted Joe back. That was the only reason Patricia was kidnapped, she said. Angela didn't care about politics or the revolution; she just wanted her boyfriend back. Alone among the SLA women (and men), Atwood allowed herself some eye-rolling iconoclasm about the self-serious rituals of the SLA. DeFreeze believed in conditioning exercises for the group, even in the tight confines of the house. But Angela drew a line. "I never do push-ups!" she said to Patricia with a giggle.

Even in her straitened circumstances, Patricia turned out to be a savvy judge of her keepers. Angela remained a ditzy actress. Nancy Ling worshipped DeFreeze as if he were some kind of god. Mizmoon preached revolution and bragged about violence. (Patricia heard Mizmoon boasting that she had killed a chicken with her bare hands in a bathtub.) Emily Harris was grim-faced and withdrawn. Camilla Hall was rarely around the house in Daly City, because the comrades recognized that she was the least known to the authorities and thus had the greatest ability to circulate aboveground.

After the first couple of days, DeFreeze wanted to set up a structure for Patricia's captivity. Besides himself, he wanted only three people to have contact with her. That way, if she were released, she would not be able to identify all of them. In addition, DeFreeze recognized that he had no rapport with Patricia, so he thought that others might have better luck getting information out of her. The first was Angela Atwood, of course, because she had already more or less adopted Patricia. The second was Nancy Ling—mostly employed to keep an eye on Angela. DeFreeze wanted to make sure that Patricia always remembered that she was a prisoner of war.

Cinque's third designee was Willy Wolfe. This, too, made sense. Wolfe, the physician's son who had gone to prep school, came from a background most similar to Patricia's. Their shared social class distinguished them from everyone else at Northridge Drive. DeFreeze figured right on this score.

In his gentle, soft-spoken way, Wolfe (whom Patricia knew as Cujo) set about providing Hearst's political education. He gave her a copy of the SLA's urtext—George Jackson's *Blood in My Eye*. He also talked about the prison at Vacaville—how poorly the inmates were treated, especially when it came to medical care. (He spoke with such intimate knowledge that Patricia at first thought Wolfe himself had been incarcerated there.) Wolfe sat outside Patricia's closet and read Maoist and Marxist literature to her, including *The Communist Manifesto,* Carlos Marighella's manual for guerrilla warfare, and Mao's Little Red Book. He had a favorite quotation that he recited many times. "All men must die, but death can vary in significance. The ancient Chinese writer Ssu-ma Ch'ien said, 'Though death befalls all men alike, it may be weightier than Mount Tai or lighter than a feather, but to work for the Fascists and die for the exploiters and oppressors is lighter than a feather.'" Wolfe made clear to Patricia that he was willing to die for the people. Hearst couldn't fathom Wolfe's goals, but his sincerity was unmistakable.

Patricia's moment-to-moment terror ebbed. The death threats subsided. She was not going to be executed, like Marcus Foster. The door to her closet stayed open for longer periods of time. The SLA members no longer blasted the radio so she couldn't hear what they were saying. Still, the question remained: What were they going to *do* with Patricia?

DeFreeze, sequestered in his bedroom, wouldn't say. Finally, Bill Harris decided to make a suggestion.

6

NOT JUST A BUNCH OF NUTS

Bill Harris still liked his old idea of hijacking a trailer truck full of frozen turkeys and distributing them to the needy. It would have been guerrilla theater at its best, a zany modern take on Robin Hood. Take the Butterballs from the corporations and give to the poor . . . Harris also understood that the notion was impractical, maybe even impossible. Still, he gravitated toward the idea of using the SLA to redistribute wealth. Certainly, he thought, that kind of thing had a better chance of rallying public support, to say nothing of generating good press, than, say, murdering an African American school superintendent.

What, Harris wondered, if they could accomplish the same goal in a different way? What if the SLA didn't have to steal the food at all? What if the SLA could force old man Hearst to give away the food? Everyone always thought of ransom as something that the kidnappers demanded for themselves. What if the SLA demanded that the ransom for Patricia Hearst be paid . . . to the poor?

Harris brought up the idea at one of the long, meandering group rap sessions in the Northridge Drive house, where the SLA members gathered in a circle and chewed over their ideas. DeFreeze was interested, but he also liked to keep his options open, so he didn't want to commit to just a single ransom demand. He decreed that the SLA would demand that Hearst feed the poor as an initial gesture of good faith. Then, if and only if DeFreeze found Hearst's effort satisfactory, the SLA would make a true ransom demand.

In any event, the group decided to proceed and set about refining the demand. How much food? Given to whom? Where? When? There were long meetings into the night about these issues. Meanwhile, Patricia's parents, as well as the FBI and the waiting world, heard nothing from the kidnappers after the initial, vague communiqué. Again, days passed.

DeFreeze came to like the idea of a food giveaway so much that he decided to issue the demand himself. He would make a tape recording in his own voice rather than just rely on another stylized Nancy Ling communiqué. Further, DeFreeze combined the demand for the food giveaway with their most powerful propaganda tool—Patricia Hearst herself. There would be two tape recordings delivered to KPFA on February 12: one from DeFreeze, to outline his initial demands, and the other from Hearst, to establish that she was alive, healthy, and well treated.

Drawing on Mizmoon's research skills and Nancy Ling's rhetoric, DeFreeze recorded a half-hour stem-winder. DeFreeze had a powerful speaking voice that belied his diminutive size, and his words, especially at the beginning, had an undeniable punch. "To those who would bear the hopes and future of our people, let the voice of their guns express the words of freedom. Greetings to the people, fellow comrades, brothers and sisters," he began. "My name is Cinque, and to my comrades I am known as Cin. I am a black man and representative of black people. I hold the rank of General Field Marshal in the United Federated Forces of the Symbionese Liberation Army."

As usual, the SLA imbued its rhetoric with the faux authority of an imaginary legal system: "Today I have received an order from the Symbionese War Council, the Court of the People, to the effect that I am ordered to convey the following message in behalf of the SLA, and to insert a taped word of comfort and verification, that Patricia Campbell Hearst is alive and safe." DeFreeze went on, "The SLA has arrested the subject for the crimes that her mother and father have, by their actions, committed against we, the American people, and oppressed people of the world."

DeFreeze gave a lengthy summary of the business interests of the "ultra-right Hearst Corporation," including its newspapers, magazines, television stations, and real estate. He then spent nearly as long excoriating Catherine Hearst for her role on the Board of Regents of the University of California, which supports "through its investments the murder of thousands of black men and women and children of Mozambique, Angola and Rhodesia, murder designed to destroy the spirit that all humanity longs for."

At last, DeFreeze turned to his actual demand. "Before any forms of negotiations for the release of the subject prisoner be initiated, an action of good faith must be shown on the part of the Hearst family," he said. "This gesture is to be in the form of food to the needy and the unemployed, and to which the following instructions are directed to be followed to the letter," which was a reference to a written description of how the food giveaway should take place that was also included in the package for KPFA. The demand (crafted mostly by Nancy Ling) reflected the obsessive, meticulous style of the SLA.

Hearst was to provide "$70.00 worth of meats, vegetables, and dairy products" to all people in California who had "welfare cards, social security pension cards, food stamp cards, disabled veteran cards, medical cards, parole or probation papers, and jail or bail release slips." The food was to be distributed in seven of the biggest cities in the state, and "there must be at least 5 stores as distribution points within each community, we suggest such stores as Safeway and Mayfair." In addition, "the meat, vegetables, and dairy products must be of top quality." The food giveaway must begin in one week, on February 19, and last for four weeks so the recipients "will not be forced to stand waiting in long lines."

As always with the SLA, there were instructions for the media as well. The SLA symbol of the "seven-headed cobra" must be displayed in all communications. The full texts of the statements from Cinque and Patricia Hearst must be printed. "The news media is warned," the statement went on, "that all attempts to mislead the public concerning the intentions of the SLA, or to confuse the public by withholding or omitting sections of the tape or SLA documents jeopardizes the prisoner." (The package for KPFA also included copies of the original SLA constitution from August 1973 and a sixteen-point statement of goals, starting with "to unite all oppressed people into a fighting force and to destroy the system of the capitalist state and all its value systems.")

The initial demand for the food giveaway was detailed, comprehensive, and completely insane. If taken literally, it would entitle millions of Californians, by no means all poor, to $70 worth of free food. (The demand covered individuals who were receiving Social Security benefits, many of whom, of course, were not impoverished.) The demand called for the Hearst family to obtain millions of dollars' worth of "top quality" food and then, in essence, to occupy supermarkets in much of the state to give it all away. According to initial estimates, full compliance would cost the family approximately $400 million (more than $2 billion in 2016 dollars).

Still, the demand for the giveaway, and all the other documents, hardly registered with the public at first because it was overshadowed by the voice of Patricia Hearst.

Patricia made her recording in her closet cell on February 8—four days after she was kidnapped and three days before the tape was released. (The delay occurred because the SLA took several days to work out the details of its giveaway demand.) DeFreeze held the microphone of the reel-to-reel tape recorder. He didn't write out a script but gave Patricia paragraph-by-paragraph instructions on what to say in her own words. Her statement was in no way voluntary, but the way she phrased her captors' sentiments offered hints about her unsettled psychological state.

Her first four words became famous: "Mom, Dad, I'm okay." Some people thought her breathy monotone suggested that she had been drugged, but that was the way Patricia always spoke—with a flat

In December 1973, Randolph Hearst summoned a photographer from his newspaper, the *San Francisco Examiner*, to his estate in Hillsborough to commemorate the engagement of his daughter Patricia to Steven Weed. Randolph and his wife, Catherine, had reservations about their daughter's marriage plans. So, in short order, did Patricia.

The three kidnappers crept up to the stairs on the left of the house at 2603 Benvenue Avenue in Berkeley before knocking on the door to apartment 4. As they dragged Patricia to their car, her fuzzy slippers fell to the ground. Earlier, they had carjacked a convertible from Peter Benenson, who had been grocery shopping. They put him on the floor of the backseat, and Bill Harris, after a considerable struggle, put Patricia in the trunk, shown here.

Shortly after the kidnapping, Steven Weed, who was beaten in the attack, appeared before reporters with Catherine Hearst in front of the family mansion in Hillsborough.

On January 10, 1974, Joe Remiro (in white, on left) and Russ Little (in white, on right) were arrested and charged with the murder of Oakland school superintendent Marcus Foster. One motive for the kidnapping of Patricia Hearst, on February 4, was to free Remiro and Little.

Six of the SLA kidnappers, top row, left to right: Camilla Hall, the poet and artist from Minnesota; Willy Wolfe, whom Patricia called "the gentlest, most beautiful man"; Donald DeFreeze, the prison escapee who appointed himself General Field Marshal Cinque. Bottom row, left to right: Angela Atwood, the New Jersey–born actress; Nancy Ling Perry, the tiny spitfire and propagandist; Patricia "Mizmoon" Soltysik, onetime lover of Camilla Hall and in-house researcher.

Randolph and Catherine Hearst made frequent appearances before reporters in their driveway in Hillsborough. In one communiqué, Patricia said, "Mom should get out of her black dress, that doesn't help at all."

In response to demands from Patricia's kidnappers, the Hearsts agreed to fund a food giveaway program, called People in Need, in the Bay Area. Some of the food distributions turned into riots.

This iconic photograph of Patricia, taken by Mizmoon Soltysik in front of the SLA symbol of a seven-headed cobra, became one of the most famous images of the 1970s. Patricia's expression is inscrutable, as subject to as many interpretations as the larger tale of her captivity. She looks steely or terrified; her lips are pursed in determination or defeat; she could be battle ready or battered. Shortly after the photo was taken, DeFreeze ordered Mizmoon and Ling to cut Patricia's hair. Thereafter, Patricia usually wore wigs out of doors.

During the robbery of the Hibernia Bank on April 15, 1974, the SLA comrades positioned Patricia so that her photograph would be taken by the security cameras. "First person puts up his head," Hearst yelled at the customers, "I'll blow his motherfucking head off!"

In the immediate aftermath of the Hibernia heist, federal law enforcement officials disagreed about whether Patricia should be arrested for bank robbery. They compromised and decided to seek to hold her as a material witness, as indicated in this early wanted poster. Note the FBI's use of her engagement photograph, with Steven Weed cropped out.

WANTED BY THE FBI

BANK ROBBERY
INTERSTATE FLIGHT - POSSESSION OF HOMEMADE BOMB, ROBBERY, RECEIVING STOLEN PROPERTY, ASSAULT WITH FORCE

RE: DONALD DAVID DE FREEZE   PATRICIA MICHELLE SOLTYSIK   PATRICIA CAMPBELL HEARST
NANCY LING PERRY   CAMILLA CHRISTINE HALL   MATERIAL WITNESS

TO WHOM IT MAY CONCERN:

The FBI is conducting an investigation to determine the whereabouts of these individuals whose descriptions and photographs appear below. Federal warrants charging robbery of a San Francisco bank on April 15, 1974, have been issued at San Francisco, California, for Camilla Hall, Donald DeFreeze, Nancy Perry, and Patricia Soltysik. A material witness warrant in this robbery has been issued for Patricia Hearst, who was abducted from her Berkeley, California, residence on February 4, 1974, by a group which has identified itself as the Symbionese Liberation Army (SLA). The participants in the bank robbery also claim to be members of the SLA.

DONALD DAVID DE FREEZE
N/M, DOB 11/16/43, 5'9" to 5'11",
180-180, blk hair, br eyes

PATRICIA MICHELLE SOLTYSIK
W/F, DOB 5/17/50, 5'3" to 5'4",
110, dk br hair, br eyes

PATRICIA CAMPBELL HEARST
W/F, DOB 2/20/54, 5'3", 110,
lt br hair, br eyes

MATERIAL WITNESS

NANCY LING PERRY
W/F, DOB 9/19/47, 5', 95-105, red
br hair, haz eyes

CAMILLA CHRISTINE HALL
W/F, DOB 3/24/45, 5'6", 125,
blonde hair, blue eyes

If you have any information concerning these individuals, please notify your local FBI office, a telephone listing for which can be found on the first page of your directory. In view of the crimes for which these individuals are being sought, they should be considered armed and extremely dangerous, and no action should be taken which would endanger anyone's safety.

Very truly yours,

C. M. Kelley

Clarence M. Kelley
Director

When the comrades fled their apartment on Golden Gate Avenue in San Francisco, they left taunting messages on the walls for their pursuers from the FBI. Patricia scrawled this slogan of the Cuban revolution and signed it with her nom de guerre, Tania.

Following the successful Hibernia Bank robbery, Mizmoon Soltysik took this triumphant group portrait of the SLA. Back row: Emily Harris (Yolanda), Willy Wolfe (Cujo), Donald DeFreeze (Cinque), Bill Harris (Teko), Camilla Hall (Gabi). Front row: Patricia Hearst (Tania), Angela Atwood (General Gelina), Nancy Ling Perry (Fahizah).

On May 16, when a clerk at Mel's Sporting Goods caught Bill Harris shoplifting, Patricia fired dozens of rounds of ammunition across this busy Los Angeles street to help Bill escape.

On the afternoon of May 17, the Los Angeles Police Department surrounded the small house at 1466 East Fifty-Fourth Street and demanded that the six SLA comrades inside surrender. After neighbors were evacuated, a ferocious gun battle ensued, with thousands of rounds of ammunition exchanged, and then the house was destroyed by fire. In the end, Donald DeFreeze, Willy Wolfe, Camilla Hall, Nancy Ling Perry, Angela Atwood, and Mizmoon Soltysik were all killed in the inferno. The house itself was destroyed, as is evident from this aerial photograph.

affect that gave the impression she was slightly disengaged. (Her voice somewhat resembled that of Jacqueline Kennedy Onassis, who was also a product of a private girls' school education.) "I had a few scrapes and stuff, but they washed them up, and they're getting OK. . . . I'm not being starved or beaten or unnecessarily frightened. I have heard some press reports, and so I know that Steve and all the neighbors are OK and that no one was really hurt." She went on, "I'm kept blind-folded usually so that I can't identify anyone. My hands are often tied, but generally they're not. I'm not gagged or anything. I'm comfort-able. And I think you can tell that I'm not really terrified or anything and I'm OK." The diction was distinctly Patricia's own. And the state-ment was true. By February 8, she was rarely in any kind of restraints.

Most of the tape recording was devoted to Patricia's statements about her captors—assigned sentiments expressed in her own words. "These people aren't just a bunch of nuts," she said. "They've been really honest with me, but they're perfectly willing to die for what they are doing. And I want to get out of here, but the only way I'm going to is if we do it their way. And I just hope you'll do what they say, Dad, and just do it quickly." She made the same point several dif-ferent ways: that the SLA was sincere and that her father should meet their demands.

Patricia made several references to the arrests of Little and Remiro, without exactly suggesting that the SLA would trade their freedom for hers. "I am a prisoner of war and so are the two men in San Quentin," she said. "I am being treated in accordance with the Geneva Conven-tion, one of the conditions being that I am not being tried for crimes which I'm not responsible for. I am here because I am a member of a ruling class family, and I think you can begin to see the analogy. The people, the two men in San Quentin, are being held and are going to be tried simply because they are members of the SLA and not because they've done anything. . . . Whatever happens to the two prisoners is going to happen to me."

Patricia's words about Little and Remiro were elliptical, but she concluded with a clear request to her parents. "I'm telling you why this happened so that you will know and so that you'll have something to use, some knowledge to try to get me out of here," she said. "If you can get the food thing organized before the 19th, then that's OK, and it would just speed up my release. Today is Friday the eighth, and in Kuwait the commandos negotiated the release of their hostages, and they left the country. Bye." (In this and subsequent communiqués, the SLA made references to events in the news to prove that the stated dates of the recordings were accurate.)

The town of Hillsborough was devoted to the tasteful display of wealth. It banned sidewalks, commercial businesses, apartment buildings, houses smaller than twenty-five hundred square feet, and lots of less than half an acre. Even by the lofty standards of Hillsborough, the French provincial house at 233 West Santa Inez Avenue stood out for its grandeur. Built in 1914, the ten-thousand-square-foot structure had twenty-two rooms, nine bedrooms, and a garage with an apartment for the chauffeur. Until Patricia was kidnapped, few were even granted the privilege of seeing the house, for it was camouflaged from the street by full-grown Monterey pines, flowering plum trees, rhododendrons, and camellias (the last a nod to the southern roots of the lady of the house).

The house was also fraying a little around the edges, like the Hearst family itself. The small pool needed work, and the bathhouse was falling apart. With the youngest of the family's five daughters nearly out of high school, the Hearsts had put the place on the market, just before the kidnapping, for $400,000 (roughly $2 million in 2016 dollars). There were no takers. Unbeknownst to the public, and certainly to Patricia's kidnappers, the Hearsts had less disposable cash than many supposed. And now, suddenly, their cherished privacy had vanished. Dozens, then scores, of journalists and their support personnel camped on the edge of the driveway. The phone company ran new lines into the property for the journalists' phones, which were nailed to trees by the street. At first, Catherine Hearst tried to preserve a measure of propriety by treating the reporters as guests. She directed Emmy Brubach, the family cook, to distribute homemade asparagus soup to the waiting throng, helping them ward off the February chill.

Suddenly, too, the big house seemed very crowded. Randy and Catherine sequestered themselves within its walls, waiting for news, along with Emmy the cook and their live-in housekeeper. (The chauffeur's residence was vacant and made available to reporters to use the facilities.) The other Hearst sisters came home, and Gina brought her husband, Jay. Patricia's cousin William Randolph Hearst III, known as Will, also set up shop in the house. Twenty-four years old and a Harvard graduate, Will was known as "the cool Hearst," the only one with a modicum of familiarity with the counterculture, and he served as a kind of interpreter for the communications from the kidnappers. On Saturday, February 9, Steven Weed was discharged from the hospital, and he moved into one of the bedrooms as well.

The FBI's Charlie Bates made nightly pilgrimages to Hillsborough, to report on progress in the investigation (or mostly the lack thereof), where he joined the lower-level agent who was living on the premises. (The agent's main job was to answer the Hearsts' home telephone, which rang more or less continuously with calls from journalists, friends, and cranks.) The FBI command post was in the library, where the agents stored their .38-caliber revolvers on the mantelpiece below a Della Robbia ceramic dating from the Renaissance. The big house quickly became claustrophobic, with all the bodies in such proximity. A river of scotch and red wine lubricated the proceedings.

The psychics soon followed. Catherine Hearst was the most religious member of the family, but she also had a weakness for the paranormal, which was exacerbated by her worry about her daughter. Randy, too, was willing to try anything to find Patricia. So when several callers suggested that they had supernatural abilities to locate missing persons, the Hearsts, desperate for any information, took several up on their offers. Shortly after the kidnapping, Patricia's sister Gina and her husband, Jay, went to Los Angeles to meet with Peter

Hurkos, who called himself "the world's foremost psychic" and made multiple guest appearances on Johnny Carson's *Tonight Show*. (Steven Weed, who was more skeptical, referred to Hurkos as Swami Number 1.) Gina and Jay brought Hurkos one of Patricia's nightshirts, which he ran his hands over and announced that he could not immediately locate her. But he asked to keep one of Patty's shirts, just in case the spirits changed their minds. At the same time, a former astronaut named Ed Mitchell provided the assistance of his "parapsychology" research center in Palo Alto. Mitchell told Randy that he was in touch with twelve people from various parts of the globe, and they all concurred that Patricia was being held in a house near a large body of water, probably in a beach community.

Swami Number 2 (as Weed dubbed her) was Helen Tully, of Nutley, New Jersey. The FBI, revealing its desperation (and lack of leads), actually embraced Tully as a source of information. Agents asked Randy Hearst and Weed to bring the bloody shirt Weed had worn on the night of the kidnapping to Tully, who was ensconced at a hotel near the San Francisco airport. Tully brought along her psychiatrist, who purported to place her in a deep trance while she held the shirt.

"You are at the apartment now," the psychiatrist murmured to Tully. What did she see?

"Yes, I see them. They are driving north. They are in a great hurry." (The kidnappers drove south, and slowly.) But she reported that it was too dark to see the license plate. Undeterred, the psychiatrist told Tully, who was still purportedly in a trance, that she had infrared glasses that allowed her to see in the dark. Tully then proceeded to announce a series of letters and numbers, which two FBI agents dutifully recorded. Tully droned on for almost two hours, and Randy Hearst, stressed and exhausted, fell asleep on the floor of the hotel room. (The FBI declined Tully's request to be placed in the trunk of a car and driven around Berkeley, as Patricia had been.) Tully's leads also went nowhere.

Yet another psychic, the Dutch-born Jan Steers (Swami Number 3), actually moved into the Hearst mansion briefly, to sense Patricia's vibrations, but he was also eventually sent packing.

The FBI welcomed still one more psychic, who took agents around Berkeley, looking for a blue Pontiac that the spirits had informed her was related to the kidnapping. No luck.

For all the people assembled in the house, the actual responsibility for responding to the kidnappers belonged to just one man—Randy Hearst. On the surface, he seemed almost comically ill-suited to the role—an overfed plutocrat whose cosseted existence could scarcely differ more from the lives of the criminals holding his daughter. And he did make mistakes, especially at the beginning. But the kidnapping of Patricia also turned out to be transformational for her father. He learned a great deal about an alien and dangerous world, and by the time his daughter came home, he had become a different man.

For starters, Randy felt compelled to respond to the tape of Patricia's voice, so he and Catherine stepped up to a forest of microphones on February 13. This would become a familiar tableau: Patricia's parents, standing in their crescent-shaped driveway, responding to the latest developments in the case. Randy wore tweeds, Catherine a black dress appropriate for mourning. On this occasion, Randy addressed his daughter directly. "Patty, I hope you're listening," he said. "We're really pleased to know you're OK." (Her father's frequent references to her as Patty, which were broadcast around the world, condemned her to a lifetime of being referred to by that sobriquet, even though she always preferred for strangers to call her Patricia.) "You sounded a little tired or like you were sedated, but you sounded all right and I'm sure that the people who have you are telling the truth when they say they are treating you under the Geneva Convention," he went on.

Randy Hearst was not especially articulate, but his concern for his daughter was obviously genuine. He was used to saying what was on his mind, and he did so in this long-distance negotiation as well. "It's a little bit frightening, because the original demand is one that is impossible to meet. However, in the next twenty-four to forty-eight hours, I'll be trying my best to come back with some kind of a coun-teroffer that's acceptable. It's very difficult because I have no one to negotiate with, except through a letter that generally comes two or three days later than we expect it." He made one more point: "No one's going to bust in on them or start a shoot-out." Randy's voice nearly broke when he said, "Hang in there, honey."

Catherine was already weeping when she leaned in to speak after her husband. "We love you, Patty, and we're all praying for you," she said. "I'm sorry I'm crying but I'm happy you're safe, and be strong. I know God will bring you back."

Once Randy returned to the house, however, he realized that he made the SLA's ransom demand sound like an invitation to a business negotiation. So a couple of hours later, he returned to the microphones and apologized for his previous remarks. He said he wasn't trying to bargain down the price for his daughter's freedom. "Obviously, I don't see how I can meet a four-hundred-million-dollar program," he said. "But I just want these people to know, these members of the SLA, I'm going to do everything in my power to set up the type of program they're talking about."

The question, then, was, how in the world was he going to do that?

Randy led a rarefied existence, but he had the good fortune to own a journalism company, which had access to people at all levels of society. So when he put out the word that he needed access to expertise in food banks, he received answers in hours. Look, he was told, to Seattle.

When Congress killed the supersonic transport project in 1971, the fortunes of Boeing's home city took a sharp turn for the worse. Local churches felt compelled to start food banks, and by 1974 a woman named Peggy Maze ran a network of them, called Neighbors in Need,

across the state of Washington. A Hearst company functionary tracked
Maze down within a day or two of the SLA's demand. Uncomfortable
with placing the fate of the project (and Patricia) in the hands of a
woman, the functionary asked Maze about her boss. She didn't really
have one, but the Washington secretary of state, A. Ludlow Kramer,
had taken an interest in her work. So within a matter of hours, Kramer
and Maze found themselves across the dining room table from Randy
Hearst in Hillsborough. Could they create a food giveaway program
virtually overnight? Hearst asked. Kramer and Maze said they could,
and they decided to call their creation People in Need.

Kramer was tall and taciturn, with a vague resemblance to Abra-
ham Lincoln. Maze was short and voluble.

"No one can make a dollar go farther than I can," Maze boasted.
Hearst was impressed. He also had no other options, so he asked the
pair to take the next step in organizing the giveaway, which was to
meet with what he called "the groups."

In their communication demanding the giveaway, the SLA had
listed more than a dozen community and political groups that were
to participate in and monitor the process. This proved to be a savvy
move. The groups ranged from the Black Panthers and the United
Farm Workers to local operations like the Glide Memorial Church in
San Francisco. Several of these organizations, like the Panthers and the
UFW, immediately refused to be associated with the SLA because of
its responsibility for the assassination of Marcus Foster. But most of
the others, including the American Indian Movement and the United
Prisoners Union, agreed to take part, mostly by contributing members to assist in the distribution of food. Most important, the participating groups helped validate the operation. Their involvement
marked a turning point in the brief history of the SLA—a crucial step
in the laundering of its reputation.

The *Berkeley Barb,* the alternative weekly that served as the unofficial paper of record for the Bay Area counterculture, reflected this
change in the SLA's public image. Following the kidnapping, and the
demand for the food giveaway, the *Barb* heaped praise on the SLA.

The group has "pulled off a devastatingly successful action, under-scored the extent of poverty in this state, and written a few pages of American history," one article noted. "Terror has always been a tool of government and has a legitimate use in actions taken by guerrilla groups against repressive governments. . . . The life of each Vietnam-ese peasant is just as valuable as the life of Patty Hearst, who is another non-combatant caught up in a war." *Barb* headlines from this period included "SLA, We Love You" and "How Can I Join?" In this way, the kidnapping of Hearst, and especially the food giveaway, became such important, high-profile national events that they pushed the SLA's involvement in the Foster murder from the public consciousness. After only three months, this heinous event, amazingly enough, was on its way to being forgotten.

On the same day that Kramer and Maze visited Randy, the SLA released another tape from Patricia. Her voice was more relaxed, her message conciliatory, at least in part. "Dad, Mom, I'm making this tape to let you know that I'm still OK and to explain a few things," she said. "First, about the good-faith gesture. There was some mis-understanding about that, and you should do what you can, and they understand that you want to meet their demands. . . . They were not trying to present an unreasonable request. It was never intended that you feed the whole state. So whatever you come up with is basically OK. And just do it as fast as you can, and everything will be fine."

But there was an edge to Patricia's voice in this new tape, too, a kind of confidence that had not been apparent before. She displayed impatience—not with her captors, but with her parents. "And so, I mean, Dad, you shouldn't listen or believe what anybody else says about the way I'm being treated, this is the way I'm being treated," she said, in language that sounded more ad-libbed than rehearsed. "And I'm not left alone, and I'm not just shoved off somewhere. I mean, I am fine. Also, since I am an example, and it's really important that everybody understand that, you know, I am an example and a warning. And because of this it's very important to the SLA that I return safely. And so people should stop acting like I'm dead. Mom should get out of her black dress, that doesn't help at all." The shot at her mother's outfit could never have been scripted by anyone else; it was pure Patricia.

Randy chose to see the encouraging signs in Patricia's tape and moved ahead to fund People in Need. First, though, there was a matter of some awkwardness. Randy Hearst was less wealthy than people thought. William Randolph Hearst, the Chief, had not only excluded his five sons from managing the Hearst Corporation but controlled their financial destinies as well. Worried that his hard-drinking sons might squander the family fortune, the Chief tied up most of the Hearst fortune in trusts controlled by professional money managers, not members of the family. Randy and his brothers had access to splendid family resources, like the San Simeon and Wyntoon estates, but they didn't own them—or much else. Even with the SLA acknowledging that People in Need didn't need $400 million, the giveaway still required a big infusion of cash, and Randy had to scramble.

After a series of quick negotiations with his bankers, Randy was able to return to the driveway, with the still-black-garbed Catherine by his side, to announce the official launch of People in Need. "Arrangements have been made for two million dollars to be delivered to a tax-exempt charitable organization approved by the Attorney General of California, capable of making distribution for the benefit of the poor and needy," he said. "Of this amount, half a million dollars represents my own sum. This happens to be a substantial part of my personal assets." Randy arranged for the other $1.5 million to come from the William Randolph Hearst Foundation. (Two million dollars is roughly $10 million in 2016 dollars.) He announced further that he had retained William Coblentz, a well-connected San Francisco attorney, "to see that Russell Little and Joseph Remiro get a fair trial and receive due process in all phases of the proceedings." Randy knew that the SLA had not yet directly linked Patricia's fate to that of Little and Remiro, but he believed this gesture in their direction represented another manifestation of his good faith.

In his awkward way, Randy tried to signal to the SLA that his consciousness was being raised as well. "My own feeling is that this can be quite successful," he said of the food giveaway. "However, I do feel that the real problems go much deeper than food and go into jobs and job placements. Possibly later we can do something about that, but at this time we'll look into some of it."

Kramer and Maze spent their first couple of days in San Francisco working out of the offices of the Hearst Foundation, but they knew they would need a major facility where they could collect and then distribute the food. Maze asked for help from Joseph Alioto, the mayor of the city and an old acquaintance, who directed them to a cavernous, unused World War II–era warehouse on the bay, in a neighborhood known as China Basin. (The warehouse is close to the current site of the San Francisco Giants' ballpark.) Maze also contacted the distributor she had used in Seattle, who began ordering food to be sent to the warehouse and then distributed to the poor.

Like everything regarding the Hearst case, the creation of People in Need, and its location in China Basin, had received a great deal of publicity. The walls were plastered with photographs of Patricia bearing the words "This is what it's all about." In short order, the warehouse became a magnet for people: volunteers, who wanted to pack boxes; donors, who wanted to drop off food; and curiosity seekers, who just wanted to be part of the scene. More to the point, because it was common knowledge that Kramer and Maze had $2 million to spend, that money became a magnet for every hustler in the city.

Soon after Maze settled into her office at China Basin, a trio of men, all wearing dark suits and dark glasses, arrived unannounced.

The leader introduced himself as the Reverend Jim Jones, who ran an organization called the Peoples Temple.

"You're an outsider," Jones told Maze. "This operation should be run by local people." With a slight edge of menace, Jones said he should be the one to run the program and manage the $2 million.

Maze, who happened to be a San Francisco native, told Jones that she was fully capable of running the giveaway, and she showed Jones and his colleagues to the door.

Another pair of early visitors were Joseph X Polite and Leonard X Vaughn, two members of the Nation of Islam. They informed Maze that they served as local distributors for several food providers and expressed the view that PIN should buy food through the Nation of Islam. Maze passed, explaining that she was using her distributor based in Seattle. But the two men declined to take no for an answer and made their way to Hillsborough, where they secured an audience with Randy Hearst, who had an open-door policy for almost anyone who purported to have a connection to the kidnapping. Without saying so directly, the two men suggested that a congenial relationship with the Nation of Islam might ingratiate the Hearsts with the kidnappers and their allies. Randy responded by calling Maze and ordering her to buy some food from the two men. Maze bought some eggs, which was only the beginning of her problems with the Nation of Islam.

The human traffic in the China Basin warehouse reflected the raffish mix of San Francisco in the mid-1970s—from hippies to Teamsters. Cigarette and marijuana smoke drifted toward the ceiling of the hangar-like building. For this reason, the most unusual early visitor to the warehouse was a woman who appeared out of place in this environment, if not in the rest of the United States. She looked to be in her mid-forties, and she wore her hair in a prim bob and had on a skirt that draped well below her knee. She approached Maze, who was briefing half a dozen or so new volunteers.

"God sent me," the woman said.

All the heads swiveled toward her at once.

She explained to Maze that she was an accountant who wanted to serve in that role for PIN. Her conversation, like her initial remark, was just a little off-kilter. Her professional background, like her appearance, appeared to be entirely conventional. Her most recent job, she said, was to keep the books at a country club. She lived in Danville, a distant suburb of San Francisco, but she was willing to make a full-time commitment to the work of PIN. She also mentioned that she had a son, and his father was a "Hollywood movie star" whom she was not permitted to name. At this point, Maze could not be too picky, especially for those with real skills, like this woman. PIN was already a cauldron of eccentricity, so what was one more odd duck in the mix?

So Sara Jane Moore, who would attempt to assassinate President Gerald Ford nineteen months later, was kept on to tend the books of People in Need.

THREE HUNDRED BALD MEN

Improbably, in just a few days, the warehouse at China Basin began to fill up with food. Teamsters driving forklifts dodged ex-cons loading cartons of milk on pallets. Several dozen Cal students volunteered out of solidarity with their kidnapped classmate. (This gesture had some poignancy because none of these volunteers actually knew Patricia; her closed-off life with Steve Weed did not allow for friendships with fellow students.) DeFreeze originally demanded that the giveaway start on February 19, but Patricia's subsequent tape recording indicated some flexibility on the date. The PIN leadership planned the first deliveries for Friday, February 22. The project was coming together.

Then, again, the impulsiveness of DeFreeze crushed hopes of a smooth beginning. On February 21, he released a new tape that excoriated Randy Hearst's $2 million plan. This was, of course, unfair and irrational, especially because Patricia's last tape had all but endorsed a modified version of DeFreeze's original $400 million proposal. But the general field marshal, marinating in anger and plum wine, operated by his own rules, and he threw the whole PIN plan into doubt. "The Hearst empire has attempted to mislead the people and to deceive them by claiming to put forth a good faith gesture of $2 million," DeFreeze said. "This amount is not at all a good faith gesture but rather is an act of throwing a few crumbs to the people, forcing them to fight over it [*sic*] among themselves." He also revised his earlier demand to limit distribution to certain specified groups, like welfare recipients. Now, he insisted, the food should be given to anyone who asked for it.

DeFreeze then repeated much of what he had said in earlier communications about the Hearsts' assets. "The Hearst Foundation is a front for the Hearst fortune," he said. "The foundation donates $3 million a year to established charities to maintain its legal status as a foundation. The $1.5 million proposed to be coming from the foundation is nothing more than half of what the foundation is legally required to donate annually." Here, again, the *Berkeley Barb* backed the SLA cause, writing, "Randolph has been willing to undertake a heartless deception concerning the extent of his wealth, even at the risk of his daughter's life." Of course, DeFreeze didn't know (or didn't care) that Randy Hearst's personal wealth was a great deal less than he imagined; nor did DeFreeze acknowledge that the foundation might have had other priorities besides paying off his extortionate demands. Still, for the moment, Patricia's presence in the Daly City closet gave DeFreeze the leverage in the standoff.

His new demand was for an additional $4 million for PIN—for a total of $6 million. In addition, DeFreeze tied Patricia's fate even more directly to those of Little and Remiro. If Hearst did not provide the additional $4 million, DeFreeze said, "all further communications shall be suspended," and Patricia would remain a prisoner of war "until such time as the status of our captive soldiers is changed."

DeFreeze was so mercurial—alternately enraged and disengaged—that it was often difficult to see why anyone paid attention to him. He often seemed like a drunken fool. But his statement on February 21 contained a peroration that had an undeniable, if malevolent, power, and it helped explain why, for all his faults, he could still captivate his followers. During the previous week, press reports had identified Cinque as the escaped convict Donald DeFreeze. But DeFreeze, in his tape, used his blown cover as a metaphor for his place in the world. "You know me," DeFreeze said, so you think you can dismiss me. "You know me," so you think you don't have to repent for your own misdeeds.

"To this I would say yes—you do indeed know me," DeFreeze went on. "You have always known me. I'm that nigger you have hunted and feared night and day. I'm that nigger you have killed hundreds of my people in a vain hope of finding. I'm not that nigger that is no longer just hunted, robbed and murdered. I'm the nigger that hunts you now.

"Yes, you know me. You know us all, I'm the wetback. You know me, I'm the gook, the broad, the servant, the spic.

"Yes, indeed, you know us all, and we know you—the oppressor, murderer and robber. And you have hunted and robbed and exploited us all. Now we are the hunters that will give you no rest. And we will not compromise the freedom of our children.

"Death to the fascist insect."

Still, if the SLA had had to rely only on DeFreeze's intermittent eloquence alone, its reach would not have extended beyond his bedroom. What made the SLA something more than a product of DeFreeze's imagination were the women by his side: Patricia "Mizmoon" Soltysik and Nancy Ling Perry. They were the muscle behind the assassination of Marcus Foster, the kidnapping of Patricia Hearst, and the "actions" that followed.

Mizmoon Soltysik and DeFreeze were a kind of prototypical couple for their milieu in Berkeley. Mizmoon was white and middle-class, and DeFreeze was black and poor, and they shared something more than their radical politics—a deep loathing for their fathers. (This was common among the SLA comrades.) Born in 1950, Mizmoon was the third of seven children raised in a small house near Santa Barbara, and in her early years she did her best to conform to her parents' expectations. She excelled as a future farmer in 4-H, as a cheerleader, and as a high school student, earning a 3.83 grade point average. She was even her mother's designated representative to take her siblings to worship in the local Catholic church. But Mizmoon's desire to start dating in high school soured her relationship with her father, a pharmacist, and his violent rages about this and other subjects ultimately compelled her mother to seek a divorce, just as Mizmoon was graduating from high school. She rejected her father's politics but inherited his ferocity.

She pieced together three scholarships to pay her tuition at Berkeley, but like many students in that era she soon felt more at home in the political scene than in the classroom. Soltysik had a part-time job as a janitor in the Berkeley Public Library, and she found a sense of community there among the researchers, activists, and hangers-on who used the library as their base. Mizmoon learned to use the library as well as clean it, and her research skills defined her role in the early days of the SLA. She dropped out of college as a junior, in 1971. She dated women and men, usually African Americans, but then fell in love with a white woman—Camilla Hall.

Of all the members of the SLA, Hall represented the least likely revolutionary. She was born in 1945 to a Minnesota family tormented by misfortune. Her father, a Lutheran minister, and mother, a homemaker who also taught art, had four children, and three of them died of childhood diseases—two of congenital nephritis, one of polio. Camilla tried to compensate for her parents' losses; she was named class clown in her senior year of high school. She went on to the University of Minnesota and did social work after graduation. Her politics, like her personality, were earnest and conventional. She took her work seriously, writing home about her efforts on behalf of a troubled eighth grader, "I'm having a hard time keeping an emotional distance from my client. I'm human and I get emotionally involved." Noting that her parents were about to sell the family home, outside Minneapolis, she wrote them a letter that might have been more revealing than they realized. She said she had thought about moving back to the house, "but not until I'm married and have some kids—and who knows when that will be? (i.e. don't hold your breath)."

Hall was gay. She never came out to her parents, but like untold numbers of closeted young people she moved away, in her case to California. She tried to sell her drawings at a small gallery and wrote poetry for women's publications. In the Bay Area, Hall no longer had to hide her sexual identity, and her poems displayed her new freedom:

> I will cradle you
> in my woman lips
> kiss you
> with my woman lips,
> fold you to my heart and sing,
>> Sister woman,
>> you are joy to me.

Hall found a job as a gardener for a small park in Berkeley and reveled in her communion with the natural world (the subject of several of her poems). She represented what would soon become an archetype: the arty lesbian out to make her gentle way through the galleries and gardens of Berkeley.

Hall's downfall began when she fell for Patricia Soltysik, who, for a time, reciprocated her affection. In the joyful first days of their relationship, Hall wrote a poem in honor of her lover, whom she dubbed Ms. Moon and then rewrote as Mizmoon. Patricia was so taken with the appellation that she went to the trouble of legally changing her name to Mizmoon Soltysik.

They were an odd couple—the brooding Soltysik, who was small and wiry, and the airy Hall, who was zaftig and ungainly. Mizmoon spent most nights in their apartment, which featured a poster of a Vietnamese woman bearing a machine gun, but she was never fully committed to the relationship. Even when she lived with Hall, Mizmoon insisted on seeing other people, including men. Hall tried to talk the language of revolution, but she had trouble even pretending that she was a radical. "Revolution has to be social as much as political," she wrote to her parents, "but it's going so slowly that it doesn't seem like a revolution at all . . . very gradual consciousness raising would probably be a better term."

Like most SLA relationships, the union between Mizmoon and

Hall was up-and-down. Mizmoon pulled away from Hall in late 1972, writing to her sister, "But, much as I want Camilla to be happy and get what she wants, I'm not into being her lover. Saying yes, though, about sex things, just has to come 'for real' from me." Hall moved out of their apartment and vagabonded around Europe for a while, hoping to get Mizmoon out of her system. Still, when Hall returned from Europe in February 1973, Mizmoon went to Denver to greet her. The reunion went poorly, and they made their ways separately back to Berkeley. A few weeks later, DeFreeze took Hall's place in Mizmoon's apartment and in her life.

By the summer of 1973, Mizmoon Soltysik and Donald DeFreeze had a new roommate—Nancy Ling Perry. More than anyone except DeFreeze, Ling came to be the public symbol and voice of the SLA—a tiny spitfire who backed up her revolutionary rhetoric with gunfire. The trio represented the molten core of the SLA. During that summer, the three of them began separating themselves from the outside world. They spent weeks in seclusion as they began to define their malign creation. They typed up a series of manifestos and communiqués; they created the SLA and planned the murder of Marcus Foster.

Nancy Ling Perry, who preferred to be called Ling or later by her code name of Fahizah, did most of the writing, which was only one of the paradoxes about her. She was a frantic, prolific propagandist, a writer of great urgency if not refinement, yet she was also a street person, nearly homeless, usually unemployed, except when squeezing oranges at Fruity Rudy's, a juice stand near the Peking House dumpling cart in Berkeley. Like Mizmoon, she came from a conservative background; her father managed a furniture store in Santa Rosa. Also like Mizmoon, she was a dutiful daughter through high school, a cheerleader and outstanding student; at her father's urging, she sported a Barry Goldwater button in 1964, the year before she graduated. Unlike the Soltysik home, the Ling residence was serene, and Nancy had warm relationships with her parents and brother. But after a year at Whittier College (Richard Nixon's alma mater), Ling, again like Mizmoon, made her way to Berkeley and turned her life upside down.

At twenty-six, Ling was a little older than Mizmoon and significantly more experienced. Shortly after she arrived at Berkeley, Ling fell in love with Gilbert Perry, a talented African American jazz musician. Ling horrified her parents by marrying Perry when she was twenty and their fraught relationship began her descent to the dark side of local life. Perry made little money (while cheating on his wife with a multitude of women), and Ling supported him, at first as a topless waitress and blackjack dealer at a sleazy bar in San Francisco's North Beach district. She also sold pot, worked as a call girl, and shoplifted. Ling was political in the vague sort of way that most students were in those days, but more than other members of the SLA, Ling also indulged in the spiritual side of the 1960s; she became a devotee of astrology and the *I Ching*. Another difference from her future colleagues was that Ling was more into drugs, including LSD, cocaine, and whatever commercial pharmaceuticals she could find to abuse.

Ling and Perry didn't divorce for years, but their stormy reunions became less frequent over time. By the early 1970s, Ling mostly socialized with black men, including one, Chris Thompson, who lived for a time in Peking House. Through Thompson, Ling met Willy Wolfe and through Wolfe became a visitor to Vacaville prison. She was also a lover, for a time, of both Russ Little and Joe Remiro, so it was no surprise that Little suggested she move in with Mizmoon Soltysik and Donald DeFreeze.

In the summer of 1973, the trio brooded together, their resentments simmering. Mizmoon whipsawed between DeFreeze and Camilla Hall, and between men and women, as she seethed behind her mop and pail at the library. Ling was weary from the long struggle with her husband and her overindulgence in drugs, and she had become alienated from her work at Rudy Henderson's fruit cart. (She had fallen in love with Rudy, too, and he disappointed her like all her men. When Ling was hitchhiking, a driver offered her a stolen television for $150. She presented the deal to Rudy, who bought it. When the TV turned out to be defective, Rudy insisted that Ling go to San Francisco to turn tricks until she had the money to refund his purchase price.) DeFreeze was the most embittered of the group. As a fugitive, he was trapped in the small apartment, with little prospect of ever leading a meaningful life. He missed his children, who appeared lost to him forever. He had no money, no job, no future.

In the summer of 1973, the three of them divided the labor of creating the SLA. Mizmoon, with her knowledge of the library, handled research; Ling did the writing, while DeFreeze presided and drank plum wine. His main contribution appears to have been lending his authenticity to the group as a black man and a felon. Together, as a trio, they assassinated Marcus Foster in November 1973. They planned the kidnapping the following February, and Mizmoon and Ling served as DeFreeze's confidantes during the long wait in the safe house in Daly City, with their captive secured in the closet.

Notwithstanding the broadside from DeFreeze on February 21, the people at PIN decided to go forward with the food giveaway the next day. They did accede to one new demand: anyone who wanted the food could line up and receive it.

The event was without precedent in American history. Even during the Great Depression, no one had tried, on short notice, to feed thousands of people. What made the moment even more extraordinary was that it took place because of something else that had never happened before in the United States: a political kidnapping. The nation had always prided itself on the nature of its civic discourse; lone gunmen might assassinate our leaders, but this was not a place, like Europe or South America, where political outlaws kidnapped their adversaries or robbed banks. So the Hearst kidnapping and its aftermath suited the hallucinogenic moment, where America looked less like itself and more like a foreign country.

The country was reeling in February 1974. On the sixth, two days after Patricia was kidnapped, the House of Representatives voted to authorize the Judiciary Committee to hold hearings on the impeachment of President Nixon. On February 20, Reginald Murphy, the editor of the *Atlanta Constitution,* was also kidnapped, and the ransom demand came from something called the American Revolutionary Army. (The kidnapper turned out to be more emotionally unstable than politically motivated, and Murphy was released unharmed after two days. Randy Hearst later hired Murphy to run the *San Francisco Examiner.*) With the Arab oil embargo still in place, California, the most car-besotted state in the nation, instituted gas rationing; inflation was raging, unemployment rising. Also on February 20, Patricia Hearst turned twenty years old, which the journalists stationed outside the house in Hillsborough commemorated with a ten-foot-long sign that said, in red letters, "HAPPY BIRTHDAY PATTY FROM THE NEWSMEN." Against this backdrop, the food giveaway began.

PIN announced that the first distribution would take place in four places—minority neighborhoods in San Francisco, Richmond, East Palo Alto, and East Oakland. (Sara Jane Moore, despite her dowdy appearance, turned out to be a zealous turf fighter in the fledgling organization, and she more or less appointed herself public spokesperson for PIN as well as its chief bookkeeper.) Using the expertise they developed in Seattle, Kramer and Maze quickly mastered the process of getting food delivered to the warehouse in China Basin. Getting the food out the door and into the hands of the needy was more difficult. They had less experience with that kind of work and fewer local contacts who appeared able to get the job done. This led Kramer and Maze, in the improvisational ballet that was PIN, to agree to hand out the food in sites owned by the Nation of Islam.

The distribution was supposed to begin at noon on February 22, but it was just after dawn when thousands of people started lining up waiting for the deliveries. In the confusion of that first day, the PIN trucks didn't even leave the warehouse until early afternoon. The crowds stirred impatiently. With cell phones not yet invented, and little in the way of communication coming out of China Basin anyway, the restlessness of the crowds turned to truculence and then to anger. The boxes, all stenciled with the seven-headed logo of the SLA, were supposed to contain a great deal of food: a rack of lamb, a beef roast, a "picnic" ham, a packet of four steaks, a roasting chicken, and either a box of frozen fish or a pork roast, as well as a dozen eggs, a quart of milk, boxes of macaroni and cheese dinners, potatoes, onions, fresh fruits, two boxes of rice, fresh vegetables, flour, instant cocoa mix, and canned milk. (Not all boxes contained everything, but full boxes weighed about twenty-seven pounds.) In three of the cities, the distribution went chaotically but peacefully. The Oakland location was another story.

By 1974, Your Black Muslim Bakery, as it was called, was already a kind of landmark in Oakland. Yusuf Bey (born Joseph Stevens) had a talent for making bean pies and a friendship with Elijah Muhammad, the leader of the Nation of Islam. Bey had opened the establishment in 1971 in response to Muhammad's suggestion that he produce goods in accord with Muslim dietary laws, with no refined sugar, fats, or preservatives, as well as the Nation of Islam's imperative for black pride, self-help, and personal discipline. Bey also earned a reputation, like the Nation of Islam itself, for rough treatment of adversaries. Allegations of extortion, abuse, even rape, behind the closed doors of the bakery surfaced from its earliest days.

On the morning of February 22, roughly five thousand people lined up on the sidewalks leading to the bakery, where the PIN trucks were supposed to deliver the food packages. Waiting for hours, the crowd spilled into the street, blocking the way of the first truck that arrived in the afternoon. The driver sat on his horn, and someone in the crowd threw a bottle through his window. A riot ensued.

As more trucks arrived on the clogged streets, people stopped them and began forcibly removing the goods. The scene quickly degenerated. People threw food from the trucks into the crowd, and heavy items—especially the frozen meats—became weapons. Twenty-one people were treated in hospitals. Gangs of kids followed those lucky enough to snare some food and relieved them of the bounty. The trucks were emptied within an hour, and thousands of those waiting received nothing at all. Television cameras captured the chaos.

For the Hearsts, the aftermath of the fiasco in Oakland added insult to injury. One woman lost an eye when someone threw a rock through her car window, and she sued Randy Hearst, PIN, and the city of Oakland for $1 million. The proprietors of the bakery asserted that they were forced to distribute food from their own stocks to keep those waiting outside from rioting. Specifically, they made the improbable claim that they had doled out 150,000 pounds of fish and 820 cases of eggs. In light of this, the bakery presented PIN with a bill for $154,000—a transparent attempt at a shakedown of a deep-pocketed patron. Kramer had a starchy sense of rectitude, and he wanted to give the bakery owners nothing. But Randy, worried about offending any potential ally in the effort to free Patricia, approved a payment of $99,026. According to Kramer's admittedly imprecise estimate, about nine thousand people received some food on the first, disastrous day of the giveaway. But the real question, on the night of February 22, was whether the program could continue at all.

On the night of the Oakland fiasco, Randy Hearst called Bill Coblentz, his street-savvy lawyer, begging for ideas that might save the project and thus Patricia. Coblentz, in turn, placed a call to a young private investigator named David Fechheimer, the deputy to Hal Lipset, the PI who was handling security at the PIN warehouse. Coblentz's question was simple: How the hell could they fix this thing?

Fechheimer had an idea: Delancey Street.

John Maher was born in New York in 1940 and grew up there as a child heroin addict and street hoodlum. He moved to Los Angeles and cleaned up his life with the help of Synanon, the cultlike drug treatment program. After Maher moved to San Francisco, he wanted to help addicts like himself, but he sought to do it in a way that reflected both the rigor of Synanon and the off-kilter sensibilities of his adopted home. So in 1971, Maher founded the Delancey Street Foundation, one of the most effective, and also one of the quirkiest, drug treatment programs in the nation.

Maher scraped together funds to buy the former Russian consulate, in tony Pacific Heights, where he spent several years fighting neighbors who wanted to evict Delancey Street. Maher took the toughest cases—long-term drug addicts, recently released prisoners, gang members, and hopeless alcoholics. He treated them with a dizzying combination of deference and discipline. Sometimes Maher picked them up from prison in a Rolls-Royce, but he insisted that they shave their heads, live under his supervision, and work seven days a week. Maher took no government money and started a business that reflected the local values: a posh restaurant, called Delancey Street, fully staffed by his residents.

On the afternoon following the Oakland fiasco, Fechheimer convened a meeting with Randy Hearst, Bill Coblentz, and Maher at the Delancey Street restaurant, which was located on San Francisco's fashionable Union Street. Hearst wore a tie; Maher showed up in his customary outfit of a buckskin jacket over a white cashmere turtleneck. Fechheimer explained the problem. PIN needed a genuine security force that could protect both the warehouse in China Basin and the various distribution centers. Hustlers and crooks were lusting after Hearst's money, and PIN needed a force that would not just stop them but intimidate them from even trying. Could Maher's Delancey Street residents help?

Maher pondered. "I have three hundred men and thirty trucks, and I'm willing to help you, but I have two conditions," he said. Hearst, Coblentz, and Fechheimer leaned forward to hear the terms.

"We will not accept any payment, and we will not accept any publicity," Maher said. The three men stammered that those conditions appeared acceptable. Maher excused himself to use the pay telephone in the restaurant. Within a few minutes, dozens of bald-headed ex-goons appeared, in a surreal parade, marching down Union Street. They were reporting for their assignment to China Basin.

The Delancey Street residents mostly stopped the wreckage and pilfering—though a truck with food for four thousand people was hijacked the following week. Still, Randy Hearst had to deal with the other, new disaster on his hands—DeFreeze's demand for an additional $4 million.

So Randy changed tactics. His initial impulse had been simply to accede, as best he could, to whatever the SLA demanded. But that approach failed to produce Patricia's release and also yielded an escalating series of demands. So Randy took a harder line, in part because he had no other choice; he didn't have another $4 million. Not that he expected Cinque to understand, but Randy didn't even control the company or foundation that bore his name; his father, the Chief, had seen to that. And the professionals in charge were loath to funnel any more money in the direction of lunatics like DeFreeze and Ling.

Randy was grim-faced as he took to the microphones on his driveway. "The size of the latest demand of the SLA is far beyond my financial capability," he said. "Therefore, the matter is out of my hands." With that, Charles Gould, Hearst's second-in-command at the *Examiner* (and the day-to-day boss of the place), stepped in to make a statement. He said the Hearst Corporation was prepared to contribute an additional $4 million to People in Need "provided Patricia Hearst is released unharmed." It was a dramatic change in the Hearst bargaining position, which Gould underlined. "Two million dollars will be contributed immediately upon the release of Patricia and two million more will be contributed in January 1975." In other words, the Hearsts would provide no additional funds as long as Patricia remained a captive. As Randy trudged away from the reporters, he was despondent.

Back in the house, Steven Weed sat with his stockinged feet perched on top of the dining room table. If there was one point of unanimity among the protagonists in the kidnapping, including the Hearst family, the FBI, even the SLA and eventually the public, it was contempt for Patricia's erstwhile fiancé. Ironically, the Hearst family and the SLA had basically the same complaint about him: cowardice. Randy and Catherine had what they called a "manliness test" for their daughters' beaux; Steve, with his droopy mustache, slouching demeanor, and superior attitude, had failed that exam even before the kidnapping. Now the Hearsts felt that Weed's cowardice might have cost Patricia her life. "Whatever happened to the real men in this world, men like Clark Gable?" Catherine asked Steve one day. "No one would have carried my daughter off if there'd been a real man there." (Among themselves, Patricia's captors sneeringly made the same point.)

Trying, as always, to prove that he knew more than anyone else, Weed sought to position himself as simultaneously inside and outside the Hearst camp. He saw himself as a potential bridge to the kidnappers, so he didn't want them to think he was fully part of the establishment. For its part, the FBI also resented this supercilious attitude, and agents questioned him repeatedly and gave him a lie detector test, suspecting that he was holding back some of the truth of what happened on Benvenue. They grilled him about everything in his background, including the time at Princeton that he played quarterback for a team from Students for a Democratic Society in a touch football game against a team from ROTC. (Weed wasn't in SDS but played as a favor for a friend.) This was yet another waste of time in the FBI investigation.

As the situation with the kidnappers was deteriorating, Weed compounded the problems with a tone-deaf interview with Marilyn Baker, the reporter covering the story for KQED, the local public television station. Weed's targets included Catherine Hearst. "Patty and I always thought her mother was so hypocritical," he said. "She'd say one thing to your face and another behind your back. Like, if you asked her if she liked a new dress, she'd tell you how beautiful it was, then you'd hear her telling the cook, 'Isn't it awful?'" (He also complained that the Hearst household provided store-bought rather than homemade cookies.)

About Randy Hearst, Weed said, "Actually, we disagreed somewhat over the importance of divulging his finances. He does not seem to understand how people, even very intelligent people, could fail to understand his financial status. One of the problems, though, is that Mr. Hearst is getting too much advice—from friends, relatives, the authorities, even the cook."

Of the FBI, he said, "Unfortunately, they're almost comical. Mr. Bates comes in and sits down. He's poured a drink, then Mr. and Mrs. Hearst and whoever just sit down and chat. The comical part is how adept Mr. Bates is at not telling us anything." Did he trust the FBI? "To a point. I do not believe that the FBI wants Patty to die, but I think the SLA would be wrong to trust them entirely."

Weed even offered faint praise to his fiancée: "Oh, she's pretty, you know, the prettiest of any of the Hearsts' daughters. But then none of them are raving beauties. She's a bright girl, too. Not brilliant, of course, but reasonably bright. She's a simple girl. The simple things please her. She rarely got angry and then it would all be over in a few minutes. She has a very good character, too."

Finally, Baker asked if Weed was willing to take Patricia's place as a hostage. (Russ Little's father, the military mechanic in Florida, had publicly offered to take Patricia's place.)

"It uh . . . It depends on the circumstances. I wouldn't rule it out."

Weed's petulance and arrogance infuriated the Hearsts, of course. Privately, Randy called him an "egocentric pain in the ass." But Weed's interview also drew the notice of a different audience. Fourteen miles away, in her closet in Daly City, Patricia Hearst had been granted a television, and she was now following her own story with close attention.

"I'M A STRONG WOMAN"

The restrictions on Patricia in Daly City were loosened within a few days of the kidnapping. The first to go were the restraints on her wrists. She was blindfolded for a while, too, so she couldn't identify her captors. When she was allowed to take her blindfold off, the SLA members she could see wore ski masks. At first, the SLA had blasted music into the closet so Patricia couldn't hear their conversations, but then they let her listen to the news. They gave her a television and books, starting with George Jackson's *Blood in My Eye*. Before long, though, the door to the closet stayed open almost all day, which was the most important change of all.

And so Patricia's long conversations with members of the SLA began. Often they talked at her, especially DeFreeze, but sometimes they engaged in real conversations. Patricia was scared and weak and at times could barely stand up, but she was curious and attentive, too, especially once it became clear that the SLA had no intention of killing her. This was no indoctrination, formal or otherwise; the SLA wasn't organized enough for such an undertaking, and there was no apparent point anyway. As DeFreeze told Patricia from the beginning, they didn't expect to keep her around for very long. It's just that the SLA were *talkers,* and Patricia was, very literally, a captive audience. The three people assigned to her—Angela Atwood, Nancy Ling, and Willy Wolfe—generally spoke to her while sitting cross-legged on the floor by the door to the closet. (The house was carpeted but unfurnished.) In one remaining concession to operational security, the SLA members did continue to refer to each other by their code names in front of her, so Patricia knew her keepers as Gelina, Fahizah, and Cujo.

All of the members had assignments. Camilla Hall, Mizmoon's erstwhile lover, bought food and supplies for the group. Bill and Emily Harris also left the house occasionally to do errands, like buying disguises and conducting surveillance—mostly to see if anyone in the neighborhood was looking for them or casing 37 Northridge Drive. Mizmoon and Ling catered to DeFreeze, listening to his diatribes, researching his ideas, and writing his communiqués. As for the general field marshal himself, he spent long hours sequestered in one of the three bedrooms, brooding, drinking, and listening to music. One day, DeFreeze stunned the comrades by announcing that the SLA had a "national anthem"—a jazz tune called "Way Back Home," by the Crusaders. (When DeFreeze cited "Way Back Home" in one of the communiqués, the Crusaders were, predictably, horrified.)

Patricia had a different relationship with each of the three SLA members assigned to her. Ling spoke to her the least but made an important point: Patricia had more to fear from the FBI than from the SLA. This might have been true. In a press conference shortly after the kidnapping, William Saxbe, the attorney general, acknowledged that the FBI might launch a raid to free Patricia. It was true, too, that except for DeFreeze's growls at Patricia on the first day or two, the SLA never threatened to kill her. She was always told that she would be used as a bargaining chip; the terms of a prospective deal would never be clear to Patricia (or to the SLA), but the idea was always to use her to advance the SLA's goals, not to do her harm. But Ling and the others repeatedly asserted that they would defend themselves if the FBI or other law enforcement sought to extract Patricia by force. In such a gun battle, the cross fire could prove lethal. DeFreeze had also told her on the night of her capture that the FBI was the real threat to her safety. The SLA was not going to kill Patricia, but she might well die in an FBI raid.

The SLA was so obsessed with the idea of an FBI invasion that one day DeFreeze came to Patricia's closet with a bizarre idea. She dreaded his visits, because he was the most confrontational of her captors and the most contemptuous of her parents. ("Your mommy and daddy are insects," he said once. "They should be made to crawl on their hands and knees like insects if they want you back.") On this occasion, though, DeFreeze had a gift for Patricia. In light of the probability of a confrontation with the FBI, DeFreeze said Patricia deserved a chance to defend herself. He presented her with a sawed-off shotgun, and for the next three days she was given instructions on how to break it down, hold it, and shoot it. (Thanks to her outings with her father, Patricia already had a good idea about how to use a shotgun.) DeFreeze also presented her with a gas mask, to use in case the FBI lobbed tear gas into the house. He didn't give her ammunition at this point, but he said when the time came, he would provide her with the special SLA shells that were laced with "Ajax," which was his code word for cyanide. What to make of this gesture? Patricia was terrified at the idea of an FBI raid, especially at the thought of participating in a gun battle. But what kind of kidnapper gives his hostage a gun? The simultaneous hostility and trust from DeFreeze—the idea that she was both an enemy and a comrade—proved predictably unsettling.

By comparison, Patricia's time with Angela Atwood was a relief. Angela sat by the closet door and jabbered—"gesticulating, rolling her eyes and making like an actress playing to the galleries." As Patricia recalled, "She was full of joy, in contrast to all the others, who always were so intent and serious about their revolution." After Patricia's baths, Angela would dry her hair and then comb it out and style it, as if they were a couple of kids at America's most surreal slumber party. One night, when Patricia was still blindfolded, she was awoken by loud noises outside her door—the sound of a radio playing Kool and the Gang's "Jungle Boogie," a big hit at the time. Angela opened the door a crack and whispered, "Oh, I wish you could see this. We're all having so much fun."

"What's happening?" Patricia asked.

It was Willy Wolfe, Angela said. "Cujo is wild! He's dancing naked all over the place! He's so marvelous, you should see him!"

Angela listened to Patricia's complaints about her mother, whom she described as domineering and reactionary as well as addicted to pills and booze. (Catherine's politics had never previously been of particular interest to Patricia.) For her part, Angela spent a lot of time talking about her boyfriends, Little and Remiro (whom she called Osceola and Bo), and how much she missed them. Angela fixated on the injustice of their arrest for the murder of Marcus Foster. The government's announced theory was that Little and Remiro had been the gunmen, which they were not. (Patricia didn't learn the truth about who killed Foster until much later.) By dwelling on the government's mistaken scenario for the killing, Angela and the others avoided the larger point that Little and Remiro had been part of the conspiracy to murder the school superintendent. Still, as with the claims about the dangers of an FBI raid, the SLA's statements to Patricia about Little and Remiro had a measure of truth.

And then there was Willy Wolfe, who spent the most time of all with Patricia. He was tall, gawky, and clumsy, especially in the tight confines of the house, but he was strong, too, his limbs sinewy from scaling mountains. Wolfe wore his earnestness without the ferocity of Mizmoon and Ling or the menace of DeFreeze. He talked politics with Patricia, explaining the process of his own radicalization, which came about largely through his visits to Vacaville prison. He told how he smuggled clandestine literature, like George Jackson's work, to the prisoners. Wolfe's family didn't have the wealth or notoriety of the Hearsts, but Willy and Patricia—alone among the people crammed into the small house—shared a social class.

They talked about their lives, and Patricia's caustic side emerged in the conversations, especially when she confessed her disappointment with her fiancé. Even before the kidnapping, Patricia told Willy, she had wanted to break the engagement. It gnawed at her that Steve had said, "Take anything you want!" Steve was a wimp, "unmanly," so he stood in unspoken contrast to the revolutionaries, like Wolfe, who put their principles into action. Willy and Patricia spoke the same language, often deep into the night.

———————

Willy Wolfe grew up in the bucolic Connecticut town of New Milford, where his father was an anesthesiologist and his mother a homemaker. His childhood had more than the normal quota of troubles. After his mother came down with a mysterious paralysis, his parents went through an ugly divorce. At the age of six, Willy lost part of his foot in a lawn mower accident and walked ever after with a limp. He was a dreamy, inattentive student who graduated number 148 in his prep school class of 194 students. Willy came from a long line of Yale men, but he failed to be admitted. He set out west to Berkeley instead, hoping to study archaeology. Despite his later associations, Wolfe was always described as possessing a kind of sweetness—a soft-spoken, off-kilter charm that made people want to take care of him. He read more Thoreau than Marx.

While he was still in his first year at Cal, in 1972, he began tutoring at Vacaville and visiting Peking House, where he moved in and became a kind of mascot for the commune. At first, Wolfe knew little about politics and nothing about prisons; he didn't know much about women either, because he was almost certainly a virgin at that point. Wolfe ingratiated himself with his new roommates by sharing his love of the outdoors, especially mountain climbing. "I wasn't much of a climber at first," Russ Little, who lived there, recalled, "but I loved being outdoors with Willy, who, clumsy as he was around the house, was like a goat in the mountains." In short order, the people of Peking House taught Wolfe about politics; he told them about Vacaville. For the denizens of Peking House, the reelection of Richard Nixon in November 1972 deepened their alienation from conventional politics and reinforced George Jackson's call for apocalyptic change. They decided they would be revolutionaries, dedicated to the overthrow of the entire structure of American society. Even Wolfe, who had spent the previous summer as an aspiring scientist looking for fossils in Wyoming, now foresaw Armageddon.

Throughout 1973, Wolfe drew closer to Remiro and Little. They taught him to shoot at the rifle range. After DeFreeze escaped, Wolfe worked as a sort of runner for him, attending meetings of the Oakland school board to keep an eye on Marcus Foster. Wolfe knew next to nothing about the local political scene, and his garbled renditions of the controversy over police in schools contributed to DeFreeze's decision to go forward with the assassination in November. Wolfe had portrayed the controversy over the police as a life-and-death struggle between black and white Oakland, with Foster on the side of the oppressors. In fact, the issue was far more nuanced, and Wolfe, like DeFreeze, was shocked at the universal revulsion that followed Foster's murder.

Shaken by the assassination, Wolfe returned to his father's home in Pennsylvania over Christmas and weighed leaving the SLA. Foster's death jarred his confidence in DeFreeze. But after Remiro and Little were busted in January 1974, DeFreeze told Bill Harris to call Wolfe in Pennsylvania and summon him back. They needed his help, but mostly they needed his cash. (Besides, DeFreeze explained to Harris, Wolfe was weak and privileged, and he might talk to the authorities. It would be better to keep him under their direct control.)

Harris had mixed feelings about DeFreeze's demand. At that point, Bill barely knew Cinque (or Nancy or Mizmoon), but he did know Wolfe. He thought Willy was a good kid, kind of naive, and certainly ill-suited for a life underground. He had no experience with the kinds of "actions" that the SLA was contemplating. Harris recalled a conversation with Willy on the steps of Peking House, shortly before he went back east. "I don't know," Willy had said. "I think I might be a liability. If someone comes at me, I don't know if I could shoot them." Bill had reassured him at the time. "Oh, we're not going to have to shoot anybody," he said. "This is just armed propaganda." But now they had passed that point. Bill was asking Willy to return to a shooting war.

Bill knew, too, that Willy had fallen for a young Swedish woman and was thinking of going overseas to meet her. A trip across the ocean would keep Wolfe out of trouble, and he could put this whole strange episode behind him. Bill had a measure of humanity and a smidgen of common sense. A friend would give Willy a pass. But Bill was too caught up in the revolutionary spirit of the SLA to see himself as Willy's friend. Bill was now a soldier, and unlike when he was a marine, he believed in the cause. He received orders from his commanding officer, Cinque, and he followed them.

As for Willy, he had told his father, on January 10, that he was moving to Sweden to get married. But the following day, Wolfe received three collect phone calls from Bill, who had been directed by DeFreeze. Harris talked his young friend into returning to California—to join the battle and, more to the point, help finance it. Willy told his father that instead of going to Sweden, he was leaving immediately for New York, to visit a sick friend. Instead, Willy went west.

At some level, as Wolfe joined the team that kidnapped Patricia the following month, he knew he was joining a doomed crusade. He had enough sense to recognize the folly of the SLA but not enough sense to avoid being drawn back in. "I don't like to see you going along with the colossal rip-off of our brothers and sisters around the world," Wolfe wrote in an eerily prophetic letter to his mother back east. "Please stop kidding yourself. America is heading for either Communism or 1984. I hope you won't be a passive enemy of the people in the struggle for a decent life, and if 1984 does come, I'm a dead man."

In the first hours after her capture, Patricia had told DeFreeze the truth when she denied knowing about the Hearst family's finances. Catherine regarded the subject as vulgar, and Randy would never have thought to engage with his children on such matters, especially because they were all girls. Patricia knew that her family lived comfortably but not ostentatiously, but that was about all she knew.

So when Patricia heard her father's public statements about the limits of his personal wealth, she didn't know if he was telling the truth. But DeFreeze and Mizmoon had done research, and they assured Patricia that her father was lying. And they had scores of facts—or what appeared to be facts—to back up their view. DeFreeze gave Patricia long disquisitions on the Hearsts' business interests, and he made it sound as if Randy Hearst had many millions. In contrast, all Patricia knew was gathered from Randy's vague words, uttered with Catherine by his side. *Half a million dollars represents my own sum. This happens to be a substantial part of my personal assets. . . . The size of the latest demand of the SLA is far beyond my financial capability.* Angela, Ling, and Willy—the ones assigned to play the role of Patricia's friends—as well as DeFreeze rolled their eyes at her father's poor-mouthing. He was a Hearst! How could anyone believe that he didn't have the money they were demanding?

Patricia didn't know what to think, and it wasn't as if she were in a position to receive a dispassionate analysis of the evidence. The closet door might have opened, but the front door certainly had not. She was a prisoner, and while she was allowed to listen to some news reports, her captors remained her primary source of information. And DeFreeze made such specific assertions on the tapes, claiming, for example, that Randy had "a silver mine and thousands of acres of land in Mexico, acreage in Hawaii, and 70,000 acres of timberland in Northern California valued at millions of dollars." How was Patricia supposed to argue with that? And though their personal styles differed—from the hard-assed Ling to the sweet-voiced Willy—the message from all of them was the same: that her father was acting like a capitalist pig, that he was nickel-and-diming the SLA, and that his cheapness was taking money out of the mouths of the poor. Patricia couldn't help but notice, too, that all of the SLA demands were aimed at helping those in need, not enriching themselves. That thought stuck with her as well.

In all, during the long hours in the house in Daly City, the SLA started saying things that made sense to Patricia. The real danger came from the FBI. Little and Remiro were being framed. The SLA—starting with Cujo—was fighting for a better world. Patricia listened, and she talked, too. She was not what the SLA expected. She was curious and feisty. She laughed in the right places, especially at Weed's expense. In short order, Angela, Ling, and Willy told their comrades, *You're not going to believe this, but we like her.*

After Randy Hearst rejected DeFreeze's demand for an additional $4 million on February 22, the two sides said nothing to each other for nine days, the longest gap so far between communications. In typical fashion, DeFreeze had not gamed out a strategy. He had failed to plan what to do if Hearst refused the latest demand. Now that Hearst had done just that, DeFreeze was stumped. Further, thanks largely to the Delancey Street volunteers, the next PIN distribution on February 28 went more smoothly. The third distribution the following week, which expanded to twelve sites, went even better. (PIN stopped announcing the distribution sites in advance, which limited crowds and the potential for unrest.) Thousands were being fed. The absence of chaos, and the silence of the protagonists in the kidnapping, took the story out of the headlines. In addition, the news media were momentarily distracted by yet another plague to beset San Francisco. A strike by municipal workers paralyzed the city, leading, for example, to 426 million gallons of untreated sewage being discharged into the city's beloved bay.

Randy Hearst could not abide the silence, so he tried to break the logjam on March 3, the day before the one-month anniversary of the kidnapping. He had nothing new to offer, just a request for the kidnappers. Back in front of the cameras in his driveway, his still-black-clad wife by his side, Randy asked the kidnappers to allow some kind of direct communication with Patricia. He again flattered the SLA by invoking the Geneva Convention—as if the kidnappers were a national army. He addressed his daughter directly: "Of course, it's ridiculous to think that under the Geneva Convention we would be allowed to go in and see you . . . but under the convention, you are allowed to write from time to time to other people. See if they'll let you send us a note or something to let us know you're OK." Catherine added, "Patty, honey, your father's doing everything in his power, and I want you to know that millions of people all over the world are praying for you. I know it's been a long time, sweetheart . . . but keep up your courage, and you keep praying."

Though the Hearsts did not realize it, their statement played into DeFreeze's hands. At this point, he knew he wasn't going to get Little and Remiro released. He had lost interest in the food giveaway, even though it was finally running smoothly. Despite the rhetoric of the communiqués, the SLA was not a vehicle for social or political change; it was a spectacle, an instrument for getting attention for its own sake. This was why DeFreeze demanded that all the communiqués be printed in full. Randy's silence deprived the SLA of the oxygen to keep the story alive. Now DeFreeze had the opportunity to rally his troops to respond to Randy's statement of March 3.

Inside the SLA house, DeFreeze whipped up a volcanic reaction to Randy's latest. As Cinque saw it, Randy was now making demands of his own, instead of figuring out how to comply with the SLA's. The comrades had already proved several times that Patricia was alive and well. There was no need to provide any letters from her. This was just a stalling tactic or, more ominously, a way for the FBI to track down the location of the safe house. DeFreeze spread the word that they should prepare for an FBI raid at any moment. Training began immediately. As in the Concord house, the comrades ran and jumped around the tiny enclosed space, in a series of drills designed to simulate a gun battle with the authorities. But something was different this time. There was another comrade watching, cradling a weapon, and taking a bead on the imaginary FBI intruders. Patricia Hearst was now part of the army. From her first day in captivity, she had been told that the real threat was from law enforcement; it made a kind of sense for her to join the collective self-defense.

DeFreeze knew he had the potential for a propaganda coup on his hands, so he directed a kind of symphonic SLA message for the next recording, with four different voices speaking for the group. On March 9, a female caller alerted a local radio station to look for a package taped to the toilet of the women's room of Foster's, a well-known restaurant in San Francisco. The package contained a tape recording and Patricia's automobile club card. The first voice on the tape marked the public debut of Angela Atwood, which was a revealing choice on DeFreeze's part. He had chosen Patricia's confidante. As a way of welcoming Patricia into the fold, and easing her way to becoming a public spokeswoman, pairing her with Angela made sense.

Still, Angela's part of the recording was an embarrassment. "My name is Gelina and I am a general in the Symbionese Liberation Army," she began, announcing her rank, just as General Field Marshal Cinque had done. The former actress knew little about politics, so her words served mostly to convey the rage of the leaders—DeFreeze, Mizmoon, and Ling. She began by excoriating those groups on the political left that had failed to rally to the SLA's banner. When DeFreeze emerged from his bedroom to storm around the house, the perfidy of the Black Panthers (as well as Angela Davis and Jane Fonda, who had both also denounced the SLA) was a favorite theme. "There have been many of the Left who, without a clear understanding, have condemned the actions of the SLA, and the people's forces who have chosen to fight rather than talk," she said. "It has been claimed that we are destroying the Left, but in truth an unarmed and nonfighting Left is doomed." What made Angela's remarks more excruciating was that this ordinarily well-spoken woman adopted an African American accent. DeFreeze was always defensive about the absence of actual African Americans in the SLA, so Angela's feigned accent was his dubious attempt to address the problem.

The gist of Angela's message was certainly theatrical: that "communication between POW Patricia Hearst and her family will come after the immediate creation of the necessary mechanisms whereby Russell Little and Joseph Remiro can communicate via live national TV with the people and the SLA concerning the full scope of their physical health and all the conditions of their confinement." In other words, Angela sought to take the next logical step in the SLA's obsession with the media—that prisoners in San Quentin be permitted to speak to the nation, as in an Oval Office address.

The real bombshell came in the next part of the tape. The voice was recognizably that of Patricia Hearst, with her breathy rich-girl diction, but her tone was sharper, more irritated, and the target of her ire was obvious. "Mom, Dad," she began, "I received the message you broadcast last Sunday. It was good to hear from you after so much silence. But what you had to say sounded like you don't care if I ever get out of here."

Patricia's words neatly recapitulated what she had been told daily, sometimes hourly, for the past five weeks. All the themes were there: the perfidy of the FBI; the SLA's attraction to the media; and above all her mother and father's stinginess with regard to the poor. "I'm beginning to feel that the FBI would rather that I get killed. . . . The SLA are not the ones who are harming me. It's the FBI, along with your indifference to the poor, and your failure to deal with the people and the SLA in a meaningful, fair way. . . . I'm telling you this now because I don't think the FBI will let any more words from me get through to the media." This last was absurd, because the whole recording was immediately broadcast worldwide. She also took a swipe at her mother: "Mom, I can't believe that you've agreed with the 'out of my hands' stance of Daddy's program. I just wish that you could be stronger and pull yourself together from all these emotional outbursts.

"Whether consciously or not, the news media has been assisting the FBI for its now overt attempts to set me up for execution," Patricia said, "first, by promoting a public image of my father as a bereaved parent who has done all he can to meet the demands of his daughter's kidnappers, and who now awaits her supposedly long overdue release. In fact, the SLA demands have not even been approximated, and they have made it very clear that until the good faith gesture is completed, negotiations for my release will not begin. Second, the media, with cooperation from my parents, has created a public image of me as a helpless innocent girl who was supposedly abducted by two terrible blacks, escaped convicts. I'm a strong woman, and I resent being used this way." She added, "I have been reading a book by George Jackson called 'Blood in My Eye.' I'm starting to understand what he means when he talks about fascism in America."

Again, Patricia was working off an outline prepared by her captors, but her enthusiasm for the task appeared noticeably greater than in her earlier tapes. "While I have no access to ammunition, in the event of an attack by the FBI, I have been told that I will be given an issue of cyanide buckshot, in order to protect myself," she said. "I no longer fear the SLA, because they are not the ones who want me to die. The SLA want to feed the people, and assure safety and justice for the two men at San Quentin. I realize it is the FBI who want to murder me."

After Patricia stopped speaking, Angela took the microphone back for a moment to inform the "US government-inspected super-pigs that those you have hunted are now hunting you." Then it was Nancy Ling's turn to offer a revolutionary call, specifically in a female voice. "We women know the truth as it has been revealed in our own lives," she said. "We turn our rage toward the enemy in a direct line, down the sights of our guns." This was a first gesture toward the nascent feminist movement, and such sentiments within the SLA would become more prominent over time.

DeFreeze closed the March 9 tape recording in his usual pretentious manner. "This is General Field Marshal Cinque in command," he intoned. "I call upon oppressed people of all colors to arm themselves in defense of their own freedom while they still have the chance."

After a month in Daly City, Patricia had established some kind of relationship with virtually all members of the SLA. Angela Atwood, Nancy Ling, and Willy Wolfe were her assigned keepers, and DeFreeze and Mizmoon kept a controlling eye on her as well. Camilla Hall, the zaftig poet, was an occasional presence, flitting in and out of the house.

That left Bill and Emily Harris, the newest recruits to the SLA banner. For all his bluster and compulsive talking, Bill was baffled by the situation. Bill loved the food giveaway; it was more or less his idea, after all. But none of the others seemed interested in PIN anymore, except as a means for berating Randy Hearst. With his minuscule attention span, Bill didn't even have the patience to read or listen to the communiqués. All he knew was that DeFreeze and the others were now talking mostly about their coming clash with the FBI. He barely knew these people, and now he was on the brink of joining them in an apocalyptic showdown with the FBI. Was that really the only way this thing could end?

Bill barely spoke to Patricia. He wanted nothing to do with her and didn't want to get to know her and then perhaps feel sorry for her. He understood she represented the means to an end—to win the release of Little and Remiro and, as a bonus, to feed the poor people of the region. But it quickly became clear that the release was never going to happen, and the food giveaway had run its course. Hearst said he was finished throwing money at it. Now Bill thought the SLA needed an exit strategy—something other than a climactic gun battle.

Emily was closer to the radical SLA core, more willing to risk a showdown with the authorities. She didn't have anything to do with Patricia either, but for a different reason from her husband's. Emily had a ferocity that Bill lacked, and she was more willing to see Patricia as a potential casualty of war than as an actual human being. Taciturn where Bill was volatile, thoughtful where Bill was impulsive, Emily had a more explicitly political agenda than he did. But she, too, wondered, what was the plan? What were the next steps? Had anyone even thought about those questions?

The answer, in short, was no. DeFreeze regarded the March 9 tape, starring the indignant voice of Patricia Hearst, as a triumph. Everything else would have to wait. And as the SLA stumbled into an uncertain future, there was another issue threatening the fragile equilibrium at 37 Northridge Drive: sex.

9

THE BIRTH OF TANIA

At first, Patricia Hearst's kidnapping was reported as a story largely outside the political tumult of the 1970s. The press and the public appeared to regard the crime through the prism of celebrity rather than politics. The kidnapping was so sensational and aberrational that it existed apart from the other conflicts that were convulsing the country. It was a story for tabloid newspapers (which still existed in large numbers in those days), for *People* (which published its first issue the month after the kidnapping), and for *Newsweek* (which put Patricia on the cover seven times). For these outlets, any political implications were secondary to the drama of an heiress in captivity.

In any case, the SLA was a political orphan; even the radical Left never wanted to be represented by these irrational outlaws. At a time when politically motivated bombings were commonplace, the embrace by the SLA of assassination and kidnapping marked them as too crazy even for their putative allies in the counterculture. Because of the murder of Marcus Foster, the SLA was already a pariah in the Bay Area, scorned by the Black Panthers and other stalwarts of the movement. Even the Weather Underground, which could usually be counted on to embrace the most extreme and violent revolutionary forces in the country, couldn't bring itself to muster any enthusiasm for the SLA. Following the kidnapping, Bernardine Dohrn, one of the leaders of the Weather Underground (who at the time was a fugitive on the FBI's most wanted list), issued a communiqué stating, "We do not comprehend the execution of Marcus Foster and respond very soberly to the death of a black person who is not a recognized enemy of the people." Still, Dohrn expressed a kind of grudging respect for the kidnapping itself. While calling for no harm to come to Hearst, she said, "We must acknowledge that this audacious intervention has carried forward the basic public questions and starkly dramatized what many have come to understand through their own experience: It will be necessary to organize and to destroy this racist and cruel system."

As it turned out, though, the kidnapping became emblematic of the political evolution of the country during the 1970s—in precisely the opposite way that the SLA intended. Far from setting off a foco-style Marxist rebellion among the proletariat, the kidnapping of Patricia Hearst fueled the backlash against the Left. And paradoxically, the target of that backlash was the Hearst family as much as the SLA.

Randy Hearst was never known for strong political views— Catherine was the real conservative in the family—but he was the one who took the lead in responding to the kidnappers. His only priority was to save his daughter's life. And if that meant trying to negotiate with the kidnappers and meeting some of their demands, he resolved to do so with alacrity. But from the beginning, Randy's conciliatory press conferences drew a hostile reaction from the ascendant conservative movement and its tough-on-crime leadership. Ten days after the kidnapping, William Saxbe, the attorney general whom President Nixon installed after Elliot Richardson and his deputy resigned in the Saturday Night Massacre, opened a news conference by denouncing Hearst's plan to offer concessions to the kidnappers. This was also when Saxbe said the FBI might try to free Patricia. A policy of avoiding confrontation, he said, would amount to a "dereliction of duty."

Randy Hearst responded fiercely to the attorney general's broadside. "Mr. Saxbe is not the father of Patricia," he said in another driveway press conference. "I'm going to do what I can to get her out . . . and to make a statement that you're going to bust in and shoot the place up . . . is damn near irresponsible." In this way, the Hearsts became the symbol of the overly lenient parents of the era and a counterpoint to the Republican administration's voice of discipline and order.

It was left to Ronald Reagan, the governor of California, to distill the change in mood. As a member of the Board of Regents for the state's universities, Catherine Hearst had been Reagan's staunch ally in his crackdown on student activists across the state; still, the governor believed that the family was becoming weak in the face of the threats to Patricia. Reagan expressed disgust with the Hearsts' concessions to the criminals in a characteristically pungent way. For starters, he said his administration would remain committed to the prosecutions of Little and Remiro. But Reagan's most memorable statement came just after the People in Need food distribution began. On March 6, Reagan was the guest speaker in Washington at a private luncheon of the Bull Elephants, a club of influential Republicans. Asked about the PIN program, he said, "It's just too bad we can't have an epidemic of botulism." A shocked congressional aide leaked the remark to a reporter. The governor dismissed his quip as a joke, but as usual Reagan had tapped into a powerful stream of public sentiment. With a single remark, Reagan managed to convey disgust with the freeloaders in the ghetto as well as their indulgent benefactors in the suburbs. In the dangerous and disorderly aftermath of the 1960s, the country was full of people who were repelled by the radical criminal element and anyone, including Patricia's terrified parents, who pampered the lawbreakers.

Reagan's comment about the food giveaway (even in the unlikely event it really was a joke) would reverberate until Patricia was freed. Reagan understood the desire for a strong hand in a nation losing its grip. To a growing conservative audience, the People in Need program stood for a shiftless and lazy underclass that preferred handouts to hard work. To Reagan and his supporters, the Hearsts were a family that displayed weakness rather than strength in a crisis. And as Patricia's taped words became more supportive of her captors, she too became anathema to what was then known as the silent majority. A strong and honorable woman held firm in the face of adversity, but one who embraced the illicit and licentious values of the SLA, even under pressure, deserved no sympathy.

Perhaps the clearest symbol of how far the SLA lived from conventional American morality was this: just about the only people in the SLA who were not sleeping together were the ones who were married to each other, Bill and Emily Harris.

"Bill and I have quit our jobs and moved with people who are serious about destroying and building," Emily wrote to her parents in Illinois. "I can no longer relate to the aspirations you have for creating a comfortable life for yourselves because they ignore the tortured lives that others lead in an attempt to survive." A man she had met during her prison visits had opened her eyes. "One person in particular—a beautiful black man—has conveyed to me the torture of being black in this country and of being poor." Emily's transformation was personal as much as political. "Bill and I have changed our relationship so that it no longer confines us, and I am enjoying relationships with other men. I am in love with the black man I referred to earlier and that love is very beautiful and fulfilling."

Bill had a very different view of Emily's love affair with the prisoner (which was consummated, like many in those days, in visiting areas of the correctional institution). The relationship infuriated him, and the coldness between them persisted in the close confines in Daly City. Still, between the Harrises and the half a dozen other comrades, most of the sexual permutations were tried at one point or another. DeFreeze lived first with Mizmoon, then Nancy Ling, and then both of them. In Daly City, Ling, the former sex worker, announced that she had embraced celibacy, though she occasionally slept with Bill. Camilla was still devoted to Mizmoon, who sometimes reciprocated. Once, amid the tense waiting for something to break in the standoff over Patricia, there was a four-way romp in the bathtub involving DeFreeze, Angela, Bill, and Emily. Only Willy Wolfe, the awkward New Englander, was too shy to join in the collective high jinks.

For the SLA, there was a political theory underlying the sexual dynamics of the group. They believed that sex was a basic human need, like food or shelter. Like those other necessities, sex should be shared in an egalitarian manner. This was especially true in a safe house, where it was impractical for the comrades to circulate normally in the broader society. Later, in an interview he prepared when he was still on the run, Bill Harris explained the concept this way:

> You can't just let people drop by a safe house to socialize. So far as sex was concerned, we had to get all of our sexual and personal needs met by comrades within the cell. Everyone realized that at this time there was no room for exclusive relationships because each of us had to help the other comrades meet their sexual needs and maintain harmony within the cell. We wanted to learn to love each other on an equal basis and on many levels, including sexually. We tried not to focus on just one or two people who we might have subjectively liked best. We had a need to develop collectively and sex was just one of them.

This, in any event, was the theory. Predictably, the sexual merry-go-round had failed to maintain harmony within the house. Sexual tensions and rivalries among the comrades were epidemic, especially in the claustrophobic confines of 37 Northridge Drive. And these pressures were layered on top of the fear of an FBI raid and the uncertainty about what to do with Patricia. As with economics, a sexuality based on sharing worked a lot better in theory than in practice. (In one way, the SLA departed from the norms of the counterculture. None of them used drugs after Patricia was kidnapped, though DeFreeze was devoted to his wine. This abstemiousness was due more to lack of funds than to moral qualms.)

The SLA's putatively egalitarian approach to sex involved group discussions on the subject. The agenda sometimes included who was sleeping with whom and who wanted to sleep with whom. On one occasion, about a month into Patricia's captivity, Angela went to the group to report on a request. Patricia wanted to have sex with Willy Wolfe. Should the comrades allow it?

To a great extent, the facts surrounding the kidnapping of Patricia Hearst are undisputed. There is almost no disagreement about what happened when she was removed from her home or when she was confined to the closet in Daly City. The question of the relationship between Patricia and Willy Wolfe is another matter entirely. On this issue, Patricia's version and that of the surviving members of the SLA are in irreconcilable conflict.

According to the SLA, the issue first arose during a conversation between Angela and Patricia. Angela asked Patricia if she ever got horny. Patricia replied that she did. Angela then asked whether she was interested in anyone among the comrades. Yes, said Patricia, she wanted Cujo—that is, Willy Wolfe.

In keeping with the SLA practice for decisions affecting the group, Angela brought the issue to the comrades for discussion. Five of the eight comrades in the Daly City house were women, and they shared a feminist sensibility; they deplored rape and embraced sexual self-determination for women. But the group, including the women, split on the question of whether Patricia and Willy should sleep together. Angela and Nancy Ling were closest to the two and watched the relationship between them develop. They said it was up to Patricia and Willy to decide whether they wanted to have sex, and it was not the group's function to interfere with their choice. The other two couples (Bill and Emily Harris and Mizmoon and Camilla Hall) were opposed. They made an obvious point: the only reason that Patricia was among them was that she had been kidnapped. They said that even if the sex with Willy was consensual, the group was leaving itself open for Patricia to charge later that she had been assaulted. DeFreeze sided with Angela and Ling, so that very evening Willy went into the closet for his first assignation with Patricia.

Thus, according to the SLA, began a tender love affair between two young people thrown together under extraordinary circumstances. In light of the bond between them, they also decided it was time for Patricia to have her own code name. (In the first days after the kidnapping, the SLA referred to her as Marie Antoinette; later, they called her Tiny, which was fitting because her slender frame shrank to under a hundred pounds in captivity.) Willy bore a passing resemblance to Che Guevara, the South American revolutionary who had been executed by the Bolivian military in 1967. An East German woman named Haydée Tamara Bunke Bider fought by Che's side in Bolivia, and she too lost her life in the struggle. Bider had taken the nom de guerre of Tania. So, Willy Wolfe decided, would Patricia Hearst.

Patricia's version of her relationship with Wolfe, recounted in her later testimony and her book, differs in every significant particular.

One day, about three weeks into her captivity, Angela whispered to her, "Cujo wants to get it on with you. You know, he wants to fuck you." Later in the same conversation, Angela turned the proposal into a fait accompli. "You'll be getting it on with Cujo," she said. Still blindfolded in front of the comrades, weak from her confinement in the closet, Patricia felt powerless to protest. She had thought that the SLA's much-touted adherence to the Geneva Convention would prohibit such a thing, but now, to her horror, she realized that was not the case.

Later, she was brought to a group session, with the comrades seated in a circle on the floor, to discuss the issue of her relationship with Wolfe. In her version of the meeting, the conversation was precisely the opposite of the SLA account; the group was addressing Willy's desire to have sex with Patricia, not her wish to have sex with him. "Free sex was one of the principles of the cell," she was told. "No one was forced to have sex in the cell. But if one comrade asked another, it was 'comradely' to say yes."

"So we want you to know," Angela said, "you can fuck any of the men in the cell that you want to."

"Or any woman!" Camilla Hall said, to raucous laughter.

Patricia, in her account, complied wordlessly, and Willy followed her into the closet that night. "The door was shut, we took our clothes off, and he did his thing and left."

But worse was in store. Three days later, Angela informed her, "Cin wants to fuck you." Patricia wrote in her book that she had dreaded this moment above all. Appalled as she was, Patricia offered no protest to this either. "I would have been accused of racism, for I had unprotestingly submitted to Cujo, and I knew that among these people there was nothing worse than being guilty of racism." She submitted to the two men for a simple reason. "My thoughts at this time were focused on the single issue of survival." (The members of the SLA who are still alive deny that DeFreeze ever had sex with Patricia.)

Patricia's description of the beginning of her relationship with Willy Wolfe is more persuasive than that of the SLA. At the time, which was the beginning of March, Patricia had been a hostage confined to a closet for about a month. At that point, she had seen none of her captors' faces, including Wolfe's. She was weak and emaciated. Advocates for the SLA version of events point out that the group consisted mostly of women, all committed feminists, who would never have countenanced any kind of sexual assault in their presence. But these women had already participated in a kidnapping and prolonged detention, so the idea that they scrupulously followed other laws seems dubious. Even Angela Atwood, Patricia's ostensible friend, might have seen what she wanted to see in Patricia and Willy's relationship, rather than recognize the power the SLA held over its captive. In short, according to modern conceptions of consent, it is difficult to imagine how anyone in Patricia's situation could be deemed to have voluntarily slept with one of her kidnappers. Everyone agrees that Patricia had sex in the closet with Willy Wolfe, and it seems equally clear that the sex was not consensual, at least at first. If Patricia had sex with DeFreeze, that too was surely nonconsensual, but the evidence is less clear about whether such an encounter took place.

Also around the one-month mark of her captivity, Patricia's behavior, in private and in her taped statements, changed. She had a television in her closet at this point, and she was able to follow the coverage of her kidnapping. She saw her parents' press conferences. (Thus, her admonition to her mother to stop wearing black.) She saw the food riot in Oakland. She heard Attorney General Saxbe embrace the idea of an FBI raid. One day, frustrated by the media circus that her kidnapping had become, she told Angela, "I don't wanna go home." At first, Angela paid the remark little heed, thinking it was just a reaction to the raucous media scrum outside the mansion in Hillsborough. But then Patricia said it again. At the same time, she was speaking of Steve Weed with nothing but contempt. Her ties to her former life were fraying. At first, no one in the SLA took Patricia's words literally; they believed she did want to go home but was just expressing frustration about how the people in her former life were handling her release. But then Patricia kept saying it—*I don't wanna go home.* Her evolution from empathy to sympathy to comradeship was gradual, but that evolution did take place.

On March 13, Governor Reagan announced he had reappointed Catherine Hearst to a new sixteen-year term on the Board of Regents. Even though Reagan disdained the Hearsts' accommodating approach to the kidnappers, the governor knew that he could needle the outlaws by keeping their captive's mother on his team. As Reagan intended, the members of the SLA were appalled by Catherine's reappointment. But so was Patricia. Her mother embraced the right-wing governor who had disdained the food giveaway in such ugly terms. Patricia saw the reappointment as another sign that the family had abandoned good faith negotiations and, thus, her.

Randy understood the political dynamics of the situation better than Catherine, and he worried that her acceptance of the reappointment would put Patricia at risk. But Randy never discussed the issue with his wife, much less insisted that Catherine turn down the job. Still, the night of the reappointment, he grumbled to a group assembled at the house, "Reagan's a jackass. That's like a slap in the face to the SLA and it could make them angry enough to hurt Patty." Catherine had not consulted her husband about her decision to accept reappointment, and it became an early sign of how Patricia's kidnapping drove her parents apart.

When Patricia started expressing her reluctance to return to her former life, late in her first month of captivity, Angela was the only comrade who paid much attention. But as the days passed and Patricia repeated the sentiment, others also took note. Angela talked it over with Ling and Wolfe, the two other comrades who knew Patricia best. They saw from the beginning that Patricia was nothing like her mother. In their view (and they were far from wrong), Patricia was a kind of rebel even before they kidnapped her. They talked to DeFreeze about her. Look, they said, this is a girl who did drugs, who fucked her high school teacher, who chose Berkeley over Stanford. Maybe she really could be one of us.

DeFreeze was intrigued. He had no interest in Patricia as a human being, but he saw her through the prism of his obsession with public attention. If Patricia joined the SLA, it would be a monumental propaganda coup, which DeFreeze pronounced *coop*. In *Blood in My Eye,* George Jackson had singled out the Hearst newspapers for criticism. ("It's really annoying to hear blacks express right-wing traditionalist political ideals. I mean, the same kind of spiel that you get from . . . Hearst.") And now here was the prospect of a Hearst in the SLA! The negotiations with the family, such as they were, were going nowhere.

People were losing interest in the story. If Patricia were to change sides, DeFreeze thought the potential for media coverage was enormous.

But as usual with the SLA, there was an absence of orderly thinking, especially on the part of their leader. At the same time that DeFreeze was considering whether to recruit Patricia into the SLA, he was still obsessing with the group about ways to spring Little and Remiro from San Quentin. (The pair was actually housed in the prison's death row for a time, which they viewed as an intimidation tactic.) During the all-day and all-night conversations among the comrades, the topics ranged inconclusively between Patricia's future, Little and Remiro, and the dire need for cash. Then, with characteristic impulsiveness, DeFreeze made a decision. No one was sure why, but the general field marshal suddenly became convinced that a raid on the house in Daly City was imminent. They had to move—right away.

DeFreeze gave Camilla Hall the assignment of finding a new apartment, with one specific instruction. There was no more need for the walk-in closet for Patricia—that is, for Tania. She would live among the rest of the comrades now.

DeFreeze wanted to move to the city, where the SLA might be able to blend in and circulate as they could not in suburban Daly City. At least in theory, that meant the comrades could recruit new members, in service of the uprising that was supposed to follow their insurrection. Camilla found a shabby two-bedroom apartment (with a Murphy bed) at 1847 Golden Gate Avenue, in the Western Addition neighborhood of San Francisco. (To the amusement of the comrades, the apartment was only a little more than a mile from FBI headquarters, at 450 Golden Gate Avenue.)

On the night of March 21, the SLA members folded Patricia's diminutive frame into a newly purchased thirty-gallon garbage can for the ten-mile drive into the city. When they reached the apartment, DeFreeze decreed that the Murphy bed would belong to Tania, while the rest of the comrades could make do with whatever combination of beds, couches, and floor space they could find. (Later, Patricia would describe the Murphy bed as being in a closet, but it was clear that the nature of her captivity had changed dramatically.)

By the time the group moved, Patricia was becoming a full-fledged member of the SLA. But there was still one problem. As Willy and Angela told Patricia, Bill and Emily Harris still opposed the idea of Patricia's joining the group. Patricia had to convince the Harrises that she belonged. So one evening, shortly after they settled into Golden Gate, Bill sat by the foot of the Murphy bed and listened to Patricia make her case for membership. Still wearing a blindfold so she could not see the comrades, she told Bill her old life was gone. Her mother was a drunken reactionary. Her father betrayed her. Steve Weed was a clown and a parasite. According to Bill and Emily, Bill tried to talk Patricia out of her infatuation with the SLA. As long as she was with them, he said, the group was an all-but-certain target for an FBI raid. That was bad for Patricia and bad for them. If she were to go home, she would save her own life, and the SLA members would have a chance of fading into the woodwork. Eventually, though, Bill gave up in frustration.

A day or two later, according to Patricia's recollection, DeFreeze sat down by the Murphy bed and said, "Tiny, you remember what I told you about the War Council thinking about what to do with you?"

With her blindfold still in place, Patricia said yes.

"Well, the War Council has decided that you can join us, if you want to, or you can be released and go home again." (Patricia and the surviving members of the SLA confirm that this conversation, as well as several others like it, took place.)

So DeFreeze gave Patricia the choice to leave. But did he mean it? In her book, Patricia said no, that the offer was just a ruse. The real choice he was offering was "to join them or to be executed. They would never release me. They could not. I knew too much about them. He was testing me and I must pass the test or die." Nonsense, said her captors. She had a real choice, and she chose to stay.

In any event, she told DeFreeze, "I want to join you."

"That'll mean, you know, you never can go back to your old way of life. You'll be an urban guerrilla, fighting for the people."

"Yes," she replied, "I want to fight for the people."

DeFreeze went on to say that Patricia would have to convince each of the comrades that she was worthy of membership. She could remain only if the vote were unanimous. So Patricia spent the next few days trying to convince each member of the cell of her bona fides. As she made the circuit in the cramped apartment, she heard the comrades' own reasons for going underground with the SLA. Nancy Ling said DeFreeze had saved her from a life of drug abuse. Camilla Hall said she hoped to organize an army of homosexuals to join the revolution. Willy Wolfe said the SLA represented just a small part of a people's rebellion that was brewing around the globe. Her friend Angela acted as a kind of campaign manager, advocating among the comrades on her behalf.

Patricia's only real problems were the Harrises, who remained skeptical. Emily reminded Patricia of the costs of a life in the shadows. Emily confessed how much she missed her prison lover, whom she could no longer see or contact. Bill, who was miserable in the close confines of the apartment, simply could not believe anyone would choose to sacrifice a life of wealth and ease for this threadbare and perilous existence. Patricia later asserted that her passion for joining was a subterfuge, because she truly believed that the real choice was join or die. But the SLA saw only a woman on fire with revolutionary passion.

At last, on the night of March 31, eight weeks after she was kidnapped, the comrades gathered for a final decision. Patricia was invited to sit in the circle with them. It was a remarkable scene— the fine-boned heiress waiting in supplication before the collection of bedraggled misfits. The windows were covered (as they always were) by filthy Indian bedspread material. A small arsenal of sawed-off shotguns and handguns, with the ever-present rounds of cyanide-laced bullets, stood in readiness against the walls. A bare lightbulb drooping from the ceiling illuminated the proceedings. With great solemnity, the general field marshal asked, "So you want to be an urban guerrilla and a soldier in the Symbionese Liberation Army?"

"Yes," Patricia said.

"Are you ready to renounce your past and become a guerrilla soldier in the Symbionese Liberation Army?"

"Yes," she said.

The verdict of the comrades had been unanimous. Tania could join them.

"Okay," DeFreeze said, "take your blindfold off."

Suddenly, for the first time, she saw the faces that went with the voices of her tormentors turned teammates. "As General Field Marshal, I welcome you," DeFreeze said. "You are now a guerrilla fighter and a soldier in the Symbionese Liberation Army!"

A couple of days later, Willy gave Patricia a memento to welcome her as a comrade. He said an archaeologist friend had given him two charms that he had found on a dig in Mexico. Willy braided and waxed a rope for the charm, which Patricia wore around her neck. Willy made a similar rope for his own charm. The matching keepsakes symbolized their union.

Now it was time to plan a bank robbery.

STAY AND FIGHT

The comrades had never been flush, but before the kidnapping most of them at least had jobs, which allowed them to make ends meet. Bill Harris worked at the post office, Emily at Cal, Mizmoon at the Berkeley Public Library, and Ling at the juice cart. (Of course, DeFreeze, as a prison escapee, couldn't seek work, and besides he'd scarcely ever held a real job anyway.) But the collective decision to go underground eliminated their regular sources of income. Despite DeFreeze's hopes, Willy Wolfe's return from Pennsylvania added nothing significant to the SLA coffers. In short order, the comrades were desperate. They practically lived on mung beans and black-eyed peas—"poor people's food," they called it.

Camilla Hall, the one SLA member who could still move somewhat freely aboveground, was the group's lone source of funds while they were in Daly City. On March 1, she withdrew the last $1,565 from her savings account at her bank in Berkeley. (The FBI knew both that Hall was affiliated with the SLA and where she had a bank account, but the bureau neglected to monitor the branch closely enough.) Three days later, Hall sold her 1967 Volkswagen, which Wolfe drove during the kidnapping. In an extraordinary coincidence, Hall sold the car to a local dealer who in turn sold it to a clerk in the FBI's steno pool. The car sat outside the bureau's offices for weeks before it was finally recognized. Still, Hall's largesse could go only so far. Even crammed into a single small apartment, nine people generated considerable expenses.

So the SLA began thinking about robbing a bank for the most venerable of reasons: that's where the money was.

But that wasn't the only reason. The comrades had been talking about robbing a bank even before the kidnapping, but their rationale evolved after Patricia emerged from beneath her blindfold. DeFreeze recognized what a dramatic statement it would be if she participated in a stickup. Bill Harris and Angela Atwood were deputized to search for an appropriate target, but their checklist included more than just the chances for a quick strike and clean getaway. Unlike virtually all other putative bank robbers, they sought out a bank that possessed a relatively new form of technology: a security camera that could be activated by bank staffers in the event of a robbery. (Security cameras that took video did not yet exist.) If Patricia were part of the team inside the bank, they could show, not just tell, that Patricia had joined the SLA.

Before the robbery could take place, though, the SLA had to go about the business of informing the world that Patricia—that is, Tania—was now one of them. They did this in an extraordinarily cruel way.

With her blindfold gone for good, Patricia had a chance to explore the Golden Gate apartment for the first time. She was not impressed. The place was filthy. The comrades remained pack rats who hoarded news clippings (especially about themselves) and seldom threw anything away. They washed their clothes, when they washed them at all, in the bathtub. (Still, DeFreeze prohibited the comrades from wearing blue jeans, or dungarees, because he said black people disdained them.) Thanks to his work at the post office, Bill Harris had developed considerable expertise in stealing credit cards and other forms of false identification, so the comrades all had several alter egos. In a further effort to obtain useful documents, the SLA also made a practice of stealing unattended purses, which was especially important, given the gender breakdown of the group. Patricia also saw an extensive collection of wigs and theatrical makeup, which Angela (the former actress) had assembled to use for disguises. And there were weapons—lots of them. Shotguns (some sawed-off), handguns, carbines, and hundreds of rounds of ammunition were jammed into the closet near the Murphy bed.

In light of DeFreeze's obsession with publicity, he wanted a photograph of Patricia to go with the announcement of her conversion. He set the scene with care, even employing a gender-based division of labor to create the right backdrop. He assigned a sewing project to the women, who carved a large black-felt version of the seven-headed cobra and stitched it onto a red blanket, which they hung on the wall. The group had a primitive Polaroid camera and an aspiring photographer in Mizmoon Soltysik.

For the photograph, the comrades dressed Patricia in combat-style fatigues and handed her a sawed-off M1 carbine. Between her father's lessons and her drills with the SLA, Patricia had developed a level of comfort with the weapon, and she cradled it with ease. DeFreeze choreographed the session as Mizmoon snapped a few precious frames of instant film. Patricia's complexion is clear, and her hair still fashionably shoulder length, with a beret perched rakishly on the side of her head. The rope with Willy Wolfe's Mexican charm is barely visible around her neck. Another long gun is perched on the floor against the flag. When DeFreeze approved, Mizmoon snapped the official portrait. For the 1970s, this image of Patricia Hearst became a kind of *Mona Lisa,* and nearly as famous. Her expression is inscrutable, as subject to as many interpretations as the larger tale of her captivity. She looks steely or terrified; her lips are pursed in determination or defeat; she could be battle ready or battered. (Shortly after the photograph was taken, DeFreeze ordered Mizmoon and Ling to cut Patricia's hair; the woman known as Tania then mostly wore wigs out of doors.)

Later, DeFreeze directed all the comrades to pose for Mizmoon's camera in front of the same flag. The resulting image is overexposed and a little out of focus, but the personalities do assert themselves. Five comrades stand in front, while three kneel below; all wield weapons. With her tidy shoulder-length hair and polo shirt, Emily Harris looks like the open-faced midwestern college student she recently was, albeit one with an ammunition belt slung across her chest. Willy Wolfe is next to her, the tallest by far, his boyish face with a half smile suggests that he understands, at some level, what a ridiculous enterprise he has joined. In the middle is DeFreeze, doing his best to scowl and suggest leadership. Next to him is Bill Harris, wearing a comically fake mustache and beard, and on the far right is Camilla Hall, clearly out of place, looking as if she had never held a weapon before (which might well have been the case).

In the front row, Patricia kneels on the left, her hair now shorn and wrapped in a bandanna, her gaze directed off camera. In the middle is Angela Atwood, the former actress, who looks graceful and cheerful, even in what must have been an uncomfortable crouch. Finally, on the right is Nancy Ling, the bantam-sized terror, whose face is fuzzy but whose energy is apparent. At one level, the overall effect is more comic than sinister, for the group appears like a collection of cartoon radicals or guests at a Halloween party who threw their costumes together at the last minute. But such an idea is misleading, too, because the group, for all their vanity and ineptitude, had killed before and would kill again.

Reading the SLA's pompous and impenetrable communiqués was bad enough for Randy and Catherine Hearst, but enduring the silence from their daughter's captors, through almost the entire month of March, was worse. They reacted in different ways. Catherine withdrew—to her church, to visiting priests and close friends, and to the bottle. She rarely said a word to the press, though she did volunteer one day to a reporter, "They can hide her from everybody else but not from Almighty God."

Randy self-medicated as well, but he otherwise took an opposite tack, exploring worlds that had scarcely existed in his gilded life. He went to Vacaville several times, to meet with prisoners who professed to have some influence on DeFreeze. One time at the prison, Randy even sat down at a typewriter and took dictation from a prisoner who claimed that his message would prompt DeFreeze to free Patricia. (It didn't.) Randy engaged in weeks of fruitless negotiations with prison officials in an effort to allow Little and Remiro to make a live broadcast, as the SLA had demanded. Randy also met with the volunteers who were packing boxes at the PIN warehouse in San Francisco, as well as with the community groups that formed the coalition behind the PIN food giveaway. The leaders of these groups were as skeptical of Randy as he was of them. When Hearst hosted Russell Means and Dennis Banks, of the American Indian Movement, for lunch at a downtown hotel, the two men insisted that their bodyguards taste the food first, to make sure that they weren't being poisoned.

After the last PIN distribution, on March 25, Ludlow Kramer and Peggy Maze returned to Seattle, shell-shocked by their surreal month in San Francisco. But Randy still wasn't willing to give up on using food for the poor as a lever to win Patricia's freedom. He traveled to New York, to persuade the Hearst Corporation to put $4 million in escrow for a further food giveaway, which would take place in the event Patricia was released.

On March 29, after Randy returned home from a long day at Vacaville, Sara Jane Moore (and her five-year-old son) showed up at his front door in Hillsborough. Unbeknownst to Randy, the erstwhile bookkeeper for PIN had had a stormy departure from the program. Unnerved by Moore's increasingly imperious behavior, Ludlow Kramer and Peggy Maze asked a beefy apprentice private investigator named Jack Palladino to fire her and escort her from the China Basin warehouse, which he did. The next day, however, Moore returned and locked herself in her office. Several hours of negotiations, which included threats to break down the door, finally prompted her to surrender. Moore then nominated herself to go to Hillsborough to present Randy and Catherine with a collection of news reports about the PIN operation as a kind of tribute to them and their daughter. Her real agenda for show-ing up uninvited was to ask for a job in any of the Hearst enterprises. When Randy put her off, the matronly eccentric filibustered, while her son wandered around the big house. It took almost three hours, but the Hearsts eventually managed to shoo Moore out the door. Her visit was just another annoyance for Randy in his full-time effort to free his daughter. In the process, he became something that he had studiously avoided, even with his famous name: a public figure. Still, none of Randy's efforts seemed to matter to the SLA.

Then, finally, out of the blue came a breakthrough, or so it appeared. On April 1, Nancy Ling (in disguise) went to a florist and ordered a bouquet delivered on that day to John Bryan, the editor of an underground newspaper called the *San Francisco Phoenix*. Ling also provided an envelope to be included with the flowers. It contained two documents, as well as half of Patricia Hearst's driver's license. The first document came in the now-familiar communiqué format. The subject was "negotiations and release of the prisoner," and the text was brief:

Herein enclosed are the Codes of War of the Symbionese Lib-eration Army, these documents as all SLA documents are to be printed in full and omitting nothing by order of this court in all forms of the media. Further communications regarding subject prisoner will follow in the following 72 hours. Communications will state the state, city and time of the release of the prisoner.
Signed: I.I. Unit 4
General Field Marshal Cin, SLA

The codes of war themselves were also included, consisting of typical long-winded SLA gibberish—stating, in essence, that betrayal of the comrades would be punished by death and that lesser offenses (such as "tortures or sexual assault on either a comrade or people or the enemy") would be subject to unspecified "disciplinary action." The florist's truck broke down, so the bouquet and envelope were not delivered until the following day, April 2. Still, the message seemed clear. Within seventy-two hours, the SLA would announce the release of Patricia Hearst. In Hillsborough, there were cautious celebrations. Anne Hearst moved out of Patricia's old bedroom, to make room for her homecoming. The cook prepared matzo ball soup, Patricia's favorite.

But DeFreeze, Mizmoon, and Nancy Ling—the dark heart of the SLA—had sprung a macabre April Fools' Day joke. The communiqué, which was supposed to arrive on April 1, operated exactly as designed—to raise the hopes of the Hearsts, only to crush them in short order. This was SLA guerrilla theater at its most sinister. For when Ling delivered the communiqué to the florist, Patricia had already recorded her statement that would shock the world. In keeping with the SLA practice of delivering written statements to newspapers and tape recordings to radio stations, Patricia's tape went to KSAN on April 3.

She began by protesting too much: "I would like to begin this statement by informing the public that I wrote what I am about to say. It's what I feel. I have never been forced to say anything on any tape. Nor have I been brainwashed, drugged, tortured or hypnotized or in any way confused. As George Jackson wrote, 'It's me, the way I want it, the way I see it.'"

As the rest of the recording made clear, there was no way that Patricia wrote it all herself. The passages of pidgin Marxism, in tone and structure so similar to previous communiqués, bore the stamp of the SLA theoreticians—Nancy Ling, Mizmoon, and to a certain extent Angela Atwood, all interwoven with the paranoia of Donald DeFreeze. At the same time, there was little doubt that the voice on the tape revealed a different Patricia Hearst from the haunted young woman who barely possessed the energy to read her first recordings in captivity. Gone, too, was the bored monotone of her previous life.

Her speech was firm and clear, her cadence brisk. Many of the words sounded like her own. And they were, in every sense, revolutionary.

Her statement, as shocking an utterance as any made by an American during the 1970s, defined the terms of the debate over Patricia's state of mind. Had she really enlisted with the SLA? Was her behavior voluntary, or was she brainwashed or otherwise forced to join with her captors? Were her denials of coercion by the SLA believable—or more proof that she'd been coerced? Complicating matters further, the SLA possessed considerable sophistication in manipulating the media. DeFreeze and company recognized what the arguments about Patricia's state of mind would be and sought, in advance, to preempt and refute them.

On the tape, Patricia denounced those who were once closest to her, each in turn, starting with her father. "Mom, Dad, I would like to comment on your efforts to supposedly secure my safety. The PIN giveaway was a sham. You attempted to deceive the people. You were playing games—stalling for time—time which the FBI was using in their attempts to assassinate me and the SLA elements." Of course, this was both wrong and unfair. Randy never stalled for time but rather wanted her home as soon as possible. Then Patricia turned to her mother. "My mother's acceptance of the appointment to a second term as a U.C. regent, as you well knew, would have caused my immediate execution had the SLA been less than 'together' about their political goals. Your actions have taught me a great lesson, and in a strange kind of way, I'm grateful to you." Fairly or not, Patricia's snide sarcasm about her mother had the ring of sincerity.

Next she moved on to Steven Weed, and here the words appear closest to Patricia's own: "Steven, I know that you are beginning to realize that there is no such thing as neutrality in time of war." She expressed a measure of sympathy for the repeated FBI interrogations that Weed had undergone: "We both know what really came down that Monday night [February 4]. But you don't know what's happened since then. I have changed—grown. I've become conscious and can never go back to the life we led before. What I'm saying may seem cold to you and to my old friends, but love doesn't mean the same thing to me anymore. My love has expanded as a result of my experiences to embrace all people. It's grown into an unselfish love for my comrades here, in prison and on the streets. A love that comes from the knowledge that no one is free until we are all free. While I wish that you could be a comrade, I don't expect it. All I expect is that you try to understand the changes I've gone through."

And here Patricia came to the crux of her statement: "I have been given the choice of (one) being released in a safe area, or (two) joining the forces of the Symbionese Liberation Army, and fighting for my freedom and the freedom of all oppressed people. I have chosen to stay and fight."

But Patricia wasn't finished, though her statement at this point meandered into a bizarre rant about automation, of all things. Addressing her father, she said, "You, a corporate liar . . . tell the poor and oppressed people of this nation what the corporate state is about to do, warn black and poor people that they are about to be murdered down to the last man, woman and child. . . . Tell the people that the entire corporate state is . . . about to totally automate the entire industrial state, to the point that in the next five years all that will be needed will be a small class of button pushers."

As Patricia worked to her conclusion, she introduced a name that would become nearly as familiar as those given to her by her parents: "I have been given the name Tania after a comrade who fought alongside Che in Bolivia for the people of Bolivia. I embrace the name with the determination to continue fighting with her spirit. There is no victory in half-assed attempts at revolution. I know Tania dedicated her life to the people. Fighting with total dedication and an intense desire to learn, which I will continue in the oppressed American people's revolution." She paid a final tribute to Little and Remiro: "Even though we have never met, I feel like I know you." In her final words, she invoked the unofficial motto of the Cuban revolution. "It is in the spirit of Tania that I say, '*Patria o muerte, venceremos!*'" Fatherland or death, we shall triumph!

After the tape played, Randy and Catherine could not bring themselves to hold one of their driveway press conferences. They were too upset. Inside, Catherine confessed to a friend, "I think they killed Patty. I know she's dead already." Reporters on the endless stakeout in front of the house caught Randy as he was arriving. "We're more or less shocked over this thing," Randy said. "And until we know more about it, we don't have anything to say." Then he walked inside, and for the first time in his daughter's fifty-nine days in captivity Randy Hearst wept. The next day, he and Catherine left for a respite at the Mexican villa of their friend Desi Arnaz, the actor and singer.

This moment at the beginning of April was a high point for the SLA. The comrades had forced Randy Hearst to spend millions to feed the poor, and his daughter had astonished the world by announcing her preference for them over him. Of course, the group still had no long-term goals or plans, but at this time its tactical proficiency trumped its strategic ineptitude. The SLA always planned individual actions with skill and care. So it was with the kidnapping of Patricia on February 4, and so it was with the robbery of the Hibernia Bank on April 15.

Patricia acted like a full-fledged comrade after her communiqué became public on April 3, and her captors treated her as if her conversion were sincere and total. Bill Harris taught her how to lace bullets with cyanide. DeFreeze showed her how to assemble a pipe bomb—a frightening undertaking in any circumstance, but especially in a small apartment and with the general field marshal's unsteady hand. The group conducted daily drills in the apartment, including calisthenics and weapons training with their unloaded guns. (DeFreeze thought the loud clicking of inserting ammunition clips might arouse the suspicions of neighbors.)

For a target, Bill Harris and Angela settled on the Hibernia branch in the sleepy Sunset district of the city. Wedged between Golden Gate

Park and the Pacific Ocean, Sunset in those days consisted mostly of single-family homes populated by Irish and Italian families. (Joe Remiro, the only SLA member from San Francisco, grew up in Sunset.) The business district along Noriega Street was lightly traveled, especially compared with busier parts of the city, and the Hibernia Bank at Noriega and Twenty-Second Avenue had security cameras. Later, much was made of the fact that the president of Hibernia was a local aristocrat named Michael Henry de Young Tobin, whose daughter Trish was Patricia's best friend in Hillsborough. But there is no evidence that Patricia volunteered this information to the comrades, so this particular coincidence was unintentional.

The robbery had enormous stakes for the SLA, not least because the preparations consumed the last of their funds. Between April 11 and 13, Camilla Hall and Emily Harris used an identification card in the name of Janet Cooper to rent the four cars to be used in the operation. On the night of the fourteenth, DeFreeze ordered a final splurge for dinner—steak and potatoes for everyone. He did so, he announced, because the SLA coffers would soon be refreshed.

The primary objective for the robbery was money, but the propaganda value was nearly as important. In casing the bank, Bill had studied the location of the security cameras. The plan was for Patricia to stand the entire time in full view of the lenses. DeFreeze ordered her to wear a brown wig that looked like her hair at the time of the kidnapping. He didn't want anyone to doubt that it was actually Patricia Hearst inside the bank. What's more, DeFreeze wanted to make sure everyone knew Patricia's weapon was loaded; her assignment was to fire a round into the ceiling and shout, "This is Tania!" Even the date of the operation—April 15, tax day—had symbolic significance for what the SLA called an expropriation, not a robbery.

DeFreeze designated two teams—an inside team, which would conduct the actual robbery, and an outside team, which would act as lookouts, detain the police, if necessary, and supervise the getaway. The inside team was the SLA core—DeFreeze, Mizmoon, and Nancy Ling—joined by their prized recruit, Patricia Hearst. Camilla Hall also went just inside the bank door. On the outside were Bill and Emily Harris, Angela Atwood, and Willy Wolfe. For communication during the robbery, DeFreeze gave each comrade a code number, from one (himself) to nine (Hearst). The plan was to arrive shortly after the bank opened, make their score, display Patricia, and leave. They didn't want to get caught, so they knew they had to work fast. The goal was to be in and out of the bank in ninety seconds.

On the morning of the fifteenth, Camilla Hall, who was driving the inside team, took a meandering route that traversed Golden Gate Park. Patricia had not been outdoors (except inside a garbage can) in more than two months, and the sight of grass and trees was so beautiful to her that she almost wept. Fear, too, played a part. She was both terrified and electrified.

The outside team parked across Noriega from the bank, and Hall stopped around the corner with the inside team. Camilla Hall began the action by opening the door to the bank, and then DeFreeze, Hearst, Ling, and Mizmoon filed inside. As she was walking through the front door, Ling accidentally dropped her ammunition clip in a great clatter and stooped to collect the bullets. DeFreeze stepped over her and shouted to the eighteen employees and six customers, "This is a holdup! The first motherfucker who don't lay down on the floor gets shot in the head!"

On the second floor of the bank, in a break room, Jim Smith, the branch manager, heard the commotion. At 9:51 a.m., he punched a silent alarm, which triggered two high-speed cameras with wide-angle lenses to begin shooting four pictures per second. (Spliced together, these photographs can resemble a jerky motion picture; in all, each security camera took about four hundred pictures of the robbery.)

DeFreeze kept to his assigned role of standing by the front door. Ling gathered her ammunition and controlled the customers and employees, yelling, "SLA! SLA! SLA! Get down on the floor!" With balletic grace, Mizmoon vaulted over the partition that separated the customer area from the tellers. She stepped over the employees, who were prone on the floor, and started removing cash from the drawers. While Mizmoon extracted cash, DeFreeze found the bank security guard and removed the .38-caliber revolver from his holster. (One passerby thought the entire event was a scene from *The Streets of San Francisco,* which was actually shooting an episode nearby.)

Everything was going perfectly—until Nancy Ling panicked. This was her pattern. In November, she had fired wildly at Marcus Foster and succeeded only in grazing him. In February, she had taken needless potshots at the students next door to Patricia's apartment on Benvenue and missed again. This time, while Mizmoon was collecting the money and the employees and customers lay motionless, two new customers walked in the door. When Pete Markoff, a liquor store owner, and Gene Brennan, a pensioner, stepped inside, Nancy Ling started to blast her machine gun. Fortunately, her aim again proved less than lethal. She hit Markoff in the buttocks and Brennan in the hand, and they retreated, bleeding, to the sidewalk. (Both survived.)

Inside the bank, Patricia's fear translated into adrenaline. She took her place, as planned, in direct view of the security camera and tried to absorb the chaotic scene unfolding around her. She then remembered her assignment and tried to cock her carbine to shoot at the ceiling. But the bolt jammed as she pulled it back. (It seems that in tampering with the bullets to apply the cyanide, she had changed their shape, which blocked the gun's proper functioning.) Panicking and worrying about disappointing her comrades, she blurted out, "This is Tania. . . . Patricia Hearst."

Then, recovering her equilibrium, she joined the others in ordering the customers and employees not to move. "First person puts up his head," Hearst said, "I'll blow his motherfucking head off!"

The robbery took just about as long as planned, and the SLA group inside the bank stepped over the bleeding body of Pete Markoff and got into the getaway car, still driven by Camilla Hall. The SLA's two vehicles raced about ten blocks away, where the comrades had earlier stashed the other two rental cars. The group made the change into the switch cars and drove carefully, well within the speed limit, back to the apartment on Golden Gate. Seven comrades raced up to the third-floor apartment to count the loot, while Mizmoon and Emily Harris drove the two cars to a parking garage on the other side of town, where they left them.

Inside the apartment, a raucous celebration began. Angela dumped the bag of money on top of a blanket spread out on the floor. As she began to gather the cash into a heap, Angela stuffed a $20 bill in her mouth and said, "It looks so good I could eat it!" Once Mizmoon and Emily returned, the group began the count. The total was $10,660.

Someone thought to turn on the radio, to check on the coverage of their triumph, but they found only music: the O'Jays' hit "For the Love of Money."

PART THREE

COMMON CRIMINALS

Euphoria prevailed. In the small apartment, the comrades gazed happily at the disorderly pyramid of the oppressor's cash. The security guard's gun boosted the SLA arsenal. The pigs seethed. The public gawked at villains they could not see. The tinny AM radio blared danceable soul. For a day or two, it was very heaven to be young and a member of the Symbionese Liberation Army.

The comrades' strike inside the bank had gone according to plan and taken just about ninety seconds. Photographs from the security camera surfaced almost immediately in the news media, and the images of Patricia wielding her military-style M1 carbine became nearly as famous as the one of her in front of the SLA flag. Close examination would reveal that her dark hair was really a wig—a 1970s-style flip—but there was no question about the identity of the woman in the photograph. Closer study would reveal Willy Wolfe's Mexican charm. Patricia's expression was blank, as usual, but she went through her paces with a confident swagger. Her short dark raincoat looked rakish. Like her comrades inside the bank—the frenetic Nancy Ling, the athletic Mizmoon Soltysik, the regal Donald DeFreeze—Patricia radiated outlaw glamour.

The SLA had shocked the world and gotten away with it. The haul was massive. For the first time, they felt rich. The injuries to bystanders were inconsequential and irrelevant (at least as the comrades saw it). The police were concentrating their search in the area where the SLA abandoned their cars—in other words, miles away from the safe house on Golden Gate. No one had noticed they had switched cars. As usual, DeFreeze had no real plan about what to do next, much less in the long run, but for the moment the SLA thrived.

At this point, DeFreeze and the others treated Patricia as a full-fledged comrade, for better or worse. She and Willy Wolfe operated as a couple, in the sense that any SLA pair was a couple. They slept together and regarded each other as partners, but they also honored the SLA prohibition on sexual exclusivity. They were expected to participate in comradely sex with others who sought them out. In this context, Patricia and Bill Harris had sex for the first time in the Golden Gate apartment.

The heiress was even treated as an equal when it came to the proceeds from the bank robbery. DeFreeze wanted to avoid the risk that the police might seize the full $10,000-plus take, so he split it into chunks of $1,000 and gave one to each comrade, including Patricia. In the event that they had to take off in different directions, following a police raid, DeFreeze wanted to make sure that they would all have means to support themselves until they could regroup.

The prized trophy from the robbery was the security guard's .38-caliber Smith & Wesson revolver. The SLA already had plenty of guns, thanks largely to the collection Remiro and Little had amassed before they were arrested. But this weapon was liberated directly from a pig, so DeFreeze took some time before deciding what to do with this precious spoil of the class war.

Patricia could never be sure how the mercurial field marshal would react to anything, so she had worried after the robbery that she would be punished for failing to shoot her gun into the ceiling. She needn't have been concerned.

With some ceremony, DeFreeze presented the security guard's gun to her. "This is for you, Tania, your personal sidearm," DeFreeze said. "Keep it on your person at all times and learn how to use it." Unlike the shotgun that Patricia was given in Daly City, the Smith & Wesson came loaded with ammunition. Henceforth, like all the other comrades, Tania would always be packing heat.

The bank robbery cleaved Patricia Hearst's public image along the lines of the larger divisions in the country. In small circles of the Left, she became a folk hero—a renegade who had traded the life of an aristocrat for that of a renegade. The *Barb* celebrated Patricia's apparent conversion under the banner headline "PATTY FREE!" "Patty Hearst has said her last goodbye to America's ruling class, to a life of privilege, wealth and power, and has joined the guerrillas of the Symbionese Liberation Army in their war against the 'fascist corporate state,'" the paper wrote. "Her decision to commit herself to armed struggle was clearly her own, based on her own observations and experiences while being held hostage." Ads in the paper offered posters of the famous Tania photograph. When the Women's Collective of the Weather Underground placed a bomb in the federal building in San Francisco, its communiqué said the action was "inspired by the SLA."

Patricia herself achieved a kind of perverse stardom. The sheer strangeness of her situation and the mystery about her true feelings made her an almost irresistible antihero. The more the establishment turned against her, the more she found favor in the counterculture.

At the same time, the establishment was transforming her image from victim of the radical underground to enemy of the state. Especially in San Francisco, the mood had soured on the protesters and the loudmouths and especially the criminals who were turning their city into a battleground. Through the early months of 1974, the Zebra killers continued to stalk white victims. Joseph Alioto had been elected as an old-fashioned liberal—Hubert Humphrey considered him as a running mate in 1968—but the mayor could not abide the descent of his city into lawlessness. After another Zebra murder on April 16, the day after the Hibernia robbery, he announced that the police would take a new "extreme" measure. Henceforth, they would stop all black men who resembled a generic sketch of the Zebra killers. Worse yet, the police would give "Zebra cards" to all blacks who passed inspection—an ugly echo of the pass laws in apartheid South Africa. In response, civil rights protests enveloped city hall. A federal judge halted the police crackdown after a week: the killers remained on the loose.

Now, in addition to the Zebra and Zodiac threats, as well as run-of-the-mill mayhem plaguing the city, there was the robbery of the Hibernia Bank. Two carloads full of revolutionaries, provisioned like an invading army, had besieged a local bank in a quiet neighborhood. Far from fearing exposure, the bandits sought it, placing their unmasked faces in direct view of the cameras. They sprayed automatic weapons fire at innocent bystanders, who were, by some miracle, only injured rather than killed. Even for San Francisco, this kind of quasi-military operation in broad daylight represented a new low. It was intolerable behavior in a civilized society and the latest problem for the mayor to address. Alioto ordered the police "to activate a special investigative team to devote full-time to tracking down the kidnappers of Miss Hearst." He called the SLA "killers, extortionists, and third-rate intellectuals" and insisted, "We have indulged them long enough." As the historian David Talbot wrote of this moment, "The city seemed to crackle with madness."

Even San Francisco politicians turned on Patricia. She might have been a kidnap victim at the beginning, but now she looked like a rich kid who had decided to take out her grievances on the establishment. At a press conference, Attorney General Saxbe asserted that Patricia "was not a reluctant participant" in the bank robbery. Thus, in his view, she and her SLA allies were "common criminals." Evelle Younger, the California attorney general, went even further. He berated the FBI for being "timid" in its search for Patricia. "I think the moment of truth has long since passed for Patricia Hearst," he said.

Back in Hillsborough, Randy and Catherine tried to hold an increasingly precarious and lonely middle ground. Unlike the Berkeley radicals, the Hearsts couldn't embrace Patricia's transformation into a celebrity outlaw, and unlike the establishment politicians, her parents couldn't reject her as a criminal. Rather, in a driveway news conference to respond to the denunciations, the Hearsts continued to insist their daughter was a victim. "Mr. Saxbe is not aware of all the facts in this matter. Despite his point of view, our daughter is still a kidnap victim," Randy said. Still, Randy sensed the public shift against Patricia. "No matter what she says and does, as long as she is under the control of the SLA, we know she is not acting of her own free will. . . . Whatever legal problems are in her future, we will be there for her."

The bank robbery underlined the continuing failure of the FBI search for the kidnappers. In the seventy days between the kidnapping and the bank robbery, the SLA had been taunting the authorities, and now they were embarrassing the bureau. Far from covering their tracks, the rotating cast of SLA spokesmen had been boasting about their successes. Their names and faces had been publicly known for weeks. And as the Hibernia operation illustrated, the group had remained in the Bay Area, right under the noses of dozens of FBI agents working the case. Yet law enforcement had made basically no progress since day one.

The FBI maintained a stoic public profile about its investigation, insisting that unspecified progress was being made. On his nightly pilgrimages to Hillsborough, Charlie Bates, the San Francisco special agent in charge, made similar claims, promising Randy and Catherine that the SLA would soon make a mistake that would lead to its capture. But behind the scenes, the sad truth was that the FBI had no idea where Patricia and the comrades were. Under J. Edgar Hoover, the bureau had placed special reliance on the use of informants, whether of Communists or of bank robbers. But the FBI had no entrée into the tight-knit world of the SLA. Agents had photographs and fingerprints of the comrades but no way to identify their location.

Bates was the public face of the investigation, but his subordinate Monte Hall supervised the day-to-day work. A World War II veteran from the hills of Pennsylvania, Hall had a no-nonsense style and a belief in the power of numbers in an investigation. With every available agent at his disposal, Hall cleared out nearly an acre of space in the FBI offices at 450 Golden Gate Avenue and created a series of labor-intensive assignments for his agents. Recognizing that the SLA was moving from place to place, Hall established a "water gas" program, where his men would track down and interview all tenants who signed up for new apartment rentals and utility services. It yielded nothing. Hall also learned of DeFreeze's passion for plum wine, so he sent agents to liquor stores to look for regular buyers of what he thought was an exotic beverage. Plum wine turned out to be sold in five thousand outlets in the Bay Area, so this line of inquiry was similarly unfruitful—as were, of course, the insights of the Swamis 1, 2, and 3. On another occasion, Hall received a tip that a major SLA operation was imminent. At great expense, he rented a Bell Ranger helicopter to provide surveillance over San Francisco. When nothing materialized, Hall gave FBI clerical employees free rides to thank them for their hard work.

Perhaps the most bizarre FBI initiative came from its enduring faith in the power of informants. A prisoner at Vacaville put out the word that he could locate the SLA, but only if he were given a few days of freedom. The FBI persuaded the California authorities to give the man a furlough, and the bureau even supplied him with a car, though it rigged the vehicle so that it could not travel at a very high speed. The bureau employed an elaborate ruse to persuade the inmate to return to prison rather than flee. Shortly after he was released from custody, agents took him to a trailer that had been fitted out to look like a medical clinic. A man in a white coat told the would-be informant that he was injecting him with a slow-acting poison. He would die if he did not return in a week for the antidote. Agents also put a transponder in the inmate's car so they could track his movements. One night they lost him—only to find him, several hours later, making out with a woman in the car. In any event, the fake-poison story was apparently good enough to make the man return to prison, though his adventure outside prison walls produced no useful evidence about the SLA. As the agents later acknowledged, he had just conned them into giving him a few days of freedom.

The man who would ultimately decide whether Patricia would be charged in the bank robbery was Bates's counterpart in the Department of Justice—James Browning Jr., the U.S. attorney in San Francisco. The job of top federal prosecutor in a big city is usually a patronage plum awarded to a close ally of the home-state senators of the president's party. But Browning had obtained the job in an unusual way. A veteran street-level prosecutor in the relative backwater of San Mateo, Browning had won the appointment simply by writing a letter to Senator George Murphy, the senior Republican in the state in 1970. At forty-one, tall and lean, thoroughly apolitical, Browning had the instincts of a trial lawyer. If the evidence was there, he'd charge anyone—including Patricia Hearst.

Browning and Bates were friends, and they worked together on dozens of investigations, but they were in conflict over the Hearst case. Through his nightly pilgrimages in Hillsborough, Bates had become close to the Hearst family. (He even slept over on occasion.) Bates felt Randy and Catherine's pain as they agonized over the fate of their daughter. During many long, boozy nights in the mansion, Bates came to see the case, and even the evidence in the bank robbery, through the eyes of the Hearsts. Their exclusive concern, understandably, was Patricia's well-being, and it came to be Charlie Bates's as well.

Jim Browning, the prosecutor, never met the Hearsts, and he saw the facts of the case differently. The U.S. attorney also had his offices in 450 Golden Gate Avenue, and the two men developed a ritual for every time a new communiqué arrived from the SLA. Browning would take the elevator to Bates's FBI suite, and the two men would huddle over a tape recorder and parse the words. Listening to Patricia's first few statements, Browning shared the view that she was a terrified victim. But he sensed the transformation in her tone. Browning didn't buy Bates's argument that Patricia was forced to join the SLA.

And then, finally, there was the bank robbery itself. Together, the two men studied the herky-jerky motion picture created by splicing the security camera photographs together. Patricia didn't look coerced to Browning. Her weapon looked just like those wielded by Ling, Mizmoon, and DeFreeze. She yelled at the customers just as the others did. To every appearance, Patricia had her assignment inside the bank, and she completed it. Like the trial lawyer he was, Browning didn't cotton to complicated explanations for evidence that was right in front of him. He thought it wasn't his business, or a jury's, to ask *why* a criminal chose to break the law; the system was designed to identify and convict those who committed crimes. Yes, Patricia had been kidnapped, but she had also robbed the bank. His job, Browning thought, was to prosecute bank robbers. Bates was unpersuaded.

Then, nine days after the robbery, came the communiqué of April 24, 1974.

After Steven Weed moved out of the Hearst family mansion, he continued his quixotic, independent investigation of the kidnapping. In early April, Weed tried to make connections in the radical exile community, hoping to find a country that might grant asylum to the SLA, if they freed Patricia. One of his contacts suggested that Régis Debray, the originator of the foco theory (whose books had been found in the Concord house), might be willing to help. As a bonus, Debray had known the original Tania and could speak about her character and motivations. Weed's acquaintance called the singer Joan Baez, a friend of Debray's, who agreed to contact the Marxist theoretician, who was living in Mexico. Debray indicated some interest in trying to help. Weed then ran the idea by Randy Hearst.

"We need a goddamn South American revolutionary mixed up in this thing like a hole in the head," Randy replied.

Randy's skepticism notwithstanding, Weed took off for Mexico during the second week in April and secured an audience with Debray, who agreed to write a letter, which Steve brought back with him to California. "To Patricia Hearst," the letter began, "I just received a visit from your friend, Steve. It is at his request . . . that I take the liberty to intervene in a situation in which the spirit, methods, and intentions are obviously foreign to me."

The letter went on in an arch, Marxist academic style, but the gist was that Debray asked to be informed whether her conversion to the SLA cause was genuine—for Patricia to "assure me that you have consciously and freely chosen to take the name and follow the example of Tania." Debray said that the original Tania's intellectual development had been the result of "years amongst the workers" and study of "the theory of scientific socialism and the reality of the actual world." He explained, "You will understand that we must be cautious to protect the moral integrity and the international purity of her commitment." When Weed returned to the United States, he released the letter and held a news conference where he said the video of the bank robbery suggested to him that Patricia had been coerced into participating.

There was something almost poignant about Weed's desperate journey to find an intellectual voice who might persuade the SLA, and his fiancée, to change course. But the idea was doomed from the start. From DeFreeze on down, the comrades parroted Marxist lingo more than they understood it; especially by the time they were on the run, they operated more by instinct than by thought. And Weed, an object of derision inside the SLA, was the worst possible intermediary at this point. So the Debray letter and Weed's press conference prompted a scathing response, which came on April 24.

"Greetings to the people. This is Tania," Patricia began, her voice clear and steady. "On April 15, my comrades and I expropriated $10,660.02 from the Sunset branch of the Hibernia Bank." (DeFreeze had told her to add the two cents to confuse the bank's auditors.) "Casualties could have been avoided had the persons involved kept out of the way and cooperated with the people's forces until after our departure. I was positioned so that I could hold down customers and bank personnel who were on the floor. My gun was loaded, and at no time did any of my comrades intentionally point their guns at me. Careful examination of the photographs which were published clearly show that this was true.

"I am obviously alive and well. As for being brainwashed, the idea is ridiculous to the point of being beyond belief." It was as if Patricia had eavesdropped on the debates between Bates and Browning over her state of mind (as well as Weed's public comments) and then set about refuting every argument the FBI man made in her defense.

To be sure, Patricia also mouthed some SLA political verbiage that still sounded contrived coming from her. "Consciousness is terrifying to the ruling class," she said. "And they will do anything to discredit people who have realized that the only alternative to freedom is death; and that the only way we can free ourselves of this fascist dictatorship is by fighting, not with words but with guns."

But Patricia's tone became venomous when the subject turned to Weed, whose name she could barely bring herself to utter. "As for my ex-fiancé, I am amazed that he thinks that the first thing I would want to do, once free, would be to rush and see him. I don't care if I never see him again. During the past few months, Steven has shown himself to be a sexist, ageist pig. Not that this is a sudden change from the way he always was. It merely became more blatant during the period when I was still a hostage. Frankly, Steven is the one who sounds brainwashed."

This broadside certainly had the ring of authenticity. At the time of the kidnapping, Patricia was, as she later said, "mildly suicidal" at the thought of marrying Steve. Now, whether prompted by her relationship with Willy Wolfe, or by a broader political consciousness, or (as she later claimed) by the continuing threat of death for disobedience, Patricia was at her most convincing in her denunciations of the man with whom she had recently shared her life.

She concluded with the words that would become her signature: "To those people who still believe that I am brainwashed or dead, I see no reason to further defend my position. I am a good soldier in the people's army. *Patria o muerte! Venceremos!*"

The April 24 tape ended with a brief, menacing postscript from
DeFreeze. The field marshal wanted to make clear that the stakes in
the SLA's battle with the authorities were life and death. "Regarding
the two people shot in the bank, we again warn the public any civilian
attempting to aid or to involve or assist the enemy of the people in any
manner will be shot without hesitation," he said. "There is no middle
ground in war. Either you are with the people or with the enemy."

The April 24 communiqué converted Bates to Browning's point of
view—almost. The two men compromised. The U.S. attorney would
issue arrest warrants for all the SLA comrades, including Patricia. But
while the others would be subject to arrest for the robbery, Patricia
would be charged as a "material witness." This meant that if the FBI
or the police located Patricia, she could be held like any of the others.
At that point, based on further investigation, the FBI and the U.S.
attorney could then decide whether to charge her with the bank robbery or to release her as an unwilling participant in the crime.

In light of this decision, Patricia Hearst made her debut on a
wanted poster, with her image displayed alongside pictures of Donald DeFreeze, Nancy Ling Perry, Camilla Hall, and Patricia Michelle
Soltysik, "aka Mizmoon." (The authorities still lacked photographs of
Bill and Emily Harris, Angela Atwood, and Willy Wolfe.) The text
noted, "THESE SUBJECTS ARE TO BE CONSIDERED HEAVILY
ARMED AND EXTREMELY DANGEROUS." The poster did not
reveal that the photograph of Patricia came from her engagement
announcement, on her parents' lawn in Hillsborough, less than six
months earlier. In the picture, as in Patricia's life, Steven Weed had
been cropped out.

The exhilaration over the bank robbery passed after a few days,
replaced by DeFreeze's paranoia as well as the claustrophobia created
by nine bodies in a small apartment. This time, DeFreeze had a new
idea about how he was going to advance the cause. He would begin

recruiting new members by ringing doorbells and introducing himself to strangers as General Field Marshal Cinque of the SLA.

Even by DeFreeze's standards, this was a lunatic notion. He was perhaps the most wanted man in America, and his photograph had been all over the news. Still, it galled DeFreeze to fancy himself a leader of black people when all of his followers were white. Now, he thought, it was time to reach out to African Americans, and most of the neighbors in the Western Addition neighborhood happened to be black. He believed he could build on the outlaw sensibility he had cultivated with the food giveaway and the bank robbery. DeFreeze told Angela Atwood and Bill Harris to accompany him on his rounds and stand behind him as he made his pitch to whoever happened to open the door. (Harris, characteristically, thought DeFreeze's idea was madness, though he did comply with the order to tag along.)

The trio wandered the streets three times in late April, carrying the Jehovah's Witnesses' publication the *Watchtower* as a cover for their proselytizing. They would spot African American people who looked hip and "jam" them, as DeFreeze said. He would follow them to their homes and knock on their doors—"lightning meetings," he called them. Once inside, Cinque would identify himself and seek recruits.

The most incredible thing about DeFreeze's door-to-door campaign was that it worked. None of the people who answered the door reported the encounters to the police, and one family, which happened to belong to the Nation of Islam, became a crucial ally.

The young woman of the house called herself Jamellea, and DeFreeze persuaded her to come visit the safe house on Golden Gate, which was about a block from her apartment. When Jamellea did visit, she brought an entire delegation with her—three adults and three children. As soon as the group arrived, one of them, Brother Ali, asked to meet the famous Tania.

"There she is," DeFreeze said, pointing.

"She doesn't look like her," Ali said.

"Smile for the man, Tania," DeFreeze said. "People don't recognize you unless you smile, like in your pictures." (For her part, Patricia was shell-shocked by the visitors because she had not been in an apartment with outsiders since the day she was kidnapped.)

The visitor named Rasheem raised an embarrassing question. "Where are all the blacks?" he asked the man he knew as Cinque. "I don't see any blacks here except you."

DeFreeze deployed his fantasy, which he had shared with Patricia after her kidnapping, that there was actually a bigger SLA out in the world. "Oh, this is the white unit," DeFreeze told Rasheem. "I'm here just to help them get organized and trained 'cause these brothers and sisters are going to lead the other white units." The black units, he said, were training elsewhere.

For a few days, Jamellea and the others (including the children) were regular visitors to the Golden Gate apartment, and they treated DeFreeze with the kind of deference he enjoyed. At one point, the woman who called herself Retimah told him that her children referred to him by a code name—Jesus. This pleased him.

DeFreeze decided that the heat from the bank robbery was growing too intense for the comrades to remain at Golden Gate, so he gave his new friends an assignment. Over the next couple of weeks, he supplied them with cash to buy three used vans, all for a total of about $2,000. Then, in late April, DeFreeze told the new recruits to find the comrades a new place to live, one farther from the FBI offices. They rented a two-bedroom place at 1808 Oakdale Avenue, in Hunters Point, another run-down part of town. Before the May rent was due on Golden Gate, DeFreeze announced that the comrades would be moving. Pack rats as always, they filled the station wagon for two round-trips to the new apartment. Even before they moved, the Golden Gate apartment was a stinking mess, overrun by cockroaches, and they left behind a mix of trash and food that prompted other tenants to complain within a couple of days of their departure.

When they were finished emptying the place, the group wanted to leave a message for their pursuers that displayed their trademark theatrical flair. So they dumped a mass of documents and keys (including the keys to the cars used in the robbery) into the bathtub and then filled it with a toxic brew of chemicals. On the wall of the bathroom, they left the following message:

WARNING!
TO THE FBI, CIA, DIA, NSA, NSC AND CBS:
   There are a few clues in this bathroom. However, you will have to wait until they are dry. An additional word of caution: ½ (one-half) lb. (pound) of cyanide (potassium cyanide) crystals has been added to this "home brew." So, pig, drink at your own risk.
   There are also many additional juicy SLA clues throughout this safe house. However, remember that you are not bullet-proof either.
   Happy hunting, Charles!

The taunt was directed at Charles Bates of the FBI.
   The comrades also covered the walls of the apartment with graffiti. One scrawl was in the unmistakable, private girls' school handwriting of Patricia Hearst:

Freedom is the will of life.
Patria o muerte, Venceremos.
   Tania—

Alerted by neighbors who noticed the cockroaches coming from the third-floor apartment, the police broke down the door on May 2. But by then the comrades had been gone for days.

By the time the comrades were settled in the apartment in Hunters Point, the jubilation of the bank robbery had passed. The Nation of Islam recruits brought food, and the comrades continued their daily rounds of calisthenics and battle drills in the slightly less cramped conditions of the new apartment. But DeFreeze never liked the apartment on Oakdale Avenue. He recognized the folly of placing eight white comrades in a virtually all-black neighborhood. They would call attention to themselves when they ventured outdoors.

Between slugs of plum wine, DeFreeze waxed fatalistic. He told Patricia that he was the only one of the comrades who had a criminal record, but now they were all wanted for bank robbery. Before the Hibernia action, the others had the option of going back to their bourgeois lives, but now they had passed the point of no return. They were fugitives—forever.

Then, suddenly, DeFreeze had an announcement. They were leaving for Los Angeles.

SHOWDOWN AT MEL'S

By the time the authorities discovered the Golden Gate safe house, with the taunting graffiti on the walls, DeFreeze and the comrades had already concluded that it was only a matter of time until they were caught in San Francisco. DeFreeze decided to flee to the place he knew best—Los Angeles, his former home. Of course, it wasn't clear what the SLA would do once they were there, but Cinque figured he could maneuver more easily in a place where he knew the terrain. He wanted a measure of control over his surroundings. What he found in Los Angeles was something very different.

The cash from the bank robbery dwindled faster than the comrades expected. After paying for the vans, rent on two apartments, food and supplies for nine people, DeFreeze had to start cutting into the $1,000 grants he had made to each of the comrades. Worse still, the stress of fugitive life was getting to everyone, especially with the repeated, furtive, nighttime moves. DeFreeze's mood turned consistently apocalyptic. The revolution, he promised, was just around the corner, though he conceded that the comrades might not survive to see the victory. Ling and Mizmoon, the truest believers, responded to his discourses with ever more reverent behavior toward the field marshal. Angela Atwood, theatrical as ever, also welcomed the approach of Armageddon. Talk of death—their own as well as their enemies'—was constant. Camilla Hall, weary and still overweight, struggled to keep pace, physically and emotionally. The Harrises quarreled, as always, and Bill kept talking about leaving the sinking ship without ever making a move to do so. Patricia and Willy kept to themselves, their worry sheltered by their now-recognized union. As a group, the comrades were not so much retreating to Los Angeles as spinning out of control.

Thanks to the purchases by the Nation of Islam recruits, the comrades had three vans at their disposal. DeFreeze decreed that they would travel in separate vehicles and rendezvous at a spot he designated in South Central Los Angeles, his old neighborhood. But first he had to decide how to divide up the comrades for the long journeys south. He said he wanted three teams of three, with each team equally strong in case they had to take action independently. He said he wanted to separate the lovebirds—Patricia and Willy Wolfe—so they would maintain their focus on the tasks at hand. In the end, DeFreeze assigned Angela Atwood and Camilla Hall (who was clearly the weakest link) to his car; Willy would go with Mizmoon and Nancy Ling; and Patricia would travel with Bill and Emily Harris. These assignments would turn out to be the most consequential decisions DeFreeze ever made.

And so, late on the night of May 8, the caravan set off. They staggered their departures so they would avoid calling attention to themselves, but they all took the same route, shunning I-5, the major north-south highway, and instead taking the less-traveled Route 99 most of the way. Driving through the night, careful to observe the speed limits, they passed through the agricultural heart of the state, the Central Valley, before they hit the sprawl of Los Angeles. Bill Harris took the first turn at the wheel of the battered Chevy van, with Emily next to him and Patricia in the back, next to a small arsenal of weapons covered by a blanket. Then Emily drove. Before dawn, Patricia did some driving, too.

The three SLA vehicles linked up later in the morning. DeFreeze appeared in his red-and-white van, which had the odd feature of dainty curtains on the windows. Nancy Ling was deputized to find the group a place to live, and she returned to report that she had located a house at 833 West Eighty-Fourth Street, in South Central, for the modest sum of $70 a month. When the comrades assembled there, they saw why the price was so low. Even by the modest standards of the comrades' living conditions in San Francisco, the place was a wreck—a three-room shack with no electricity and thus no hot water, in the heart of the ghetto. Even with the big score at the bank, the comrades couldn't help but notice the downward trajectory of their living conditions. They had gone from a comfortable suburban house in Concord, to a modest home in Daly City, to a pair of seedy apartments in San Francisco, to this hovel in Los Angeles. The dismal regression offered a vivid counterpoint to DeFreeze's promises of imminent victory.

There was no furniture, no stove, no refrigerator, no cooking utensils. Emily Harris and Camilla Hall snuck out to a grocery store and returned with canned spinach and okra, which they attempted to flavor with another purchase, canned mackerel. The comrades who could stomach the mixture ate it cold. Patricia, her weight already below a hundred pounds, lived on crackers and Kipper Snacks, a different kind of canned fish. As in San Francisco, the black neighborhood made it difficult for anyone but DeFreeze to leave the house without drawing attention. Mostly, they stayed inside, doing their military drills and calisthenics in desultory compliance with their established custom. DeFreeze added instruction in knife fights to their daily ritual.

Bill Harris didn't bother to hide his revulsion at the Eighty-Fourth Street house or his frustration at DeFreeze's increasingly apparent estrangement from reality. "This is just one more reason for leaving this stupid group!" he fumed to Emily. Yet, as with his earlier bouts of dismay, Bill never followed through with his determination to break ranks. Sensing Harris's disgruntlement, DeFreeze made the only placating gesture he could afford at this point. On the spot, General Field Marshal Cinque promoted Harris to the rank of general in the SLA; henceforth, Harris would be known to the comrades as General Teko.

After the group settled in Los Angeles, the three-person teams remained intact for brief forays outside the walls of the house. On one occasion, Bill, Emily, and Patricia set out to find a woman named Utommu, who was the mother of the lover Emily had taken during her prison visits, before she and Bill joined the SLA. After a considerable search, they found Utommu, who lived in the area, and Emily went inside to talk to her alone. As Patricia recalled, Emily came out of the house practically skipping with joy. The mother had informed Emily that her lover would soon be released from prison. They would soon be together again. Notwithstanding the Harrises' theoretical belief in open marriage, Bill seethed at this news.

After just a few days, he was desperate to find any excuse to leave the shabby house, so he volunteered to take his team to do errands—to buy food, collect supplies, even pay parking tickets. One day, DeFreeze announced that the comrades would need heavy clothing for future combat actions. He wanted them to get long johns, heavy socks, and thick pants. Bill prepared to take his team—that is, Emily and Patricia—on the mission to the store. Just before they left, though, Mizmoon said she thought Patricia should stay back at the house, because she was too weak and too recognizable. Better, Mizmoon argued, to send Angela with Bill and Emily. As Mizmoon said, "Gelina would be much better on this action and safer, too."

But Patricia—who was, at this point, very much Tania—protested the idea that she should be excluded from any SLA action. "That's not fair," she argued to DeFreeze. "I'm capable enough now to be backup on this operation and I'm on their team and it's only right that I fulfill my responsibility as a member of Teko's team. We're supposed to stay together on all actions and I want to do my part."

Bill and Emily weighed in on Patricia's behalf. "She's our comrade, and we trust her," Bill told DeFreeze. "We'll be safer with her in case something happens."

DeFreeze took Patricia's side. Tania would go shopping.

Shortly before 4:00 p.m. on May 16, 1974, Patricia (having donned a curly dark wig) joined Bill and Emily Harris in DeFreeze's red-and-white Volkswagen bus on a round of errands in nearby Inglewood. On the front seat was an envelope with cash to pay a parking ticket, but perhaps understandably, in light of what followed, the three comrades never got around to mailing it.

Even through the windshield, the sun felt good. Emily drove, Bill rode shotgun, and Patricia squatted in the back on the floor, next to DeFreeze's pile of weapons. The windows were open, and a cool breeze lifted the spirits of three people who had mostly been cooped up indoors since February.

Taking their time and enjoying the escape from the dreadful house on Eighty-Fourth Street, the three comrades drifted from store to store. First, they bought four bags of groceries at a supermarket for $33.06. Next they went to a clothing store, where they bought six pairs of Levi's jeans for $81.41, thus disregarding DeFreeze's edict against dungarees. They went to a stationery store, where they bought nine five-by-three notebooks, as well as batteries, chewing gum, aspirin, a newspaper, and cigarettes. (Like most of the comrades, Patricia had become a chain-smoker since her kidnapping.) At all of these stops, Bill and Emily had gone inside the stores, and Patricia had waited in the van, with the curtains drawn. At a stationery store, Bill heard the radio playing the Crusaders' "Way Back Home"—the SLA national anthem. When Bill reported the news to Patricia, they agreed that it was a positive omen, perhaps even a sign that the SLA was gaining strength.

Bill noticed a place called Mel's Sporting Goods, on Crenshaw Boulevard, where he thought he could find the other items DeFreeze wanted. He told Emily to pull the van into a parking lot on the opposite side of Crenshaw, a busy four-lane street with a concrete divider. Bill checked that the curtains on the van windows were drawn before he and Emily headed toward the store. Both were armed with handguns.

"Stay in the van," he said to Patricia at 4:10 p.m. "We'll be right back."

As in the previous three stops on the afternoon of May 16, the Harrises enjoyed the chance to browse in a store, the kind of normal activity that had been off-limits for a long time. They wandered around for a while, eventually going to the camping supplies section and picking up a sweater, sweatpants, several pairs of socks, and a watch cap. Just before they were going to check out, Bill noticed a shotgun shell bandolier for sale. He believed in what he called armed propaganda, and he liked the bold look of a belt of shells strapped across his chest. Still, he didn't want to call attention to himself by buying anything related to weaponry. So he slipped the item in his pocket.

Tony Shepard, a clerk on duty at the store, was a twenty-year-old college sophomore majoring in police sciences. As it happened, he used his job as a form of training for his future career in law enforcement. By habit, he glanced up at the convex mirror by the checkout counter as Bill and Emily approached, and he noticed Bill slip the bandolier in his pocket. At that point, though, Shepard did nothing. From his studies, he knew that the crime of shoplifting does not actually take place until an individual leaves the store. So he carefully stepped to a different counter, where he kept a pistol and handcuffs just for situations like this one. Once he had armed himself, Shepard sidled close to the counter where Emily was paying the bill of $31.50 with two $20 bills.

As Bill Harris stepped out the door, Shepard yelled out, "Hey, Bill!" Harris turned around, but the clerk was calling to Bill Huett, his boss at the store, to back him up. Shepard then asked Harris to step back inside Mel's.

"Are you going to pay for what you have in your pocket?" Shepard asked.

A wanted criminal armed with a weapon, Bill was determined to be neither arrested nor frisked. He bolted. But Shepard and his boss tackled him on the sidewalk. Emily tried to pull the men off her husband. A third store employee jumped on the pile, then so did a schoolteacher who happened to be passing by. The brawling heap of people rolled into the gutter, in a vaguely comic melee.

Then, from the bottom of the pile, Bill Harris reached into his pocket, and a voice in the scrum called out, "He's got a gun!"

As Patricia waited in the van, she pulled the curtain back and saw Bill and Emily walk across the street toward the store, but then she closed the curtain again. She noticed that Bill had bought an afternoon newspaper at an earlier stop, and she leafed through it while she waited. And waited. The visit to Mel's seemed to be taking an unusually long time. At last, she moved the curtain again to see what was going on and grasped the situation instantly. Bill and Emily were in trouble. They were being assaulted by a group of men, presumably from the store.

What should Patricia do?

The tableau at Mel's Sporting Goods marked the crossroads of Patricia's captivity, the moment when she had the greatest number of options before her. The key to the van was in the ignition. She could have slid into the driver's seat and gone anywhere she wanted—to a friend, a hospital, or home—and left the Harrises to fend for themselves. She could have turned herself in to the police and explained that she had been coerced into participating in the Hibernia Bank robbery. Or, simply, she could have opened the door, walked away, and called for help. She could even have done nothing at all and waited to see how the fight would end. But Patricia Hearst did none of those things.

Reacting instinctively, she later said, based on her SLA training, she whipped the blanket off the cache of guns next to her. She grabbed the heaviest, most dangerous weapon she could find. It was Bill Harris's submachine gun, which Patricia had never before trained with or fired. (This was the very gun she had posed with in the famous "Tania" photograph.) Pointing the weapon out the van window, she aimed in the general direction of the fight across the street, pulled the trigger, and sent thirty deadly rounds in the direction of Mel's store. The first bullet whizzed within inches of Bill Harris's head. Later fire hit the divider in the middle of the street, and other bullets shattered Mel's plate glass window. Miraculously, no one was hurt, though it was a very close call. One bullet hit the chest of a store clerk, but it was blocked by the ballpoint pen in the man's pocket.

But Patricia wasn't finished. When she emptied the ammunition clip in Bill's machine gun, she drew another weapon—this time, her own semiautomatic carbine. Still firing wildly across a busy street, she squeezed off three more shots, trying to free her comrades.

As the bullets started flying, everyone but Tony Shepard fled for his life.

"Dude, you better get out of here," Bill Harris said to him. "You're going to get killed."

"No shit," Shepard whispered to Harris, who had dropped his gun in the chaos. Shepard released his grip on his captive and crawled on his belly to a position of relative safety behind a concrete telephone pole. Bill raised his head to make sure that Patricia had stopped firing, and then he grabbed Emily by the hand and raced across traffic back to the van. Shepard had managed to apply a single handcuff to one of Bill's wrists, and it dangled as he jumped into the driver's seat of the van and gunned the engine.

Shepard then fired his own gun twice at the van. Then, still determined to pursue an early police apprenticeship, he jumped into his own car, which was parked in the same lot. Harris swung north for a block on Crenshaw, and then he made a hard right onto Imperial Highway, another divided street, with traffic lights. Shepard followed. As in so many movies that were filmed in this area, the chase was on.

Bill didn't know Los Angeles at all and had no idea where he was going. The underpowered Volkswagen was wheezing, but Bill kept blowing through traffic lights, his tires screeching. The seats had been removed from the back of the van, so Patricia bounced around on the floor as Bill peeled east on Imperial. Even during this crisis, Bill and Emily found time to bicker.

"What did you take?" she demanded.

"Nothing," Bill said.

"You must have taken something."

"Nothing. Just a little bandolier that I thought we could use."

"Jesus Christ," Emily replied. "That was stupid."

"How was I supposed to know the store had a fucking junior pig?"

Determined to ditch the persistent Shepard, Bill made a right turn onto a side street, drove a few more blocks, and then slowed to a stop. Shepard pulled over several car lengths behind them.

As soon as Bill stopped the van, he grabbed a weapon from the stash in the back and made a menacing procession toward their pursuer. Recognizing that he was outgunned, Shepard fled.

Suddenly it was quiet. Bill and Emily were standing alone with their weapons at the ready. They knew dozens of people had seen the shoot-out and surely the plate numbers on the van had been called in to the police. They could hear sirens in the distance. The trio needed a different car—right away.

They noticed that a couple had just parked a Pontiac Trans Am, a classic California muscle car, a few feet away from the van. Bill walked over and pointed his gun at the occupants.

"We're SLA. We need your car," Harris said.

"Fuck you," the man said.

"Dude," Bill explained, "I don't want to do this, but the cops are on their way here to kill us."

The man reluctantly handed over the keys, and Patricia moved the rest of the weapons from the van into the Pontiac. (In the frenzy of the moment, no one thought to remove the envelope with the parking ticket.) Bill, Emily, and Patricia jumped in the Pontiac, and Bill drove off.

Just two blocks later, in the middle of an intersection, the engine died.

"Shit!" Bill said.

The trio found a Hispanic father and son standing by a Chevy Nova station wagon.

"We need your car," Bill said, waving his gun, the single handcuff still dangling from his wrist. "We need it right now. We're the SLA."

The father said, "Sure, sure," and handed Bill the keys.

"Just a second," the owner of the Chevy said, in heavily accented English. He had a lawn mower in the back. Could he remove it before they took the car?

Bill agreed, and Emily and Patricia transferred the weapons a second time.

At least the Chevy appeared to be in decent working order, and for the moment there appeared to be no one in pursuit. Bill drove through the streets of Inglewood, heading nowhere in particular.

Bill, Emily, and Patricia discussed their situation. They were fine now, but the police were sure to follow their trail from the VW van to the Pontiac to the Chevy. They would need another car to lose the police.

They took the Chevy to a shopping center, hoping to find another vehicle that might cause the police to lose their trail. They saw a hippie type getting into a camper, which seemed especially appealing because it could serve as a mobile hideout. Bill pulled his gun, and unlike the previous two carjack victims the hippie registered real fear. He started weeping hysterically. Bill gave up on him and his camper. "Don't call the cops!" Bill instructed, but he realized that the cops would soon know of their latest encounter as well.

By this point, they had traveled to Lynwood, another small city within Los Angeles County. They recognized that just stealing cars out from under people was doing them no good. The victims were surely calling the police as soon as the trio took off. It was nearly seven o'clock, and the sun was beginning to set. They needed a safer ride—soon. Just then, as they cruised the residential streets of Lynwood, Emily spied a Ford Econoline van with a "For Sale" sign in the window. The sign gave a phone number and an address, which happened to be right where they were. Emily knocked on the door and in her most polite midwestern voice asked for a test-drive of the van.

An eighteen-year-old high school senior named Tom Matthews

answered the door. A test-drive was fine, Matthews said, but he had to come along. He was asking $2,500 for the van.

Emily took the wheel of the van, with Matthews next to her. A pair of benches lined the sides in back, with a beanbag chair plopped between them. Emily steered the van a couple of blocks to where Bill and Patricia were parked in the camper.

"Do you mind if my friends come along?" Emily asked.

Matthews said sure.

Bill and Patricia approached the car, and Bill pulled a machine gun from inside his coat.

"We're SLA," Bill told him. "We need to borrow your van. Just get in the back. If you don't do anything funky, you won't get hurt."

Matthews's eyes bulged at the sight of the gun, and he scampered to join Patricia in the back. "As long as I don't get shot, I don't care what happens," he said. He crouched down under the same blanket that covered the weapons.

It had been only a little more than an hour since the shoot-out, but Bill, Emily, and Patricia now had their fourth vehicle—and, for the first time, a hostage.

The situation was different in another way, too, for Tom Matthews possessed a rare, almost surreal equanimity. He fit a California archetype, that of the surfer dude, except that he wasn't a surfer. He was a baseball player, a first baseman at Lynwood High School, and as he told his kidnappers, the first day of the state play-offs was tomorrow. "I just need to be back for the game," he said.

Bill, Emily, and Patricia were immediately taken with their hostage. A big sports fan himself from his Indiana days, Bill took a shine to the lad and quizzed him about his team's prospects in the championships. Giddy and energized by the chaos of their adventure, Bill decided to share a secret with Matthews.

Pointing to Patricia, Bill said, "Do you know who this is?"

Matthews stared.

"This is Tania!" Bill said. Matthews had been following coverage of Patricia's kidnapping in the news.

"Holy shit!" he said.

Patricia beamed at him.

The atmosphere in the van turned almost chummy as Emily drove through the city. The three comrades had a problem. Bill still had one wrist stuck in a handcuff, with no key. Did Tom have any idea where they might find a hacksaw?

Matthews knew of a hardware store nearby, but when Emily went inside, there was no appropriate blade. Matthews then directed them to a Montgomery Ward, where Emily found a tool that she thought could do the job. In the parking lot, she handed the saw to Bill, who struggled using his right hand to saw through the cuff on the left, but all he succeeded in doing was to make the cuff tighter and tighter on his wrist, which started turning blue. "Here," Matthews said. "You're going to cut off your hand. Gimme that."

Crouching in the back of his van, Matthews used the saw to slice the cuff off Bill's wrist. When he was finally liberated, the three comrades cheered. Patricia gave the young first baseman a kiss on the cheek.

Matthews cradled the shredded handcuff. "Can I keep this as a souvenir?" he asked. The comrades agreed.

The police found the Volkswagen van within minutes of the comrades' first car theft. The unmailed parking ticket, found on the front seat, gave the authorities a priceless clue. The ticket said the violation had taken place in front of 835 West Eighty-Fourth Street, next door to the safe house. The police also identified the gun that Bill had dropped in front of Mel's. It had been purchased by Emily Montague Harris, in Oakland, on October 13, 1973. Witnesses to the car thefts informed police that the perpetrators had identified themselves as the SLA.

So by the time the trio set off in the van with Tom Matthews, the radio was blaring news that the SLA had brought its unique brand of theatrical violence to Los Angeles. The story dominated the airwaves.

Earlier in the week, DeFreeze and Bill had agreed on a fallback location for a rendezvous in case the comrades found themselves on the run. After Bill was extricated from the handcuff, Emily drove the van to the Century Drive-In movie theater, a landmark for local cinema buffs, which was located in Inglewood. The plan called for a meeting at midnight, when the first to arrive would indicate his location by placing an upside-down cup on a speaker stand. Bill figured that the news reports about Mel's would prompt DeFreeze and the other comrades to flee Eighty-Fourth Street and activate the backup plan.

"You'll meet our friends," Bill told Matthews. "We'll join up with them and you can have your van back. You'll make the game, no problem." He even offered gas money to the hostage, but Tom declined the cash.

In the meantime, the four people in the car—including at this point three of the most wanted criminals in the United States—watched a double feature. The first movie was *The New Centurions,* a drama about the Los Angeles Police Department, and Matthews noted that the comrades cheered each time an officer was shot. They then watched *Thomasine & Bushrod,* an all-black takeoff on *Bonnie and Clyde.*

No one in the group was paying a lot of attention to the movies, and Bill and Emily kept getting out of the car—to buy snacks, to check if anyone was watching them, and to exorcise their nervous energy. This gave Matthews and Patricia a chance to chat as they shared the beanbag in the back of the van.

Curious and ingenuous, Tom had a lot of questions for Patricia— like what was the deal with the bank robbery? Was she a willing participant, or did the SLA have their guns trained on her to make her behave?

"I was totally into it," Patricia said. "No one made me do anything. We rehearsed. I wanted to be a part."

How about the food giveaway?

Oh, she said, my father just used that as a tax break.

And what happened at Mel's?

"I saved my comrades," Patricia said. "I was so proud when I saw them running across the street."

At another point, Bill told Patricia to make sure her carbine was not loaded. He didn't want any accidental shootings in the car. Patricia took the opportunity, while unloading her gun, to show Matthews how easily she handled the weapon. She pulled out a couple of rounds of ammunition. "See that?" she said, pointing. "That's where we put in the cyanide."

Though she was barely two years older than Tom, she took an almost maternal interest in him, patting his head to make sure he wasn't scared by the bizarre situation. "I was kidnapped, too, and under a blanket," she said. "You'll be okay."

Indeed, Matthews seemed a great deal less scared than Patricia had been when she was seized. He even displayed his cheeky humor. At one point, when Bill and Emily returned to the car, Bill groused that he had received a hamburger when he ordered a cheeseburger. Tom was comfortable enough at that point to needle Bill. "You were just involved in a shoot-out and you're worried about whether you got a hamburger or a cheeseburger?"

But as midnight passed, there was no sign of the other comrades. DeFreeze had not shown up at the fallback. After the theater closed, Emily took off on a meandering drive through the Hollywood Hills, then on to Mulholland Drive. At some point in the middle of the night, they found a secluded spot, and all went to sleep for a few hours. Patricia made sure Tom was covered with the blanket.

At dawn, Bill decided that they needed another car, not least because they wanted to return the van to Tom so he could make his baseball game. So on the morning of May 17, Emily and Patricia posed as hitchhikers, and the two attractive young women had no trouble getting a ride. A man named Frank Sutter, driving a late-model Lincoln Continental, picked them up, and the pair engaged him in a provocative conversation about taking them to Las Vegas. Their chitchat with the driver allowed Bill to come up behind them, with his machine gun, and force Sutter into the backseat, under the blanket. (Bill waved to Tom Matthews to return to his van. Matthews made it to his game that afternoon, which his team won, 1–0.)

Now riding in their fifth car, the trio went to look for a newspaper with classified advertisements to find a sixth. They spent several hours trying to track down a working but cheap used car. Eventually, they found an aged Plymouth Valiant and removed $250 in cash from Sutter's wallet to pay for it. They returned the Lincoln to Sutter and took off in the Plymouth.

Bill had heard on the radio news that thanks to the parking ticket the police had raided the Eighty-Fourth Street house but found that it was empty. It was a relief that DeFreeze and the other comrades had not been busted, but they still had no idea where they were or how to reach them.

Emily had had a summer job at Disneyland, and she recalled that there were motels directly across the street from the amusement park, in Anaheim. She said they would be good places to blend in with the tourists. It was nearly dusk on May 17 before Bill, Emily, and Patricia found one and checked into a room.

The first thing they did was turn on the television.

LIVE ON TELEVISION

A t 5:30 a.m. on May 17, the LAPD and the FBI set up a joint command post near 835 West Eighty-Fourth Street, the address on the parking ticket. They began stopping everyone who came from that direction, and one person reported that he saw white people going in and out of the house next door. Several residents also said they had seen two vans parked in front of that house, including one that was red and white. The authorities had identified the SLA safe house in Los Angeles.

The FBI, hungry to bring its embarrassing failed investigation of the kidnapping to a conclusion, descended on Eighty-Fourth Street in force. The LAPD, however, guarded its turf more zealously than the local police in San Francisco, so tension between the bureau and the cops became a recurring theme of the events on May 17. For one thing, the only crimes that had taken place in Los Angeles were shootings and car thefts, and those were local matters, not federal offenses. In addition, the LAPD had a reputation for ferocity that far exceeded that of the San Francisco cops or any police force in the nation. This was due, in part, to a special unit, created in 1967, that appeared custom-made for the challenge—a quasi-military detachment called Special Weapons and Tactics, or SWAT. The team included thirty-seven officers in five-man squadrons, dressed in commando garb and armed with AR-180 semiautomatic weapons, AR-15 semiautomatic rifles, 12-gauge shotguns, tear gas guns, a .243-caliber long rifle, and .45-caliber pistols.

For the initial action against the SLA on May 17, the FBI and the LAPD reached an uneasy compromise. The scene would be nominally under the control of the FBI, but officers from both departments would take part in the siege. First, they evacuated the entire block around 833 West Eighty-Fourth Street. Then, just after 8:00 a.m., the LAPD SWAT team deployed to the front of the house, and the FBI SWAT group deployed to the rear. At 8:55, an LAPD officer with a bullhorn announced, "To those inside the house at 833 West 84th Street: this is the Los Angeles Police Department. We want you to come out the front door with your hands up. We want you to come out immediately. You will not be harmed." There was no response.

After eight minutes of silence, the FBI supervisor ordered the LAPD to launch twelve canisters of tear gas into the house. A few minutes later, the FBI busted down the back door and found the place empty. Clearly, though, the SLA had been on the premises very recently. There was no furniture, but there was plenty of evidence. There were three suitcases containing clothes, as well as gas masks, women's wigs and handbags, shotgun ammunition, SLA literature, and handwritten notes about how to leave the house in a hurry. The significance of some evidence in the Eighty-Fourth Street house could not be fully appreciated at once. There was a work sheet dividing up lookout duty for nine soldiers as well as a grocery list and prices for dehydrated food with the prices divided by nine. Clearly, then, nine people had lived there and fled in a hurry. But who were they? And where did they go?

The LAPD immediately put out the word that witnesses had seen a pair of vans associated with the house. Shortly after noon, two uniformed officers on regular patrol on East Fifty-Third Street decided to take a look in an alleyway that was sometimes used as a dumping ground for stolen vehicles. (This was about five miles from the house on West Eighty-Fourth Street.) The officers found two vans matching the description of those used by the residents of Eighty-Fourth Street. The license plates showed that one van had been purchased on May 7 in San Francisco by Ali Bey (who was one of the SLA's Nation of Islam recruits) and the other had been purchased around the same time by a person using a fake name.

The neighborhood around East Fifty-Third Street in Los Angeles was even rougher than the one around West Eighty-Fourth. Most of the buildings were one-story frame and stucco houses, many of them abandoned or boarded up. Foot traffic was rare. Suspicion of the police was high. Plainclothes officers began circulating in the neighborhood, trying to determine where the owners of the vans might be staying. In short order, the LAPD identified four houses where the SLA might be holed up. But the information was sketchy, and no one wanted to take any chances with a heavily armed and dangerous group of outlaws.

There was again the matter of turf. The FBI and the LAPD had collaborated on the raid of the Eighty-Fourth Street house, but the attack had been unsatisfactory, and maybe dangerous. They had different training and different rules of engagement, and neither wanted to be worried about the other if bullets started flying. So at 2:00 p.m., William Sullivan, the special agent in charge of the FBI's Los Angeles office, showed up at the local precinct for a summit meeting. By this point, the Hearst operation had been one of the largest and most complex kidnapping investigations in the history of the FBI and certainly one of the biggest embarrassments for the bureau as well. In light of this, Sullivan informed the local police commanders that the FBI SWAT team members would be moving into position near the newly discovered vans, and they would handle any confrontation with the SLA. The LAPD brass on the scene begged to differ. In short order, the two sides were screaming at each other.

The LAPD officer in charge of the SWAT operation was Daryl Gates, a legendarily gruff figure who would later go on to run the department. At the time, Gates was at Parker Center, the LAPD headquarters, and after he heard of the confrontation, he decided to put an end to it. He knew that the FBI could not handle the situation alone; the bureau would need LAPD officers to block traffic, summon fire and ambulance support, and isolate the confrontation. Gates decided to use that advantage to exclude the FBI altogether. "Tell Bill I understand how he feels," Gates told his subordinate, who was facing down Sullivan in the precinct house. "But if there is any shooting in Los Angeles, it's going to be done by the LAPD."

With that, Gates ordered two elite units of SWAT officers (totaling seventeen men), backed up by more than two hundred other police personnel, to assemble at a staging area near Fifty-Third Street and await his further orders.

Events moved so quickly on May 16 that the news media never caught up. But the shoot-out at Mel's and the chase that followed gave local television stations the chance to mobilize the following morning. In those days, most local stations sent out camera crews to shoot film that had to be developed back at their studios. But KNXT—which stood for "experimental television"—possessed a new technology that allowed it to broadcast live from the field through a microwave transmitter attached to the top of a small truck. The technology was so new that the team at KNXT is said to have invented its name: the Minicam.

KNXT (later renamed KCBS) would become a national prototype for local news in America. This happened, in part, because Mary Tyler Moore's aunt happened to work as the business manager of the station, and she shared tales of the station's lead anchor, Jerry Dunphy—who served as the model for the hapless Ted Baxter. But the station was also a journalistic and ratings leader, with a strong institutional commitment to securing scoops. For KNXT, the Minicam was a not-so-secret weapon. Bill Deiz, a thirty-year-old correspondent for KNXT, wanted to deploy the new technology when he showed up for work on the morning of May 17 to cover the biggest story the city had seen in a long time: the sudden, thunderous arrival of the Symbionese Liberation Army in Los Angeles.

The shoot-out the previous afternoon, with the trail of stolen cars, galvanized law enforcement, the news media, and the public. All were obsessed with the same questions: Where was Patty Hearst? Was she one of the gun-toting outlaws who terrorized a sporting goods store? The authorities were inundated with purported sightings of the heiress turned bank robber, but none panned out. The police were being cagey about any leads they might be following, but when it came to tracking the Los Angeles Police Department, KNXT had another distinctive asset at its disposal. In addition to its exclusive access to a Minicam, Bob Long, the assignment manager for the station, and his colleague Jeff Wald had cultivated a local eccentric named Jeff Webreck, who in a later day would be known as a hacker. Webreck lived in the Hollywood Hills, near the crossroads of radio transmissions in the city. He had located the crystals that allowed him to track confidential police transmissions. Webreck permitted KNXT to shadow the cops.

Deiz began the day covering briefings on the search for the SLA at various police stations around the city. As with all routine stories, motorcycle couriers took the film back to the KNXT broadcast center. He was told to keep in touch with the office, to receive further instructions. (Like most reporters at the time, Deiz kept a pocketful of change to use in pay phones.) Webreck had picked up news that the police were converging on a house at Fifty-Fourth Street and Compton Avenue. Deiz was told to get there to meet the Minicam truck, which was staffed by Rich Brito, a cameraman, and Rey Hernandez, a technician.

When the KNXT team arrived, they saw that the police had surrounded a small yellow stucco house at 1466 East Fifty-Fourth Street. They set up their truck on Compton, and Deiz took his microphone, with a long cable, and began threading his way between buildings to get as close as possible to the focus of police attention. Through an alleyway, he was able to stand so that Brito's camera could get a clear shot of both him and the building behind him. The crew on the scene began transmitting pictures back to the station.

But there was a problem. KNBC, the top competitor to KNXT, had shown up on the scene with an old-fashioned live television truck, the kind used for sporting events and political conventions. KNBC also had one of the early news helicopters hovering overhead. Given KNBC's late arrival, there was no way that station could get on the air with a clear shot of the scene, but its presence interfered with the KNXT electronic signal, which had to be beamed directly to a tower on Mount Wilson, about thirty miles away. The situation was a journalistic standoff. KNBC couldn't get its own picture on the air, but it could stop its competitor from doing so. After a few minutes, Bob Long called his counterpart at KNBC and proposed a deal. If KNBC would shut down its operation on Fifty-Fourth Street, KNXT would share its live signal. KNBC agreed, and soon the picture of Bill Deiz crouching in front of the shabby little yellow house was being broadcast on both major stations in Los Angeles.

Within minutes, other stations in the city asked to receive the KNXT live feed as well, and then stations around California, and then the whole country, plucked the signal from the sky. In less than an hour, the scene in front of 1466 East Fifty-Fourth Street became a landmark in the history of television journalism. To that point, networks had only broadcast live events where they could lay cable and plan in advance. Thanks to the Minicam, the Hearst kidnapping led to the first unplanned breaking news event broadcast live around the entire United States. Suddenly modern technology made real one of the famous counterculture slogans of the era: the whole world was watching.

News of the shoot-out at Mel's hit the airwaves on the evening of May 16. The comrades heard the news on the radio that night, and DeFreeze issued an order to vacate the Eighty-Fourth Street house. By the time the remaining comrades packed up—and they left a great deal behind—it was after midnight on May 17, so there was no point in trying to meet up with the Harrises and Patricia at the fallback location at the drive-in. It was a moment of maximum desperation for the remaining six—DeFreeze, Mizmoon, Nancy Ling, Angela Atwood, Willy Wolfe, and Camilla Hall. They had no contacts and no idea where to go. They took off in the two remaining vans and just drove around South Central in the middle of the night. They stopped at 1466 East Fifty-Fourth Street for the most basic of reasons: the light was on.

The house resembled many in the neighborhood—built in the 1940s of stucco, framed with wood, with two bedrooms, all on one floor. This model happened to be painted yellow, though not recently, and its condition was dismal. The house was elevated about three feet off the ground, and the entrance was from a wooden porch. The most distinctive feature of 1466 East Fifty-Fourth Street was the sturdy stone wall in front of the porch, facing the street. The house was unusual in another way, in that it had a rotating cast of residents. Many houses in the neighborhood were occupied by struggling but stable working-class African American families. In 1466 East Fifty-Fourth Street, men, women, and children came and went at all hours of the day and night. It was a flophouse, so when Donald DeFreeze knocked on the door at about 4:00 a.m. on May 17, the intrusion was less bizarre than it might have been elsewhere.

Christine Johnson and Minnie Lewis, both in their mid-thirties, answered the door. Freddie Freeman, Johnson's boyfriend, and a seventeen-year-old girl were also awake in the front room. They had all been drinking wine, playing dominoes, and listening to the radio. DeFreeze got right to the point.

"I saw your lights, sisters. My name is Cinque. I need your help," he said. He said he and some "white friends" were being pursued by the police, and they needed a place to stay "for a few hours." Seeing the women hesitate, Cinque offered them $100, which was accepted. Cinque then introduced his comrades to their hosts as "soldiers of the SLA." As Patricia and the Harrises had done with the stolen car victims the previous day, DeFreeze made no attempt to hide their identity. A collective fatalism had come over the whole SLA enterprise. They were who they were, and they would not pretend otherwise. For weeks, if not months, DeFreeze had preached that surrender was not an option, and his subordinates had internalized his position. So they joined him in barreling forward, trusting that they would somehow continue to foil their pursuers or die in an honorable conflagration.

After handing over the cash, DeFreeze began unloading the two vans; the comrades produced an extraordinary arsenal. (The amount was especially remarkable because they had just left another significant amount of weaponry behind at Eighty-Fourth Street.) They brought more than a dozen guns and more than four thousand rounds of ammunition to Fifty-Fourth Street. Specifically, the SLA stash included the following:

- four M1 .30-caliber carbines, all illegally converted into machine guns;
- a Browning .30-caliber semiautomatic rifle;
- a Remington .244-caliber semiautomatic rifle;
- seven sawed-off 12-gauge shotguns;
- two Mauser double-action automatic pistols;
- a military model Colt .45 automatic pistol;
- two .38-caliber revolvers. One, a Smith & Wesson known as the blue steel "Chief's Special," was DeFreeze's personal sidearm. The other, a Rossi, was the gun used to kill Marcus Foster. (At the time, Patricia still had possession of the group's other .38-caliber revolver, which had been liberated from the security guard at the Hibernia Bank.)

In addition, there were boxes and bandoliers of ammunition, some with cyanide tips, as well as cardboard boxes full of documents, suitcases, and sleeping bags. The people inside the house might have been shocked by the size of the arsenal, but they quickly turned their attention to making money off DeFreeze, who had a lot of immediate needs. Shortly after dawn, he gave the seventeen-year-old $20 for a quick trip to buy sandwich ingredients, beer, and cigarettes. Two young children materialized from a bedroom, and they were given sandwiches to take to school. DeFreeze and Willy Wolfe (the only male SLA members on the premises) took half-hour turns monitoring the sidewalk in front of the house, while the four SLA women chatted up the residents and took catnaps. All morning, people came and went, and DeFreeze never hid his identity or his goal—to "start a revolution," as he informed one visitor.

Cinque also wanted to hide the two vans that brought the comrades to Fifty-Fourth Street. Freeman showed him the secluded alley about a block away that was frequently used as a temporary home for stolen vehicles. DeFreeze and the man hustled the two vans into the alley, but the SLA leader would soon recognize the folly of relying on a drunken stranger for advice on operational security. The police knew about the stash in the alley, and that was where the uniformed officers discovered the vehicles around noon. They radioed in the information, which prompted the arrival of the SWAT team, with its dozens of backups. The vise was tightening.

By early afternoon, the scene inside the house had turned increasingly surreal and crowded. Minnie's children returned from school to find Nancy Ling making Molotov cocktails in the kitchen. One of the children, who was eleven years old, recognized DeFreeze, who introduced himself as Cinque, from television. When the boy asked him his name, DeFreeze replied that the boy should go into the bathroom and lie down in the tub if he didn't want to get killed. The boy fled out the back door instead. An older man named Clarence Ross settled in with a pint bottle of whiskey. At another point, Christine Johnson and a woman named Brenda got into a fistfight. Impressed with the seventeen-year-old Brenda's skills, the comrades asked if she wanted to join the SLA. A male friend of hers arrived, and DeFreeze asked him to go buy them a car. He gave the fellow $500 in cash, and he never returned with a car or the money. More than a dozen people passed through the house over the course of the day, and DeFreeze disclosed his identity to virtually all of them.

The presence of the SLA during the afternoon of May 17 was such an open secret that DeFreeze practically became a neighborhood tourist attraction. At one point, an eighteen-year-old woman showed up because she had heard that the SLA was there and she wanted to meet them. She found DeFreeze drinking a jug of Boone's Farm wine (apparently because plum wine was unavailable). He told the woman there was probably going to be a shoot-out, and he was prepared to die. Still, he said, "We're going to take a lot of motherfucking pigs with us." In the middle of their conversation, Christine Johnson walked into the kitchen, started to say something, then passed out, snoring, on the floor. DeFreeze carried her back to the bedroom, and the woman visitor left.

At about 4:00 p.m., Mary Carr, the mother of Minnie and the grandmother of the children in the house, walked in on the chaos. She had heard about what was going on and wanted at least to extract her grandchildren before they were caught up in violence. When Carr arrived, her daughter and another woman were passed out in drunken stupors. Brenda said the SLA women were making bombs in the other bedroom. Appalled, Carr confronted DeFreeze about the dangers his people were creating. The field marshal tried to mollify the furious grandmother, telling her that black people needed to stick together. But Carr had no interest in DeFreeze's brand of revolution, and she grabbed her two grandchildren and stormed off. (Unbeknownst to Carr, there was still another child left inside the house.)

Holding their hands, Carr walked over to Compton Avenue, where the police were assembled. At that point, the cops had narrowed the search for the SLA down to four houses in the neighborhood. Carr settled the issue. She gave the cops the specific information they needed. She said the SLA was holed up in a yellow frame house, which she said was the fifth one in from the corner.

———

In response to Carr's information, the SWAT commander on Compton sent two teams to the yellow frame house, one group of nine officers toward the front door on Fifty-Fourth Street, the other of eight toward the back, in an alley. Sergeant Al Preciado, a thirty-four-year-old eight-year veteran of the LAPD, led the team going to the front door. Preciado crouched down and started to make his way along Fifty-Fourth Street toward the fifth house. But when Preciado reached the *fourth* house, he realized this was the yellow one. Carr had miscounted. Preciado didn't want to risk being seen and was trapped behind the stone wall in front of the target structure.

Preciado could clearly make out the voice of Donald DeFreeze, issuing instructions. "We are not going to surrender," he said. "We are going to fight to the death." Preciado heard furniture being pushed around to block sight lines into the house. (The SWAT team by the back door, near the kitchen, could see a refrigerator being pushed to block the window.)

At 5:44 p.m., Preciado gave the signal to Sergeant Jerry Brackley, who had a bullhorn at the ready.

"Occupants of 1466 East 54th Street," he said, "this is the Los Angeles Police Department speaking. Come out with your hands up. Comply immediately and you will not be harmed."

The response was silence.

Brackley made a second announcement.

A moment later, the front door opened. An eight-year-old boy stepped outside and froze, too afraid to move. After a few moments, he stepped off the porch, and officers hustled him to the command post on Compton Avenue. The boy told the officers that there were two men and four white women, all heavily armed, inside the house.

Two more surrender announcements followed.

The door opened again, and the elderly man named Clarence Ross put his hands up and walked slowly down the stairs off the porch. Questioned by the officers, he denied seeing any weapons inside the house.

In the first nine minutes of the standoff, the police made eighteen surrender announcements, and all were met by silence.

The LAPD had the house completely surrounded, but the FBI did have one agent on the scene. He was the keeper of a German shepherd "sniffer dog," who had been primed with the scent of Patricia Hearst. The dog's assignment was to identify Patricia, alive or dead.

APOCALYPSE ON
FIFTY-FOURTH STREET

To Patricia Hearst, Disneyland really did look like a magic kingdom. Emily Harris had driven the thirty miles to Anaheim, with Patricia curled up, exhausted, in the backseat. In the passenger seat, Bill kept boasting that they had outsmarted the cops once again. Patricia was disgusted with the newly promoted "general" Teko. It was his imbecilic decision to shoplift the bandolier from Mel's that started the day's mad cascade of events. Who was he to brag about anything?

Still, the sight of Cinderella's castle filled Patricia with melancholy. Like so many California kids, she had visited Disneyland and had fond memories of the park's gleaming world of make-believe. The contrast between her last visit and this one struck her as more than bizarre. She wondered if she would ever go to such a place again. She had begun a new chapter in her life, and she could not know if she could ever again show her face in public without a disguise. As committed as she was to her new life, she was now also both a fugitive and a refugee.

Bill told her to crouch down in the backseat while Emily went to the motel's front desk to rent a room. This was to keep Patricia from being recognized and also because the police might be looking for a man and two women traveling together. It was also a money-saving move. (Motels charged more for three people than for two.) The three of them were down to their last few dollars, and they had lost the groceries and clothes from their shopping trip when they abandoned

DeFreeze's van, several vehicles ago. All they had were the clothes on their backs and their weapons.

When Emily turned the key in the door, the motel room looked as good as San Simeon to Patricia. There were clean sheets on the two double beds. There was a shower with hot water. There was no trash strewn on the floor. There was a color television set. Compared with the dumps where they had been staying in San Francisco and Los Angeles, this was paradise.

Just before they checked in, they heard on the radio that the police had surrounded the SLA. Bill turned on the television in the room, and it looked as if a police siege were about to begin. At first, the three of them thought they were watching film of the raid on Eighty-Fourth Street, which had taken place that morning. But they quickly realized the target was a different house, on a different street, and this broadcast was live. It was just after 5:30 p.m.

Steven Weed continued his quixotic independent investigation of the kidnapping, even after his efforts only seemed to make matters worse. His journey to Mexico to coax a letter out of Régis Debray had ended in humiliation. Instead of leading to Patricia's release, the Debray letter prompted her communiqué of April 24, which included her most cutting and hostile rejection of the man she now referred to as her *former* fiancé. Weed's arrogant style put off everyone, including the Hearsts and the FBI. But there was no disguising that he was in a great deal of pain. Worried about Patricia's well-being, stung by her public rejection of him, he traveled California alone, trying to figure out what had happened to his girlfriend.

He had a compulsion to keep giving interviews to the press, too, and this led to the final breach in his relationship with Patricia's mother. In May, Weed talked to *Newsday* about his relationship with the Hearst family. He had said many of the same things before—that Vicki had been a poor student of his, that Patricia had a troubled relationship with her mother—but Catherine decided she had had enough of him. When Steven called the house in Hillsborough to say that he would be visiting friends in Southern California, Randy answered the phone. "What the hell is it with you?" Randy yelled at Weed. Anytime Weed was around a reporter, Randy said, "You just bubble like a yeast cake! I don't want you coming around here even to pick up your mail. You just aren't housebroken!"

As it happened, Weed was in Los Angeles on May 16. He was tracking down psychiatrists who might give him insight on what Patricia was going through as a captive and fellow traveler of the SLA. On that night, he had dinner with a psychiatrist and his girlfriend, and then the pair drove him to a peculiar little hotel nestled along the coast, in the bluff between Santa Monica and Malibu. Sitting alone at the bar after dinner, Weed proceeded to get roaring drunk as the television began showing reports about the shoot-out at Mel's. As he later recalled, "I was too drunk to know if I had actually heard the bulletin or merely imagined it."

Depressed and hungover, Weed spent most of the next morning on the beach, intentionally cutting himself off from news reports. He roused himself to make it to the airport at 3:15 p.m. for a short flight to San Diego, where he was going to visit friends. He read about the shooting at Mel's while on the airplane. He arrived at his destination in San Diego at around the same time that Patricia, Bill, and Emily checked into the motel in Anaheim. Like them, he turned on the television around 5:30 p.m.

On the afternoon of May 16, Randy Hearst took a call from a man claiming to be a former Brazilian police officer with a special expertise in freeing political prisoners. He offered to help free Patricia, if Randy would put up $37,000 to set up an office for him in San Francisco. Randy demurred, though it was by no means the most outrageous scheme he had encountered over the previous four months.

By this point, the crowds of reporters outside the mansion in Hillsborough had thinned. PIN had closed down. There had been no communiqués since April 24. Randy still talked to almost everyone who had a theory about his daughter—the psychics, the profiteers, the cops, the purported jailhouse informants—but there was less urgency. Patricia's status had changed. It was one thing to recover a kidnap victim and something very different to track down a criminal. The journalists out front started averting their eyes when Randy and Catherine passed by. Only the rivers of alcohol flowing through the house were unchanged.

John Lester, a local news reporter for a San Francisco station, had quit his job in the spring to work as the Hearsts' liaison with the rest of the press corps. He spent his days in the mansion, transmitting interview requests and generally keeping Randy and Catherine apprised of what the reporters were thinking. On the night of the sixteenth, the couple had dinner with friends, stopped by their country club, where their younger daughters, Anne and Vicki, were rehearsing a performance for a musical revue, and returned to Hillsborough after midnight. Lester gave them the news about the shoot-out at Mel's and the possibility of Patricia's involvement before the couple went to bed.

In the morning, Catherine and Randy showed up early in the room that they had turned over to the FBI agents who were still living with them. As always, Catherine was immaculately turned out in a black dress. Randy, having suffered a long, sleepless night, appeared unshaven and still wearing his pajamas. They heard the news about the raid on the empty house on Eighty-Fourth Street. According to the FBI, that location had clearly been used by the SLA, but the occupants had vanished. Charles Bates, the lead FBI agent, usually checked in with the Hearsts after any major development in the case, but he didn't contact them on May 17. To the family gathered in the house, the silence from Bates felt ominous.

The family spent the day puttering nervously about their home. Shortly after 5:00 p.m., Emmy, the family cook, burst into the room where Randy, John Lester, and the FBI agents were sitting. "Mr. Hearst," she said, "it's on the television. A house in Los Angeles is surrounded." The question hung heavily: Was Patricia inside?

Randy shook his head and said, "We might as well turn it on." Lester did, at about the same time as Weed was starting to watch in San Diego and Patricia was doing the same in Anaheim.

Catherine couldn't bear to participate in the vigil. She retreated to the music room, where she played Hank Williams's "Your Cheatin' Heart" on the piano.

At 1466 East Fifty-Fourth Street, the first surrender announcement came from a police bullhorn at 5:44 p.m. In the following eight minutes, the eight-year-old boy and then Clarence Ross left the house, while the LAPD kept repeating instructions to the SLA to leave the house peacefully. There were no responses.

The LAPD had a decision to make: whether to attack or to wait. It was clear that the SLA comrades were heavily armed. It was getting dark. Crowds were gathering. Given the rocky relationship between the LAPD and the black community, there was risk to the officers when so many were sitting in place for so long in South Central. A broader conflagration was always possible. The Watts riots of 1965, which were triggered about five miles away, were less than a decade in the past. In the end, the decision might have been dictated, simply, by the DNA of the Los Angeles police. Another department—perhaps the one in San Francisco—might have opted for caution. But aggression, not patience, fueled the L.A. cops.

At 5:53 p.m., a SWAT officer named Kenny Rice fired two 509 Flite-Rite CS tear gas projectiles through a side window of the house. The flash from the gun lit up the entire street. Other SWAT team members could hear the canisters bouncing around the walls and then the hiss of the gas dispersing.

Suddenly automatic weapons fire began pouring from the house.

The biggest police gun battle ever to take place on American soil had begun, and it was on live television.

Most of the bullets, in both directions, were flying directly over Al Preciado's head. Kneeling behind the stone wall in front of the porch, he heard the SLA machine-gun fire aimed at the officers hidden behind cars and buildings on the far side of Fifty-Fourth Street. The return fire by the police headed toward the front windows. A similar exchange of fire was taking place in the rear.

In those days, LAPD officers had to purchase their own weapons, and Preciado had invested in an Armalite AR-180 semiautomatic assault rifle, a civilian version of the M-15 carbine that was used by American troops in Vietnam. (The AR-180 was especially popular with the Provisional wing of the Irish Republican Army, which dubbed the gun "the widowmaker.") The magazines for the gun held twenty rounds, and Preciado had stashed five of them in his uniform before approaching the house. When the bullets started flying, he inched toward the corner of the stone wall and managed to point his gun toward one of the front windows. In short order, he had exhausted his ammunition—one hundred bullets.

"I need more ammo!" he shouted to his colleagues who had taken over the house next door.

Along with the gunfire, the police continued to lob tear gas into the house, to no effect. In light of the failure of the gas to chase out the criminals, the officers assumed (correctly, as it turned out) that the comrades possessed modern military-grade gas masks, like the ones they left behind in the house on Eighty-Fourth Street.

In a matter of minutes—that is, by 6:00 p.m.—the SWAT teams were running low on ammunition, especially tear gas canisters. The FBI SWAT agents, who were waiting impatiently at the Compton Avenue command post, volunteered their tear gas projectiles, but a quick inspection revealed that their 37-millimeter projectiles would not work in the LAPD's 40-millimeter launchers. So the LAPD allowed the FBI team to take a position across the street from the house and fire sixteen gas projectiles at the house (and about sixty rounds of regular ammunition as well). Nothing succeeded in suppressing the fire coming from the house, and after a few minutes LAPD officers hurried the FBI agents off the scene.

At the command post, the volume of shooting from the house prompted a new worry. What if the SLA busts out and starts shooting up the street? There were still many civilians in the area, and large numbers of spectators—looky-loos, in LAPD argot—had assembled by the police barriers. (The LAPD later estimated the crowd in the area at four thousand.)

In light of the continuing, violent standoff, the SWAT team members on the scene decided they needed to escalate the confrontation. "We need fragmentation grenades!" they told their on-site commander, John McAllister.

At that moment, Daryl Gates, who had overall charge of the SWAT teams, was in a police car speeding from headquarters to the scene. Hearing the request for the grenades, he thought, *Jesus . . .*

A fragmentation grenade is a military antipersonnel weapon that sends metal shards flying in all directions upon detonation. The LAPD did not possess them, as Gates quickly informed his subordinates, but the request itself underlined the desperation of the situation.

The firing didn't stop—from any direction. The comrades were shooting mostly the automatics, from both the front and the back of the house, where the second team of SWAT officers was sending round after round into the structure as well. Still pinned down behind the stone wall, Preciado was being resupplied with magazines that fellow officers slid across the driveway from the house next door. He emptied them almost as fast as he got them—as many as twenty-five magazines, or five hundred shots, from this one officer alone. And still the SLA fought back.

Stymied, the SWAT officers tried to go over the top. At 6:30, Jerry

Brackley (the bullhorn operator) climbed to the roof of the house next door. He tried to fire a tear gas canister into a side window, but the gun misfired. He raised his head to make a second attempt, and a burst from a machine gun missed him by inches. Brackley fell backward to avoid the shots, and a spotter in a police helicopter reported on the LAPD radio band that he had been hit. In fact, Brackley was unhurt, but the report rattled and inflamed his colleagues. In fact, amazingly, despite the intensity of the shooting on both sides, there were no injuries—at first.

When climbing down from the roof next door, Brackley discovered, to his amazement, that there were still three female civilians, huddled on the floor, who had refused earlier police entreaties to vacate the premises. Brackley insisted that they leave, and he lifted each one out the window on the opposite side from the shooting. "Don't leave my dogs behind!" one woman yelled. Three terrified dogs were scampering around the house. But the cops refused to remove them, saying they didn't have time "to go around saving animals."

As the standoff approached the one-hour mark, with no end in sight, the officers in the back of the house decided to escalate the confrontation. At great risk to themselves, they rose from behind the concrete barriers that were protecting them and threw two canisters of a different model of tear gas into the house. Federal 555 riot tear gas was both more toxic and more flammable than the CS gas that the police and the FBI had been using. The effect was nearly immediate. Black smoke appeared from a window in the rear of the house. The police held their fire for a moment so Brackley could make another announcement. "Come on out," he said. "The house is on fire. You will not be harmed."

At 6:45—sixty-one minutes after the first announcement—the front door opened. "Okay, we got one coming out," Brackley said.

It was Christine Johnson, one of the residents of the house. She was so drunk that she had slept through the gun battle. She awoke only when the bed caught fire. She staggered out the door, and a SWAT officer, gambling with his life, rushed up on the porch to take her to safety.

Between the fire and Johnson's exit, most officers on the scene figured that the confrontation was nearing an end. But the gunfire from the house continued, now coming almost exclusively from the rear. At 6:47, Brackley tried again. "Come out," he said, "you will not be harmed. The house is on fire. It's all over. Throw your guns out the windows. You will not be harmed." He received more gunfire in response.

Months earlier, back in the comparative serenity of the house in Concord, Joe Remiro had drawn up instructions about what to do in case the cops made a direct assault. They called for the comrades to station themselves in the crawl space underneath the house. At the moment of truth, the comrades appear to have remembered Remiro's advice. As smoke filled the interior, the comrades pried a floor heater from its moorings, opening a hole to beneath the house. There they kept firing their guns at the police at the rear through the air vents.

For the six comrades, the situation was now beyond desperate, beyond horrific. Tear gas enveloped them. Fire closed in on them. Gunfire rained down on them. Three of them—DeFreeze, Mizmoon, and Nancy Ling—might have known, when they gunned down Marcus Foster, that they would probably lose their own lives. But even their route to this moment seems difficult to fathom. DeFreeze was a low-level hood, Mizmoon an industrious library denizen, Ling a spaced-out sex worker. None seemed destined for an inferno.

For the other three, their ambush borders on the tragic. Angela Atwood wanted to be a star, not a revolutionary martyr. A year earlier, Willy Wolfe was scouring for archaeological relics, not firing machine guns. And Camilla Hall, the lovelorn poet, was tending the flowers in a Berkeley park. Even at this moment, a chatty letter to Hall's parents back in Minnesota was in her pocket. ("Dear Mom & Dad, How are you? I've been thinking about you a lot & hoping that all is well with you. I get a lot of strength from our love & it really helps keep me going.") With the fire closing in on them, they could have fled, but the comrades stayed together, fighting, to the end.

By 6:50 p.m., the smoke billowing out of the house was so thick that the police could scarcely see the windows. At that moment, the SWAT officers in the back caught their first clear sighting of an SLA member. Nancy Ling had climbed through a small space that family dogs had used to go beneath the house, to escape the heat of the day. She rose from a crouch, fired a pistol in the direction of the police, and was then immediately hit by seven bullets, producing two fatal wounds in her back, four nonfatal wounds in her legs, and one nonfatal wound in her arm.

Camilla Hall followed Ling out of the crawl space, guns in both hands. Before Hall could get all the way out, a police bullet shattered her skull, tearing off a large portion of her head. She fell to a prone position, and her comrades pulled her lifeless body by the legs back into the house.

At 6:58 p.m., the walls and roof of the house collapsed. The pop-pop of unused ammunition exploding inside the gutted residence—which made a different sound from ammunition fired from a weapon—continued for a few more minutes. Then the guns were silent. At 7:02, the police decided it was safe for firefighters to begin to extinguish the blaze. By the time they did, not a single wall in the house remained intact.

"Look!" said Bill Harris, pointing to the television in the motel room. "Look, it's live! That's our people in there!"

Patricia watched, trembling, from the floor. Emily sat on one bed, her faced etched with the horror of the scene. Bill bounced around the room, changing the channel, looking for new angles, swearing at the injustice of it all.

"We should go up there and help our comrades," he told the two women. "We could blast the pigs from the rear and fight our way in, so our comrades can escape."

"It's no use, Teko," Emily, always more levelheaded, said. "We'd be so outnumbered, we'd just be killed and it would serve no purpose."

"We should go anyway. . . . We should die with our comrades."

"No," Emily replied. "Cin would want us to live and fight on. That's what we've got to do."

"Oh, I wish I was there with them," Bill said, punching the bed.

Patricia watched in silence as flames began licking the sides of the house. "Come out," they heard Sergeant Brackley say, "it's all over."

As the machine guns still roared, Bill cheered.

But then there was silence as the house disintegrated into ashes.

Bill and Emily embraced on the bed as Bill wailed. "It's all my fault. . . . If it weren't for Mel's . . . I killed them. . . . Oh, I wish I were there. . . . I wish I were dead, too."

Emily tried to comfort her husband, telling him that they lived to fight on another day.

Overwhelmed, Patricia went into the bathroom and locked the door. "I was a soldier, an urban guerrilla, in the people's army," she thought. "It was a role I had accepted in exchange for my very life. There was no turning back. The police or the FBI would shoot me on sight, just as they had killed my comrades."

Emily coaxed Patricia out, and the three watched the postmortems on television. As it happened, they were the only living people on earth who knew the answer to the question that the reporters were asking each other: Was Patricia Hearst inside that house?

The scale of the battle on Fifty-Fourth Street was enormous. According to a subsequent investigation by the LAPD, the SWAT team fired more than fifty-three hundred rounds of ammunition in a little more than an hour of fighting. The police used eighty-three tear gas canisters. The number of rounds fired by the SLA comrades could not be determined with precision; it was probably between two and three thousand. The fire department could not pinpoint the precise cause of the fire, though it appeared likely that the tear gas played an important role. (A two-gallon can for gasoline was also found with a bullet-hole puncture, which was another possible source of the blaze. Two pipe bombs, with blasting caps, were also found inside the house, but they had not exploded.) In addition to 1466 East Fifty-Fourth Street, twenty-three homes in the area were damaged. The houses on either side of 1466 also burned to the ground. The three dogs next door were killed in the fire.

The barrages of bullets from both sides inflicted little damage on their intended targets. No police officers were hit, and only a handful suffered minor injuries. Ling and Hall were killed by police. Angela Atwood, Willy Wolfe, and Mizmoon died of burns and smoke inhalation, though Mizmoon had also suffered nonfatal gunshot wounds. DeFreeze suffered a fatal bullet wound to the temple. It remains unclear whether he died from suicide or from police gunfire. By the time the bodies were removed from the rubble, all had been severely burned.

As the battle was winding down, Steve Weed jumped in a car in San Diego and raced to the scene to find out if Patricia had been inside the house. One of his hosts thought it would be safer if she drove, and she gave Weed two Valiums for the trip north to Los Angeles. They were stopped at the security perimeter, and some in the crowd recognized Patricia's former fiancé from his television appearances. "Tania's found her brown sugar now an' she don't need no more of his shit!" one of them taunted.

In Hillsborough, Randy heard that Weed had shown up at the scene. Like his wife, Randy had had enough of the young man. "I should go down there and level that asshole," Randy said to the family and friends who had joined him. "He's a real jerk. Leveling him would be like striking out the pitcher."

Five bodies were initially removed from the scene. Thomas Noguchi, the chief medical examiner for Los Angeles, scheduled a news conference for 2:00 p.m. on Saturday, May 18, to announce the identities of the dead. (Noguchi, who was known to covet publicity, delayed his announcement so it would not conflict with the Preakness stakes.) As he informed Catherine by phone a few moments before he told the world, Patricia was not among the dead. He identified DeFreeze (aged thirty), Wolfe (twenty-three), Atwood (twenty-five), Mizmoon (twenty-four), and Ling (twenty-six). The Hearsts, and Steve, could be thankful.

But the following morning, searchers on the scene found a sixth body that had been buried. Another morning of tense waiting in Hillsborough gave way to relief when Noguchi said the sixth corpse was that of Camilla Hall, aged twenty-nine. "They died compulsively," Noguchi said. "They chose to stay under the floor as the fire burned out. In all my years as a coroner, I've never seen this kind of conduct in the face of flames."

So Patricia was not dead.

But where was she?

PART FOUR

"THE GENTLEST, MOST
BEAUTIFUL MAN"

This is what we have to do," Patricia said after she and the Harrises observed the carnage on television. "We need to go up there to L.A. and do a search-and-destroy mission on the cops."
"Fuck it," she said. "If we're going to go out, let's go out in a blaze of glory."

The shoot-out at Fifty-Fourth Street cemented Patricia's transformation into a committed revolutionary. She was kidnapped on February 4. On March 31, she convinced the comrades of her worthiness to join the SLA; on April 3, she sent the communiqué in which she vowed to "stay and fight" under her new name of Tania; on April 15, she participated in the robbery of the Hibernia Bank; on April 24, she sent the communiqué that mocked the idea that she had been brainwashed; on May 16, she fired her machine gun (and another gun) at Mel's to free Bill Harris from the clutches of his pursuers; on May 17, she watched her comrades, including Willy Wolfe, die excruciating deaths.

Patricia closed the door to her former life. The police were already after her in connection with the bank robbery, and now she would be wanted for the Mel's shooting as well. Her conversion from victim to perpetrator was complete. And besides, she asked herself, who had her real interests at heart? Starting from the day of the kidnapping, the comrades had warned Patricia that the only real threat to her life came from the police. The SLA was not going to harm her; the FBI, and its allies in law enforcement, were. DeFreeze made the point over and over again. That's why he gave her a shotgun, way back in Daly City—to protect herself in the event of an attack by the cops or the FBI. Well, the raid happened, just as DeFreeze and the others had predicted, and the police wiped out everyone they found. They would have shot her too if they had had the chance. Patricia had every reason to believe that the cops would now keep trying to kill her. Back in Berkeley, the *Barb* reached the same conclusion. Under the headline "War Has Come Home: The First Massacre," the paper wrote, "To the disappointment of both the police and spectators, Tania's body wasn't found in the rubble. The police were disappointed because she was fast becoming a dangerous, elusive, and identifiable revolutionary symbol."

Patricia was alive only because of several improbable twists of fate. If, back in San Francisco, Cinque had not assigned Patricia to the same team as Bill and Emily . . . If Bill weren't going stir-crazy in the Eighty-Fourth Street house and thus volunteered to run errands . . . If DeFreeze had accepted Mizmoon's recommendation that Angela, rather than Patricia, join the Harrises on the errands in Inglewood . . . If Bill hadn't been caught stealing the bandolier at Mel's, causing the split with the other comrades . . . If the other comrades had met up at the drive-in, as planned, and persuaded Bill, Emily, and Patricia to rejoin them . . . If the comrades had all stuck together, as they had done from hideout to hideout, month after month, then Bill, Emily, and Patricia would also have been inside the house on Fifty-Fourth Street. And they would all be dead.

So Patricia, in the grip of a cold fury, wanted revenge, even more than her remaining captors turned colleagues. She lived off cigarettes and snacks. Days and nights of hiding in grimy motels and squalid apartments gave her a sickly pallor, but adversity, for the woman called Tania, made her stronger. In this, there was, despite everything, a hint of her former life. In Hillsborough, and on the many stops on her academic journey, she sensed that she could shape the world to her liking. Then or later, Patricia was not one to be thwarted. So when the LAPD had thwarted her in the most public and gruesome way, she vowed, in the irrational cadence of the SLA, that they would pay.

The Harrises had no similar expectations. Emily was nearly catatonic with grief and fear; Bill was in a state of garrulous paralysis. He was a great one for jabbering about how he was going to commit acts of violence, but he had never followed through. Bill never fired a gun at anyone (not even in Vietnam). So even though their political fanaticism exceeded hers, they told Patricia to stand down. There would be no retaliatory, and suicidal, raid against the police. Bill and Emily were hardly experienced or competent revolutionaries, but they had lived among radicals and rebels long enough to expect that the police—the man—was always going to strike back. That's what happened. It was time now to regroup. It had never been more difficult to answer the paradigmatic question for the SLA: What now?

For one thing, there was no SLA, not anymore. Joe Remiro and Russ Little were locked up in San Quentin, awaiting trial for the murder of Marcus Foster. DeFreeze, Mizmoon, Nancy Ling, Atwood, Wolfe, and Hall were dead. For the moment, even Bill and Emily recognized the absurdity of suggesting that the two of them and Patricia amounted to an "army" of any kind. They were fully in survival mode. The revolution would have to wait.

After watching the shoot-out, on May 17, the trio spent the weekend in the motel by Disneyland. Then, with their finances dwindling, they fled south about fifteen miles to the sleepy little city of Costa Mesa. They found a dingy residential motel and rented a room with a hot plate and a black-and-white television for $40 a week. Together, on the following Tuesday, they watched the L.A. district attorney announce that he had brought charges against the three of them for kidnapping (of Tom Matthews), armed robbery, assault to commit murder, and a variety of other charges.

Bill, Emily, and Patricia were the most wanted criminals in the United States, and they were stuck, without allies, in Orange County, which was then the citadel of California conservatism. The Bay Area called out to them. Of course, they had no real idea what they would do there, but there had to be more options, and more friends, than in Ronald Reagan's Southern California.

They waited until Memorial Day, May 27, to make their getaway so they could disappear into holiday traffic for the nine-hour journey to San Francisco. They were still driving the barely functioning 1964 Plymouth Valiant, which they had purchased with the $250 they had stolen from Frank Sutter, their last carjacking victim. For the journey north, Patricia assumed her customary position in the backseat, under a blanket. Bill had lost his sidearm in the confrontation at Mel's, so he took Patricia's .38. A red satchel held the rest of their weapons.

Somehow the car limped all the way to San Francisco. Emily drove to Broderick Street, on the edge of the Haight-Ashbury district, which had, like the counterculture, degenerated into a crime-ravaged ruin. There the car died. The three of them got out and pushed the vehicle to a service station, where Bill put down a deposit for repairs. He returned to find Emily and Patricia waiting on a park bench. At that moment, this heiress to millions and her two friends had a total of $5 among them.

Bill remembered that a gay couple who had been his and Emily's upstairs neighbors back in Bloomington had a house nearby, on Oak Street.

Bill knocked on the door, and his old friend Mark blanched at the sight of the criminal.

"What are you doing here?" Mark said. "The FBI was just here yesterday, asking about you!" Agents were tracking down virtually everyone the Harrises had ever known.

Terrified, Mark agreed to let the trio stay for one night in a basement storage space that had once been a coal bin. Mark threw some blankets down the stairs, and they slept on the bare concrete floor. Every time it seemed that their accommodations could not get any worse, they found a new low. In the morning, Mark sent them on their way with $50 in cash. They spent the next night in a motel near downtown, and then Bill decided they needed a more permanent base. He sent Emily off to Oakland to find an inconspicuous pad in the neighborhood where Peking House had been. Their car was still in the shop, so they made their way to Oakland by bus—with the duffel bag full of clanking weapons at their feet. Patricia was still wearing her fluffy curly wig, but now she had freckles, too, courtesy of a makeup pencil donated by the gay couple.

Their new apartment was on Walnut Street in Oakland, and their arrival marked a turning point in Patricia's association with the Harrises. Everyone in the SLA had been treating Patricia as a comrade since the bank robbery in April; she had her own weapons and responsibilities like everyone else. But the Walnut Street apartment was the first time Bill and Emily left Patricia alone. When the Harrises went on errands, or jogging (they were early adopters of that fad), Patricia had the apartment to herself and could come and go as she pleased. "I was being left alone for hours, sometimes for most of the day," she later wrote. "I suppose I could have walked out of the apartment and away from it all. But I didn't. It simply never occurred to me. My fear of the police outweighed my hatred for the SLA." Whether or not Patricia hated the SLA at that point, she behaved like what she was—a fugitive. Through the following months, Patricia would make the same choice again and again—to remain with her comrades and to avoid law enforcement. She recognized that police officers who once might have seen themselves as her rescuers were now her pursuers, and she never tried to persuade them that she still needed saving.

Still, tensions were high among the three survivors. Bill and Emily fought all the time, as they usually did, and Patricia sulked and brooded. Rejected sexually by Emily in Oakland, Bill turned to Patricia, who, as she recalled, complied uncomplainingly. Still, the sexual energy of the SLA members dropped precipitously. The struggle for survival trumped the quest for satisfaction. And money, far more than sex, remained their principal preoccupation. Emily spent most of the cash from their gay friend on the security deposit for the Oakland apartment, and the rest went for cigarettes and food—beans, mostly. Bill talked about robbing another bank, mugging a prosperous-looking man on the street, or purse snatching. But it was just talk. By June 3, they were again down to about $20. Fortunately, they could still afford a newspaper, which informed them of a startling event that had taken place the previous day.

By the time the comrades were killed in Los Angeles, the SLA had become accustomed to its isolation within the counterculture. The murder of Marcus Foster marked them as irrational and untrustworthy. Most groups and individuals on the left wanted nothing to do with the "army." This repudiation from their nominal peers first became evident during the food giveaway, when even hard-core activists like the Black Panthers refused to participate in any activity initiated by the SLA. In response, the comrades nursed grudges against these groups and individuals like Angela Davis and Jane Fonda who spoke out against the SLA's tactics. By June, Bill and Emily took a perverse sort of pleasure in their lonely stand against what they regarded as the weak-willed counterculture establishment. They fought on alone, though it was never clear to what end.

Therefore it was a considerable surprise when Bill, Emily, and Patricia received a rare message of solidarity from fellow outlaws on May 31. A bomb went off at the Los Angeles office of the California attorney general. (There were no injuries.) The Weather Underground took responsibility and in a communiqué dedicated the attack to "our sisters and brothers" in the SLA. The gesture was encouraging, but irrelevant to the trio's everyday struggles. The Harrises didn't know anyone among the Weathermen, and they had no way of contacting them for support, leaving them still stuck in dismal isolation.

But on June 3, the newspaper said that the previous day, unbe-knownst to the trio, there had been a rally of commemoration and support for the SLA members killed by the police. It took place in what was dubbed Ho Chi Minh Park, near the Cal campus, in Berkeley. (Willard Park was the official name.)

By Berkeley standards, the rally was modest, drawing perhaps four hundred people, and it featured none of the big names or organizations active in the Bay Area. It did, however, include some of the people who genuinely knew and cared about the departed comrades—as they illustrated with their stage decoration. The front of the small speaker's platform was lined with bottles of Akadama plum wine, in commemoration of the general field marshal's favorite beverage.

There was one principal speaker on the occasion—Kathy Soliah (pronounced *SOUL-ee-ah,* with emphasis on the first syllable). Soliah was long and lean, and she possessed the long straight hair and tinted aviator glasses that were the signature of glamorous counterculture figures like Gloria Steinem, whom Soliah resembled. She came by her dramatic presence honestly, because she was an actress, which was how Bill and Emily knew her. Kathy Soliah was Angela Atwood's best friend. They both had leading roles in the local production of *Hedda Gabler,* and they worked together as waitresses at the Great Electric Underground in downtown San Francisco. Both were fired there, after protesting demeaning treatment from their bosses. In politics and life, Kathy and Angela were soul mates, and Kathy Soliah came to Berkeley on June 2 to mourn the loss of her friends and comrades.

"When I first met her," Soliah told the crowd about Angela Atwood (Gelina), "she wasn't very political, but she was always on the right side." Later, she realized that Atwood had gone underground with her comrades in the SLA. "Angela, Camilla, Mizmoon and Fahizah [Nancy Ling] were among the first to fight so righteously for their beliefs and to die for what they believed in." She went on, "Cinque, Willie, Camilla, Mizmoon and Fahizah were viciously attacked and murdered by five hundred pigs in LA while the whole nation watched. I believe that Gelina and her comrades fought until the last minute. And though I would like to have her here with me right now, I know that she lived and she died happy. I am so very proud of her."

Soliah had a message, too, for Bill, Emily, and Patricia, the sur-vivors. "SLA soldiers, although I know it's not necessary to say, keep fighting. *I'm* with you. And *we* are with you." Gazing out at the crowd, Soliah said, "I am a soldier of the SLA."

Reading Soliah's remarks in the newspaper, Bill saw a route to sal-vation.

Kathy Soliah was born twenty-seven years earlier and raised in Min-nesota, and her background resembled those of the other women com-rades. Her family moved when she was young to Palmdale, California, which was still a small desert town and not yet part of the greater sprawl of Los Angeles. She belonged to the pep squad for the football team, but her real passion was the stage, and she played leading roles in school plays throughout high school. Her father was a gym teacher as well as a football and track coach at the high school, and his prize pupil was his son Steve, Kathy's younger brother. The intertwined fates of Kathy, Steve, and Josephine Soliah, the baby of the family, would be a major theme of the post–May 17 SLA.

In the late 1960s, Kathy went to the University of California at Santa Barbara, where the political culture was less famous than the one at Berkeley but every bit as extreme and volatile. There she met and fell in love with a fellow student named Jim Kilgore, who was an accomplished athlete, an aspiring sportswriter, and a budding revolu-tionary. The couple moved to Berkeley, where they were soon joined by Steve Soliah, who ran track in college and bonded with Jim over their love of sports. For a time in the early 1970s, Kathy, Steve, and Jim Kilgore lived together.

The Soliah siblings and Jim Kilgore were more than friends. Along with a handful of others, they were, in the argot of the era, a cell. Their group was known to some as the Revolutionary Army, but it never had a formal name, like the Weather Underground; still, their chosen form of political expression was the same—to set off explosives, after working hours, in symbolically resonant locations around California. In an era when there were dozens of bombings a year in the state alone, this kind of behavior was less aberrational than it appears today, if not less dangerous. This cell emerged from the same aggressive, frustrated corner of the counterculture as the SLA, and they expressed themselves in similarly theatrical terms. In other words, the alliance between the Revolutionary Army and the surviving SLA members was a natural one.

To make ends meet, Kilgore and Steve Soliah worked as house-painters for a company run by a recent Cal grad named Michael Bortin. Kilgore and Bortin filled a Berkeley garage with bomb-making material, and one of their confederates later admitted that the group had set off about a dozen bombs in 1971 and 1972, albeit without causing casualties. Their partner in this project was another young radical named Willie Brandt. His girlfriend, Wendy Yoshimura, rented their bomb-making facility for them.

Kathy Soliah's friendship with Angela Atwood connected the two groups most directly, but the radical world was small enough that there were other points of overlap. (For example, Kathy Soliah had taken gun training from Joe Remiro.) It was thus no surprise that Kathy—a performer as well as a radical—would take it upon herself to star in a public memorial to the lost soldiers of the SLA and to cheer on the survivors. Similarly, it was understandable that the Harrises would look to Kathy to throw them a lifeline.

Emily still had Kathy Soliah's address, so she just showed up there one day, disguised in a gray wig. Kathy wasn't home, but Emily was directed to a bookstore where Kathy worked. There, Emily made eye contact and passed Kathy a note, which said, "Meet me at the church." Twenty minutes later, the two women fell into each other's arms.

Kathy telephoned her boyfriend, Jim Kilgore, and he collected all the cash he could find—several hundred dollars—which she turned

over to Emily. Kathy said her younger sister Josephine would provide another cash infusion from her savings account. On that first day,
Kathy gave Emily enough money for Bill to retrieve their car from the
repair shop in San Francisco.

The next night, Kathy and Jim Kilgore arranged to meet Bill,
Emily, and Patricia at a drive-in theater in Oakland, where *The Sting*
was playing. Emily, Patricia, and Kathy convened in the women's
bathroom and later reassembled in Kathy's car, which was parked in
a section of the theater where a soft-core porn film called *Teacher's
Pet* was running. Kathy took the lead in the conversation, telling the
three fugitives of her love for Angela and her grief at her death. To the
amazement of the Harrises, Kathy produced $1,500, which she said
came from Josephine Soliah's savings account. Kathy told them too
about her brother Steve, who was also living in Berkeley at the time,
though he was not yet cognizant of Kathy's discovery of the SLA survivors. "He's more of a hippie than into politics," Kathy said, "so I'm
not sure I should tell him."

Their alliance cemented over the soft moans coming from the
speaker, the two cells agreed to keep in touch. The alliance revived
Bill's spirits, and he began to think about an SLA revival, even with
their diminished numbers. It galled him that the police were gloating
about the conflagration in Los Angeles. Obsessed as always with public relations, Bill wanted to tell the world that the SLA was still alive,
regardless of whether that was actually true. So after they received
the cash from the Soliahs, Bill and Emily had one more request for
Kathy—for a tape recorder.

Like approximately no one else on earth, Bill thought the world
needed to hear what the surviving members of the SLA thought about
the deaths of their comrades. While sequestered in the apartment in
Oakland, he and Emily and Patricia sketched out a communiqué that
would commemorate the departed and announce, with considerable

exaggeration, the continued existence of the SLA. They wanted a tape recorder so they could deliver the audio of their message to a radio station. Kathy provided the machine.

Bill did most of the talking, giving a droning recapitulation of the themes in DeFreeze's communiqués. In typical fashion, he spun the calamity of May 17 as a heroic stand and gave his tiny remnant a new name in the process. "This is Teko speaking," he said. "Yolanda, Tania and I extend profound feelings of revolutionary love and solidarity" to their allies. "The Malcolm X Combat unit of the Symbionese Liberation Army left the San Francisco Bay Area in a successful effort to break a massive pig encirclement." Nursing a guilty conscience about starting the fiasco by shoplifting at Mel's, Harris lied about what happened. "A pig-agent clerk named Tony Shepard, attempting to show his allegiance to his reactionary white bosses, falsely accused me of shoplifting," he said. "It was impossible to allow a verifying search by a store security guard because I was armed, and therefore we were forced to fight our way out of the situation."

As for the shoot-out, Harris said, "People witnessed on live television the burning to death of six of the most beautiful and courageous freedom fighters by cowardly, fascist insects. In most cases when an urban guerrilla unit is encircled by the enemy, it can expect to take great losses, especially if the enemy has time to mobilize a massive force." To conclude, Bill adopted DeFreeze's deranged sense of self-importance: "The pigs boast that they have broken the back of the Symbionese Liberation Army. But to do this, the pigs would have to break the back of the people"—as if "the people" had ever rallied to the SLA cause.

The tape had another purpose, which was to bid a more personal farewell to the six martyred comrades. Patricia—Tania—wanted to deliver this message. Emily insisted on drafting part of it, and the final version was a collaboration by the three survivors. Much later, Patricia would repudiate the "eulogy tape," as it became known, but it does seem to have been, at least in part, her own handiwork. Her early taped messages cannot be taken as expressions of her own views. Now

Nancy Ling and Angela, who wrote and collaborated with Patricia on her earlier communiqués, were dead. Bill and Emily had never told her what to say. And by June, Patricia was a far more independent actor—free to express herself as she wanted to be heard. And this is what she said, as it was later transcribed by the FBI:

Greetings to the people. This is Tania. I want to talk about the way I knew our six murdered comrades because the fascist pig media has, of course, been painting a typical distorted picture of these beautiful sisters and brothers.

Cujo [Willy Wolfe] was the gentlest, most beautiful man I've ever known. He taught me the truth as he learned it from the beautiful brothers in California's concentration camps. We loved each other so much, and his love for the people was so deep that he was willing to give his life for them. The name Cujo means "unconquerable." It was the perfect name for him. Cujo conquered life as well as death by facing and fighting them.

Neither Cujo or I ever loved an individual the way we loved each other, probably because our relationship wasn't based on bourgeois, fucked up values, attitudes and goals. Our relationship's foundation was our commitment to the struggle and our love for the people. It's because of this that I still feel strong and determined to fight.

I was ripped off by the pigs when they murdered Cujo, ripped off in the same way that thousands of sisters and brothers in this fascist country have been ripped off of the people they love. We mourn together, and the sound of gunfire becomes sweeter.

Gelina [Angela Atwood] was beautiful. Fire and joy. She exploded with the desire to kill the pigs. She wrote poetry—some of it on the walls of Golden Gate, all of it in the LA pig files now—that expresses how she felt. She loved the people more than her love for any one person or material comfort. . . . We laughed and cried and struggled together. . . .

Gabi [Camilla Hall] crouched low with her ass to the ground.

She practiced until her shotgun was an extension of her right and left arms, an impulse, a tool of survival. [This was a bit of an inside joke among Bill, Emily, and Patricia. Camilla was inept with firearms.] She loved to touch people with a strong—not delicate—embrace.

Zoya [Mizmoon] wanted to give meaning to her name, and on her birthday [May 17], she did. Zoya, female guerrilla, perfect love and perfect hate reflected in stone-cold eyes. She moved viciously and with caution, understanding the peril of the smallest mistake. She taught me, "Keep your ass down and be bad."

Fahizah [Nancy Ling] was a beautiful sister who didn't talk much but who was the teacher of many by her righteous example. She, more than any other, had come to understand and conquer the putrid disease of bourgeois mentality. She proved often that she was unwilling to compromise with the enemy because of her intense love for freedom. . . . She was wise, and bad, and I'll always love her.

Cinque [DeFreeze] loved the people with tenderness and respect. . . . He longed to be with his black sisters and brothers, but at the same time he wanted to prove to black people that white freedom fighters are comrades-in-arms. . . . He taught me virtually everything imaginable, but wasn't liberal with us. He'd kick our asses if we didn't hop over a fence fast enough or keep our asses down while practicing. . . . He helped me see that it's not how long you live that's important, it's how we live: what we decide to do with our lives. On February 4 [the day of the kidnapping], Cinque Mtume saved my life. . . .

It's hard to explain what it was like watching our comrades die, murdered by pig incendiary grenades. A battalion of pigs facing a fire team of guerrillas, and the only way they could defeat them was to burn them alive. . . . It made me mad to see the pigs looking at our comrades' weapons—to see them holding Cujo's .45 and his watch, which was still ticking. He would have laughed at that. . . . The pigs probably have the little Old

McMonkey that Cujo wore around his neck. He gave me the
little stone face one night. . . .

I renounced my class privilege when Cin and Cujo gave me
the name Tania. While I have no death wish, I have never been
afraid of death. For this reason, the brainwash/duress theory of
the Pig Hearsts has always amused me. Life is very precious to
me, but I have no delusions that going to prison will keep me
alive. I would never choose to live the rest of my life surrounded
by pigs like the Hearsts. . . .

Patria o muerte, venceremos! Death to the fascist insect that
preys upon the life of the people.

Once the tape was complete, the Harrises arranged a meeting with
Kathy Soliah by Oakland's Lake Merritt. Kathy gave the recording to
her brother (who had been clued in that his sister was sheltering the
trio), and Steve ferried the tape south to Santa Barbara, where he gave
the tape to still another person, who stashed it beneath a mattress
in an alley behind KPFK, the Pacifica radio station in Los Angeles.
Tipped off by a call from a phone booth, the station retrieved the tape
and played it on the air on June 7.

Notwithstanding the brave talk on the tape, Bill understood that
the best chance for the survival of the remaining SLA comrades was
to disappear for a while. Even the Bay Area, with its network of like-
minded friends, represented a life of constant threat of arrest or, like
their comrades' fate, death. Kathy had admitted her brother Steve into
the circle of Bill, Emily, and Patricia, and the trio began to spend time
with the easygoing ex-athlete. As it happened, someone had contacted
Steve Soliah, offering the surviving SLA members a route out of town
and, perhaps, into a new life.

16

JACK SCOTT MAKES AN OFFER

J ack Scott sat in his cramped apartment on West Ninetieth Street and stewed. The biggest story in years was unfolding in his old home turf, but he was thousands of miles away, on the other side of the country, on the Upper West Side of Manhattan. He was pushing paper around his desk, supposedly working on a book about drugs and sports, but he couldn't muster much enthusiasm for the subject. But the SLA—now there was a story!

Scott was a curious hybrid, very much a product of the era. He was a journalist and an activist, an idealist and a hustler, an athlete and a hedonist. He wanted to do good and do well. His mixed motives, and mixed role, played a crucial part in the fate of Patricia Hearst.

Scott regarded the shoot-out in Los Angeles as both horrifying and fascinating. He didn't know any of the SLA comrades personally, but he had dwelled in their milieu in Berkeley. In the previous decade, he had lived both sides of the divide in the American Left. He had been a good liberal and worked in an orderly way for gradual reform of the sports world. But he also knew and admired people on the militant left. The radicals were also "America's children," he told his wife, Micki, and he wanted to tell their story.

So, bored and restless, he decided to get on a plane and head west. He didn't even know at that point whether anyone in the SLA was still alive. (Patricia's eulogy tape had been recorded but not yet released to the public.) Scott checked into a Holiday Inn near Berkeley and started making calls to reach people who might know the SLA comrades. On his first night in the Bay Area, he arranged to have dinner at an Italian restaurant in North Beach with Wendy Yoshimura, who brought along Michael Bortin, an active member of the Revolutionary Army bombing cell in Berkeley. Bortin had dropped acid before the dinner, and so was less than coherent, but Scott succeeded in persuading him to put the word out that he wanted to meet people who were close to the SLA.

After Bortin, Scott checked in with his old friend Kathy Soliah. He wanted to tell the SLA story, Scott told her. Did she know anyone who knew people in the SLA? Kathy said she'd think about it, and before too long she called him back. As it happened, she did know some people. "I can introduce you tonight to people who are close to the people killed in Los Angeles," she told him. She said she would come to the hotel and pick him up with Jim Kilgore, who was also an old friend of Scott's.

At around seven, Soliah and Kilgore fetched Scott at the hotel. "These people you want to meet are nervous," she said. "They don't want you to know where they are." So Kathy Soliah placed a blindfold over Jack Scott's head for the trip to meet her friends. Scott rolled his eyes at the absurdity of the gesture, but he figured it was just typical Berkeley craziness. Plus, he knew that Kathy had been an actress, so he also chalked it up to her flair for self-dramatization. He was willing to play along. He accepted the blindfold as Kilgore began driving a circuitous route through Berkeley.

They went to an apartment in North Berkeley, and Kilgore and Soliah steered Scott to a chair in front of a table. "Are you ready?" Kathy asked him. Scott said he was.

Then, with a flourish, Kathy Soliah removed Scott's blindfold.

Jack Scott was born in 1942 and raised in Scranton, Pennsylvania, where his father ran a prosperous family tobacco business until his alcoholism drove the operation into ruin and his family into near destitution. Jack found a refuge from his chaotic home on the playing fields of his high school, where he captained the football team and set records as a sprinter. He was offered athletic scholarships to Villanova and Stanford. He spent a year at each school before a foot injury ended his athletic career and cost him his scholarship. The stark reality of college sports, where an injury could cost a student his education, left him with a sour impression. Scott spent a year in Greenland, graduated from Syracuse, then went west to Berkeley to study for a Ph.D.

Even before he received his doctorate, Scott made a national name for himself. He founded the Institute for the Study of Sport and Society, which aimed to capture and focus national attention on the exploitation of athletes in the college and pro ranks. Scott's group challenged the authority of coaches, denounced racism in sports, and questioned the medical treatment of athletes. Scott helped write Dave Meggyesy's 1970 best-selling insider's account of playing in the NFL, which described rampant drug use and violence against women. As sports editor for *Ramparts,* a counterculture magazine based in San Francisco, Scott made exactly the enemies he wanted. Spiro Agnew, the vice president of the United States and a great sports fan, denounced Scott by name for questioning the verities of the national pastimes. The most famous visitor to Scott's institute in Berkeley was Bill Walton, the UCLA center who was at the time the best college basketball player in the country; later, Walton and Scott would become close friends.

On a personal level, Scott's institute also attracted the attention of sports-minded radicals, notably Jim Kilgore (the former track star) and his girlfriend, Kathy Soliah (the daughter of a coach). Kilgore painted the Scotts' Berkeley apartment for free. Scott's circle in Berkeley also included Willie Brandt, who was one of the first members of the Revolutionary Army bombing cell to be charged, and whose girlfriend, Wendy Yoshimura, designed the sign for Scott's ISSS. Jack was never an actual member of the outlaw cell that drew these people together, but he inched close to the line on several occasions. When Brandt was arrested, Scott helped Yoshimura flee from the authorities.

In 1972, the Berkeley idyll of Jack and Micki Scott ended abruptly when Oberlin College hired a left-leaning president who wanted to shake up his athletic program. The president hired Jack as athletic director, even though he was only thirty years old. In keeping with the spirit of his appointment, Scott hired Tommie Smith, who had given the famous black-gloved salute during the 1968 Olympics, as the school's track coach. Oberlin's president was forced out after only two years, and Jack was cashiered as well, albeit with a severance package worth about $40,000. Jack and Micki decided to reopen their institute in New York, rather than Berkeley, and the couple moved there just around the time that the SLA kidnapped Patricia.

Balding, bearded, lean, and still athletic, despite his Dionysian appetites, Scott loved the attention that came with his prominence as an activist in Berkeley. The job in Oberlin, though prestigious, had been a sleepy detour. The Scotts hadn't yet put down roots in New York either, and the book on drugs and sports scarcely held Jack's attention. The SLA, in contrast, looked to be Jack's route to the big time—to fame and a book deal as well as a chance to put a human face on what were at the time despised figures. But first Scott had to make connections to the people who knew them.

Kathy Soliah had led him, in a blindfold, to where he wanted to go.

After the blindfold was removed, Scott beheld an unforgettable tableau.

Before him were the three most notorious fugitives in the United States—Bill and Emily Harris and Patricia Hearst. Scott thought he was only meeting friends or associates of the SLA. But these people, to his astonishment, were the real deal.

And what a sight they were. All three were in full battle dress—military-style jackets, watch caps, scarves, gun belts with ammunition bags, and holstered sidearms. Patricia had a bandolier draped across her chest and a .30-caliber rifle slung along her back. Bill had a submachine gun in his lap. Emily also had a bandolier and a shotgun across her knees. Guns were scattered around the rooms, like throw rugs, as decorative statements of revolutionary intent.

Bill spoke first. "This is Tania," he said, "and I am General Teko. Sitting beside Tania is Yolanda." Kilgore and Kathy Soliah hovered in the background.

Scott was mesmerized by the spectacle—amused by the costumes and petrified for his life. He knew what happened the last time the SLA comrades were gathered together: they were immolated. He imagined that he would soon hear a police bullhorn, like the one outside the house in Los Angeles, demanding that they surrender. Then, gathering his wits, he responded to the scene as a journalist.

"Tell me your story," he said. "I'll tell the world."

Bullshit, said Bill. No thanks. "We need a journalist like we need a hole in the head. What we need is your help getting out of here. The heat is too much. We've been told that you're the kind of guy who would help people in this kind of situation." Kilgore and Soliah had told the Harrises how Scott helped Wendy Yoshimura skip town when Willie Brandt was arrested. Bill, Emily, and Patricia wanted the same kind of assistance, in an unimaginably more high-profile situation.

Scott thought fast. His wife, Micki, had rented a farm for the summer in the countryside of Pennsylvania, near Jack's hometown of Scranton. He planned to use it to write in peace and quiet, away from their apartment in New York. Maybe he could install the trio there instead and interview them at leisure. In that way, Bill, Emily, and Patricia could put some space between themselves and their pursuers, and Jack might get a blockbuster article or book out of it. Harboring fugitives was illegal, but it was a risk he was willing to take.

"Look at yourselves," Scott said to the trio, "holed up in this little room, hugging your weapons. You all look so tired and pale and worried. You need fresh air and open country, an atmosphere where you won't have to be so paranoid."

Scott then added a condition that he regarded as nonnegotiable.

"You have to disarm," he said. "I can't have you bringing weapons to the farm."

Patricia, who had largely been silent up to that point, rejected this idea out of hand. "We will not surrender and we will not give up our guns," she said. Like most Americans, Scott only knew Patricia's voice from her tapes. He had no other sense of her as a person. But what he saw was a fanatic, clearly the most passionate and even unhinged of the three SLA members before him. She was fixated on revenge.

"The last time," Patricia said, referring to Fifty-Fourth Street, "shots were only coming into the house." (This was wrong, of course, because the SLA fired thousands of rounds at the police.) "The next time they'll be going both ways," she said. "We'll kill pigs this time."

In fact, Patricia had a plan to share with Scott. "We'll tell Master Bates that I'll surrender, and when they come for me, we'll kill him and the others, to avenge our comrades' deaths."

The conversation did not go well. At around 11:00 p.m., Kilgore and Soliah served what they called "Dagwoods" to the group. They consumed the thick, multilayered sandwiches eagerly, but they came no closer to consensus. (In the brief break, Scott learned from Kilgore and Soliah that the Harrises were worried about security. The two were just house-sitting in this apartment for the next couple of days. In other words, the fate of the SLA trio had to be settled fast.)

Scott tried to paint an idyllic picture of life on the farm, even though he had not yet been there himself. They could relax, take stock, and look ahead. Scott even told them about his severance from Oberlin, which he was willing to share to help support the group for a while. But Scott was firm about the weapons. He was not going to lead them into another firefight and massacre.

Tightly wound and desperate, the three would not budge. They told Scott he didn't understand the nature of revolutionary action. They were soldiers, and soldiers did not give up their weapons. Patricia escalated matters by suggesting that Scott might be leading them into a trap. "How do we know you're not a police agent?" she asked.

Scott's curiosity turned to frustration. "Fine," he said finally. "Okay, don't disarm. I'll just go back to the hotel."

No, Scott was icily informed, that would not be possible. You know we're here, Bill said, we can't let you go. Scott was now almost a hostage himself. He thought the best thing he could do was simply to go to sleep on the floor of the apartment and hope that the morning would bring some agreement. Six people—the Harrises, Patricia, Kilgore, Soliah, and Scott—spent an uneasy few hours in a kind of half sleep sprawled around the apartment in North Berkeley.

Shortly after dawn, they heard a crash outside. Bill—as General Teko—barked orders to his comrades. Emily and Patricia took up their weapons and released their safeties. Scott cowered and waited. And waited some more. At last, he defied orders and peeked out the window. He saw that a dog had knocked over a garbage can. The negotiations continued.

Morning brought more Dagwoods, which was the only food in the apartment. Kathy's siblings Steve and Josephine Soliah also joined the deliberations. Both were more levelheaded than Kathy, and the younger Soliahs recognized that Jack Scott represented the only real option for the SLA trio. First Bill, then Emily, began to buy into Scott's plan. But Patricia held firm, insisting that Scott was a police agent who would lead them into an ambush. "Tania, he's a do-gooder," Emily explained. "He's not a cop. He's sort of a peacenik. He's not one of us, but he's okay." The Harrises gave some ground on the weapons. They would leave the carbines behind and take only their pistols. Scott held firm—no guns at all.

"Let me tell you how I was raised," he said. "My mom is from Ireland, and her father was Thomas Brennan, one of the founders of the IRA. The British used to come to their house looking for IRA soldiers, and my mom's mother would greet the soldiers and ask them not to disturb her sleeping children. The soldiers always left, and there were always IRA soldiers hiding underneath my mom's bed. This is what we do in our family. We protect our friends. Trust me. This is how I was raised."

This story gave Scott an idea. He said that Patricia was obviously the most recognizable of the three, even in her wigs and makeup. Her transportation would represent the biggest challenge. His parents now managed a small motel in Las Vegas, but he said he could persuade them to come to the rescue. He would ask his parents to drive Patricia (and him) across the country to Pennsylvania. It would be the perfect cover—an elderly couple out for a drive with their young son and daughter-in-law. What cop would regard them suspiciously?

The Harrises, and eventually even Patricia, folded. They agreed to disarm for the trip to Pennsylvania.

Scott left the apartment and wandered off to the dirt running track at Berkeley's school for the deaf. He sat down on the infield and pondered what to do. He could walk away and let these strange people fend for themselves. Or he could follow through with his plan. Later, Scott justified his decision as keeping his word to desperate people; after all, in lobbying them for his plan, he had compared himself to Harriet Tubman, who led slaves to freedom on the Underground Railroad. But it seems just as likely that Scott hungered for the adrenaline rush of consorting with the most wanted outlaws in the country and perhaps making a fortune as an author in the bargain. It was typical of Scott's manic arrogance that he overlooked his own criminal culpability for harboring fugitives.

In any event, Scott returned to his motel outside Berkeley and called his parents. He explained his bizarre overnight encounter with the SLA trio and asked for their help. Both John and Lydia Louise Scott drew the same parallel that Jack did—to the efforts by Lydia's family to shield the IRA back in Ireland. They agreed to serve as couriers and to head out to Berkeley that evening.

In a frantic twenty-four hours, Jack arranged transportation for the fugitives. Jack and his parents would take Patricia. He activated his sports network to locate Phil Shinnick, a 1964 Olympic long jumper who became radicalized, in part, because he felt track and field officials had unfairly denied him a world record. Shinnick would drive Emily.

Jack Scott would fly back to San Francisco and then drive to Pennsylvania with Bill.

When Scott's parents arrived in Berkeley two days later, they repeated their willingness to serve as couriers, but they wondered if it would really be necessary. John and Lydia (who was known as Lou) shared their son's iconoclastic politics, but they also had a great deal of sympathy for Patricia's parents, their generational peers. "If you bring her to us, I bet we can persuade her to go home," John Scott told his son. Lou agreed. "If the Harrises will let that little girl go with us across the country, we'll be able to get her to go home and end all this," she said. Jack told his parents he would honor Patricia's wishes if she wanted to bring the whole macabre adventure to an end. That would be up to her.

The next morning, Jack brought his parents to the apartment to meet Patricia.

At the meeting, Jack pulled Bill aside and explained that his parents were going to try to persuade Patricia to return to her family. "Fine with me," Bill replied. "We've had a 'Ransom of Red Chief' situation with her for a while." Harris was referring to a famous short story by O. Henry where two men kidnap a child who is so spoiled and unpleasant that the criminals wind up paying the boy's father to take him back. "If Tania goes home, all the cops who are looking for her will quit. That's cool for us," Harris told Scott. "But if she does go back, call us, so we can get out of here."

That evening, John and Lou Scott, with Jack in the backseat, returned to the apartment building in their Ford LTD, a sturdy boat of a vehicle. Patricia Hearst, reluctantly disarmed, slid into the car next to Jack.

Just before John Scott pulled onto the highway, to begin the long journey east, he pulled off San Pablo Avenue and stopped the car without warning.

"Patty," he said, turning around from the driver's seat.

"Tania," she said, correcting him.

"We can take you wherever you want to go," John continued. "We can take you into San Francisco. We can take you to your parents, or to an uncle or aunt. We can go to a hospital. Anywhere you want. Or we can get on the highway and go across the country."

Patricia Hearst—Tania—replied, "Take me where-the-fuck you're supposed to, or you'll be dead, not just me."

John Scott gunned the engine and headed for the entrance to Interstate 80, heading east.

17

ROAD TRIP

First stop, Reno.

The gambling mecca, though not as rollicking as Las Vegas, was still a place where people could check into a motel at four in the morning without drawing much notice. That's what the people in the Ford LTD did. Two couples booked two rooms.

The arrival at the motel meant that Jack and Patricia, purported husband and wife, had to settle their sleeping arrangements. "I just lost the man I love," Patricia told him, closing off any advances. They slept in chaste proximity for the rest of the journey.

John Scott insisted on doing all the driving, hour after hour. Jack, who talked almost as much as Bill Harris, kept up a running commentary. Among other topics, he described his plan for a joint book with the SLA comrades, and according to Patricia, he detailed an elaborate plan where he would stash their proceeds in an untraceable account in Liechtenstein. (Jack later denied making this offer.) Patricia mostly sulked in silence. She felt very alone. She never cared for Bill or Emily Harris; she was repelled by Bill's belligerence and sexual demands and by Emily's haughty fanaticism. But Patricia had spent nearly every moment of her life with them from May to July, and she had managed to survive harrowing misadventures in their company. Now, though, Patricia was with strangers, and she had no idea what further horrors awaited her. So, during the road trip, she displayed a heightened sense of paranoia. Passing a construction site, she'd notice a worker glancing at their vehicle. "Why is he looking in the car?" she would say. "He's a pig." She tensed at the sight of highway patrol cars, even though John stuck to the speed limit and the right lane. When they stopped to refuel, Patricia hid her face when the attendants approached the car. (No self-service gas in those days.)

They stuck to I-80 nearly the whole way, taking the great northern route across the country for a trip of nearly three thousand miles. Hearst mostly ignored the two Scott men. She told them what she wanted to order at meals and not much else. She ate little, smoked a lot.

But Lou Scott's warmth and generosity won Hearst over. Patricia insisted that John and Jack call her Tania, but she did not protest when Lou (and only Lou) called her Patty. Lou confided that the Scott family had seen more than its share of problems. John's alcoholism had cost him the family business as well as their home in Scranton. Their other son, Walter, Jack's brother, was an erratic presence in their lives who claimed to work as a freelance mercenary. Lou said they would never tell Walter about Patricia, because he could not be trusted to keep their connection a secret.

Mostly, though, Lou talked to Patty about Patty. Through the long days on the road, and especially during private chats at meals, Lou kept urging Patty to go home to her parents. Lou said she understood political passion; after all, she grew up in a household filled with it, and she respected anyone who was willing to fight for the rights of others. But there came a point when the price was too high. *You're a nice girl. . . . You don't want this kind of life for yourself. . . . Your parents are heartsick with worry about you. Don't do this to them. . . . You're not the kind of person who should be around guns and violence.* Lou pleaded with Patricia to give up and go home.

Patricia was more willing to listen to this advice from Lou than from anyone else she had met since February 4, but she was steadfast in her insistence that she wanted to lead the life of a revolutionary. "There is nothing for me anymore in Hillsborough," Patricia told the Scotts. "The thought of seeing Steve Weed makes me sick. . . . I don't care if I ever see my mother again. She's a pill-popping drunk and a tool of Reagan. . . . The pigs killed the only man I ever loved. I want to make them pay for what they did to Cujo."

Hearst pointedly did not invite Jack to participate in these conversations with his mother, so he picked up most of his clues about Patricia's thoughts secondhand. On one occasion, though, Jack heard for himself another version of Patricia's reasoning—one that left him reeling in astonishment.

It was one of the last nights before they reached the East Coast. Jack was in the kitchenette of a motel preparing dinner. John was watching television. Patty and Lou were having an intense conversation on a sofa. Jack strained to eavesdrop.

"Lou, I was part of this thing from the beginning. I can't go back to my old life."

Jack's mother asked what she meant.

Patricia told Lou she had staged her own kidnapping. Nancy Ling had been her pot dealer in Berkeley. They became friends, and Patricia disclosed her true identity to her. Ling, in turn, introduced Patricia to DeFreeze, who came up with the idea of a fake kidnapping. Patricia had agreed to the kidnapping scenario because it offered her a way out of her engagement with Steven Weed. According to Hearst, Ling and DeFreeze never shared this secret with the other comrades. "Cinque was always testing people," Patricia explained. Knowing this secret allowed DeFreeze to play the puppet master with his comrades as well as the public.

Not surprisingly, Lou was baffled by this story. The kidnapping itself had been violent, and Steve Weed was obviously not in on the plot. "Weren't you afraid that Steven would get shot if he resisted?" Lou asked.

"Steven Weed?!" Hearst replied. "He was too much of a coward to resist. I knew he wouldn't."

A staged kidnapping was a win-win, Patricia explained. The SLA would get publicity and millions to feed the poor. Patricia would get out of her engagement, and Steve wouldn't get hurt.

"If Steve was so terrible, why did you get involved with him in the first place?" Lou asked.

"Two years ago, I was in high school," Patricia explained. Her peers thought Steve was a real "catch," and she became caught up in their expectations.

But Lou asked, sensibly, "Why not go to your parents about the failed engagement? Wouldn't that have been a lot simpler than getting yourself kidnapped?"

Patty said Lou wouldn't understand. "You don't know my parents," she said. "They are not like you." Randy and Catherine had never approved of Steve, and she couldn't stand the humiliation of admitting to them that the engagement had been a bad idea. Thus, she said, the kidnapping.

Jack never let on to Patricia that he heard this conversation, and he kept her account of her kidnapping to himself for a long time. He wondered, as anyone would, whether her story was true. Did Patricia Hearst stage her own kidnapping?

The answer is no.

The scenario that she outlined for Lou Scott could not have happened and did not happen. The documents seized from the house in Concord show how Patricia's name came to the attention of the SLA comrades. Bill Harris then looked up her home address in the Cal student directory. Unhappy as Patricia was with Steve, she would never have concocted a violent plot that risked her own life—or done so with the people who had just murdered Marcus Foster. It is possible that Patricia bought pot from Nancy Ling—though Steve did most of the buying and smoking—but that alone wouldn't prove anything about her kidnapping. Moreover, Ling and DeFreeze were bumbling and ineffectual, as well as malevolent, so it's extremely unlikely that they could have thought up such an elaborate double cross, much less pulled it off. And if they did, they would have told their comrades.

Still, if Patricia did not stage her kidnapping, why did she say that she did?

Jack Scott later speculated that Patricia came up with the story to get Lou off her back—that is, to persuade her to stop nagging Patricia to return to her family. That's probably the most plausible explanation, and it appears to have worked. Stunned by the tale, Lou did drop the subject during the remaining hours of the trip. Still, even though Patricia's story about the staged kidnapping was a lie, there was a kind of truth in it. It was part of her declaration of independence from her former self. Telling the story was an illustration of how far she would go to display her transformation from the person she had been. In a way, too, she was right: she was a very different person. Months earlier, Patricia was the kind of teenager who would care about the pattern of her wedding silver, or at least would pretend to care about it. Now she was the kind of young woman who would conspire with terrorists to stage a kidnapping, even if she did not actually do so.

Jack and Patricia arrived in New York City shortly after Emily Harris and Phil Shinnick. Jack flew back to San Francisco to retrieve Bill, and Micki remained in the apartment with Patricia and Emily. They would all meet up at the farm in July. So Jack headed for California, leaving Emily, Micki, and Patricia in the Scotts' third-floor walk-up at 317 West Ninetieth Street.*

Micki had never before met either of her famous guests, but she had the right temperament to make them feel welcome and safe. Jack might have maintained an athlete's intensity, but his wife had the mellow bearing of a flower child. As Patricia later wrote of Micki, "Within a few minutes I sensed that she was a nice, warm person. It was more than I had any reason to expect, given all the characters I had been meeting, but it came to me that here was a woman who was straightforward and open." Emily, too, was in good spirits. She immediately regaled Patricia with tales of her trysts with Shinnick

---

* At the time, I was fourteen years old and lived with my parents on the same block. To my knowledge, none of us ever saw Patricia or her comrades.

by the side of the road. Patricia relaxed as Micki played her favorite Country Joe and the Fish album. Patricia recalled, "For the first time in months, I had decent food and hot showers and books and magazines to read."

For a week or so, the three women established a ritual. After they woke up, Micki would walk to Broadway to buy coffee and the *New York Times* for Patricia and Emily. Though the setting was congenial, Patricia's fury had not abated. She would curl up with the newspaper, and a pen, and circle the names of her enemies, especially those she regarded as betrayers of the revolutionary cause. Angela Davis and Jane Fonda were favorite targets. At one point, Micki asked Patricia what she was doing. "Making our hit list," Patricia replied. She made clear that she was still mourning her great true love, Cujo (that is, Willy Wolfe), and she was plotting revenge, in some unspecified way, for his murder.

Patricia spent her days reading and smoking, while Emily and Micki came and went doing errands. Of course, Patricia could have walked out the door alone at any time and gone wherever she pleased, but she preferred to remain with her comrades. Micki bought her a new wardrobe, because she had traveled across the country with just a handful of clothes. Emily went to a free clinic at Bellevue Hospital for a pregnancy test (which was negative). Emily made the medical appointment under an assumed name, and the issue of aliases provided a measure of levity for the women. After the shoot-out on May 17, Bill Harris decreed that the group adopt new code names, and he dubbed Emily (formerly Yolanda) as Eva and Patricia (formerly Tania) as Pearl. But the new names never stuck, and Micki, who had no code name, was never sure what to call anyone. Patricia mostly stuck with Tania, though she also answered to Pearl and, with reluctance, to Patty.

Jack Scott had told Emily and Patricia that he wanted to hire a "baby sitter" for them (and for Bill) at the farm in Pennsylvania. The farm was in a remote place, but it was still part of the United States, and any of the three fugitives might be recognized if they circulated in the small towns nearby. Jack wanted someone who was not well-known to do the shopping and other errands and who also could be trusted to keep the operation a secret.

Toward the end of Patricia and Emily's stay with Micki Scott, a new visitor appeared at the door. Small, delicate, and reserved, she was clearly of Japanese ancestry, and she called herself Joan Shimada. She said she would serve as the group's caretaker at the farm. Emily and Patricia realized almost immediately that "Joan" was in fact Wendy Yoshimura, who would turn out to be another crucial figure in their lives.

"I was born on January 14, 1943, in Manzanar, California in a concentration camp which the U.S. government called a relocation camp," Yoshimura wrote in a personal narrative for her lawyers, some time later. "At birth I was delivered by a medical student as there were no full fledged doctors to assist with medical care." After Yoshimura and her family were released from the notorious camp, when World War II ended, they took an unusual step for the time. Her parents, who were also born in the United States, were so appalled and fearful of anti-Japanese bias in the wake of the war that they renounced their American citizenship and moved to Japan. They lived on a small island near Hiroshima, where her father worked as an interpreter for the U.S. Army and young Wendy heard harrowing tales of the atomic bomb. Once the American occupation of Japan ended, work became scarce, and the family moved back to the United States in 1957.

Wendy's father started out as a farmworker, outside Fresno, and eventually opened a garden store. Wendy was behind her peers academically—she didn't start high school until she was seventeen—but she was a skilled artist. A teacher at Fresno State encouraged her to apply to the California College of Arts and Crafts in Oakland, where she began studying in 1965. Like so many young people (and all of the SLA comrades), Yoshimura had a political awakening in the Bay Area, in her case when she took a philosophy course. "I met a man who opened my eyes to social injustice. (Obviously, it usually is a man, isn't it?)" she wrote. "Then I met another man (again!) who had the time and patience to help me understand about the Vietnam war, capitalism, colonialism, imperialism, racism, classicism, sexism, etc. etc." The second man's name was Willie Brandt.

Yoshimura and Brandt became a couple, and they made a pilgrimage together to Castro's Cuba, via Mexico, which was a difficult thing to do in the early 1970s. They also turned to even riskier pursuits. On March 30, 1972, police responding to a report of gas fumes discovered what they called a "massive" bomb factory in a Berkeley garage, which had been rented by a woman named "Anne Wong," who was later identified as Wendy Yoshimura. In the space, police found hundreds of pounds of explosives, gunpowder, fuses, blasting caps, a three-gallon oil-ammonium-nitrate bomb as well as ammunition, pistols, and rifles (including an AK-47 machine gun). Police staked out the garage and the next morning arrested three people who arrived there: Willie Brandt, Michael Bortin, and Paul Rubenstein, who was a roommate of Jim Kilgore and Kathy Soliah. In their car, police found a communiqué from the Revolutionary Army regarding a bombing of the Berkeley Naval Architecture Building, which had apparently been scheduled for that night.

It was following the arrest of Brandt, Yoshimura's boyfriend, that Jack Scott helped her flee the Bay Area. (Bortin and Rubenstein pleaded guilty to minor charges and served brief prison terms; Brandt also pleaded guilty and served longer.) Following the busts, Jack drove Wendy to Los Angeles, where the two of them flew to Philadelphia. There friends from the movement agreed to take her in, and she obtained phony identification in the name of Joan Shimada. She spent the next year or so as an itinerant, living in Pennsylvania, New Jersey, and Texas, working for sympathetic families as a nanny, and returning to California once in a while.

In July, Jack Scott tracked Yoshimura down in New Jersey, and he proposed a deal for her. He would replace her decrepit car and pay her $600 if she would serve as the babysitter for the Harrises and Patricia at the farm for the rest of the summer. Yoshimura was a fugitive, too, of course, because she had also been charged in connection with the bomb-filled garage. A job caring for the most notorious fugitives in the country was a considerable risk. But she had few options, and she remained loyal to Jack for spiriting her away after the bust in March. She agreed and joined Micki, Emily, and Patricia in the apartment on West Ninetieth Street. A few days later, the four women headed for Pennsylvania. Jack Scott brought Bill Harris from California a little while later.

The farm was owned by a New York City fireman who charged Micki Scott $2,000 for the summer rental. When the comrades arrived in tiny South Canaan Township, about twenty miles east of Scranton, the thirty-eight acres looked like a slightly weather-beaten version of paradise.

The house was straight out of Norman Rockwell—white-painted wood, with a balcony outside the second floor. The most distinctive feature was the wrought-iron design on the balustrade of the balcony. It spelled out the word "PAIX." The farm was to be a place of peace, which it seemed to be. The farmland in this part of Pennsylvania was poor, and nothing had been grown or raised on this property for years, but the barn and a windmill remained. Three ponds, one stocked with catfish, dotted the acres. Perhaps most important to the comrades, there were no other houses within view. The privacy was total.

When Bill arrived, he disrupted, in typical fashion, the serenity that the four women had enjoyed. He demanded that Wendy buy bags of sand and cement. He used these raw materials to make a primitive fitness set for the comrades—barbells and ankle weights—so they could maintain their readiness for self-defense. Bill paced off a one-mile course through the rolling hills, and he made the comrades complete it daily. Bill had reluctantly honored Jack's demand to leave his weapons at home, so he contrived exercises with broomsticks to simulate his beloved carbines. (The women found these pitiable displays absurd, but Bill did not.)

Patricia hated Bill's demands for conditioning. She never regained the weight she had lost in Daly City, but even in her nearly emaciated condition Patricia displayed remarkable toughness. She jumped every obstacle, lifted every weight, and completed every drill. As she approached the five-month mark since her kidnapping, it was clear that she owed her survival in significant part to her strength—physical, emotional, and spiritual. At any number of points along the way, she could have simply given up and yielded to despair, fear, or paralysis. But Patricia was a fighter, and though her alliances were scrambled, her determination to survive never wilted.

Jack visited the farm about once a week (with Sigmund, his aged German shepherd), and he maintained his optimism about the book project for longer than was justified. He brought steaks for the grill, and he played volleyball with the comrades and went skinny-dipping with them in the ponds. At first, Jack was so euphoric about his connection to the famous outlaws that he couldn't resist showing them off.

Shortly after he installed the comrades and their babysitter at the farm, he invited Jay Weiner, a former student of his at Oberlin and a sportswriting intern at *Newsday,* to celebrate Weiner's twentieth birthday with him and Micki. Jack said they would go to the Poconos together, but he didn't say exactly where. After a comedy of errors in New York (Micki's car was towed and had to be retrieved), Jack, Micki, and Weiner arrived at the farm on the late afternoon of July 2. Jay was not told the names of the guests at the farm, but he quickly figured out who they were. "Are they who I think they are?" he asked Jack, who confirmed their identities.

The comrades appeared starved for a new companion, and they welcomed Weiner into their midst, even though he was just a kid. (He was between his junior and his senior years in college, and his voice had not yet changed.) Informed that it was Weiner's birthday, Wendy

Yoshimura rushed to the store to buy ingredients for a cake. Emily Harris told Weiner that they "needed someone to back them up" in New York. Weiner explained that he was just a student on a summer internship, and he had neither time nor money to help. Patricia volunteered that perhaps he could learn to forge identity documents. Weiner allowed that it might be possible, but he didn't want to be involved with guns or anything involving violence.

In the course of a long, bizarre dinner, Weiner was treated to recitations of the comrades' obsessions. Patricia went on about her drunken, pill-popping mother. Bill once again displayed his guilty conscience about the incident at Mel's by stating (falsely) that he had not shoplifted, but just fought back after the clerk tried to frisk him. Making conversation with Patricia, Weiner told her that he had seen the already famous picture of her in front of the seven-headed cobra— "the one with the shotgun," Weiner said. Patricia thanked him but also corrected him. "It was a machine gun, not a shotgun." Patricia pointed out that she, too, had just had her twentieth birthday, and she sat by Weiner's side as he blew out the candles.

Weiner's visit was just pointless and weird—a tremendous security risk for no actual benefit to Scott or the comrades. Late at night, just before Weiner was preparing to return to New York with the Scotts, Emily Harris said the most sensible, and prescient, thing to him. "I'm kind of sorry we put you in the position of knowing that we're here."

But Jay Weiner was the least of the group's problems. In relatively short order, everyone was mad at everyone else. Wendy took an instant dislike to Bill, and her disdain hardened with time. She resented that he took his role as General Teko seriously and that he ordered everyone around. Wendy didn't want to do calisthenics, nor did she feel obliged to participate in Bill's spying and countersurveillance exercises. Bill and Emily's marriage was as tempestuous as ever, especially after Bill learned of Emily's roadside couplings with Phil Shinnick during their cross-country trip. Jack became frustrated by the lack of progress on the book and annoyed that he was bankrolling the farm operation with no prospect of repayment, to say nothing of any gratitude from his beneficiaries. Like his mother, Jack thought that Patricia would make everyone's life easier if she just went home. With the heat off, Bill and Emily could integrate more easily into the underground, and Patricia could gain greater attention for her causes if she spoke out publicly. Patricia, in turn, regarded Jack's attitude as patronizing, in that he failed to recognize that she was a warrior and revolutionary with no interest in surrender.

In counterpoint to the bickering around them, Patricia and Wendy developed a real friendship. "She was calm and friendly and sane," Patricia later wrote. "It was difficult to keep in mind that this quiet, cheerful young woman was a revolutionary, and a fugitive from charges involving explosives." At this point, Patricia too was an unlikely revolutionary, and they shared relatively serene temperaments, especially compared with the battling Harrises. Wendy was also a committed, knowledgeable feminist, and she provided Patricia with a stream of readings on the subject. In short order, Wendy came to return Patricia's affection. Wendy wrote to her boyfriend, Willie Brandt, who was imprisoned at the time, "I hope you'll have a chance to meet P.H. She is incredible! She amazes me! I swear only the toughest could have come out of it as she did. What an ordeal she went through!!" Wendy also watched with bemused affection as Patricia continued her habit of circling the names of her enemies in the newspaper.

Wendy's accommodating nature led indirectly to the end of the summer arcadia. Bill never came to terms with Jack's prohibition on weapons. He thought the comrades needed them for protection, but at a deeper level Bill felt demeaned, as a self-styled guerrilla, that he was denied the basic tools of the trade. So Bill persuaded Wendy to buy him a BB gun, which he regarded as technically in compliance with Jack and Micki's wishes. Bill then added target practice inside the old barn to the comrades' daily round of training exercises. In typical fashion, he layered his personal grievances onto his political activity. For his target in the barn, he sketched a long, tall silhouette—based on the rangy physique of the long jumper Phil Shinnick.

Jack and Micki were apoplectic when they found out that the comrades were shooting on the farm property. (They did not buy Bill's argument that a BB gun was not a real weapon.) They thought the sounds of gunfire, from whatever source, might pique the curiosity of neighbors and thus lead to their exposure. Micki, as the signer of the lease for the farm, was especially concerned. So Jack and Micki decided to make a change. They told the comrades that they would have to leave. Micki, this time wearing a disguise and using a false name, rented them another house about an hour away, across the New York border, in the Catskills. (Shortly after they shooed the comrades out of Pennsylvania, Jack and Micki Scott brought Jay Weiner, the sportswriting intern, back to the vacated farm. There the three of them wiped down all the surfaces where police might look for fingerprints. "We'd make good cops," Jack quipped.)

The farm in tiny Jeffersonville, New York, followed the customary trajectory for SLA accommodations—worse than the previous one. This defunct dairy operation, with a one-room farmhouse on twenty-two acres, was to be shared by Bill, Emily, Patricia, and Wendy. There was just one bathroom. In the new location, Bill instituted a revised training regimen, which featured team-based search-and-destroy missions. Patricia and Wendy would take a three-minute head start, and then Bill and Emily would chase them through the woodsy terrain and capture them. At night, they worked their way through reading material, much of it sent by Jim Kilgore, from California, via the Scotts. Along with Wendy's feminist literature, Patricia was particularly impressed with *Prairie Fire: The Politics of Revolutionary Anti-imperialism,* a manifesto that had just been published by the Weather Underground.

Still, the writing went nowhere. Jack came up with a different idea. He would recruit an outsider to conduct the interviews with Bill, Emily, and Patricia, and this person, in theory, would prompt the kind of expansive candor that they needed to produce a real book.

Scott summoned his friend Paul Hoch, who was teaching at a small college in Canada. Hoch had a Ph.D. from Brown, and he had earlier been affiliated with Scott's sports institute, where he wrote a book called *Rip Off the Big Game: The Exploitation of Sports by the Power Elite.* His politics were roughly simpatico with those of the SLA. Hoch brought a pair of tape recorders with him so that both he and the comrades could keep copies. This created the first problem. Bill didn't want recordings of his words out in the world, where they might find their way into the wrong hands, especially those of the police or the FBI. Bill's discomfort with the tapes reflected his ambivalence about the whole project. As an egomaniac, Bill liked the idea of broadcasting the success (as he saw it) of the SLA to the world. But as a half-baked revolutionary, he believed in propaganda more than journalism. As he later acknowledged, he used his interviews with Hoch to put forth the version of SLA history that he wanted to be true, but often was not. Hoch sensed Bill's mixed motives and grew frustrated.

Then Bill made the problem worse. His solution to the security issue was to insist that Hoch leave his tapes at the farm, where the comrades would transcribe and edit them. (Jack delivered them a balky typewriter.) In this way, Bill could make sure to inject his version of the SLA party line into all the interviews. Through the transcription and editing process, the interviews lurched further from the truth and more into Bill Harris's notion of successful propaganda.

This was especially true regarding Hoch's interviews with Patricia. The edited transcripts of her recorded sessions were later recovered, and they became collectively known as the "Tania interview." Much of the information could only have come from Patricia herself, but the form of expression was usually SLA-style jargon. The sentiments are recognizably hers, but the language sounds like that of the stilted SLA communiqués. The transcript includes handwritten edits by Bill but some by Patricia herself.

Asked about her parents, she said,

Everything from my upbringing, due to my class position was trying to make me declare allegiance to my parents' values and ideas. As a young woman in high school, I was more than anything embarrassed by my parents' wealth and class position.

About Steven Weed:

For about a year and a half, I was content to think about nothing but becoming a "gentle woman" and fitting into Weed's life. But in spite of reactionary attitudes, I was growing. My relationship with Steve was changing and I was becoming resentful of his patronizing attitude toward me. . . . While part of me was plotting my escape from this relationship, the other part of me was smiling for engagement pictures and cooking dinner—playing out various aspects of a role that I hated.

About her kidnappers:

At first I didn't trust or like them. . . . For a while I didn't trust anything they said to me. But I got over that level of mistrust pretty quickly. I realized that except for security information, I wasn't being lied to anymore.

About her decision to join the SLA:

My decision to join the SLA was the result of a process of political development. . . . After a couple of weeks I started to feel sympathetic with the SLA. I was beginning to see that what they wanted to accomplish was necessary, although at that time it was hard for me to relate to the tactic of urban guerrilla warfare. But how can someone disagree with wanting hungry people to have food?

Was she brainwashed by the SLA?

I couldn't believe that anyone would come up with such bullshit. . . . I feel that the term "brainwashing" has meaning only when one is referring to the process which begins in the school system, and . . . the process whereby the people are conditioned to passively take their place in society as slaves of the ruling class.

About the Hibernia Bank robbery (handwritten edits in Patricia's hand):

There were two reasons. We needed the money and we wanted to illustrate that [Tania] was alive, and her decision wasn't a bunch of bullshit. . . . We didn't go into the bank with the intention of shooting someone. That would be crazy. But we also expected people to cooperate with us and not freak out.

About a visit with her mother to her hometown of Atlanta:

Catherine is an incredible racist. . . . She went crazy. It was "nigger" and "we're in jig town now." There were no street signs in the black areas of Atlanta, and her comment about this situation was, "Niggers don't need street signs."

On her relationship with Willy Wolfe:

My personal relationship with Cujo was based on a political and military relationship. The strong personal relationship did not develop, could not develop, until after I joined the cell because there would have been no common understanding and therefore no basis of trust between us. . . . Cujo was an incredibly patient, loving and dedicated person. His experiences with the brothers in California's concentration camps played a very important part in his political development. . . . Before I got a reading light in the closet, Cujo read Stalin's *Dialectical and Historical Material-ism* and some other essays to me. He explained everything as he read, and never got frustrated if I asked a "stupid" question. . . . Cujo was a beautiful and gentle man and at the same time he was a strong and ruthless guerrilla soldier.

On sexual exclusivity in the SLA:

People in the cell didn't have exclusive relationships. There was no room for bourgeois types of personal relationships. The cell couldn't function like that on a military/political level. . . . After a while the comrades realized that our personal relation-ship was working well in the cell situation. Both Cujo and I were becoming stronger.

On her comrades:

We live for the people, and some of us died for the people. It was horrible to watch our closest comrades burned alive, but the people were able to see just how fascist this government really is, and what kind of determination revolutionaries must have to bring this motherfucker down. Our own deaths do not frighten us, for death is a reality of life, and we no longer run from reality.

Hoch made some progress with his interviews, but the comrades didn't care for him, and the book project withered.

For a time, at the New York farm, Bill and Emily stopped fight-ing, but then Phil Shinnick showed up for a visit. Shortly after his arrival, Emily and Phil went for "a walk." According to Patricia, Bill confronted Emily after Phil left.

"I went out for a jog, you know, and there you were with him, like animals, fucking on the side of the road!"

"Well, you found what you were looking for," Emily shot back.

"Yeah, well, you know, that was a breach of security, doing that in the woods, don't you?"

"Well, fuck you," Emily said. "I enjoyed myself for once."

Bill became increasingly paranoid, especially about the tapes for the "book." What if they fell into the wrong hands? What if Jack took them? What if *Jack* put the tapes in the wrong hands?

As summer faded, Bill raised a serious question. Would he have to kill Jack Scott? Did Jack know too much? Fortunately, there was always a lot more talk than action when it came to Bill Harris and violence. But even the discussion of the issue illustrated how far things had deteriorated. Late in the summer of 1974, Bill destroyed Paul Hoch's tapes. Only the typed transcripts, with hand-scrawled corrections, remained.

For his part, Jack Scott was getting fed up as well (though violence was not part of his repertoire). He had practically run through his entire severance from Oberlin, and his investment in the SLA showed no sign of paying off. And there was a new reason why Jack was eager to have the comrades out of his hair. His friend Bill Walton had been drafted by the Portland Trail Blazers and had invited Jack and Micki to share his home in Oregon. Jack needed to resolve his unfinished business with the SLA before heading west.

The rental in Jeffersonville was shorter term, and Jack and Micki told the comrades they would have to leave. Jack was so frustrated with the Harrises at this point that he left his wife to do most of the talking to them. Micki returned to the dairy farm and again suggested that Patricia would make everyone's life easier, including her own, if she surrendered. She would get a great deal more attention if she spoke out publicly as opposed to living in secret as a fugitive. But Patricia refused, telling Micki that she and her husband were "liberal pacifist pigs" for suggesting that she give up her life as a revolutionary.

Bill and Emily suggested that they return to the farm in Pennsylvania. Not possible, Micki said. The farm had been sold.

But Emily didn't believe Micki. Using an assumed name, Emily called the owner as a prospective buyer and learned that the farm was not even on the market. Micki was just trying to push the comrades out on their own. Emily confronted Micki about her lie, which poisoned relations even further. Because they knew the Pennsylvania farm was still vacant, the Harrises, Patricia, and Wendy moved back there.

But they were stuck again—isolated on the East Coast, with only their frayed relationship with the Scotts to sustain them. In Pennsylvania and New York, the comrades had no prospects of recruiting new comrades or raising money. The claustrophobia had become overwhelming. Risky as they knew it would be, they had to return to their roots on the West Coast. Using phone booths near the farm, Emily spoke with Kathy Soliah and Jim Kilgore in Berkeley. Her message was simple. We need to get out of here. Find us a safe place on the West Coast.

The message back was a puzzling one, but Bill, Emily, and Patricia had to accept it: meet us in Sacramento. There, among other things, Patricia Hearst would fall in love.

THE STREETS OF SACRAMENTO

Bill, Emily, Patricia, and Wendy spent the first two weeks of September packing up and making arrangements for their trip to California. (Their efforts to wipe the place for fingerprints were less thorough than the job done by the Scotts and Jay Weiner after their first departure.) Working out the details of the transfer to the West Coast was a cumbersome process because it required Bill and Emily to arrange pay-phone-to-pay-phone calls with Jim Kilgore and Kathy Soliah. Then, one afternoon, without warning, Jack and Micki Scott showed up at the farm to whisk Patricia away.

Jack had agreed to take Patricia west, but only as far as Las Vegas. He still thought she should surrender, and he believed California—where the search for her was focused—was the worst place she could go. He refused to deliver her into that kind of danger, so he chose his parents' place near the strip as a sort of compromise. From there, he said, Patricia could make her own plans. Accordingly, the Harrises arranged for Jim Kilgore to pick Patricia up in Las Vegas and take her to Sacramento.

After Jack dropped Micki in Cleveland to visit friends, Jack and Patricia again became a faux married couple on a cross-country road trip, albeit this time without his parents as chaperones. Jack had rented a van for the journey, stowed the files for his sports institute in the back, and planned to continue on to Portland after dropping Patricia. The trip nearly came to an early conclusion, however, when the pair crossed the border into Indiana.

A police cruiser flashed its lights to signal the van to pull over, apparently for speeding. Patricia was wearing her usual red wig, her face was painted with freckles, and she had a towel around her mid-section, to suggest pregnancy. If she had been looking for a safe way to surrender, this traffic stop was a perfect opportunity. Scott abjured weapons, so there was no physical risk to her. She could simply have identified herself to the officer and turned herself in. But as she later acknowledged, she wanted to do the opposite. She was desperate *not* to be caught so she could continue her work as a revolutionary. "I had to do everything in my power to stop myself from shaking with fright," she wrote. For his part, Scott remained cool and put his sports expertise to work by bantering with the officer about football. The cop sent them on their way. The traffic stop provided a vivid window into Patricia's state of mind—that of a woman who preferred the drama of guerrilla war to the safety of a police cruiser.

Jack and Patricia arrived in Las Vegas to find an unsettled scene at Jack's parents'. Their eccentric son Walter had just announced that he was returning from a tour in Libya as a soldier of fortune. None of the Scotts wanted Walter to see that the family was sheltering the infamous Patricia Hearst, so they hustled her off to a motel, to await her pickup by Jim Kilgore. She waited there for two days, staring at the television, watching reruns of a long-canceled series called *Sergeant Preston of the Yukon*. Patricia was alone for two days and could have done anything she wanted—called home, summoned an old friend or family member, turned herself in. But as before, she wanted to keep fighting.

Kilgore finally retrieved her, but he couldn't afford to rent or buy a car for the trip. So they had six hours to kill before their bus left for Sacramento. Kilgore was an anomaly among the comrades. He had actually read the turgid Marxist texts that the SLA used mostly as decoration in their hideouts. A former graduate student in economics, as well as a sportswriter, Kilgore had an eclectic intellect to go with his bomb-friendly politics. He treated Patricia with a slightly distant kind of respect. Kilgore was also carrying a .38-caliber handgun, so he didn't want to venture into a casino or hotel, where security guards might stop him. In the end, the two of them basically wandered the streets, until they made their way to the shabby Las Vegas bus station.

Why had they chosen Sacramento? The hurried consultations between the Harrises, Kilgore, and Soliah concluded that the Bay Area was simply too hot for the comrades. They were all well-known to the police in Berkeley, Oakland, and San Francisco, so any prolonged stay there seemed unduly risky. They could not trust that their disguises would work indefinitely. In contrast, none of the locals in the sleepy capital of California knew the three, and because the city was just ninety minutes away from the Bay Area, their allies could come and go with relative ease. In addition, the upcoming trial of Russ Little and Joe Remiro for the murder of Marcus Foster had been moved to Sacramento because of the abundant pretrial publicity in Oakland. The comrades' hope, as well as their plan, was to bust the two of them out of jail before their trial began.

The group that assembled in Sacramento was essentially a combination of two outfits, the remnant of the SLA (Bill and Emily Harris and Patricia Hearst) and the Bay Area–based Revolutionary Army bombing collective (Jim Kilgore; Kathy, Steve, and Josephine Soliah; and Michael Bortin). To the extent the new combination had a name, they called themselves the New World Liberation Front, although, confusingly, they did not always refer to themselves this way. The biggest change for the SLA survivors concerned the focus of their revolutionary efforts: they were now bombers.

In a way, it was almost surprising that it took so long for the SLA to start using explosives. Among the more extreme elements of the counterculture in the 1970s, which surely included the SLA, the bomb was the most common form of political expression. Dozens were set off every year in Northern California alone. But DeFreeze and his colleagues expressed mostly contempt for bombers, with their preference for after-hours actions that injured property but not people. "We don't bomb bathrooms," DeFreeze said, referring to the notorious Weather Underground action at the U.S. Capitol, in 1971. Under DeFreeze, the

SLA employed the more sinister methods of murder (of Marcus Foster) and kidnapping (of Patricia Hearst) to make its political points. In time, the SLA did follow the Revolutionary Army in embracing the bomb, but when they did, Bill, Emily, and Patricia gave the technique their own menacing spin.

First, though, the clan had to gather, which was not a simple matter. When Jim Kilgore and Patricia arrived on the Greyhound, they were met by Steve Soliah. Patricia and Steve had met briefly earlier in the summer, at the apartment in Berkeley where the comrades arranged for Jack Scott to take them to the East Coast. That had been a hurried, almost panicked gathering, and the two had little time to become acquainted. This time, though, would be different.

Steve Soliah wasn't tall—perhaps five feet eight inches—but he retained the coiled body of the football player he had once been. He had long straight hair, like his older sister's blond mane, but Steve's hair was dark and receding fast at the temples. He had an easy smile and an even demeanor. He was, in Patricia's words, "an easygoing young man who lived for the day's pleasures and excitements." He was political, like all the comrades in their set, but he wore his passions lightly. He listened as well as talked. He played the guitar. For a woman who had spent the summer being bludgeoned by the hectoring of Bill Harris and Jack Scott, the mellow sound of Steve Soliah's voice was like music. "He had no problem with his own ego," Patricia wrote, "and did not try to dominate, teach, or make demands. For me, that alone won my gratitude."

Kathy and Steve had rented a place on W Street in a gritty neighborhood near Sacramento's downtown. The plan was for Patricia to move in with them, while Kilgore returned to Berkeley. On her first day in town, Steve helped her settle in, and the two of them talked for hours. She said the summer had been good in many respects. She enjoyed being in the country, restoring her health in the sunshine. But the falling-out between the Scotts and the Harrises meant she had to leave. Steve asked her questions—obvious questions, in a way—that no men had thought to ask her in a long time. What was it like to be kidnapped? Was she scared? How did she feel about her parents? What was she thinking about the future?

Patricia confessed that the kidnapping terrified her. At the same time, she was disgusted with how her parents reacted to her situation— the way they had abandoned her, as she saw it. She had no interest in returning to them, or to Steve Weed. She resented how no one seemed to believe that she had become an actual revolutionary. Few people understood what was at the core of Patricia's political awakening. Angela Atwood, Willy Wolfe, and especially her newer friend Wendy Yoshimura had talked ceaselessly about the need for women to control their own destinies. Even during her quasi-isolation with the comrades, Patricia was inspired by the women's movement, which caught fire in the 1970s the way African Americans' civil rights had advanced in the previous decade. Patricia wanted—demanded—to be taken seriously, which Steve Soliah, in his quiet way, did.

On matters closer to home, Patricia told Steve that she couldn't stand Bill and Emily Harris, who at this moment were on their way to Sacramento. On Steve's first night in the apartment, Kathy and Patricia shared the only bed. On the second night, Steve and Patricia did. Still, the fluid sexual mores of the SLA remained intact. Steve sometimes also slept with Emily, and Patricia, despite everything, still occasionally spent the night with Bill.

Bill and Emily arrived in Sacramento shortly after Patricia checked into W Street. Bill immediately sought to assert himself in his usual belligerent manner, and he had a new adversary in the close quarters of the apartment. Mike Bortin, the bomb maker from the Revolutionary Army, had also moved in, and he and Bill began having epic disagreements. The difference was mostly stylistic. Bortin was one of the few people in their circle who indulged enthusiastically in drugs. ("Let's do an action on acid!" he suggested, to Bill's open disdain.) At the same time, Bortin was a physical fitness buff who lifted weights and ran up to twenty miles a day. With wild red hair, two chipped front teeth, and a tattoo of a dragon on his arm, Bortin projected a hippie-style wildness that clashed with Harris's dedication to discipline. Bill still fancied himself a marine-style revolutionary, and Bortin's impulsivity offended him. While Bill talked incessantly, Emily occupied herself with perpetual productivity—organizing the house, buying supplies, practicing quick draws in front of the mirror.

From the beginning, there were reminders that they were fugitives who could be swept up by the police at any moment. Late one night, not long after the group moved into the apartment on W Street, several police cars, with sirens blazing, pulled up by their house. On this occasion, Bill and Patricia were asleep in the same bed. The street outside was suddenly ablaze with lights, and the sound of police radios crackled for them all to hear. Bill pulled out his arsenal, and Patricia and Emily picked up guns for what appeared to be a Fifty-Fourth Street–style showdown. Listening carefully, though, they figured out that the cops were responding to a murder in the house next door. (Given the neighborhood, this news was not a total surprise; the homicide had been a knifing, so they never heard gunshots.) The comrades were relieved to learn that they were not the targets of the police action, but that still left the problem of living at ground zero for a homicide investigation. The cops would surely come knocking. One of Emily's best disguises was that of a frumpy housewife, and she answered the door in that costume when the police came by the next morning. She told the officers that she'd love to help but knew nothing. The crisis passed.

By late fall, a larger conflict threatened the group. Bill, Emily, and Patricia relied on the Revolutionary Army alumni—the Soliahs, Kilgore, and Bortin—for their day-to-day living expenses. Steve, Kilgore, and Bortin worked as housepainters, while Kathy and her sister Josephine did odd jobs, mostly waitressing. (Wendy Yoshimura, who came and went from the Bay Area, which is about an hour and a half from Sacramento, also had various jobs.) In contrast, Bill, Emily, and Patricia contributed nothing to their own upkeep. Emily busied herself with errands and household tasks. Patricia read books and issued denunciations of those (like her favorite target, Jane Fonda) who only pretended to be radicals. And Bill alienated everyone by issuing orders, while his benefactors thought of him as a moocher.

Steve Soliah returned to Sacramento about a month after his first visit and immediately went for a long walk with Patricia. He saw how her conflicts with Bill had worsened, and the tension was starting to affect her health. He arranged for Jim Kilgore to take a blood test from Patricia and submit it to a friendly doctor under an assumed name. The test appeared normal, but Steve decided to propose alternative living arrangements. Wendy Yoshimura and Emily stayed on in the apartment on W Street; Kilgore and Bortin lived on T Street; Kathy and Steve Soliah, along with Patricia, took a new apartment on Capitol Avenue. (Bill Harris rotated among the comrades, based on who could stand him at any given moment.) Steve and Patricia were now an official couple, at least in SLA-style terms.

Little by little, Patricia began to return to the outside world. One day in November, Steve took her along on one of his painting jobs. A man named Oscar Mills was renovating his house after a fire, and he found the number for Steve's painting company in the *Oakland Tribune* classifieds. When he asked for an estimate, Steve showed up in a multicolored Volkswagen Beetle with a woman whom he introduced— amazingly enough—as Tania. Steve and Tania won the job with a bid of $750, and then the two of them spent a week or so on the assignment. Later, Mills identified the other workers on the job as Jim Kilgore and Josephine Soliah. When interviewed by the FBI much later, Mills said he noticed that Tania didn't do as much work as the others, but she seemed like a poised, if quiet, member of the crew. When spoken to, Tania tended to look at Steve before answering. At one point, Mills, Steve, and Tania even went to a bank together to cash a check; Mills thought it was odd that Tania chose to stay in the car when the other two went inside, but at the time he never made the connection between the soft-spoken Tania and the famous fugitive by the same name.

Patricia's gestures in the direction of a normal life could not camouflage the group's larger sense of despair. At one level, the problem was simple: money. The comrades with jobs had barely enough to live on their own, much less to support the three SLA survivors. At one point, the comrades bought horse meat, because it was so cheap. They also did a lot of shoplifting, which was even cheaper, and they continued to steal unattended purses. Their best score came courtesy of Bill Harris's experience as a postal worker back in Berkeley. Bill knew that in the late afternoon letter carriers made the rounds of small businesses to pick up cash payments. One day the comrades followed a postman. At the last minute, Mike Bortin recognized the fellow as a former roommate (who could have recognized Bortin). They decided to run the same trick on another postal route and found a more suitable target. Kathy Soliah stopped at a mailbox and flagged down the letter carrier for a brief chat. At the same time, Steve Soliah rode by on a bicycle and reached into the open postal jeep. He grabbed parcels that contained about $1,000 in cash.

Mike Bortin had a different idea—an SLA book. Bill Harris told Bortin that they had just spent the summer in a futile effort in that direction, but Bortin, as was his custom, ignored Bill. Instead, Bortin went to Oakland and recruited Dan Siegel, a radical lawyer there, to meet with Bill, Emily, and Patricia about the idea. One afternoon, Bortin blindfolded Siegel and drove him to the Sacramento apartment to meet with the group. As it happened, Patricia was out shopping for groceries, alone, when Siegel arrived. When she returned, Siegel engaged the three SLA survivors in a serious political conversation, in which they laid out their continuing belief in the foco theory— that the bombings and bank robberies of a small vanguard would yet inspire a broader revolution. Emily put forward the theoretical underpinning of the argument, but both Bill and Patricia chimed in to support her. In the end, Siegel had nothing to offer in terms of book contacts, but he left the bizarre encounter with a firm understanding that Patricia was by this point a partner, not a victim, of the SLA.

Shoplifting and postal scores might tide the comrades over for a few weeks, but by the winter of 1974–75 it was clear that they needed more than these nickel-and-dime operations to survive, much less to advance their agenda. These undertakings involved considerable risk for small payoffs, and besides they lacked political content and received no public attention. They still thought of themselves as urban guerrillas who could at least sow chaos, if not foment revolution. Cooped up in their tiny apartments, eating horse meat, they were doing nothing of the kind. They felt as if they were just waiting around to get caught. Something had to change.

In the argot of the era, the two factions laid guilt trips on each other. The Revolutionary Army alumni were sick of supplying all the cash and getting nothing in return. Jim Kilgore and Kathy Soliah were willing to move forward, but they had no sense of where anyone was going. They were ready to resume making bombs, but even homemade bombs cost money to assemble, and there was no cash. Jo and Steve, Kathy's sister and brother, were less impassioned in their views but also frustrated with the state of affairs. Mike Bortin was always full of nutty ideas—like killing John McCone, the former CIA director, on his doorstep—but he also wasn't doing anything more than talking. All of them resented feeding and clothing the SLA comrades for months, with no end in sight. Were they supposed to do this forever? What was the point?

Bill Harris was quick to remind the Bay Area contingent that he, Emily, and Patricia had done the real suffering. They had watched their comrades die excruciating deaths. They were the objects of a nationwide manhunt. The others had choices about whether to return to civilian life, but Bill, Emily, and Patricia did not. They had committed their lives to revolutionary action. The others were dilettantes, fakes, posers . . . And so it went, night after night, in what they sometimes called "self-criticism" sessions, even though the comrades mostly used them to criticize each other.

For a while, the two groups were able to come together around the idea of freeing Russ Little and Joe Remiro. They contacted Remiro's cousin, who was a frequent visitor to the jail, and the cousin persuaded Remiro to prepare detailed diagrams of the security situation. The cousin smuggled out the diagrams, and Emily Harris hand copied them so that each comrade had a duplicate. In December, Bill Harris set up surveillance outside the jail, and other comrades took turns examining the comings and goings as well. But the idea petered out. The truth was that neither Bill nor any of the others had any idea how to break anyone out of prison. They were stymied again.

The group finally came around to the idea that their only option was to rob another bank. Back in San Francisco, the SLA had already proved it could do it successfully, even if the Bay Area group had not, so the group had some institutional expertise. To learn more, Jo Soliah took a job as a clerk in a local bank, to get a sense of how the internal procedures worked. The main question, of course, was which bank to rob. Emily Harris located the Guild Savings and Loan Association, on a sleepy street just outside the city limits. It had several advantages. There was no traffic, so a fast getaway would be easy. The small shopping plaza was adjacent to a residential area, so a car could merge into a different neighborhood right away. The county sheriffs, not the Sacramento police, were responsible for the area, and they were a small, weak police force. Few cops were likely to be in the area.

On February 4, 1975, the one-year anniversary of Patricia's kidnapping, Bill decided to check the place out and brought Patricia along with him. They took the bus both ways, and on their return trip, as they were walking to their apartment, a car slowed down near them to ask for directions. Bill put the woman off, but then she circled back. She leaned out the window again and said, "Does anyone ever tell you that you look like Patty Hearst?" The wig-and-freckles disguise had finally failed. But Bill thought fast. "Oh, people say that all the time. This is my wife, and you're right—she does look like Patty Hearst." The driver nodded and pulled away. When the woman slipped from view, Bill and Patricia bolted for home.

Like the Hibernia Bank job ten months earlier, the robbery of the
Guild Savings and Loan was meticulously planned. Bill and Emily
took the lead, but everyone pitched in. The Harrises drew up an
eight-point planning document—euphemistically called the "Bakery" list—which described all the steps necessary for a successful bank
robbery. It included guidance on "utilizing the phone book to pick all
good possibilities in general selected area" and "time inside (not being
greedy)." The final section was called "Assigning people to team posi-
tions and designating leadership":

A. Responsibilities of each position
B. Team discussion of responsibilities and coordination
C. Inter-team rehearsal
D. Final dry-run—total rehearsal

Another bit of advice was typed in on the side of the document:
"EXPECT THE UNEXPECTED."

The tensions between the two camps surfaced even in the lead-up
to the joint enterprise. The Bay Area team didn't object to Bill's planning the robbery, but they didn't want him involved in the actual
execution. Bill agreed. The plan was for Kilgore and Bortin to conduct the actual robbery, with Steve Soliah driving the getaway car and
Kathy Soliah serving as lookout. (Steve Soliah bought a junky 1956
Chevrolet Impala for the job.) Everyone agreed, as in the Hibernia
action, that the Guild operation should take no more than ninety seconds. But unlike Hibernia, the Guild was selected because it had no
security camera. Profit, not propaganda, was the objective this time.

The temperature was just climbing into the forties on the morning of February 25, 1975, when Michael Bortin, wearing a Halloween
mask and a "Big Apple" baseball cap, and Jim Kilgore, wearing a

green scarf, which he forgot to pull up around his face, entered the Guild bank. Bortin had a .45-caliber revolver, Kilgore a shotgun. Bortin announced the robbery to the one teller on duty, and Kilgore told the single customer in the bank to get on the floor.

Bortin instructed the teller to open the safe, and Bortin grabbed a bag of coins (pennies, unfortunately), and then he returned to rifle the tellers' drawers. He collected about $3,700, mostly in crisp twenties, plus a handful of blank money orders. Bortin and Kilgore bolted out in just about the allotted time, then jumped into the getaway car, with Steve Soliah at the wheel. A few blocks away, they dumped that vehicle for the switch car. Kathy Soliah watched the whole operation from a greeting card store across the street from the bank. As she later reported, the comrades were long gone by the time the police arrived.

Earlier in the morning, Emily Harris and Patricia had taken the bus to McKinley Park, near the bank, where they were waiting for Bortin and Kilgore. The pair gave the women two bags—one containing the guns, the other with the cash proceeds. Patricia struggled to carry the heavy bag of weapons, but she and Emily managed to get back on the bus for the ride to the W Street apartment. There Patricia and Emily counted the loot and destroyed the bags.

In short, the Guild action worked to perfection. The take was modest, but so, it appeared, was the risk. Because there were only two people inside the bank, the police never even suspected that the robbery was the work of a team of revolutionaries, much less those affiliated with the notorious Hibernia operation. To the cops, the robbery looked like a routine stickup, and it drew little attention in Sacramento, much less in the broader world.

The success energized all the comrades, including Patricia. Perhaps, it seemed, they had figured out a way to survive and prosper and to resume bombing operations. The first priority, then, was to find more target banks. Shortly after the Guild robbery, Patricia took on her first solo operation—casing a prospective bank robbery target. She was well suited for the role. At this moment, she was the only surviv-

ing member of the SLA to have actually carried out a bank robbery—
that is, to have held a gun on customers inside a bank. (Bill and Emily
Harris had only helped with the getaway in the Hibernia Bank job.)

Patricia went all the way to Marysville, a gold rush town about
forty miles north of Sacramento. She checked out the local Bank of
America branch and drew up a detailed diagram of the place. "There
are 2 picture window size openings in the wall separating the work
area from the teller area—no glass," she scribbled; "3 tellers were
open during a *busy* period so the 4th Window may never open . . . saw
7 employees, 5 women & 2 men, one young and nervous; manager is
fat and Black."

But in the end, the group decided not to go to Marysville. The
better option seemed to be a busy branch of the Crocker National
Bank, in Carmichael, which was a suburb just outside Sacramento.
The comrades agreed that this bank represented a significant step up
in potential spoils. A hundred thousand dollars did not seem out of
the question. (This bank had no security cameras either.) The comrades felt that they were, by this point, experienced bank robbers.
They were cautious but committed. They had a proven set of plans.
They had never been caught. The pickings were there for the taking.

What could go wrong?

DEATH OF A "BOURGEOIS PIG"

The success of the Guild bank robbery came at a moment of revived fortunes for the comrades and their allies. Finally, they were doing something other than running and hiding.

The first to take action were Russ Little and Joe Remiro, who were still awaiting trial for the murder of Marcus Foster, a year and a half earlier. Frustrated at the time it was taking the comrades to come to their assistance, Little and Remiro took matters into their own hands. On March 1, a quiet Saturday afternoon in the Alameda county jail, Little was meeting with his attorney, John Bain. They requested that Remiro join them in the conference room. One guard brought in Remiro, and a second guard brought in a chair. When the second guard opened the door to the conference room, Little lunged at him with a sharpened pencil and stabbed it four inches into the guard's neck. Remiro jumped the other guard, gouging his eye and grabbing his key ring. Remiro quickly identified the key to the guards' gun locker, where all the weapons in the jail were stored. Remiro was turning the key in the locker when the guard with the pencil sticking out of his neck managed to punch the electric lock that allowed the two other officers on duty to come to the rescue. Little and Remiro—Osi and Bo—were subdued and returned to their cells. As it happened, this attempted escape took place without the assistance of the SLA. But it came remarkably close to succeeding. (Both guards survived their grievous injuries.)

Thanks to the proceeds from the Guild bank robbery, the New

World Liberation Front (that is, Jim Kilgore and Kathy Soliah) could resume bombing. On March 20, Kilgore put a plastic bag of Tovex water gel explosive and nitroglycerin dynamite at the base of a Pacific Gas and Electric tower in San Bruno. A week later, Kilgore and Soliah threw a similar kind of explosive over the fence at a PG&E substation in San Jose. Both bombs exploded, but there were no injuries. Still, they showed that the comrades were back in business.

The wild escape attempt by the two original SLA prisoners put public attention back on the failed search for Patricia. But the renewed heat didn't dissuade the comrades from proceeding with their next bank robbery. After all, the FBI and the cops had no idea the group was even in Sacramento, so the comrades thought that a bank in a quiet suburb would be a promising target.

Their planning was even more meticulous than the preparations for the Guild job. This was a bigger bank, with more employees and likely more customers and cash, so they would need more people to pull off the heist. They would need more cars, too, so the comrades began their preparations by assembling a veritable fleet. On April 12, Kathy Soliah and Jim Kilgore went to a party in Oakland and stole a Pontiac Firebird that belonged to a fellow guest. The next day, they rented an enclosed garage on D Street in Sacramento to store this and other vehicles. On April 15, Kilgore stole the wallet of a Brian Bach, who was jogging in a park in Sacramento. Two days later, "Bach" rented a Volkswagen van. On April 16, Kathy Soliah stole the wallet of a woman named Norma Mulholland from a locker at a Sacramento health club. The next day, "Mulholland" rented a blue Ford Maverick. The group also stole a blue Ford Mustang that was parked near their T Street apartment, and then they put license plates stolen from another car on the Mustang. With the four untraceable cars in place, the comrades set the robbery for the morning of April 21.

Mike Bortin arrived from the Bay Area a few days early so they could review their plans and do a dry run. A late-night meeting at the T Street apartment exposed the kinds of problems that the comrades had previously managed to avoid. Emily cased the Carmichael bank, and Bill, who had done the planning, proposed that all eight comrades have roles in the new operation. An "invasion team" of four comrades would enter the bank and conduct the robbery. Two others would stand guard outside the bank, to gun down the police if they interrupted the robbery. And two more comrades would drive the switch cars. Bortin thought Bill's plan was madness—that it involved too many people and thus too much potential for error. Bortin proposed that he handle the robbery by himself, or perhaps with one other person. He wanted to be in charge of the operation, as he had been at the Guild bank. He was a physically powerful man who said that was what was needed. "You have to have the ability to get people out of the way . . . to intimidate them . . . to get them down," Bortin said. "Emily can't do that." Jim Kilgore agreed with Bortin, noting that the use of so many people would mark the robbery as an SLA job and thus draw unwanted attention.

But Bill was committed to his scheme, and he wanted Emily to be part of the team inside the bank, because she had found the bank and been involved in all the planning. The discussion, in typical SLA fashion, meandered and turned into a debate about feminism. Did Bortin respect women enough to allow them to be in charge? In the end, Bortin and Kilgore relented and allowed Emily to take the lead.

Early on the morning of April 21, the comrades began a complicated choreography that resulted in eight people in three apartments retrieving the four cars and distributing themselves into the appropriate teams. Bortin, Emily, Kilgore, and Kathy Soliah, who constituted the bank invasion team, took the stolen Firebird. Bill Harris and Steve Soliah, both armed, waited in the stolen Mustang outside the bank. Wendy Yoshimura drove the rented Maverick as one switch car to pick up Bill and Steve, and Patricia drove the van to pick up the invasion team. Patricia parked near a funeral parlor, a few blocks from the bank. Cradling a carbine, she waited for the invasion team to arrive so she could engineer their escape.

Bortin parked the Firebird by a fence near the bank. He and the three others, all packing weapons, headed toward their target, but

Emily hesitated, checking her watch, and by the time they arrived at the front door, they were not the first customers of the day. Bortin held the door open for the first arrival, a woman named Myrna Opsahl.

Family and church dominated the life of Myrna Opsahl, who was forty-two years old. She was born in Cheyenne, Wyoming, into a family of Seventh-Day Adventists, and as a teenager she went to Riverside, California, to study nursing at the school then known as the College of Medical Evangelists. There she met Trygve Opsahl, who had emigrated from Norway for medical school. Shortly after their marriage, in 1954, they moved to Trinidad to work as medical missionaries. Later, they settled in Carmichael to raise their four children, who were all teenagers by the mid-1970s. At this point, Trygve had a practice at a local hospital, and Myrna was a homemaker. On the morning of April 21, 1975, their son Jon, who was fifteen, stormed off to school after a tiff with his mother about whether there were any pens in the house to do his homework. She told him she would buy some that day, but Jon left without his customary "I love you."

The women of the Opsahls' church divided the responsibilities of counting the weekend's offerings and depositing the cash on Monday at the Crocker National Bank branch in Carmichael. On that Monday, one of the women scheduled to make the deposit had another engagement, so Myrna offered to take her place. She arrived at the bank, with two friends, just as it opened. As they approached, one of the three women noticed, with some curiosity, the four young people who were heading to the bank from the opposite direction. Why, she wondered, were they wearing heavy jackets—"hunting clothing," she called it— on a beautiful spring morning? Opsahl was carrying a small adding machine with two hands, so it was a natural gesture for the young man in front of her to open the door.

"Thank you," Myrna Opsahl said to Mike Bortin.

As soon as Bortin and his three colleagues walked in behind Opsahl and her two friends, he began screaming.

"Everybody down on the ground!"

He waved a .357 Colt pistol. He and his comrades put on ski masks, and the others flashed their weapons as well.

"Get the fuck on the floor! Down!" Bortin said.

Kathy moved toward the tellers, to start grabbing cash. Kilgore stood guard at the door. Emily unsheathed a sawed-off 12-gauge shotgun and began counting off the time, to keep the heist to the SLA standard of ninety seconds.

"Fifteen seconds!" she said. Emily turned to the three customers. "Get down!" she said. "Get down!"

Myrna Opsahl appeared to hesitate, perhaps looking for a place to put down her adding machine. Emily raised her shotgun, and the weapon discharged with a tremendous explosion. Opsahl crumpled to the ground, bleeding from an enormous wound in her side.

There was a stunned silence in the bank. No one moved. Opsahl did not flip backward but rather sagged to the floor. Blood pooled by her side. Her friends lifted their heads to look at her, but Bortin shouted them down. "Get your noses to the carpet!"

After the brief pause, the comrades proceeded with their plan. In an athletic move, Bortin jumped up on top of the tellers' counter. "Get your drawers open," he yelled. "Lie down! Do not look up!" Kathy Soliah, wielding a Browning 9-millimeter semiautomatic, awkwardly crawled over the counter, dropping bullets along the way, and started grabbing money.

"Thirty seconds!" said Emily.

"Where are the traveler's checks?" Bortin bellowed. "We don't have them!" a teller replied from the floor. Kathy Soliah kicked the woman in frustration as Kathy scampered from drawer to drawer, pulling bills.

"Sixty seconds!" Emily said.

Drawing on information from her sister Josephine's briefing about bank operations, Kathy remembered to search the drawers by the drive-through tellers, too.

"Ninety seconds," Emily yelled. "Let's go!"

The four bank robbers headed for the exit, stepping around Opsahl's body. As Emily squeezed through behind Bortin, she said, "You were supposed to say, 'We're the Dillinger gang!'"

Waiting nervously in the van, Patricia saw the Firebird peel out ahead of her. She followed the sports car to a deserted street, where both cars stopped. Emily, Kathy, Bortin, and Kilgore jumped from the Firebird into Patricia's van. "Go, go, go!" Bortin yelled at Patricia, who kept her cool and remembered to stick to the speed limit.

"Well, should we count the money?" Bortin said, with a kind of sneer at Emily.

"No, not now," Emily said.

"Well, you're in command," Bortin said. "Why don't you give us some orders?"

Emily, ignoring Bortin's sarcasm, told everyone to start removing their disguises. Then, for reasons Patricia didn't understand at the time, Emily said, "Maybe she'll live . . ."

"No," said Kilgore. "I saw her."

An ambulance arrived quickly at the bank to take Opsahl the twenty blocks to the emergency room at Carmichael's American River Hospital. The staff immediately recognized Myrna, because her husband worked there as a staff surgeon. An ER staffer paged Dr. Trygve Opsahl and told him his wife had been shot. The doctor raced to the ER, where he saw two of his colleagues attending to Myrna. As he later recalled the scene, "She was pale, unresponsive with fixed, dilated pupils, not breathing and no pulse or blood pressure. The EKG showed only a straight line with an occasional faint bleep. The I.V. fluids were running in at a fast pace but the blood and fluids were seeping out of her massive flank wound as quickly as it was pumped in. She was beyond

Kathy Soliah (who would later take the name Sara Jane Olson) is shown here speaking at a memorial rally for the slain SLA comrades on June 2 in Berkeley. The poster announced the event. Soliah's sympathetic public remarks prompted Bill and Emily Harris, along with Patricia, to seek her out and ask for her help in escaping the police.

Jack Scott, shown jogging with his wife, Micki, was a pioneer in protecting the rights of athletes. He also had an eye for adventure and profit, which led to his decision to shield the SLA comrades after the shoot-out in Los Angeles.

Jack and Micki Scott rented this farmhouse in the countryside near Scranton, Pennsylvania. During the summer of 1974, the Scotts allowed Patricia, Bill and Emily Harris, and Wendy Yoshimura to stay there, in the hopes that they might produce a memoir about their life in the SLA.

After Jack Scott's brother, Walter, told the FBI that Jack had hidden Patricia and her comrades on the farm, the bureau set out to interview Jack, Micki, and their friend Bill Walton, the basketball star. In a press conference in San Francisco, the trio insisted that they would never cooperate with the FBI.

On September 18, 1975, the FBI finally arrested Patricia at her home in this modest house at 625 Morse Street in a run-down section of San Francisco. As she was taken in for booking, Patricia lifted her fist in the revolutionary salute. At the time of her arrest she was living with her lover, Steve Soliah. From jail she wrote to him, "I miss you on me & around me & inside me, and all the pigs in the world can't take the way I feel away from me."

LAST HEARST	**FIRST** PATRICIA	**MIDDLE** CAMPBELL	**I.D. NO.** 106284	**BOOKING SLIP** NO. B 54214

Other info

TANIA refused **DATE** 9-18-75 **TIME** 1955 **SAN MATEO COUNTY JAIL**

ADDRESS STREET 6? Morse, San Francisco **CITY** **STATE** Cal. **PHONE** None   **SOC. SEC.** NIP **DR. LIC.** NIP **STATE** Cal.

CHARGE Bank Robbery **ON \[\] WRNT. \[\] ENROUTE XX COMMITMENT \[\]** **DOCKET-WRNT. NO.** **ARREST DEPT.** US Marshall **DOCTOR'S CARE \[\] NAME OF DOCTOR** None

SENTENCE **SENTENCE DATE** **MEDICATION \[\] TYPE AND REASON** None

JUDGE Woodruff **JUDICIAL DISTRICT** SF Federal Court **RELEASE DATE** **MEDICAL COMPLAINTS** None

SEX F **MARRIAGE STATUS** Single **RACE** W **DOB** 2-20-54 **AGE** 21 **HEIGHT** 5-2 **WEIGHT** 100 **CONDITION OF SUBJECT** cooperative

HAIR /brn **EYES** brn **BUILD** small **COMPLEXION** fair **PLACE OF BIRTH** San Francisco **CITIZENSHIP** USA **MARKS, SCARS, TATTOOS & MANNERISMS** Pierced ears, 4" scar rt. shin, 1½" scar on rt. ankle,

OCCUPATION Urban Guerilla **EMPLOYER** Self

EMPLOYER'S ADDRESS N/A **PHONE** N/A

EMERGENCY NOTIFY T. Hallinan **RELATIONSHIP** Attny. **ADDRESS** 819 Eddy St., San Francisco Cal. **PHONE** 771-6174

ATTORNEY T. Hallinan **PAROLE OFFICER** None **BONDSMAN** None **SCHOOL YEARS** 14 yrs. **TIME LIVED IN COUNTY** 9 yrs.

RECEIVED FROM: **OFFICER** P.T. KRELL **BADGE** 1624 **DEPT.** U.S. MARSHAL **PHOTO I.D.** **CHARGES:** BANK ROBBERY **COURT** FEDERAL SF, CA

SPECIAL ARRAIGNMENT INSTRUCTIONS **RELEASE DATA**

Trans. Deputy P/U From: ____

ALL PROPERTY RECEIVED FROM SHERIFF, SAN MATEO COUNTY

?5 DATE 9-19-75

Patricia Hearst

U.S. MARSHALL

W. G. Bronw (OFFICER SIGN HERE) Duty

Marsh (DEPUTY)

REMARKS:

HEREBY AU... ILE I AM C... SIGNATURE: Patricia H...

BOOKED BY Marsh SEARCHED BY

10M 2-75

When she was booked following her arrest, Patricia was asked her occupation. "Urban guerrilla," she replied. Also arrested on the same day were Bill and Emily Harris, who had been on the run with Patricia, in a stormy partnership, for more than a year.

The prosecution team: In the center is James L. Browning Jr., the U.S. attorney and lead prosecutor. Right to left: David Bancroft, who handled the psychiatric testimony for the government; Parks Stearns, the FBI case agent; Ed Davis, an assistant U.S. attorney; Steele Langford, second-in-command to Browning; and Carole Westrick, the paralegal who recognized the significance of the Olmec monkeys.

Randolph and Catherine Hearst walking beside lead defense counsel F. Lee Bailey, whose courtroom performance disappointed the family.

By the time of her trial, Patricia's appearance had been transformed. She no longer resembled a scruffy outlaw but instead looked like a well-groomed heiress.

The turning point in Patricia's trial came when the government introduced the small Mexican charms known as Olmec monkeys. Willy Wolfe died in the Los Angeles inferno wearing this monkey around his neck; the rope was charred in the fire. When Patricia was arrested, more than a year later, she was carrying her Olmec monkey in her purse (shown here, side by side with Willy's). Carole Westrick, the prosecution paralegal, wrote a note to the lead prosecutor that said, "No woman would carry around a memento from a man who raped her and couldn't stand for over a year!"

Following an extensive lobbying campaign by the Hearst family and its allies, President Jimmy Carter commuted Patricia's prison sentence on January 29, 1979. She had served twenty-two months of her seven-year sentence. To her left is Bernard Shaw, who had been hired to be her bodyguard and became her husband.

Patricia's love of dogs remained a constant in her life. Here she is, at the age of sixty, at the 2015 Westminster Dog Show at New York's Madison Square Garden. Her shih tzu named Rocket, also pictured here, won the top prize in the toy category.

saving." (In addition, the teller who had been kicked by Kathy Soliah went into premature labor and lost her baby.)

News of the death of the doctor's wife went out quickly on Sacramento radio news. After the robbery, the comrades began making their way to the Capitol Avenue apartment, and Patricia started to understand what happened. Kathy explained how she went through the tellers' drawers. Kilgore said that Emily had been nervous, fiddling with her watch on the street and delaying their entry into the bank. He said the shooting happened because Emily had been careless with her gun. It was an accident, Kilgore said, because Emily's gun had just gone off. Kilgore drew a diagram for Patricia, showing how the woman—Myrna Opsahl—had been standing between Emily and Kilgore. "If she didn't absorb the shot, I would be the one who got shot," Kilgore said.

Kilgore left the apartment, and Emily arrived, full of bravado. "So what if she got shot? Her husband is a doctor. She's a bourgeois pig." Emily went on to explain that the safety must have slipped off her gun. The shooting had surprised her.

Then Bill Harris showed up, making a show of nonchalance. "This is the murder round," he said, holding up the remainder of a shotgun shell. "If it hadn't been for good old Myrna, one of our comrades would be dead. She got all the buckshot." Harris then said he was going to McKinley Park to bury the brass casing. If it was recovered, it would have been evidence against Emily.

For all of Bill and Emily's brave talk, the comrades recognized that the death of Myrna Opsahl changed the calculus of their own situation. They had a contentious group meeting that night in the T Street apartment. Bortin was furious, arguing that Emily had jeopardized all of them with her incompetence. He had a point. The radio was saying that the Carmichael robbery was an "SLA-style" operation. Even if the police didn't have any evidence against them at this point, the comrades were now sure to face greater pressure. Coming just a few weeks after the brutal escape attempt by Little and Remiro, the fatal shooting guaranteed that the SLA would receive a renewed level of

attention from law enforcement. Alternately enraged and philosophi-
cal, Bill Harris pointed out that Governor Reagan had signed a law
restoring the death penalty in California. They had all participated
in a robbery that led to the death of a customer. That meant that all
of them, including Patricia, were guilty of felony murder, which was
punishable by execution. "But that's okay," Bill said, "because revolutionaries always die eventually, one way or another." Bortin told Bill
to speak for himself.

At last, they got around to counting the take. The main point of
robbing a bigger bank had been to produce a bigger score. They were
hoping for as much as $100,000. Bortin, Emily, and Kathy Soliah
emptied the bag and stacked up the bills. The actual proceeds turned
out to be around $15,000—a pitifully small take, considering the
implications of what they had done. No one even thought about doing
a communiqué. (There hadn't been one in a year, since Patricia's eulogy
after the shoot-out in Los Angeles.) The optimism that followed the
Guild robbery disappeared in the pool of blood in Carmichael.

At first, the comrades were too stunned by the debacle to do much of
anything. They stayed close to their apartments in Sacramento and
tried not to call attention to themselves. Then, with typical impulsivity, Bill Harris decided that the group needed an outing, so he
directed everyone to attend the Cinco de Mayo carnival in the city's
small Mexican neighborhood. The others objected, asserting that the
risk of discovery was too great, especially for such a trivial reason.
In the end, though, Kathy and Steve Soliah, as well as Patricia and
Jim Kilgore, agreed to go, but they insisted on wearing disguises and
packing weapons for protection. In their wigs and makeup, the group
made a lame attempt at celebration; their inappropriately warm clothing hid the telltale bulges by their hips. No one had much fun, but at
least no one was busted, either.

Everyone could tell that events seemed to be spinning out of control. The police had the Firebird, which contained the fingerprints of the four members of the invasion team. The cops also learned about the garage they had rented to store the fleet. There were fingerprints there, too. As Bortin predicted, the robbery's large cast all but announced to the world that the SLA had descended on Sacramento. In light of this, they knew that it was time to get out of town.

In a crisis, the comrades turned to their true north—San Francisco. They didn't have a lot of options there either, but the city at least offered possibilities for alliances and shelter. There was a critical difference this time as the group retreated west after one setback or another. Patricia's relationship with Steve Soliah meant that she was no longer tethered to the Harrises for support. The need to flee Sacramento gave her the opportunity to accomplish her long-sought goal of disengaging from her toxic relationship with Bill and Emily. (It was a chance for Patricia to escape the frantic madness of Mike Bortin, too.)

Kathy Soliah and Jim Kilgore, who were still a couple, took the lead in finding lodging in San Francisco. Using the proceeds from the bank robberies, they rented a pair of apartments in town—one on Geneva Avenue and the other on Lyon Street. There, in the uncharacteristically warm summer, something strange happened. The comrades achieved a kind of normalcy. The emotional temperature among them dropped. People were not angry all the time. Most of them took on regular jobs. Steve Soliah, Jim Kilgore, and Mike Bortin restarted their painting business. Kathy Soliah, using a fake name, began waitressing at the Sir Francis Drake hotel downtown. Wendy Yoshimura moved in with other friends, and Jo Soliah found work as well. No one saw signs of the FBI or the police. There was the usual musical chairs among the apartments, but the sense of domesticity was nearly serene.

The women enjoyed an especially positive summer. This was a moment when the feminist movement was taking hold everywhere, especially in the counterculture. Starting back on the farm in Pennsylvania, Wendy Yoshimura had introduced Patricia to the liturgy of women's liberation. Their bible was Shulamith Firestone's *Dialectic of Sex,* a dense and at times nearly incomprehensible analysis of feminism in Marxist terms. The SLA had always been dominated, at least numerically, by women, and they now began to assert themselves more directly. For example, Kathy Soliah tried to start a kind of underground railroad for women fugitives. To make sure that they were dealing with bona fide fugitives, Soliah put out the word that a special greeting was required. Callers should ask, "How many worms grow on your worm farm?" The answer would be "Two hundred an acre." The response would be "That's a lot of worms."

During this summer, Emily Harris and Kathy Soliah also established a feminist study group. As Patricia later recalled, "We had developed our own combat skills, were equal to the men in that respect, and therefore we no longer needed them to lead the revolution."

The women reevaluated their thoughts about sex, too. "Our position on equality in sexual relationships held that sex should be the end result of natural friendships," Patricia wrote. "A woman should not feel inhibited about sleeping with a woman she liked any more than she would sleeping with a man for whom she cared." Emily and Kathy became lovers during this time, though, as Patricia noted, their "relationship did not stop Bill Harris from sleeping with each of them from time to time and upon occasion with both of them at the same time. However, that did not last for very long and they sent him packing." Patricia was such a thoughtful participant in the discussions of female empowerment that the group designated her their scribe, and she occupied her days writing a manifesto of female liberation, sexual and otherwise.

The gentle musings about sexual rapture did not distract any comrades from their main goal of revolutionary violence. Indeed, the relative quiet of their new bases in San Francisco gave them a chance to regroup and restock, thanks to the remaining funds from the bank robberies. Chastened by the experience in Carmichael, the group decided to go back to bombing.

FEMINIST BOMB-MAKING

The feminist revolt among the comrades broadened the women's ambitions in the summer of 1975. Emily Harris, Wendy Yoshimura, Josephine Soliah, and Patricia Hearst wanted more than just equal and respectful treatment from their male colleagues; the women sought to establish their bona fides by demonstrating they could build bombs that were as deadly and effective as the explosives crafted by the men. Kathy Soliah and Jim Kilgore had already established themselves as prolific bombers, but the other women wanted to prove themselves, too. As usual, though, there was a complication, and also as usual it involved the combustible personality of Bill Harris.

Still unable or unwilling to find a real job, Bill spent his summer in San Francisco reading *The Anarchist Cookbook,* a famous underground best seller at the time. First published in 1971, the "cookbook" contained specific instructions for how to make bombs from scratch, as well as guides to other counterculture obsessions, like home brewing LSD and "phreaking" (making free phone calls). For all his bluster about revolutionary violence, Harris had a lot to learn, because he had never, up to that point, made a bomb. So Bill spent weeks studying and experimenting with this how-to guide and in short order fancied himself an expert.

The arrival in San Francisco of the former SLA soldiers gave Kilgore and Kathy Soliah new allies and options for their bombing campaign. The SLA team also gave their work a sinister new twist. Mindful of

Donald DeFreeze's contempt for late-night attacks on empty offices, Bill Harris wanted to bring a new level of menace to the bombing campaign. His goal wasn't just to damage property. He said he wanted to kill cops.

The new priority was sealed in a late-night meeting at the Geneva Avenue apartment with Bill and Emily Harris, Kathy, Steve, and Josephine Soliah, Jim Kilgore, Wendy Yoshimura, and Patricia Hearst. As Harris explained, in his twisted logic, killing cops would prompt a general police crackdown that would lead to a mass uprising against the whole corrupt American system. Later, Mike Bortin breezed into the conversation and, as usual, managed to annoy Bill Harris. "If you want to kill some pigs, why don't you just walk up to a pig in a uniform, put a gun to his head, and pull the trigger. It's no big deal."

Harris, the ex-marine, could not resist rising to Bortin's bait. "We've got to plan it. If you're such a hotshot, you come up with a plan, and we'll do it."

Bortin took up the challenge, and a few days later he took Kilgore and Patricia on a drive through San Francisco. He showed them a coffee shop called Miz Brown's, which Bortin described as a police hangout. If the comrades wanted cops to kill, Bortin said, this was a good place to start. Patricia sketched a map of the area, while Bortin went inside to check it out. The next day, though, Harris and the rest of the comrades rejected the idea. It was too risky. Bortin stormed off, complaining that all this group of revolutionaries ever did was have meetings. Bortin wanted action.

Kilgore's fanaticism was more refined—he didn't advocate machine-gun massacres—but he too was frustrated. Unlike Bill, Kilgore had actually done bombings, and he bridled at Bill's presumption of command. Kilgore proposed what he regarded as a simpler way to accommodate everyone's priorities. Why not bomb police stations? Kilgore said they should start with the Mission and Sunset (also called Taraval) outposts of the SFPD. This time, the comrades agreed: they decided to aim for a pair of simultaneous bombings on August 7. As Patricia remembered, the building of the bombs generated team spirit. "The components were easily purchased in separate stores. We all got busy devising and testing them in the Geneva Avenue safehouse. A new esprit de corps set in among us. At last we had something 'revolutionary' to do. A common purpose served to bind us together and to let us forget, at least for a while, our personal conflicts."

The comrades took to the task with enthusiasm. In particular, the female comrades made a special effort to show that they could contribute as much to the action as the men. Wendy Yoshimura, who had learned to make bombs with her former flame Willie Brandt, took the role of lead designer. She envisioned simple pipe bombs, which would consist of gunpowder stuffed inside two-inch pipes, attached by wires to a battery for a spark and an alarm clock as a timing device. Kilgore and Kathy Soliah spent a day driving around Marin County buying the components.

True to form, Bill Harris had a different approach. Based on his study of the cookbook, he decided he could improve on Yoshimura's design. Bill and Emily worked on his idea at Geneva Avenue—which paralyzed Patricia with fear of an accident—and then experimented with detonation devices on some old mattresses in the tiny backyard. Bill's test resulted in a small, smoldering fire and a summons to the fire department. According to Patricia, Emily told the firefighters that local kids smoking cigarettes had started the little blaze.

In the end, the comrades decided to go with Bill's design, but they settled on two all-women teams to conduct the actions themselves. Late on the night of August 7, Patricia and Jo Soliah took one bomb to the police station in the Mission, and Yoshimura and Kathy Soliah drove to the one in Sunset. Radical groups had previously attacked the Mission police station, so the cops there had prepared for the assaults by reinforcing the doors and windows and constructing a low wall around the main building. Under the circumstances, the comrades decided that the best options were symbolic attacks, in the form of bombs placed under police cars in front of the stations.

Both plans fizzled. Jo and Patricia set their timer for twenty minutes, and Jo slipped the bomb under a police car in front of the Mission station. Kathy and Wendy couldn't find an appropriate target in Sunset. The Mission bomb failed to detonate. It is a sign of the chaos in San Francisco at the time that the discovery of a bomb, albeit a dud, underneath a police car received scant mention in the news.

Determined to improve on these dismal results—and to wrest the bomb-making duties from Bill Harris—Yoshimura, Kilgore, Patricia, and Steve Soliah went up to Sonoma County to improve their skills and demonstrate the results. A day of explosions in the wilderness boosted their hopes for better results next time. Confident they had solved their design problems, they returned to San Francisco and set their sights on a new target—the police station in Emeryville, a small city nestled between Oakland and Berkeley.

The bomb was meant as an after-the-fact punishment for a police shooting of a fourteen-year-old boy in Emeryville in November 1973. Emily Harris and Steve Soliah placed their bomb under a police car on August 13, 1975. This time the comrades succeeded. The car was demolished, though there were no injuries. The next day, they returned to writing communiqués, claiming responsibility in the name of the New World Liberation Front, which served as a kind of place-holder name for all bombers in the Bay Area. "The explosion at the Emeryville Station of Fascist Pig Representation is a warning to the rabid dogs who murder our children in cold blood," the message began. Still, the comrades couldn't resist a nod to their former celebrity. They concluded their message with the words associated with the heyday of the SLA: "Death to the fascist insect that preys upon the life of the people."

Back on track, the comrades decided to pick up the pace and raise the stakes. It was time, they believed, to stop destroying cars and move on to destroying lives. Emily Harris led an expedition to the sheriff's office in Marin County, which was located in Frank Lloyd Wright's famous civic center. The plan was to stagger the explosion of two bombs, the first to blow up a police car and the second to attack the officers who came to investigate the first blast. At the same time, the group decided to launch another attack, this time against the Los

Angeles Police Department, whose officers had killed their six comrades fifteen months earlier. Jim Kilgore and Kathy Soliah went south to pick a target in Los Angeles, and Bill Harris, trying again to put his newly acquired skills to work, built an especially large pipe bomb for the occasion.

On August 20, Patricia and Steve Soliah drove across the Golden Gate Bridge to place the first bomb by the door to the Marin County complex. (Jo Soliah put the second bomb under a car in the parking lot.) The idea was for the officers to rush to the bombed car and then be immolated by an explosion next to the front door. Steve set the timer, and he and Patricia left the scene. Both bombs exploded, but in the wrong order—that is, first by the door, then under the car. No one was hurt.

As for the bomb in Los Angeles, Bill Harris built it out of three-inch pipe (instead of the standard two inches), and he filled the pipes with more than a hundred three-quarter-inch concrete nails. The nails would enhance the damage wrought by the bomb by spreading deadly shrapnel over a broad area. (Kathy Soliah bought the blasting caps to set the bomb off.)

Placing the Los Angeles bomb turned into a fiasco, however. Jim Kilgore and Bill Harris originally thought they would set off the bomb at a Veterans of Foreign Wars convention in a hotel downtown. But when they arrived with the bomb in an attaché case, they drew the attention of the guards, and the two comrades decided to leave. They began cruising the city with Kathy Soliah, whose relationship with Kilgore had hit the rocks. Indeed, as Patricia heard the story, Kathy made a disparaging remark about Kilgore's sexual prowess, and he punched her. Harris, who was driving, took Kathy's side, and Bill and Jim started brawling.

In their desire to do something with the bomb rather than simply return with it to San Francisco, Bill, Jim, and Kathy found a police car sitting outside an International House of Pancakes on Sunset Boulevard in Hollywood. The car was parked next to the restaurant's plate glass window, which had diners eating on the other side. Kilgore quickly rigged the bomb to explode when the police car drove away. It was the comrades' biggest bomb to date, and it would surely have killed the two officers in the car as well as several diners at the restaurant. But the bomb fizzled. It would have detonated if two screws had touched, but they remained separated by one-sixteenth of an inch. Kilgore, Kathy, and Bill made the long drive back to San Francisco—each refusing to speak to the others.

Again it seemed like the worst of times for the comrades. Most of their bombs had failed, and the ones that went off—in Emeryville and Marin—caused little damage and no injuries. Poisonous all-night arguments raged. Bombings and bank robberies were taking them nowhere. Their leases were expiring, and they needed new places to live. The Harrises moved into an apartment at 288 Precita, in a largely Hispanic area. Patricia and Steve Soliah took the opportunity to look for a place for themselves. One night, driving around with Jim Kilgore, they got lost in the city's twisting streets, and they stumbled on a little one-way street called Morse. At 625 Morse, they found a "For Rent" sign and wound up booking the place.

The apartment turned out to be the best living arrangement of Patricia's year and a half on the run. Wendy Yoshimura often stayed with them, but Patricia and Steve wound up living as a more-or-less-normal couple. Steve worked as a housepainter, and his earnings plus the remainder of their shares of the bank robbery money meant that they could live decently, without resorting to horse meat. More important, though, Steve treated Patricia like an independent adult, giving her space to develop her own interests, especially in feminism. In this way, the contrast to the old Steve in her life—Weed—could scarcely be clearer. Patricia complained that Steve Weed lectured her and made them spend time only with his friends; Steve Soliah listened to Patricia, and they spent time with both of their friends. (Admittedly, being a fugitive limited Patricia's social circle.) Both Steves offered Patricia escapes—from her parents, with Weed, and from the Harrises, with Soliah. Despite the privations of life on the run, Patricia was happy in the shabby little apartment on Morse Street.

During this period, in the late summer of 1975, Patricia could finally see for herself that she was accepted as a full-fledged comrade. In addition to the bombing campaign, the group wanted to keep up their marksmanship skills. Ever since DeFreeze first handed Patricia a shotgun, it was clear that she had a great facility with weapons— long and short guns. Her father's training on hunting trips had taken root. Thanks also to long hours studying gun manuals, Patricia easily learned to use the motley collection of weapons that the comrades possessed. Not surprisingly, Bill Harris fancied himself the crack shot in the group, but during that summer Patricia was chosen over Bill to lead refresher courses in the remote town of Guerneville, in Sonoma County. Patricia never gained back much of the weight she had lost, but with a gun in her hand, she projected a strength that transcended her petite size. She showed a softer side too. When Emily Harris said she was going to put her aged cat to sleep, Patricia and Steve adopted the animal, and she joined the family on Morse Street.

Patricia also worked on the manifesto for the women comrades' study group. Her work expressed the spirit of sexual liberation that was ascendant in the counterculture. "We began to destroy the attitudes that had made us think that we *had* to be monogamous—fear and passivity, the false sense of security, jealousy and power trips," she wrote. Mostly, though, Patricia expressed herself in the dialect of pidgin Marxism that made all SLA communiqués, whether written by Nancy Ling, Angela Atwood, or DeFreeze himself, nearly unreadable. "As oppressed people, women have a real stake in revolution (much more than white men) and can, therefore, better identify with and understand Third World and class struggles," Patricia wrote. "Although the pig media characterizes the Women's Movement as white and middle-class, and, to a great extent it is, we consider Feminist Revolution to be a unifying platform for all races and classes of women."

During this period, Patricia was romantically fulfilled, too. She shared a passion for the outdoors with Steve Soliah and spent long days on hiking trips through the rugged California countryside. As in Sacramento, they talked about moving together to the backcountry of Oregon. In light of their peculiar circumstances—chiefly Patricia's status as the most wanted woman in the nation—the couple had some strange experiences together. For example, at one point during this summer, Patricia contracted an ugly case of poison oak. On the evening of August 12, she and Steve presented themselves at the emergency room of San Francisco General Hospital. Patricia said her name was Amy Andrews and gave her address as 419 Masonic, which is nonexistent. An intern named Rod Perry saw that "Amy's" face was so swollen that her eyes were nearly shut. He later recalled she was vague about how she might have contracted the ailment. Over the course of about a two-hour visit, the couple behaved in a relaxed manner, like any other patient and escort, and Dr. Perry sent "Amy" on her way with a prescription ointment.

At around the same time, another hiking trip ended oddly. Patricia and Steve took a drive about twenty miles south from San Francisco to Gray Whale Cove, near the town of Pacifica. They scrambled down one of the picturesque cliffs, enjoyed an afternoon on the secluded beach, and then began to clamber back up to the parking lot. When they were about halfway up, they heard shouting from three deputy sheriffs. The lawmen asserted that the climb was too dangerous for a young woman to make on her own, so they threw a rope down for her to tie around her waist. Steve vaulted quickly up the steep incline and tried to talk the officers out of helping. His wife was fully capable of climbing up on her own. But the deputies wouldn't hear of it, and they insisted on throwing the rope. Patricia dutifully wrapped it around her waist, and the deputies hoisted her to the top. There, Steve gave her a big hug and whispered the name "Ann Silva" in her ear. (Soliah had a fake driver's license in the name of "Victor Silva.") None of the deputies recognized Patricia in her usual curly wig, and they sent the couple off with some good-natured advice about being careful.

Between bombings, the comrades achieved something close to a normal life. They were regulars at the drive-in movies that still dotted the region, and on one occasion the Harrises prevailed upon Patricia to go to an anti–Vietnam War documentary. Bill made a spectacle of himself in the theater, bellowing encouragement to the Vietcong forces on the screen. "Eat lead, pigs!" he shouted at the sight of American troops. Even in disguise, Patricia felt compelled to sink down in her seat, out of both embarrassment and fear of being discovered. Still, she had the fortitude to refuse the Harrises' perverse summons to another film.

"Ask me to do anything, ask me to rob a bank with you," Patricia told them. "But don't ask me to go to a movie theater and get arrested watching *Citizen Kane*."

FREEZE!

Walter Scott was a figure of mystery even to his own family. By 1975, the known facts about him were remarkably scarce. He was nine years older than his brother, Jack. He graduated from the University of Pennsylvania. He served in the Marine Corps during the Vietnam War. After that, the trail of his life drifted into the unknown. He told his parents that he served as an assassin for the military in Cambodia. Later he said he worked in electronic surveillance for the National Security Agency. More recently, Walter recounted, he was employed as a soldier of fortune, renting out his services as a mercenary in Libya, among other places. On his occasional visits with his parents, the only fact they discerned with some certainty was that Walter suffered from the Scott family curse of alcoholism. John and Lydia Scott loved their older son, but they knew not to trust him. One of the first things Jack's parents told Patricia during their cross-country trip was that Walter could never know of this secret mission. The Scotts were right to worry, because when Walter did find out that his brother had harbored Patricia and her comrades, the eccentric older brother provided the FBI with the first useful lead in the case.

The FBI's investigation of the kidnapping of Patricia Hearst—code-named HERNAP—was a long-running humiliation for the nation's premier law enforcement agency. For more than a year, the attorneys general, first William Saxbe and then Edward Levi, and the FBI director, Clarence Kelley, were grilled in almost every public appearance about the lack of progress. In response, they offered vague professions of confidence that the bureau would live up to its slogan—that the FBI always gets its man. In truth, neither the top brass nor the agents in the field had any idea when or whether they would catch Patricia and her comrades.

The bureau was simultaneously burdened with too many clues and too few. At one level, the comrades presented investigators with an abundance of evidence, starting with the communiqués. The FBI also learned the names of the SLA members in short order, right after the fire in the Concord house, in January 1974. The comrades then left behind fingerprints, handwriting, purchases, weapons, and ordnance in their former hideouts in Daly City and San Francisco. In messages scrawled on the walls of the Golden Gate apartment, the comrades taunted "Master" Bates, the FBI's lead agent on the case. Of course, most of the comrades died in the shoot-out on Fifty-Fourth Street, but that, too, presented investigators with another trove of evidence. Bill and Emily Harris, along with Patricia herself, had been on tens of thousands of wanted posters around the country for more than a year. How hard could they be to find?

Very hard, it turned out. For one thing, purported "sightings" of Patty Hearst turned into a national joke. She appeared to be every-where and nowhere, and agents spent a great deal of time checking out random, and incorrect, identifications of her. The people who actually did see Patricia and the comrades generally didn't know it or didn't choose to report it. For example, the woman who stopped Patricia and Bill Harris on the street in Sacramento apparently never called in a tip. Still, the bigger problem for the FBI was not lack of information but lack of trust.

The simple fact was that anyone who did know anything about the location of Patricia and her comrades refused to talk to the FBI. At the time, the bureau's reputation was still in the free fall that began after the death of J. Edgar Hoover in 1972. It was only after Hoover died that the full extent of the bureau's abuse of civil liberties became widely known. Senator Frank Church held a series of hearings during the mid-1970s that brought to wide public attention such outrages as the FBI's harassment of Martin Luther King. The people the bureau needed most in this investigation—that is, associates of the Harrises or the other comrades—were precisely the group most likely to be appalled by the FBI.

The situation was so toxic for the FBI that Charlie Bates went public with his distress about the situation. He gave a series of interviews begging for cooperation from the public. In the middle of the search for Patricia, Bates told the journalist Shana Alexander that the FBI had interviewed perhaps five thousand people in the Bay Area alone without finding a single clue to the whereabouts of the nation's most famous fugitive. "One thing bothers me terribly," Bates said. "In the sixteen-to-twenty-five age group, *everybody's* anti–law enforcement. Nobody will even speak to you! I dunno why . . . the reasons are more complicated than the problem. You knock and say, 'FBI, can I talk to you, please?' And they shout, 'Bug off!' and slam the door."

This was an apt description of the course of the Hearst investigation—until Walter Scott walked into the police station in Scranton, Pennsylvania.

It's not clear how Walter found out that his brother harbored Patricia and the other comrades. The most likely explanation is that Jack told him. Jack was an inveterate talker who liked to place himself at the center of stories. Despite Walter's obvious shortcomings, Jack wanted to impress his older brother. Against his better judgment, and under the influence of a few drinks, Jack probably could not resist sharing what was, after all, a pretty remarkable tale. It's also not clear what prompted Walter Scott to go to the authorities. The most likely explanation is that he was offended that Jack exposed their parents to the risk of arrest; of course, by informing on Jack, Walter also increased the risk to their parents. To be sure, determining the reasons underlying Walter's behavior was always a difficult undertaking. In any event, at around two in the morning on January 31, 1975, Walter Scott staggered into the Scranton police station with a story to tell.

Walter was drunk, and his story was confused. But the gist was believable enough for the local cops to summon the FBI, and agents wound up conducting an all-night debriefing as Walter sobered up. Walter did not have an exact address for the farm, but he provided enough information for the agents to locate the place within a couple of days. (Crucially, Walter also passed the FBI the names of Jay Weiner and Phil Shinnick, who had visited the Pennsylvania and New York farms.) The bureau's team staked out the farm in South Canaan and determined that it was abandoned. The agents then ordered in their forensic team, which identified the fingerprints of Bill Harris (on a piece of broken glass) and Wendy Yoshimura (on a piece of newspaper). They flew the dogs trained on Patricia's scent—the ones that were waiting to inspect the carnage on Fifty-Fourth Street in Los Angeles—to Pennsylvania. The dogs responded to the bed where Patricia had slept.

In light of these confirmations, the FBI turned the full force of its attention on the comrades' hosts on the Pennsylvania farm, Jack and Micki Scott.

By the time the FBI confirmed the Scotts' role in harboring Patricia, it was the spring of 1975. Jack had dropped off Patricia in Las Vegas in the fall of 1974. That was the last he had seen or heard of her. He had no current knowledge of her whereabouts. Jack and Micki Scott had no desire to help the FBI. They were classic examples of the problem that Charlie Bates was referring to in his complaint about public hostility to the FBI. Still, their refusal to give information presented them with a thorny legal dilemma.

When Jack and Micki learned that the FBI was looking for them, they went underground, but only briefly. They had no real hope of disappearing, and besides Jack loved the attention. And there was another reason a low profile was impossible. By this point, the Scotts were living with Bill Walton, who was one of the most famous athletes in the country and, at six feet eleven inches, with red hair, one of the most conspicuous. The two Scotts and Walton wanted to avoid testifying and also to avoid jail, which would not be an easy trick to pull off. So Jack called Michael Kennedy, a San Francisco lawyer known for representing counterculture figures.

To this point, the Hearst kidnapping had from a legal perspective been a one-sided affair. Cops, agents, and prosecutors had massed their efforts for months, albeit with little to show for it. But the Hearst case would also come to include squadrons of defense lawyers, who confronted a series of knotty and in many ways unprecedented legal challenges. Like their adversaries in the government, the defense lawyers would reflect both the best and the worst of their profession and meet with greatly varying degrees of success.

Kennedy told the Scotts to meet him at his Victorian house in Pacific Heights. Kennedy told Jack that his situation was precarious. If he went into the grand jury, he could take the Fifth and refuse to answer questions, but if he took the Fifth, the prosecutors would surely give him immunity, which would mean that he'd have no choice but to testify. If Jack refused to testify after receiving immunity, he could be found in civil contempt and jailed immediately. That, obviously, was a scenario to avoid.

Kennedy suggested one option to allow Jack to avoid both testimony and incarceration. If Scott could persuade prosecutors that he would *never* testify, even if he were jailed, that changed the legal calculus. An individual who refuses to testify under all circumstances is subject only to a charge of *criminal* contempt, not *civil* contempt. Civil contempt is automatic for a defiant witness; he goes immediately to jail, to coerce him to change his mind and provide evidence. In order to charge Scott with criminal contempt, on the other hand, the prosecutors would have to take the case to a grand jury, secure an indictment, then try to convict Scott in a public trial before a jury. That process takes months, and prosecutors try to avoid it. So Scott had to persuade prosecutors that a subpoena was futile—that he would never testify under any circumstances.

Kennedy suggested a press conference where Scott would announce his plan to defy a subpoena—forever. This was risky, because a public challenge from a witness like Scott might embolden prosecutors to call his bluff. But Scott loved making a public spectacle of himself. Kennedy summoned the media to Glide Memorial Church on April 9. (The location was no accident; Glide often served as a counterculture sanctuary, and the previous year it had been part of the coalition of groups in the People in Need food giveaway program.)

Jack and Micki Scott, alongside their lawyer and the towering presence of Bill Walton, announced at Glide that they would never cooperate with the investigation into Hearst's kidnapping. "The events of Watergate, and the U.S. involvement in Vietnam, the present economic situation and the almost daily revelations about the FBI and CIA have convinced us that we are confronted with a morally bankrupt government," Jack Scott told the overflow crowd. "We believe a position of total non-collaboration with this government is our moral responsibility. We have no intention of talking with the FBI now or in the future." (Scott also invited a photographer from *People* magazine to shoot Jack, Micki, and Bill on their morning jog.)

Remarkably, the gambit worked. Prosecutors did not force the issue with Jack. As Kennedy hoped, the U.S. attorney preferred to avoid getting caught up in a quasi-political sideshow. Also, investigators could tell that even if they did succeed in questioning the Scotts, they could not deliver what the FBI most wanted—Patricia's current location.

That still left the question of Bill Walton, who had not yet been served a grand jury subpoena. Just to be on the safe side, Kennedy thought Walton should stay out of sight for the week or so after the press conference. But lying low, as it were, presented a challenge for someone of Walton's fame (and height). Kennedy invited Walton to stay in his town house, which meant sleeping diagonally on a king-sized water bed in his guest bedroom. Walton ate only vegetarian food, which was a challenge for Kennedy and his wife to obtain in that more primitive culinary era. In the end, the prosecutors also left Walton alone, and he returned to the Portland Trail Blazers in time for the new season.

No one followed the Scott sideshow with greater interest than Randy Hearst. By this time, the crowds of reporters had long since disappeared from the house in Hillsborough. So, in a way, did the man of the house. The relationship between Randy and Catherine, fragile to begin with, broke under the strain of Patricia's kidnapping. Randy had long maintained discreet side relationships in San Francisco, and he began spending more nights in the city in 1975. He changed in other ways as well. As part of his efforts to free his daughter, Randy had talked with prisoners, radicals, journalists, lawyers—anyone who might have a clue about Patricia. Randy had always been more open-minded than his wife, and these explorations widened the gulf between them. With his old-fashioned diction and British tweeds, to say nothing of his famous name, Randy might appear to have been the last person who could penetrate the counterculture. But his curiosity, his decency, and above all his love for his daughter created allies for him in worlds very different from his own.

Immediately after the press conference at Glide, Randy tried to make contact with the Scotts. Randy reached David Weir, a reporter for *Rolling Stone,* who put him in touch with Michael Kennedy. When Jack heard of Randy's interest, he was intrigued but wary. In their time together, Patricia had denounced her mother to Jack the same way she did to everyone else. But she spoke with some warmth about her father. Despite his sour parting with Patricia and the Harrises, Jack wanted them to survive, and he understood how difficult the situation must be for Randy. Still, Jack worried that Randy's approach might be some kind of FBI trap, to elicit admissions that might allow the bureau to make a case against him for harboring a fugitive. Reassured through Weir that Randy would keep their conversation to himself, Jack agreed to the meeting. He was never one to shy away from an adventure, even if this one was just dinner.

Both Jack and Micki Scott went to the dinner at the Kennedys' town house, and it was an awkward occasion at first, but sports and alcohol lubricated the proceedings. Jack was well practiced in using jock talk to disarm his political opposites, and Randy played along in a self-deprecating way. "I was a pretty fair athlete myself," Randy said. "Look where it got me." They were several hours, and many vodkas, into the conversation when Randy turned to his real subject of interest. How was Patricia?

Jack decided to answer carefully. If the woman he had last seen six months ago was in fact Randy's daughter, he said, she was in good health.

What about her being pregnant?

She wasn't pregnant when he last saw her, Jack said. Her padded belly had been a disguise.

Randy pursued his real worry. Are you sure Cinque—Donald DeFreeze—didn't get her pregnant? Jack was sure. She was not pregnant from Cinque or anyone else.

Randy wanted to know if Patricia had really joined the SLA.

Both Jack and Micki said Patricia appeared totally committed to the revolution. This was not a matter of fakery or compulsion. She had joined the SLA.

"It doesn't surprise me," her father said. "She's always been a rebel."

Because Patricia had made common cause with her former captors, Randy was convinced he had to get her out of the country. "I can't let her go to trial," he said. "She is going to call the judge a fucking pig and then she'll be in jail for the rest of her life."

Randy offered the Scotts money to spirit Patricia out of the country—maybe to Cuba. It didn't matter where, Randy said, just to a place where she could not be retrieved and then put on trial by the U.S. government.

Jack demurred. He wasn't going to take that kind of risk for Patricia, and besides he did not even know where she was, much less how to get her to Cuba.

Now morose, and well into his cups, Randy moved on to another subject—his bitterness toward his wife. Specifically, Randy brooded about Catherine's decision to accept reappointment to the Board of Regents of the University of California in March of the previous year. He believed Patricia might have been released if Catherine hadn't provoked the kidnappers by accepting Governor Reagan's offer. "I'm going to get rid of [Catherine] as soon as this thing is over," Randy said.

Walter Scott's tips to the FBI only began with the link to his brother. Walter also gave agents the name of Jay Weiner, the college student and newspaper intern who had been treated to a bizarre birthday party at the farm the previous July.

Weiner always somehow suspected that the authorities would come calling, but he did not expect to be sandwiched between two unmarked vehicles on March 11, 1975. By this point, Weiner had transferred to a different college, but he happened to be visiting Oberlin when FBI agents slammed on their brakes in front of and behind him that evening. They asked to speak with him in a way that, in his naïveté, gave him the impression that he had no choice. They went to the office of the campus security director to talk.

Weiner laid out the story of his relationship with Jack Scott. He had been Jack's protégé, and this relationship earned him the invitation to the farm. There he had immediately recognized Patricia Hearst as one of the residents, but at first he only knew the other three as Alan (who was Bill Harris), Judy (Emily Harris), and Joan (Wendy Yoshimura). Weiner told the agents that Jack later confirmed the true identities of the three others, and Scott had told Weiner a detail about Yoshimura. She was Willie Brandt's girlfriend.

Tying Yoshimura to Brandt gave the FBI an important lead. At the time, Brandt was still locked up for his role in the Revolutionary Army bombings in Berkeley. In response to the information from Weiner, the FBI checked the log of Brandt's visitors in prison and found the names Josephine and Kathy Soliah. Someone at the FBI then figured out that Kathy gave the emotional eulogy for the SLA dead in Ho Chi Minh Park, in Berkeley, on June 2, 1974. The agents realized—at last—that the Soliah family was crucial to unraveling the whole story.

The failure to pursue the Soliahs earlier might have been the biggest mistake of the entire FBI investigation. In her speech at the park, Kathy Soliah had hardly been subtle about her ties to Hearst's kidnappers. She went on at length about her close relationship with Angela Atwood, and Soliah had said, "I am a soldier of the SLA"—which was a breathtakingly obvious clue. After Kathy's speech, agents did track her down to interview her, but she told them nothing of substance. There the matter ended, for more than a year. There was no followup, no investigation of Soliah's other contacts, no examination of her phone records or history. She was just another name crossed off a list.

But the agents now recognized that they had to learn more about Kathy and her sister Josephine. They knew Kathy had done more than just give a speech. Kathy had gone to visit the convicted bomber who was the boyfriend of the woman who had sheltered Patricia and the Harrises. A cursory check revealed no trace of Kathy or Jo or indeed of their brother Steve—no addresses or phone numbers. (Of course, their invisibility to the police had been very much intentional on their part.) This time, though, the agents showed some more initiative and paid a call on their father, Martin Soliah, the schoolteacher and coach, in his home in the desert town of Palmdale, California.

The agents first showed up on August 18, and they began a delicate cultivation of the father, who had his own complex emotions about his children. Martin was an old-school conservative, a World War II vet, who had watched with bewilderment, as many parents did in this era, as his children slipped away from him. He was appalled that Kathy was living in sin with Jim Kilgore. Martin knew just enough about his kids' politics to know that he abhorred them. But at the same time, he loved his three children, and the notion of any FBI inquiry about them was deeply upsetting to him and his wife, Elsie. Still, he cooperated with the agents, largely because they told him that Kathy was in no trouble; they just wanted to talk to her about some other people.

Martin and Elsie had very little information about Kathy, Steve, and Jo. (They had two other children who had no political involvements.) The Soliahs had an address in San Francisco for Kathy, 625 Post Street, which turned out to be a mail drop. They had a phone number in Oakland for Steve, but the person who answered said Steve didn't live there anymore. The agents kept returning to the Soliahs' home in Palmdale, asking more questions about their kids. On August 23, the Soliah parents received a letter from their daughter Jo. It was reassuring in its informality—it mentioned that Jo and Kathy had been on a camping trip—but it still listed the mail drop as the return address.

On their next visit to Palmdale, the agents made a specific request. They wanted Martin to travel to San Francisco to try to track down his children, to ask them to speak to the FBI. Martin revered the FBI, and he convinced himself that Kathy and Jo might be in danger. Talking to the FBI, he thought, would make them safer. So on August 28, Martin and an agent flew to San Francisco. Martin left a note at the drop box and went to a hotel to wait for a return call. A day passed. But then, late on Friday, August 29, Jo called him at the hotel. He invited her to dinner and told her to bring her brother and sister along.

The FBI paid for Martin's trip and booked his hotel room, which was adjacent to one for a bureau agent. It also gave Martin an invented cover story to explain why he traveled to San Francisco, but he didn't use it. Instead, Martin told Kathy, Steve, and Jo the truth. He said the FBI was looking for them, he was worried about them, and he wanted to know what the hell was going on. Each of the three younger Soliahs reacted in characteristic fashion to the news that Martin had been in touch with the FBI. As Martin later recounted to the journalist Paul Avery, Josephine began to cry. Steve said nothing. And Kathy exploded in anger. "Daddy! How could you do such a thing?" she said. "Don't you know you can't trust the FBI?!"

The Soliah family dinner turned into a seven-hour marathon of eating, talking, and wandering around the city. The kids assured their father that they were not involved in anything illegal, but they were vague about their lives. Most important, none of his three children would give their father an address or phone number where they could be reached. Steve said that he painted houses for a living. Martin urged them to return to their childhood home in the desert, to get away from the craziness of the Bay Area. Martin alternated between fear for his children, anger at them, and guilt about his own role—"the Judas goat," he called himself.

When they finally parted, Martin reported back to the agent who had accompanied him. The agent was disappointed. The Soliah kids provided few leads for the agent to follow up. The agent anticipated, correctly as it turned out, that they would never return to the mail drop at 625 Post Street, where their father had found Josephine. The number of agents assigned to the HERNAP investigation had dropped from dozens to about ten. They had to select their targets with care. So they decided to go with their last remaining lead—about Steve's career as a housepainter.

Shortly after Labor Day, Monte Hall, who ran the investigation day to day, was riding home on the BART rapid transit system, making notes for the next day's assignments. He came across the name of a nurse who had been tangentially connected to some of the people in the case. He assigned agents to follow her the next day, and they noticed that she had a new car. Through the dealer, the agents found that she had paid for the car by check, and Hall called in a favor at the bank to have them track down the check. It was a third-party check—from a small painting company.

Calling around, the agents found that the company was working a big job in Pacifica, south of San Francisco. The company had been painting a two-hundred-unit apartment complex since July. Early on the morning of September 15, a pair of agents approached the manager of the complex. They showed him a portfolio of photographs and asked if any of them resembled anyone on the painting crew. The manager identified Michael Bortin as a painter he knew as "John Henderson," who led the group of "hippie painters." He recognized a photograph of Steve Soliah, too. The manager went on to say that the crew included two young women, which was somewhat unusual for the time. In fact, the women were due to arrive any minute. The agents asked the manager to keep their visit to himself, and then they stepped out of sight to see who arrived. Kathy and Josephine Soliah showed up to start their day's work.

The agents kept up their surveillance throughout the workday. At about 5:30 p.m., Kathy and Jo left the painting site and drove into San Francisco, followed at a discreet distance by three FBI cars. The Soliah sisters got out at 625 Morse, the small one-way street close to the border with Daly City. The agents broke off their surveillance for the night—there was no way to remain unobtrusive on the narrow street—but they picked up again in the morning. There they saw Steve Soliah leave 625 Morse and travel about three and a half miles to 288 Precita, where he picked up Kathy and Jo Soliah. They drove to the painting site in the morning and returned to the same two houses at the end of the day on September 16.

The information was tantalizing but confusing for the FBI agents. The three Soliah siblings seemed to have ties to both apartments, but it was not clear who lived where, and it was equally uncertain if any of the other fugitives were located at either location. Most important, there was no sign of the biggest prize of all—Patricia Hearst.

—————

September had brought the comrades a measure of calm. Patricia's breach with the Harrises appeared to be final. The move to 625 Morse with Steve Soliah and Wendy Yoshimura allowed her to cut off contact with Bill and Emily. The Harrises never even visited the Morse Street apartment, and by the standards of San Francisco geography, the Harris home at 288 Precita was far away. They were never going to run into each other by accident, which was fine with Patricia. She spent most of her days curled up in the apartment with Wendy, reading and talking about feminism and working on the manifesto for the women's group. When Steve came home from his painting job, they would enjoy quiet dinners and then head off to bed. If the routine had continued, it might have started to resemble her household with Steve Weed, which was so violently disrupted nineteen months earlier.

Bill Harris, in contrast, had turned Precita into a veritable bomb factory.

There were dozens of two-inch pipes (several drilled to house bomb wires), blasting caps, six alarm clocks, and a copy of *The Anarchist Cookbook,* with a hand-typed insert headed, "Explosives Can Be Divided into Two Main Categories." There were two shotguns, two carbines, half a dozen pistols, and thousands of rounds of ammunition. There was a library of radical literature, which included two copies of George Jackson's *Blood in My Eye* and one copy of *Patty/Tania,* an instant book about the kidnapping. The living situation on Precita was less stable than the one on Morse, too. The place was home base for Bill and Emily, but Jim Kilgore as well as Kathy and Josephine Soliah and even Michael Bortin sometimes stayed there as well.

The agents decided to focus on Kathy Soliah, who seemed to be the key link among the players. She also appeared to be living on Precita Avenue, which was located in a busier part of the city and thus easier for the agents to watch without being detected. On the morning of September 17, the agents set up round-the-clock surveillance at 288 Precita, to monitor the comings and goings. In the morning, Kathy and Jo Soliah left for the painting job. At 10:30 a.m., the agents saw two new faces, which looked like Bill and Emily Harris. They were both short and fit, and they were heading out for a jog. After they returned, the man brought a load of dirty clothes to the local Laundromat.

At this point, Larry Lawler, the lead FBI agent on the assignment, decided to take a chance. Pretending to be a customer at the Laundromat, he walked directly by the man—the possible Bill Harris. The man didn't make eye contact with the agent, but Lawler noticed something about the man, who was still wearing shorts from his run. He had a large scar on his left knee. Lawler radioed that information back to the San Francisco field office, where Bill Harris's medical records from the Marine Corps were on file. A quick check revealed that Harris had had surgery on that knee. It looked as if the FBI, at last, had its man.

That night, the agents reconvened at the field office to decide how to proceed. There was no question in their minds that they had Bill Harris, and almost certainly Emily too, but the question was how to arrest them. In light of the bombing offensive under way, the agents were worried that the apartment at 288 Precita might be booby-trapped. If the Harrises were approached there, the agents worried that they might try to go out in a ball of fire. So the agents bet that Bill and Emily would go jogging again. They would be a lot less dangerous in T-shirts and shorts.

By 9:00 a.m. on September 18, Lawler had assigned fifteen agents to follow and arrest Bill and Emily Harris. At 10:02, Kathy and Jo left for work. At 12:50, Bill and Emily emerged in jogging clothes. Agents in the area kept each other posted on the progress of their run. At 1:12 p.m., an agent reported that the couple was heading for home. As the man and woman walked toward their front door, a car pulled up behind them, and four agents got out. "We're the FBI," Lawler said.

Bill stood still and said nothing. Emily bolted, but she was grabbed after about ten steps. "You motherfucking sons of bitches," she said. "You sons of bitches." A specialist inked Harris's fingers while he was still in the backseat of the car and did a rough comparison to a known sample. He had no doubt. "We got him," he said.

It was a good day for the FBI, but not a great one. They had been hoping to find Patricia, their real target, but no one else was inside the apartment at 288 Precita. Charlie Bates scheduled a press conference for 3:00 p.m., but he knew that the reporters would focus less on the capture of Bill and Emily Harris and more on the continuing failure to find Patricia Hearst.

Almost as an afterthought, two pairs of agents went to check out the apartment at 625 Morse. A San Francisco police officer and an FBI agent guarded the front door, while SFPD inspector Tim Casey and FBI special agent Tom Padden went around the back. Through a back door on a porch, Padden could see two women sitting at the kitchen table. Wendy Yoshimura was showing Patricia a letter she was writing to Willie Brandt, her long-ago boyfriend, who was still in prison. Wendy rose to get a glass of water from the sink. When Patricia stood up, she heard a crash—Padden breaking down the door—and the words "Freeze! FBI!" The comrades had warned her about this moment, when the FBI would come to kill her as they did Cinque and all the others. She thought about racing to the bedroom, where a shotgun was stashed against the wall. Maybe she could make a last stand the way the six others did.

In the kitchen, Padden yelled at Patricia and pointed his gun at Yoshimura. "Freeze! I'll blow her head off!"

Patricia froze. There would be no shoot-out.

Padden's eyes widened as he realized who was standing before him. "Are you Patty Hearst?" he asked her.

"Yes," she said.

Wendy identified herself as well.

"Are there any explosives in here?" Padden asked. Patricia said no.

Any weapons? Yes, Patricia said. Two carbines in the closet. Wendy said there was a shotgun in the bedroom, too. Both also had pistols in their purses.

Patricia had a request of the agent. She had wet her pants. Could she change before they left? Padden agreed.

Patricia Hearst left the apartment, and her weapons, behind.

PART FIVE

22

"THERE WILL BE A REVOLUTION IN AMERIKKKA AND WE'LL BE HELPING TO MAKE IT"

Patricia's crew-necked striped shirt and corduroy pants hung loosely as she stepped into the FBI car for the trip downtown. By the time they reached the federal building, on Golden Gate Avenue, the word of her arrest had leaked, and the street was swarming with reporters and photographers. The journalists, and their audience, had a single question: Who was Patricia Hearst at this point—kidnapping victim or defiant outlaw?

As Patricia stepped out of the car, she had an initial answer for the crowd. Turning away from the FBI agents, she flashed a big smile for the photographers. She raised her clenched right fist as high as her handcuffs would allow and brandished the revolutionary salute.

Inside the building, Patricia was rushed through the initial stages of the criminal process. She was fingerprinted. A booking photograph was taken. She was presented a form advising her of her right to remain silent, and she refused to sign the form acknowledging that she had seen it. Foremost in her mind was the admonition she had received long ago from Cinque: "Never sign anything, never say anything, when the pigs've got you." In nearby cells, Patricia heard Bill and Emily Harris talking about their own arrests, which had taken place about an hour before Patricia's.

Terence Hallinan, a lawyer, and her young cousin Will Hearst appeared, and they escorted her to a courtroom, where she was arraigned on charges of armed bank robbery and use of a firearm in a felony, in connection with the robbery of the Hibernia Bank the previous April. During the brief proceeding, Patricia removed her chewing gum and stuck it under the table. Hallinan entered a plea of not guilty on her behalf.

After court, Patricia was hustled back into a car for a trip to the San Mateo county jail, about twenty miles south of San Francisco, where she would spend the night. She arrived shortly before 8:00 p.m. She was approached by a deputy clerk named Stephanie Marsh, who began another booking procedure.

"Name?" Marsh asked.

"Patricia Campbell Hearst," she said.

"Do you use any other names?"

"Tania," Patricia said.

"Any other names?"

"None that I would tell you," Patricia replied.

Patricia then gave her address as 625 Morse Street, in San Francisco, where she had been arrested.

Height and weight?

Five feet two inches, one hundred pounds.

"Occupation?" Marsh asked.

Patricia looked at Marsh blankly.

"What is your occupation?"

"Urban guerrilla," Patricia said.

Randy Hearst had been hoping for his daughter's safe deliverance, but he had also been planning for it. Well before the calendar turned to 1975, he knew that she would be facing arrest if she surfaced, so Randy set about lining up a lawyer. His choice reflected both the new world that Randy had come to explore during the past year and a half and, in a broader sense, a father's belief in what his daughter had become.

So he did more than hire a lawyer. He invested in a clan, the Hallinan family, whose fame in San Francisco rivaled that of the Hearsts, albeit on an opposite ideological pole. The patriarch, who still pre-

sided, was Vincent Hallinan, who had made his name decades earlier, when leftist unions controlled the San Francisco docks. Vincent
defended Harry Bridges, the famed leader of the longshoremen, in a
perjury case that landed Hallinan himself in jail for six months for
contempt of court. Disbarred and then reinstated as a lawyer, Hallinan ran for president of the United States on the Progressive Party
ticket in 1952 and finished third nationally. The next generation of
Hallinans—six sons—proved just as combative. Their mother, Vivian
Hallinan, a veteran activist herself, wrote a family memoir called *My
Wild Irish Rogues*.

Vincent Hallinan had been a frequent target of the *Examiner*'s edi-
torial page over the years, but Randy Hearst, in characteristic fashion,
took a liking to the old man during Patricia's time on the lam. Given
her political transformation, Randy thought she would have a rapport
with the radical hero. Vincent was nearly eighty years old in 1975 and
rarely appeared in court anymore, so Randy also hired his son Patrick,
who was a skilled trial lawyer, to represent Patricia.

When word reached Hillsborough that Patricia had been arrested,
a Hearst representative called the Hallinan law offices. The family
had long owned a tumbledown Victorian mansion at 819 Eddy Street,
where they ran their law practice and rented space to other left-leaning
lawyers. The message from the Hearsts was that Patrick Hallinan
needed to get over to the federal courthouse right away for Patricia's
arraignment. As it happened, though, Patrick was at the moment at
an assignation with a woman friend in Napa Valley. His brother Terence Hallinan was in the office, and he volunteered to handle the job.
Lawyers pinch-hit for each other all the time, especially for routine
appearances, but when Terence arrived at the courthouse, he said nothing to Patricia about her father's decision to hire his brother. Terence
told her that *he* would be her lawyer—her only lawyer—and he began
interviewing her and learning her story. In other words, Terence stole
the biggest client in America from his brother.

Given Vincent Hallinan's notoriety, and the family's contentious
nature, the six boys learned to use their fists to defend themselves.

None of the brothers fought as much as Patricia's new lawyer, Terence, who earned the nickname Kayo, as in knockout. By the time he graduated from law school, in 1964, he had been arrested in so many brawls and in so many antiwar and civil rights demonstrations that the California bar refused to admit him. The family took Kayo's fight all the way to the California Supreme Court to win his law license.

Kayo's aggressiveness extended to the courtroom as well as the ring, and he decided his first fight would be to get Patricia released on bail.

After Steve Soliah heard on the radio that the Harrises had been arrested, he rushed to 625 Morse Street to warn Patricia that she might be next. He was too late, however, and he was collared as well. On the day of the arrests, the FBI neglected to secure the site in Pacifica where the other comrades were painting. As a result, Kathy and Josephine Soliah, as well as Jim Kilgore and Michael Bortin, heard the news and took off for new lives underground. It would be decades until some of them were recognized again in public.

In the meantime, Steve also needed a lawyer, and Emily Toback, a sometime girlfriend of Steve's, showed up at 819 Eddy Street, which was what counterculture figures often did when they were looking for legal help. A young lawyer named Steve Imhoff happened to be in his office, and Toback entreated him to meet with Soliah.

At first, Imhoff thought he might have an easy case. The only charge against Soliah at this point was that he had harbored a fugitive— Patricia. A quick investigation revealed that it was Jim Kilgore, not Steve, who signed the rental papers for the apartment at 625 Morse Street. How could Soliah be charged with harboring if he didn't even rent the apartment where Patricia stayed?

Imhoff's optimism vanished, however, when he returned to Eddy Street to meet with Kayo and Vincent Hallinan, his counterparts on Patricia's defense. The Hallinans had been debriefing their client, and they had learned about the bank robbery in Carmichael, where Myrna Opsahl had been killed. Patricia told her lawyers that Steve had served as a lookout and she herself had driven a switch car. This could be a capital case against both of them.

The early results of the FBI investigation held even worse news. Agents had executed a search warrant for the apartment at 625 Morse and discovered a wrapper full of cash in the refrigerator. The stack of currency included a single dollar that was a bait bill passed by the tellers to the bank robbers at the Carmichael bank. This bill potentially tied the residents of the apartment—that is, Steve, Patricia, and Wendy Yoshimura—to the robbery and, ultimately, to Myrna Opsahl's death. The bait bill alone wasn't enough for a conviction, but it still raised the legal stakes a great deal higher. (Steve and Patricia kept the cash in the fridge because Morse was located in a high-crime neighborhood and they were worried about break-ins.)

In the meantime, though, Patricia had made a request of her lawyers. She wanted to be able to communicate with Steve, her lover and roommate. Kayo and Imhoff agreed to serve as intermediaries. Kayo would sit with Patricia while she wrote a letter and then deliver it to Imhoff, who would pass the letter to Steve and wait while he read it and wrote one back of his own. With this system, the lawyers would maintain possession of the letters so the government authorities would never have a chance to read them. (Patricia's letters never came to light until I recently obtained copies.)

Patricia's letters from jail offer a unique window into her state of mind. During her year and a half with the SLA, Patricia read any number of communiqués, from her first message ("Mom, Dad, I'm okay") to the eulogy tape ("Cujo was the gentlest, most beautiful man"). Patricia later claimed that these messages did not represent her own feelings, that they were written for her, and that she was compelled to read them—all debatable claims. But her letters to Steve provide unmediated, and undisputed, insight into Patricia's character in the days after her arrest. The letters offer, in her looping private girls' school handwriting, the real Patricia.

Her first letter was sent on Sunday, September 21, three days after her arrest. It began, with original spellings intact,

> My dearest Brother,
>
> I'm so pissed off about what happened, it was so unreal. . . . I am glad that others are safe, though. It looks like we're in for some heavy shit and long trials. The past problems (interpersonal relationships & political differences) are only more intensified now, as you can imagine. We are in seperate cells, in isolation (they tell us that the sisters in here might try to stab us—that's such shit cuz we only feel support from them). I hope you're being treated OK. . . . I want to see you so bad, baby. When I saw you in the Federal Bld. you looked like shit, but I guess I didn't look so happy either. Only twice have I felt like crying 1. when I saw Wendy handcuffed to a leather belt that strapped under her crotch, & with her legs shackeled 2. when I saw you handcuffed & surrounded by pigs. I was just really glad that I got to come up & kiss & be close to you for those few seconds.

Patricia then told Steve about some of her visitors. On her first night in captivity, in San Mateo, her parents and sisters Vicki and Anne appeared in the visitors' area, bearing a bouquet of roses from the reporters waiting outside. She was not allowed to keep the flowers in her cell. The visit with her family was brief and awkward, but at least the Hearsts could see for themselves that Patricia had survived, albeit with a thin frame and short hair, home dyed red.

A more welcome visitor, the next day, was Trish Tobin, Patricia's longtime best friend, whose father was president of the Hibernia Bank. In keeping with jail policy, the visit was surreptitiously tape-recorded. Patricia began by asking Trish to bring Steve some books. She asked her to take *Rubyfruit Jungle,* by Rita Mae Brown, and "another book called 'The Bluest Eye.' He'd like that, too."

Tobin trod lightly, trying to get a sense of Patricia's state of mind.

She said her family would not be making any public statements on her behalf until she was released on bail. "I would just as soon give it myself in person," Patricia said, "and it will be a revolutionary feminist perspective totally. I'll just tell you, like, my politics are real different from, uh, way back when."

"Right," said Tobin.

"Obviously," Patricia said, laughing. "And so this creates all kinds of problems for me in terms of a defense." Still, Patricia said, she was very happy with her lawyer. "He's good," she said. "Like, I really trust him politically and personally and he, like, I can tell him just about anything I want and he's cool." She said Hallinan was working to get her out on bail, but "I don't want to have the bail thing where I'm a prisoner in my parents' home."

In her first letter to Steve, Patricia recounted her meeting with Trish—"I have seen Trish Tobin & she is so together!"—and said she'd be sending him the two books. Patricia then added, "I love you so much—you know that. I'm glad for all the times my eyes went darting around all over your face, and for the times I told you I love you. As long as we stay strong and free those pigs can't fuck with us. They can imprison our bodies but not our hearts & minds. I look forward to a lifetime of struggle—there will be a revolution in Amerikkka and we'll be helping to make it. Myself, in particular, helping to make a Feminist Revolution—meaning, of course, a revolution that will be both socialist & cultural at the same time."

The question of bail generally turns on two questions: Is the defendant a danger to the community? Is the defendant a flight risk? By both standards, Patricia Hearst was a poor candidate to be released on bail. On danger, she had been found in an apartment with several weapons, and she was closely tied to the Harrises, who had bomb-making equipment to go with their own large stash of guns. On flight, Patricia had been a fugitive for a year and a half, when she evaded one of the most extensive manhunts in the history of the country. In light of those considerations, no judge was going to release her.

Still, lawyers make difficult arguments all the time, and it was certainly appropriate for Kayo Hallinan to request bail for Patricia. He could say that in light of her fame and notoriety she was unlikely to flee and under the circumstances she wasn't a threat to anyone either. If Hallinan had limited himself to those arguments, he probably would have lost, but it would have been a reasonable effort. Five days after Patricia was arrested, Hallinan did make those arguments, but he went a great deal further.

To go with his motion for bail, Hallinan submitted a sworn affidavit by Patricia, which amounted to her first public statement about what happened to her during her year and a half with the SLA. She began by describing how she was kidnapped on February 4, 1974, and then placed blindfolded in a closet. For ten days, she said, "she was unable to eat . . . and unable to dispose of her body wastes." She was given liquids to drink, and "when the blindfold was removed, she felt as if she were on some LSD trip; everything was out of proportion, big and distorted." She received constant threats on her life. "After a month of this sort of treatment, she was in such condition that she could stand for only sixty seconds or so, and would then fall to the ground. . . . During all this time, she was in a constant state of fear and terror and expected at any minute to be murdered by her captors." Patricia went on,

Under the pressure of these threats, deprivation of liberty, isolation, and terror, she felt her mind clouding, and everything appeared so distorted and terrible, that she believed and feared that she was losing her sanity and unless soon freed would become insane. Meanwhile, after each meal, she felt an aggravation of this condition, and all sorts of fantastic shapes and images kept coming and going before her eyes, so that the faces of the kidnappers and jailers appeared to her as weird and horrible masks; that she was able to properly comprehend only the reiterated statement, "We are going to kill you." Finally under these pressures, her mind became more confused and distorted. Further weird concepts and images appeared before her, and she was unable to distinguish what was real and what was imaginary.

In short, according to Patricia's affidavit, she had spent more than a year in a drug-induced haze. Her recollection of everything that happened between the bank robbery (April 15, 1974) and her arrest (September 18, 1975) was "as though she lived in a fog, in which she was confused, still unable to distinguish between actuality and fantasy, and in a perpetual state of terror." Patricia swore to the truth of the affidavit "under penalty of perjury" on Monday, September 22, the day after her first letter to Steve Soliah.

It's unclear where Kayo Hallinan received the information he included in the affidavit. He certainly spoke to Wendy Yoshimura in addition to his first few conversations with Patricia. But he might simply have invented some of the assertions in the affidavit. Whatever its origins, the affidavit turned out to be a gigantic legal miscalculation. Most important, Patricia's reported statements were untrue. For starters, the SLA comrades did not use the kinds of drugs that would produce the effects described. Moreover, during the period described in the affidavit, Patricia had read communiqués, shot up Mel's Sporting Goods, helped rob two banks in Sacramento, written out detailed plans to rob others, and traveled back and forth across the country. Patricia later claimed that she was coerced into taking these actions, but she never said she was in the nearly catatonic state described. Further, the affidavit was terrible legal strategy. A sworn affidavit locked Patricia into a version of her captivity before her attorneys had a chance to investigate. It was beyond reckless for Kayo Hallinan to commit Patricia to a kind of insanity defense before he knew much about what his client had done for a year and a half on the run. And the affidavit was prepared in service of a motion for bail that was des-

tined to fail, which it did. Hallinan had taken a huge risk for less than
no payoff for his client.

The disastrous nature of the Hallinan affidavit would reveal itself
over time. For the moment, though, Patricia was most interested in
communicating with Steve Soliah, and she passed her next letter to
him after Steve's own bid for bail had been turned down.

In Patricia's first jailhouse chat with Trish Tobin, she had told her
friend that she was willing to put up Steve Soliah's bail money. She
had not known at the time that the authorities recorded these conversations, and prosecutors used Patricia's statement to deny Steve bail.
(Defendants are supposed to put up their own bail money, which they
will lose if they fail to appear.) In her next letter to Steve, Patricia
apologized profusely for hurting his chances for bail.

"My dearest Brother," Patricia wrote, "I heard all the gory details
about your bail reduction hearing. I feel like shit! When I talked to
Trish (she was one of my first visitors) I didn't know that they were
taping in the visiting room. . . . I found out about ½ hr. later & now
my love & concern (I'm sure *that* didn't come across) for you turns up
as the reason for why your bail shouldn't be reduced to a so-called 'reasonable' amount. I'm so sorry I want to die. . . . Oh, baby, I love you
so much & I want to be with you so fuckin' *bad*." Patricia had learned
to express herself in the coarse rhetoric of the SLA. Looking ahead to
Steve's further efforts to reduce his bail, she wrote of the prosecutors,
"So hopefully, lover, they have indeed cut their own throats & will
soon be swimming in their own blood."

At this moment, about a week after she was arrested, Patricia began
to recognize the enormity of her legal problems and the degree of
her loneliness. "I'm going to have to go through a whole lot of shit
soon . . . a whole lot. But I'm doing my best to keep it together. I am
smoking like crazy, though, but there's nothing else to do," she went

on. "Oh shit—why am I talking like this . . . to you of all people!!!!
It's the isolation from you & Wendy who I love so much & that old
SLA guilt trip that we all struggled so hard against to defeat & destroy
in ourselves. Power to the people, and Power to those who have the
strength to keep their minds free of dogma—to those who do not
allow themselves to become slaves to something 'greater than themselves' (i.e. guilt tripping & martyrdom) Love you! I guess I can't say
it enough it isn't the same as showing it, anyway!"

In light of Patricia's description of her mental state in her affidavit, the judge in her case, Oliver Carter, ordered an independent
psychiatric evaluation, to see if she was fit to stand trial. (This would
be the first of many such examinations Patricia would endure.) In her
next letter to Steve, she described the experience. "Hello my beautiful lover," she wrote. "I'm really going through hell with all these
'shrinks' comming to see me. Every interview & psych. exam means
that I'm totally drained by the end. After each session I feel like shit!"
Patricia complained that she wasn't able to exercise in jail. "But I tell
you, babe . . . you won't be feeling a weak, flabby lady in your beautiful arms. And believe me that's where I want to be. I miss you on me
& around me & inside me, and all the pigs in the world can't take the
way I feel away from me. You know . . . one thing being in here has
done for me is to make me not afraid of having a child . . . the way I
love you I can't put into words. The thought that we may never see
each other again or embrace each other . . . I can't stand thinking that.
I'm doing everything I can so that we can be together again—on our
terms . . . you know what I mean? I love you—Pearl."

In sum, during her first week in captivity, Patricia offered a public clenched-fist salute; gave her occupation as "urban guerrilla";
described her "revolutionary feminist" perspective; and employed the
rhetoric and sentiments of the SLA in her letters to Steve Soliah. All
these actions pointed to the conclusion that Patricia had become and
remained a willing and enthusiastic revolutionary. In her conversations with her parents, she was cordial but guarded. Still, Randy and

Catherine had to recognize that their daughter was, at least for the moment, a very different young woman from the one they thought they knew.

Patricia's parents saw, too, that her criminal case was off to a rocky start. Kayo had blundered forward with the affidavit to no discernible gain and considerable potential risk. Following that debacle, Kayo had no apparent plan for how to proceed. Even though Kayo had only been Patricia's lawyer for about a week, it looked to Randy that he was in over his head. Randy also had second thoughts about giving Patricia an ideological soul mate for a lawyer; perhaps, given her continuing and destructive embrace of the SLA, that was the worst thing he could have done. For her part, Catherine Hearst found Kayo's politics distasteful and his persona vulgar. So Randy started searching for a replacement, and he began with the most famous lawyer in the world.

23

"YOUR EVER-LOVING MOMMA AND POPPA CARE ABOUT THE TRUTH"

The calendar insisted that autumn had begun in Mississippi, but on this September morning in 1975 it was still summer inside the women's jail in Jackson. Five years earlier, Carolee Biddy had reported her six-year-old stepdaughter missing, setting off a search that involved hundreds of people and transfixed the state. In time, though, Biddy told police she had found the girl dead and then, fearing she would be blamed, hidden her body by a reservoir. After she led the police to her body, she was convicted of manslaughter and sentenced to twenty years. She had exhausted her appeals and was now looking for a legal miracle. So she summoned the lawyer who was sitting in front of her, wedged into a damp three-piece suit—F. Lee Bailey.

He was only a little more than forty years old at that time, but he had been famous for a decade. Indeed, his name had evolved from proper noun to noun. To be an "F. Lee Bailey" was to be a swashbuckling gun for hire, a skilled legal mercenary, capable of freeing the accused from the most dire predicaments. His cases had titles rather than names—the Boston Strangler, the Fugitive. (Biddy was "the Mississippi housewife.") Unlike famous defense attorneys of the past (Clarence Darrow, for instance), Bailey had no identifiable politics; his only causes were his clients and himself. He had become a "brand," before that term came into wide use. Bailey pioneered the use of the polygraph as an investigative tool and later turned that interest into a syndicated television program, *Lie Detector,* starring himself. By 1975, he had nurtured his growing legend by writing a pair of memoirs, both best sellers, which he promoted on all the major talk shows.

But there were darker aspects to Bailey's reputation. He won a lot of cases, especially early in his career. (He saved Albert DeSalvo, the Boston Strangler, from execution in Massachusetts, and he persuaded the Supreme Court to grant Sam Sheppard, the Cleveland doctor who became known as the Fugitive, a new trial, which he won.) But Bailey lost a lot too. (Biddy's conviction and sentence were upheld.) Bailey's hunger for money dwarfed even his lust for fame and led him into business dealings that might charitably be described as questionable. In 1973, Bailey was indicted for mail fraud with a former client, Glenn W. Turner, who was the creator of the Dare to Be Great self-improvement scheme. The case against Bailey was eventually dropped, but his financial travails continued. A pilot during the Korean War, Bailey bought a troubled helicopter company that, under his leadership, remained troubled. Then there was the matter of temperament. As a group, trial lawyers abound with self-confidence, but Bailey's belligerent arrogance transcended the norm. In part, this was due to his prodigious thirst for alcohol, which he did little to hide. (The first line of his second memoir is "Heavy trials make me thirsty.") Bailey's business partners, and wives, came and went.

On that morning in 1975, Bailey was in the visiting room talking with Carolee Biddy when the warden interrupted them. "A fellow who said his name is Randolph Hearst is on the phone for you," he said. Bailey took the call, listened to Randy ask him to represent his daughter, and took off for the local airfield.

Bailey flew his own planes from client to client around the country, so he jumped into his two-engine Aero Commander for the long trip from Mississippi to San Francisco. In a cab from the airport that night, Bailey asked the driver what he thought about the Patty Hearst case. "Everybody knows they will bring in some expensive hotshot to get her off," the driver said. "Like F. Lee Bailey."

The cab deposited Bailey at the high-rise in Nob Hill where Randy and Catherine had moved after finally selling the house in Hillsborough.

Randy Hearst had a clear sense of the magnitude of Patricia's legal problems. She was under indictment in San Francisco federal court for the robbery of the Hibernia Bank, but that was just the beginning of her potential exposure. There was also her machine-gun spree at Mel's Sporting Goods and the kidnapping of Tom Matthews. But even that was not the worst of it. In their first late-night conference, Randy confided to Bailey that his biggest worry for his daughter involved the robbery of the Crocker National Bank, where Myrna Opsahl was killed.

At the moment, the evidence against Patricia and the other comrades was weaker on Carmichael, compared with Hibernia and Mel's. The presence of the bait bill in her refrigerator on Morse Street was troubling but on its own was not enough for prosecution. The government did not yet have a witness who could identify who did what in the Carmichael robbery. But Patricia had admitted to Kayo that she and the other comrades robbed the bank where Opsahl was killed. Opsahl's death exposed all of them, including Patricia, who only drove the getaway car, to a potential capital case—that is, to a death sentence. Randy told Bailey that whatever he did as Patricia's lawyer, he had to keep her potential liability for Carmichael at the center of his thoughts. Bailey agreed.

The following day, Friday, September 26, 1975, Bailey traveled to the San Mateo county jail for his first meeting with his new client. (In Patricia's strangely unworldly way, she had never heard of the famous lawyer.) Bailey, in typical fashion, did more talking than listening. He told Patricia that he required complete control of her defense. Neither she, nor her parents, could tell him what to do. Bowled over, as most people were, by Bailey's self-confidence, Patricia just nodded meekly. One of Bailey's diktats took effect immediately. There would be no more passing of letters between Patricia and Steve. Indeed, Bailey wanted no contact at all between his client and those people who were part of her life as a revolutionary. Henceforth, her visitors would be limited to family and friends like Trish Tobin, who belonged to her pre-SLA life.

For his next trick, Bailey would try to work his blustering magic on the prosecutor.

Jim Browning, the U.S. attorney in San Francisco, was going through a divorce at the time of Patricia's arrest, and his personal life was in some disarray. A meticulous dresser, Browning liked to keep his shoes well shined, but he couldn't keep up with the task in his new bachelor life. So Browning switched to patent leather, which Bailey noticed when they met for the first time.

"Where'd you get the fag shoes?" Bailey asked. In public and private, macho posturing was always part of his rhetorical arsenal.

Notwithstanding Bailey's pugnacious opening, the meeting between prosecutor and defense lawyer was cordial. Browning invited Bailey to watch the surveillance tape of the Hibernia Bank robbery. "Patty looks like she is behaving very purposefully and voluntarily, with a lot of verve," Browning said. The prosecutor half expected Bailey to make some kind of overture for a plea bargain. Given the unusual circumstances surrounding Patricia's participation in the bank robbery, Browning might have agreed to dispose of the case if Patricia had agreed to plead guilty to a lesser charge. But Bailey made no move in that direction. Rather, he said Browning should dismiss the case against Patricia altogether. If he did, Bailey promised, Patricia would agree to testify against all the remaining SLA members.

In a way, each man's position made sense. Browning saw the Hibernia case as a simple one: Patricia, with a handful of others, committed an armed robbery, as the photographs from the security camera made clear. Federal prosecutors indict, try, and convict bank robbers. At the same time, there was some justice in Bailey's argument that Patricia's culpability, if any, was considerably less than that of the people who kidnapped her. Why should Patricia Hearst face a jury before Bill or Emily Harris did? (Bill and Emily were indicted in state court for Patricia's kidnapping, but their trial was months off; the Harrises were never charged in connection with the Hibernia robbery because of lack of evidence; they did not appear in the security camera photographs.)

In any event, Browning was never going to dismiss the charges outright. For starters, he believed that Patricia was guilty—that she made a knowing and voluntary decision to participate in the robbery. Her behavior after her arrest reinforced Browning's confidence. His ego played a part, too. Few prosecutors would walk away from the chance to try such a celebrated defendant, particularly against the most famous defense lawyer in the country.

The political zeitgeist, as reflected by the Ford administration's Justice Department, also compelled the government to bring Patricia to trial. By that fall, the legacy of the 1960s had grown even more toxic; San Francisco was crazier than ever. When Patricia was arrested, there had already been fifty bombings in California alone in 1975. After-hours explosions at power plants, government offices, and corporate headquarters became so routine that they scarcely received any news coverage. And it wasn't just bombings. On September 5, 1975, two weeks before Patricia was arrested, Lynette "Squeaky" Fromme pointed a .45-caliber handgun at President Ford as he walked through a park to the state capitol in Sacramento. A member of Charles Manson's crime "family," Fromme was wrestled to the ground by a Secret Service agent before she could get off a shot.

Then, on September 22, just four days after Patricia was arrested, Sara Jane Moore came a great deal closer to killing the president. The matronly bookkeeper volunteered to become an FBI informant while working with Randy Hearst's food giveaway the previous year. Still obsessed with the Hearst case, she circulated among the activists she had met in the China Basin warehouse and then provided leads to the FBI. Moore purchased a .38-caliber Smith & Wesson revolver and waited for President Ford outside the St. Francis hotel, in the heart of downtown San Francisco. As Ford walked from the hotel to his limousine, Moore fired a shot that just missed the president's head. She tried to get off a second round, but a Vietnam veteran named Oliver Sipple knocked her down, potentially saving the president's life. (In the ensuing publicity, Sipple was outed as homosexual. He came to feel that this disclosure ruined his life, an illustration that San Francisco, in the mid-1970s, had yet to become a fully welcoming haven for gay people.)*

Patricia's saga was caught up in the backlash against the violence and disorder of the era. In the weeks after her kidnapping, in 1974, she was portrayed sympathetically, as the tragic victim of political zealots. But her voice in the communiqués and her role in the bank robbery transformed her into an outlaw. Saxbe, the attorney general at the time, spoke for many when he said he regarded her as a "common criminal." As she remained on the lam for month after month, sympathy for her withered. By 1975, she was no longer a symbol of wounded innocence but rather of wayward youth. Many people of her generation had disappeared from good homes and resurfaced in communes and cults. They had rebelled and blamed society for their troubles. Now society was blaming them. Patricia was just another privileged youngster who had turned her back on all that was wholesome about her country. She just happened to be kidnapped first.

Most top trial lawyers have lesser-known deputies. They handle the gritty details of courtroom work, make sure the right motions are filed and deadlines are met. They hold the hands of the clients (and their families) after the top man rushes through town on the way to another engagement. Bailey's surrogate was J. Albert Johnson, a life-

---

* Moore's motive for trying to kill the president was never clear. She served thirty-two years in prison before being released in 2007. Her current whereabouts are unknown.

long friend as well as an enduring colleague. For Patricia, Al Johnson became more than a lawyer; he became a confidant, mentor, and father figure.

Bailey and Johnson grew up, literally, on opposite sides of the train tracks in Waltham, Massachusetts. Johnson was raised by aunts and uncles in a sprawling and impoverished Irish Catholic family. To make a few cents, he would prowl the tracks with a burlap bag, collecting stray lumps of coal to sell. On these rounds, Johnson would sometimes look up at a big white house on a hill, where a boy stood silently in a Little Lord Fauntleroy suit. The rich boy was Francis Lee Bailey, whose father edited the local newspaper and whose mother ran nursery schools. Most exotically, for Al Johnson, Lee Bailey was a Protestant, among the first he had ever met. In winter, they both found their way to the frozen ponds, and they bonded over hockey.

Bailey went to Harvard for two years, dropped out to fly planes for the Marine Corps in Korea, then returned, without a college degree, to start Boston University School of Law. Johnson's career was more earthbound. He went to Northeastern, then worked his way through Boston College Law School as a state police officer. After Bailey graduated first in his class, he joined the law firm where Johnson was working but then struck out on his own. They started working together again on higher- and higher-profile cases. Together, in 1971, they won an acquittal in the court-martial of Captain Ernest Medina, who was charged for his role as the commanding officer of the unit that committed the My Lai massacre. (Bailey then hired Medina to be a supervisor in his helicopter factory in Michigan.)

Johnson was a first-rate lawyer in his own right, often trying cases by himself for high stakes. In September 1975, he gave the closing argument in a first-degree murder case in Dedham. At the time, most people in the Massachusetts legal community knew that Johnson's most celebrated role was as Bailey's second-in-command. So once the summation in the murder case was over, the judge took it as his duty to summon Johnson to the bench and report that he had just received a phone message from Lee Bailey, saying he had been hired to defend Patty Hearst and wanted Johnson to join him right away. Al did.

Bailey and Johnson played off each other. Bailey's face was set at a perpetual sneer. He regarded everyone, friend or foe, with a sort of icy disdain. He repelled intimacy and wore his finely cut suits, and their vests, like armor. Johnson, with his round face, made everyone a friend, even when he fought them in court. (In San Francisco, he became a drinking buddy of Monte Hall, the FBI agent who ran the day-to-day operations of the Hearst investigation.) Bailey viewed his clients as a means to an end—their exoneration and his glory. Johnson, in contrast, sometimes fell in love with his clients, especially with Patricia Hearst. In a tape-recorded visit to Patricia's cell, Catherine Hearst raved about Al Johnson. "Al is really crazy about you," she said. "He really likes you. He hates himself for being emotionally involved, you know."

After Steve Soliah was denied a bail reduction because of Patricia's comments in the jail visiting area, everyone knew that the government recorded the conversations there. Still, these tapes provide a vivid picture of Patricia's relationships as her life took a major turn. In a way, her time in jail before her trial mirrored her time in the closet in Daly City. In both circumstances, she was confined in a small physical space and exposed only to those who wanted to impart a specific understanding of the world. And in both situations, at the ages of just nineteen and twenty-one, respectively, Patricia's will bent to the wishes of her interlocutors. She responded to benevolence; it was the kindness of Willy Wolfe and Angela Atwood, far more than the bluster of Donald DeFreeze, that led Patricia to join the SLA. To put it another way, she responded rationally to her surroundings in Daly City, and she did the same in San Mateo.

This was not a matter of proselytizing by her family and friends. Mostly, they just showed Patricia a lot of love, and this was especially true of her mother. Before and during her time with the SLA, Patricia groused endlessly about her mother, and much of what Catherine heard on the communiqués was painful. But none of it dimmed her love for her daughter, which came through in her frequent visits to jail.

At one point, Catherine was complaining about some inaccurate news reports regarding Patricia's younger sister Anne. In her soft southern accent, Catherine said, "They don't care about the truth. Nobody does anymore. You have to learn that the thing in life is that nobody except for maybe your ever-loving Momma and Poppa care about the truth." Patricia absorbed this love and, in short order, returned it. This, too, was a rational choice, not least because the looming court case made clear that staying with Steve Soliah would lead to prison; the path of her parents would, they all hoped, bring her freedom. In the closet, she became a revolutionary; in the jail cell, she became a Hearst.

The conversation was mostly family chitchat. They talked a great deal about the many family dogs. (Dogs would be a recurring interest in Patricia's life.) There were occasional catty remarks about other Hearst relatives. Regarding one of Randy's brothers, Patricia asked, laughing, "What does Uncle Dave do, by the way?" Her father answered, "Oh, well. He doesn't do much, really." Another time, Patricia's younger sister Anne recalled making a faux pas on Randy's recent birthday. She bought their father a copy of *The Times We Had: Life with William Randolph Hearst,* by Marion Davies, who was the Chief's mistress. Anne recalled, "I thought, well, he'll never buy it himself, but maybe he'll just want to look through it, you know, and look at the pictures and stuff or something."

"Well, Mom and Dad both had a fit, right?" Patricia said.

"It was really disastrous," Anne replied.

There were glimpses, too, of 1970s culture in the conversations. Patricia told Anne, "I put on one of those mood rings, you know, that's supposed to change colors." She then let other prisoners and even some of the deputies try it on. "The deputy puts it on and it turns blue, and she takes it off and an inmate puts it on and it turns violet," Patricia said. "And then I put it on. It turns gray."

"How rude," Anne said.

"It means I've got very cold hands," Patricia said.

Another time, Patricia told her cousin Will that an instructor had come to the jail to teach the inmates how to do a new dance.

"What's the Hustle?" Will asked.

"It's this dance," Patricia answered.

There were glimpses, too, of the rarefied world in which Patricia's family and friends lived. To pass the time, Patricia taught herself to crochet, and she began making scarves and hats. "Maybe there's something I can take on my trip—a muffler or a hat or something," Trish Tobin said. Patricia asked about the vacation.

"I'm going skiing for about six weeks in January," Tobin said.

"Where are you going to be?" Patricia asked.

"Switzerland," Tobin said.

Such conversations were powerful advertisements for Patricia's former life. As she weighed her future, Patricia chose between a world where people went skiing in the Alps and one where they ate horse meat and slept in crawl spaces. As in Daly City, Patricia's transformation did not take long. In her first days in jail, she was writing to her lover that "there will be a revolution in Amerikkka and we'll be helping to make it." Less than a month later, she was asking her sister Anne for makeup: "I'll tell you what I want—liner, mascara, lip gloss."

Patricia and her family were venomous whenever Steven Weed's name came up. After the shoot-out and Patricia's last communiqué, with its paean to Willy Wolfe, Weed drifted out of the Hearsts' orbit for good. Ironically, at that time both Weed and Patricia set about doing the same thing—writing books that would exploit the notoriety of the kidnapping. The comrades' publishing initiative with Jack Scott came to naught, but Weed and a coauthor had just about completed a manuscript when Patricia was arrested. Her family, never fond of Weed in the first place, were appalled at what they regarded as a breach of family confidentiality and an attempt to profit from Patricia's misery. She soon joined in the insults of Steve Weed and also stopped mentioning Steve Soliah to Trish Tobin or anyone else. When Trish said that Weed was trying to get some of his property out of the apartment on Benvenue, Patricia responded, "Oh, wow. You know, it's going to take one hell of a surgeon to extract his head from his fucking ass, because that's where it is." After an excerpt of Weed's book ran in *McCall's* magazine, Patricia told her father, "It's horrible. You know it's like about half of it is totally lies, another quarter of it is just half-truths, and then the other quarter of it is just about him."

"Oh, boy. Yeah, I know," Randy said.

"Jerk," said Patricia.

Still, as Patricia rejoined her family and social class over the course of these conversations, her life with the SLA remained a looming, if unacknowledged, presence. There was the time, for example, when Catherine was telling her daughter about a duck-hunting trip that she and Randy had just taken to a rural burg north of Sacramento.

"Oh, Marysville is the worst town," Catherine said. "We were driving around to find a grocery store and we went around the block. And there were three stores selling water beds. Can you imagine, in Marysville?"

Patricia laughed.

"And there was a dog-grooming thing with a French poodle on the front parlor—really nice looking," Catherine went on. "And who in the world, up in Marysville, you kept thinking, would bring their dog in here to be groomed?"

"I'm sure people do, you know," Patricia said. "I'm not that surprised."

"But you would think farmers would have hunting dogs," Catherine said.

Patricia answered, "But I mean, it's not all like that, you know, like they have houses and regular people up there."

Patricia wasn't just complaining about her mother's snobbery, for she was actually more than familiar with the commercial life of little Marysville. Just a few months earlier, as Tania, she had cased the Bank of America branch there. Patricia could have informed her mother with certainty that Marysville had more than just farmers; indeed, according to Patricia's notes for her comrades, the bank alone had "7 employees, 5 women & 2 men, one young and nervous; manager is fat and Black."

24

MORE EXCITED THAN SCARED

J udge Carter, ladies and gentlemen," Browning began his opening statement. "The government's evidence will prove that the Hibernia Bank, the Sunset branch thereof, located at the corner of 22nd Avenue and Noriega Streets, in the City of San Francisco, was on April 15, 1974, at approximately 9:40 to 9:45 in the morning, held up by five persons who went inside the bank. The evidence will show that these five persons consisted of one male and four females, one of whom was the defendant Patricia Campbell Hearst."

It was February 4, 1976, coincidentally the second anniversary of Patricia's kidnapping. After a week of jury selection, the trial had begun. As a courtroom presence, Browning was anti-charismatic. His words sounded as if they came from an interoffice memo ("the Sunset branch thereof"). He mumbled. Still, there was method to his mildness. His message to the jury was that this was a simple case that required no special insight to resolve. He didn't need charisma; he had facts. Browning described the witnesses who would testify for the government—mostly the customers and employees of the bank. They all saw Patricia inside the bank, wielding her weapon. To Browning, that evidence was the heart of the case.

"The five individuals were the male Donald David DeFreeze, who later identified himself as Cinque," Browning said, "Camilla Hall, Patricia Soltysik, Nancy Ling Perry and the defendant Patricia Hearst." Browning said, "The evidence will show that the five entered almost as a group. The evidence suggests that Perry entered first, followed by Hearst, and then Hall and Soltysik and then DeFreeze at the rear." Browning left unspoken the haunting fact that all the comrades who had been inside the bank with Patricia had been dead for more than a year and a half.

Browning turned to the incident, a month after the bank robbery, at Mel's Sporting Goods. Browning added an incriminating new piece of evidence to the bizarre story of Patricia's fusillade to help Bill Harris escape his pursuers. "The evidence will show that these casings and fragments were fired from the same sawed-off M-1 semi-automatic .30-caliber carbine as was later recovered over a year later in the defendant's residence at 625 Morse Street, in the City of San Francisco," he said.

How would the government prove its case? Browning said much of the evidence would come from the words of the defendant herself. He said the government would introduce the communiqués in which Patricia boasted about her role in the Hibernia robbery. ("On April 15, my comrades and I expropriated $10,660.02 from the Sunset branch of the Hibernia bank," she had said. "Casualties could have been avoided had the persons involved cooperated with the people's forces and kept out of the way.") The government would also introduce the testimony of Tom Matthews, the high school baseball player whom Patricia and the Harrises kidnapped after she shot up Mel's. Matthews would recount how Patricia bragged about her involvement in the Hibernia job. Finally, Browning said, the government would show the jury the "Tania tapes"—the transcripts, often in Patricia's own hand, of the interviews for the aborted book project. (Bill Harris, ever the pack rat, had held on to the transcripts when he moved from Pennsylvania to Sacramento to San Francisco. The FBI seized them when he was arrested.)

Following his statement, Browning moved quickly through his first witnesses. The manager of the Sunset branch described the interior of the bank and his view of the robbery. An FBI agent explained the workings of the security camera and introduced the images, spliced together, of the events of April 15, 1974. Various customers, employees, and bystanders told the jury about the scene at the bank. Bailey cross-examined little, because he conceded that Patricia was inside the bank during the robbery. His defense was built around her state of mind, and on that issue the case quickly came to a critical crossroads.

The conventional wisdom in jury selection holds that the defense should avoid veterans of the armed forces, who are believed to be harsh and unforgiving. But Bailey surprised the prosecutors in the Hearst case by agreeing with alacrity to seat William Wright, a retired air force colonel, who had served in the Korean War. Bailey took a risk on Wright, betting that his fellow Korean vet's receptivity to the defense theory of the case would trump his inclination to support the government.

During the troubled Korean conflict, more than a thousand American service members were taken prisoner. While in captivity, some of the Americans made statements that were supportive of the Communists. Several pilots who had been shot down even made broadcasts on North Korean radio confessing that American forces had engaged in germ warfare, which was demonstrably untrue. A former newspaperman named Edward Hunter, who went to work for America's fledgling intelligence agencies, invented the name for the practice of coercive persuasion that produced these results: brainwashing.

The concept took hold more in the popular imagination than in the medical literature. The notion that an authoritarian government, or group, could exert mind control over even reluctant adversaries was a familiar trope of the Cold War. *The Manchurian Candidate,* a novel by Richard Condon, published in 1959, was a political thriller about a Korean War prisoner who is brainwashed into becoming an unwitting assassin for a Communist conspiracy. George Romney, the Michigan governor who was running for president in 1967, asserted that he was "brainwashed" by American military leaders about progress in the war in Vietnam. The term, a description more than a diagnosis, came to mean the process of forcing someone to believe something he or she didn't want to believe.

That was the basis of Bailey's defense—that the SLA used mind control techniques to force Patricia to become a bank robber against her will. Thus, she lacked the requisite criminal intent to be convicted for it. Bailey's first major undertaking, then, was to ask the judge to prevent the prosecution from introducing Patricia's statements before the jury. According to Bailey's theory, the communiqués, the statement to Tom Matthews, and the "Tania tapes" interviews were all involuntary on Patricia's part. She was compelled to make them—like a statement that had been coerced by a police officer who failed to give *Miranda* warnings. Because courts kept such statements from the jury, Bailey argued, the judge should keep Patricia's "involuntary" statements from the jury as well. On February 9, less than a week into the trial, Bailey persuaded Judge Carter to halt the government's presentation of its case to the jury and hold a hearing on whether Patricia's statements were voluntary. For that proceeding, Bailey called his first witness—Patricia Hearst herself.

The ceremonial courtroom of the San Francisco federal building was cavernous, with more than 250 seats, and all of them were occupied (as was an overflow room) when Patricia took the stand. The hearing, which was conducted outside the presence of the jury, was the first time she told her story in public since her kidnapping transfixed the country two years earlier. Her parents watched attentively, Catherine still wearing black.

Patricia remained painfully thin, but she was otherwise transformed from the woman who flashed her fist at the cameras on the day of her arrest, almost five months earlier. Al Johnson had taken over the task of choosing her makeup and wardrobe; Patricia now looked like a college student arriving for a job interview—conservative suit, modest heels, clear nail polish, neatly cropped hair. Her voice, though, remained the same as the one on the communiqués—a lockjaw monotone that always seemed, despite everything, kind of bored.

"For the record, Miss Hearst," Bailey began, in his gruff conversational manner, "you are the defendant in this case?"

"Yes," Patricia said.

Bailey led her through the statements that the government planned to introduce. He began with the communiqué after the bank robbery.

"Can you tell us who was talking first about the idea of making a tape?" Bailey asked.

"Cinque," Patricia said.

"What did he say, what did he want to accomplish?"

"He said a tape was going to be made about the bank robbery."

"Did he say for what purpose the tape was to be made?" Bailey went on.

"To say that I participated in it," Patricia replied.

The testimony might well have been accurate, but Patricia's deadpan style sapped it of much emotion. She did elaborate somewhat when she talked about her encounter, along with the Harrises, with young Tom Matthews.

"Now, I'm referring to your state of mind at the time you made these statements: What did you believe would have happened to you if you had not told Mr. Matthews what Bill Harris wanted you to tell him?"

"That I would have been killed," Patricia said, with her usual lack of affect.

"Can you tell me approximately how many times . . . that you had been told that a lack of cooperation would mean that you would be killed?"

"Hundreds of times," Patricia said.

Browning had a low-key style, but he did sometimes display a prosecutor's instinct for the jugular, as when he rose to cross-examine the defendant. His point was to show that Patricia acted voluntarily, and he did not limit himself to discussion of the Hibernia operation.

He showed Patricia the "Bakery" document, which was the SLA's step-by-step guide to committing bank robberies. She said she didn't recognize it. So he showed her another document.

"Let me direct your attention to a subsequent page, which appears to be a diagram," Browning said, "and at the top it's labeled 'B of A Marysville.' Do you recognize that handwriting?"

"I wrote it, it's my handwriting," Patricia said.

"Do you recall the circumstances under which you wrote that sentence?"

Bailey vaulted out of his chair to object. He said the testimony was beyond the scope of the hearing. The judge let Browning press on.

"Do you recall, Miss Hearst, when you wrote the sentence, 'Saw seven employees, five women, two men, one young and nervous. Manager is fat and black'?"

Bailey again sputtered a series of objections, arguing that Browning's questions related to matters outside the scope of the hearing. The real reason Bailey was objecting, though, was that Browning was pressing on the area of Patricia's greatest vulnerability. He was showing Patricia the report she provided to the other comrades after she cased the bank in Marysville. That document was part of the comrades' research that led to the robbery of the bank in Carmichael and the death of Myrna Opsahl. Bailey knew this line of questioning, if permitted, could lead his client to incriminate herself in a capital crime. He tried to get Judge Carter to cut off this line of questioning, saying, "You're forcing her to answer these questions which could expose her to further charges, and I will not permit her to do it." But Browning shot back, "Mr. Bailey has waived any privilege against self-incrimination by putting the defendant on the stand."

The judge let Browning proceed. "The issue in this case involves the subject of coercion," the judge said, "and there's a whole course of conduct here that has to be evaluated, not just one incident." Carter noted correctly that Browning's questions dealt precisely with the issue of whether Patricia was an independent actor.

Bailey had little choice but to take a most embarrassing step. "I will advise the defendant to invoke her constitutional rights," he said. "Miss Hearst, you are instructed to refuse to answer on the grounds that it might tend to incriminate you." The jury was out of the courtroom and sequestered from press coverage, so they were not around at that point to see Patricia take the Fifth. Still, this was a self-inflicted wound by the defense; a hearing intended to limit prosecution evidence wound up showing the world that Patricia still had plenty to hide.

Judge Carter then rejected Bailey's attempt to limit the prosecution's introduction of Patricia's statements. Oliver Carter was one of the lesser lights of the federal judiciary. When Harry Truman appointed him to the federal bench, in 1950, Carter was only thirty-nine years old. Over the years, the judge became best known in the legal community for his chronic inability to reach decisions in civil cases. And though he was only sixty-four at the time of Hearst's trial, Carter was sick with heart disease and weary of the job. (He dozed off on many an afternoon, which produced a mordant kind of consensus between the opposing lawyers. One day, Steele Langford, a deputy to Browning, whispered to Bailey that the judge had fallen asleep again. "What should we do?" Langford asked. "Let's wake him up if we need him," Bailey said.)

Still, Carter had ample reserves of common sense. He could tell when he was being played. Bailey was simply inventing reasons to keep incriminating evidence from the jury. "The Government has established that the statements made by the defendant after the happening of the bank robbery, whether by tape recording or by oral communication or by writing, were made voluntarily," Carter ruled. The decision was a rebuke to Bailey and a warning about how the judge would handle the rest of the trial.

It didn't take long for the government to finish the rest of its case. Anthony Shepard was the aspiring police officer who was working as a clerk at Mel's Sporting Goods. He testified about how he caught Bill Harris shoplifting, chased him out of the store, tackled him, and then applied a handcuff to one of Harris's wrists. At that point, Shepard explained, Patricia's machine-gun fire from across the street caused him to drop his hold on Harris and allow him to escape.

Browning asked Shepard what happened after the second burst of gunfire.

"He said, 'Hey, we better get out of here,'" Shepard answered.

Then?

"The last time I was looking up he was jumping over the center divider proceeding toward the van," Shepard said. He then explained that he ran for his life to escape Patricia's gunfire.

The star witness for the government was Tom Matthews, the preternaturally cool high school first baseman who seemed to regard his experience as a kidnap victim as a sort of lark. On May 16, 1974, following the shoot-out at Mel's, Emily Harris had come to Matthews's front door and asked to see his van, which had a "For Sale" sign in the window. After they drove a block or two, Patricia and Bill Harris had joined them and pulled a gun. Bill said the trio needed Matthews's car. Matthews testified that Bill said, "If I did not do anything stupid, they wouldn't hurt me. I said that was fine as long as I don't get shot."

Matthews was so spacey that he didn't recognize his famous kidnappers at first. Bill explained that the woman in the car was Patty Hearst—"'Tania,' and both of them smiled," Matthews said. He understood that he was being kidnapped at this point, albeit in unusually cheerful fashion. He went on to describe their surreal journey from store to store to find a hacksaw to remove the handcuff on Bill Harris's wrist. Matthews admitted on the stand that he kept a shard of the handcuff as a souvenir.

Tom and Patricia spent a long time chatting in the back of the van. Matthews described a very different Patricia from the demure woman sitting in court. At that moment in Los Angeles, she had been in full badass regalia, with a black wig, leather jacket, hiking boots, and (of all things) green plaid pants. In the van, she showed Matthews the M1 machine guns that were lying next to her and that she had just used to spray Mel's facade. What was more, she displayed her prowess with those weapons, removing a bullet from the chamber, placing it into the clip, and then putting the clip back into the weapon.

"Do you know why she did that?" Browning asked.

"No, I don't," said Matthews. Browning's implication was that Patricia was just showing off.

The two chatted in the van about the bank robbery, and she refuted everything her defense now wanted the jury to believe. "She said she was a willing participant," Matthews testified. She said, contrary to some news reports, that none of her comrades had pointed their guns at her during the robbery. As for the incident at Mel's, "Patricia Hearst said she was lucky she saw the struggle going on, because at the time she was reading a newspaper. She looked up, saw the struggle going on, so she fired at the store."

The theme of Matthews's testimony was that the Harrises and Patricia made congenial company during their eleven hours together. Jurors smiled as Matthews recounted watching the double feature at the drive-in, as Bill, Emily, and Patricia waited in vain for their comrades to show up. Indeed, Matthews was so relaxed in their company that after the last show at the drive-in he curled up and went to sleep. It was hardly the behavior of a terrified victim. For that reason, the testimony was damaging for Patricia's case. Bailey's defense was based on the notion that Patricia lived in fear for her life at every minute. Thus, she was like a robot programmed by her evil masters in the SLA. Matthews, in contrast, made the Harrises and Patricia sound like a groovy trio. They weren't even scary enough to keep Tom Matthews awake.

Bailey compounded the damage of Matthews's testimony in his cross-examination. He tried to play up the terror of the encounter, but Matthews wasn't buying. "You thought that if you offended them in any way, you might be harmed?" Bailey asked.

"Correct," Matthews answered.

"Would you say that made a deep impression on you at the time you heard the threat?"

"Not really."

"In other words, you did not much care whether you would get shot or not?"

"No, I was more excited than I was scared."

"Were you excited with the idea of an interesting adventure?"

"Yes, I was."

"In other words, you considered yourself fortunate to have been in that place at that time," Bailey asked, with some incredulity.

"Yes," Matthews said, prompting robust laughter in the courtroom. His dreamy equanimity was funny, to be sure, but his testimony left the clear impression that if he was having a good time on his adventure with the SLA, so was Patricia Hearst.

On February 13, the government rested.

Patricia never wanted to testify at her trial. As she returned to the embrace of her family, albeit in jail visiting rooms, she wanted nothing more than to put the SLA experience behind her. She was also exhausted from talking to psychiatrists. The first group was assigned by Judge Carter to determine if she was mentally fit to stand trial; they found she was. The next were representatives of the prosecution and defense, who were examining her to determine her state of mind at the time of the bank robbery. Patricia was not a reflective person in the best of circumstances, and she loathed the process of revealing her thoughts and feelings to these strangers. Hearsts, especially her mother, regarded any form of soul baring as vulgar. The last thing Patricia wanted to do was repeat this process in a public courtroom, with the whole nation watching.

Bailey didn't much care what Patricia thought, one way or the other. He had a job to do, and he left his deputy Al Johnson to explain his decisions to the client. During a boozy, mid-trial dinner with the journalist Shana Alexander, Bailey explained how he and Johnson dealt with Patricia. "Right now we are brainwashing her in reverse, using the good cop–bad cop approach," Bailey said. "Frankly, it's not hard. She has a lot of confidence in Al, and she has no deep political convictions. She's easy meat." In their visits to Patricia in jail, Patricia's family was doing the same thing, though with less cynicism.

Patricia tolerated her brief testimony in the hearing about whether her statements were voluntary, but she hoped that she would not have to return to the witness stand. Bailey could have defended the case without her testimony. The government conceded that she had been kidnapped, and Bailey cleverly began the defense case with the testimony of Steve Suenaga. He was Patricia and Steve's neighbor on Benvenue who stumbled into the kidnapping and wound up beaten and tied up on the floor of their apartment. Suenaga's testimony convincingly established that Patricia had been the victim of a terrifying crime.

Of course, Patricia's own testimony would chronicle her ordeal in a much more vivid way. But there was a major risk if she took the stand. In her testimony at the hearing, Judge Carter had already shown that he would allow Browning to cross-examine her about her involvement with other crimes besides the Hibernia Bank—especially the fatal bank shooting in Carmichael. When Browning asked questions about Carmichael, Patricia took the Fifth. Few scenes are more damaging for a defendant than refusing to answer questions on the grounds of self-incrimination. But the jury wasn't present for the hearing. The question, then, was whether Judge Carter would allow Patricia to be cross-examined about other crimes if she testified in front of the jury.

Bailey convinced himself that the answer was no. Carter often gave vague and confusing responses to the lawyers, and sometimes he changed his mind. But Bailey still chose to interpret a brief exchange with the judge during the hearing as a definite ruling that he would limit Patricia's cross-examination. Based on that purported assurance, Bailey called his client to the witness stand, this time with the jury in the courtroom.

Bailey, as was his custom, was living on the edge throughout the trial. He was smoking at least two packs of Benson & Hedges cigarettes a day and, according to Shana Alexander, drinking about ten highballs every day as well—Bloody Marys or margaritas at the court's lunch break, scotch and soda at night. Bailey's cockiness and thirst for cash led him to shortchange preparation, too. Instead of walking Patricia through her testimony on the weekend before she was to take the stand, he took advantage of a three-day break to fly to Seattle to give a paid speech at a meat packers' convention and then to Los Angeles to give another one at a legal seminar.

Still, in spite of everything, when Patricia returned to the witness stand on the morning of February 17, she was an excellent witness, much better than earlier during the hearing. She was clear and focused. Bailey pulled salient details from her background to illustrate what kind of person she was before she was kidnapped. Patricia noted that when she was a student at Menlo College, before she started at Berkeley, there was a political demonstration.

"There was a strike?" Bailey asked.

"Yes," she said.

"And during the strike, what did you do?"

"I went to class."

Patricia gave a terse but vivid description of her kidnapping. "I was in the kitchen," she testified, "and Angela Atwood came up and I screamed, and she grabbed me and put a pistol in my face and told me to be quiet." Bailey took her from the scene at Benvenue to the car on Tanglewood Road and then to the long drive to the closet in Daly City. Blindfolded, she listened to DeFreeze rant about her parents. Bailey played the jury her voice on the communiqués, and Patricia described how DeFreeze "started telling me what to say." At one point, she said, DeFreeze came to the closet and said he had heard Patricia was not cooperating.

"What did he do to you?"

"He pinched me."

"Where?"

"My breasts and down."

"Your private parts as well?"

"Yes."

Through tears, she told of a pair of rapes. Bailey asked what Willy Wolfe did.

"He came into the closet and he closed the door and—"

"Did he make you lie down on the floor?"

"Yes."

"And then what did he do?"

"Had sexual intercourse," said Patricia.

A week later, according to her testimony, DeFreeze did the same thing.

The comrades told Patricia that her parents botched the food give-away. "I was told that my parents weren't doing anything except trying to humiliate people and trying to provoke the SLA to kill me," she said. In time, she was placed in a garbage can and transferred to the apartment on Golden Gate Avenue, in San Francisco.

Bailey asked why she wanted them to think that she had joined the SLA.

"So I could stay alive."

"Were you convinced in your own mind at the time that if you did not join, that they would dispose of you?"

"Yes."

She described the Hibernia robbery, before which DeFreeze "said that he was going to keep an eye on me and that if I messed up in any way, that I'd be killed." After the robbery, Patricia described the comrades' flight to Los Angeles. Here, Bailey breezed by a clear weakness in her story—the shoot-out at Mel's Sporting Goods. "When you saw the struggle with Bill Harris on the ground, what did you do?" Bailey asked.

"I picked up his gun and started firing," Patricia said.

"Did you fire at anything in particular?"

"Well, I was trying to fire, like, up at the top of the building." Bailey elided the key question *why* she fired to free her comrade.

As for Tom Matthews's testimony, Patricia didn't try to refute it. Bailey asked her why she smiled at the young man.

"Because whenever I met someone, I was supposed to smile," she said, "so it would be easier for them to recognize me from the photos that had been printed." The truth might have been simpler than this tortured explanation. Maybe she smiled because, as Matthews suggested, she was enjoying herself.

Patricia described how, after the death of the six comrades on Fifty-Fourth Street in Los Angeles, she fled with the Harrises to Costa Mesa and then back to San Francisco. She taped her final communiqué, which described Willy Wolfe as "the gentlest, most beautiful man I've ever known."

Bailey asked her, "Did you have anything to do with the authorship of what you said on that tape?"

"No."

"Is there anything on there that's your own words?"

"No," Patricia said. "I might have changed a phrase to make it easier to read but none of it was my own words."

Bailey rushed through Patricia's experience from her trip with Jack Scott and his family across the country in June 1974 to her arrest in San Francisco in September 1975—what the press came to call "Patty's lost year." The themes of her testimony remained the same—that she made no judgments independently of her SLA masters and that she lived in constant fear of being killed for disobedience.

Prosecutors rarely cross-examine. Defense lawyers generally call few or any witnesses, preferring instead to make their cases by cross-examining those witnesses offered by the government. Defendants themselves rarely take the stand. So a career prosecutor like Jim Browning had little experience cross-examining a defendant, which is what he began to do on February 19—the day before Patricia's twenty-second birthday. Browning was dreadful.

The U.S. attorney began by asking about the books in Patricia's apartment on Morse Street. "These books were predominantly, at least, about social and political problems, weren't they?"

Patricia agreed, and the jury could only have concluded, *so what?*

Browning accused her of exaggerating her injuries in the kidnapping. He asserted that her engagement with Steven Weed had been troubled. He showed her the sworn affidavit, prepared by her first lawyer, Terence Hallinan, in which Patricia claimed that she had been drugged by her captors. Under Browning's questioning, she admitted that the affidavit was largely false. But she asserted that she simply signed what Hallinan wrote down for her. Regarding her statements on the communiqués, to Tom Matthews, and on the Tania tapes, she maintained her insistence that she made them all under threat of death. As for why she never simply called her parents or tried to return to them, Patricia said, "I felt that my parents wouldn't want to see me again." Patricia became almost cocky on the witness stand, displaying a savvy understanding of the rules of evidence.

When Browning asked her an open-ended question about the dangers she faced, she knew how to volunteer information that the prosecution wanted kept away from the jury. "San Simeon was bombed," she said, referring to an incident that took place just days earlier on February 12, in the middle of the trial. "San Simeon was bombed, my parents received a letter threatening my life if I took the witness stand," she testified. "They wanted a quarter of a million dollars put into the Bill and Emily Harris defense fund." As Patricia knew, this information was technically irrelevant, but it was also likely to generate sympathy from the jurors, who were sequestered and sheltered from news coverage. (A letter from the New World Liberation Front took credit for the San Simeon bombing, in which no one was hurt. In this era, many people used the NWLF name, and the bombing was never solved. There is no evidence that the Harrises, who were in jail at the time, had anything to do with it.)

The only effective moment for Browning was nonverbal. At one point, he handed Patricia the weapon she had carried inside the Hibernia Bank. She took the weapon in her manicured hands and inspected it like a skilled marksman. Her proficiency drew an astonished "wooo" from the courtroom. Unintentionally, Patricia proved she was no naïf when it came to guns. Browning asked her how she knew this weapon was her own.

"By the stock and by the bolt," she said. Patricia knew the lingo too.

On several occasions, Browning made the classic trial lawyer's error—asking questions to which he did not know the answers. Trying to minimize her hardships in Daly City, Browning said, "You were given a toothbrush, I take it?"

"It was just the same toothbrush that everyone used," Patricia said, drawing a sympathetic murmur in the courtroom.

Likewise, Browning walked into a trap on the subject of Willy Wolfe and displayed antediluvian attitudes about sexual violence in the process. "Was it a forcible rape?" Browning asked.

"Excuse me," Patricia said.

"Was it a forcible rape? I mean, did you struggle? Or was it one in which you submitted because of your fear?"

"I didn't resist, no."

Pursuing the issue, Browning said that Patricia had said she "thought highly of him."

Bailey jumped up to say Patricia had never said that about Wolfe.

Patricia agreed. "I didn't say that at all," she stated.

"Well, what did you say?" Browning asked.

"I said I had a strong feeling about him."

"Well, what was that feeling?" Browning said, unwisely.

"I couldn't stand him," Patricia said.

At the defense table, the lawyers tried to suppress their smiles.

Reeling from the evident failure of his cross-examination, Browning struggled to recover the momentum he had established during the prosecution's case. Patricia had successfully batted away all of his questions about the Hibernia robbery itself. Browning's only hope was to expand the range of questioning to include such subjects as the fatal bank robbery in Carmichael and the bombings across Northern California. Bailey had already announced that Patricia would refuse to answer any questions on those subjects. The issue, then, was whether Judge Carter would allow the prosecutor to ask them.

The judge had earlier temporized on this issue, but on February 23, a week into her testimony, he came down in favor of the government. Browning could ask Patricia about her criminal activity during her year on the run. The ruling was clearly correct. A defendant who takes the stand puts all of her behavior at issue; she can't pick and choose what she wants to answer. During a brief recess, Patricia suggested to Bailey that she just answer the questions about her lost year; she thought the jury would understand her predicament. But Bailey believed that the risk of any admissions tying her to the fatal bank robbery was simply too great.

"Miss Hearst, you testified earlier, I believe, that you had come back across the United States with Jack Scott and they dropped you off in Las Vegas," Browning began. "I ask you now where he dropped you off in Las Vegas, please?"

Bailey had scripted Patricia's answer during the recess. "I refuse to answer on the ground that it may tend to incriminate me and cause extreme danger to myself and my family," she said.

Browning knew that Bailey had injected the issue of "extreme danger," even though it had no justification in law. "If Your Honor please," Browning said, "may the Court advise counsel and the jury that 'extreme danger' to herself and her family is not a legal basis for refusing to answer the question."

The judge agreed, saying, "I will instruct this witness to answer the question. I've already ruled under the circumstances that she's not entitled to raise the Fifth Amendment in these circumstances."

Browning tried again. "Miss Hearst, where were you dropped off by Jack Scott in Las Vegas?"

"I refuse to answer."

"Who met you in Las Vegas?"

"I refuse to answer."

"How long were you in Las Vegas?"

"I refuse to answer."

In all, Patricia refused to answer forty-two questions in front of the jury, until Judge Carter showed some mercy and told Browning to stop. She had refused to answer questions about Steve Soliah, Jim Kilgore, and the New World Liberation Front. She refused to answer questions about her use of phony identification cards and about her trip to the emergency room with Soliah, to treat her poison oak. Browning once baited Patricia into an answer, when he showed her a page from the Tania tapes transcript. Patricia had crossed out a sentence that said she was "sexually attracted" to Willy Wolfe and substituted "wanted to fuck."

Flustered and angry, Patricia said, "That's not exactly how it happened."

Hearing Patricia take the Fifth repeatedly, the jury was left to assume the worst about her behavior during her lost year. In calling Patricia to the stand, Bailey had gambled that Judge Carter would keep those incriminating subjects off-limits, and he had lost. So in the end, Bailey's decision to call Patricia to the stand backfired. Testimony that began with such promise for the defense concluded in a fiasco.

THE SEARCH FOR OLD McMONKEY

The spectacle of Patricia's taking the Fifth in front of the jury ruined her testimony, but Bailey still kept his eye on his main priority—protecting his client from being charged with the death of Myrna Opsahl. So in the middle of Patricia's own trial, Bailey negotiated a side deal for her.

While she was being tried for the Hibernia Bank robbery, the U.S. attorney in Sacramento charged Steve Soliah with participating in the Carmichael robbery. The prosecutor's motives in that case were transparent. The idea was to convict Soliah, or persuade him to plead guilty, and then turn him into a witness against the other participants. Three of the Carmichael robbers—Michael Bortin, Jim Kilgore, and Kathy Soliah—were fugitives at the time. Bill and Emily Harris were awaiting trial for kidnapping Patricia. No one had yet made a deal with prosecutors to turn on the others, but Bailey worried about being the last one in line, especially because Patricia was the highest-profile target in the group.

So Bailey took the rare, if not unprecedented, step of offering Patricia's testimony on Carmichael to prosecutors while she was still being tried for Hibernia. His client would agree to a full debriefing with prosecutors in the evenings, after her days in court were over. For her statements in these sessions, she would receive "use immunity"—that is, prosecutors could not use her statements against her, but they could use them to prosecute others. In practical terms, the deal amounted to a near guarantee that Patricia would never be prosecuted for Opsahl's death. In short, Bailey was hedging Patricia's bets. She might be convicted in Hibernia, but she wasn't going to go down in the more serious case in Carmichael. All she had to do was go upstairs to the FBI offices, after the end of long days in the courtroom, and tell the agents exactly what happened in April 1975.

Patricia's cooperation with the FBI—making her, in effect, a government informant—marked the next step in her political re-evolution. Her version of the Carmichael job never changed. She told the FBI that Bill Harris and Steve Soliah were the lookouts. Michael Bortin, Jim Kilgore, Kathy Soliah, and Emily Harris were inside the bank. Patricia herself drove the switch car, which took the invasion team back to their residence in Sacramento. There, according to Patricia, Emily had acknowledged that her gun killed Mrs. Opsahl, and that Emily had called her "a bourgeois pig." As Patricia and Bailey knew, the comrades' collective effort on the robbery made them all potentially liable in a capital case for Opsahl's murder.

Bailey's strategy of separating Patricia from her life in the SLA, and especially from her lover Steve Soliah, continued to pay off. He had stopped the exchange of letters between them, and he made sure Patricia didn't run into Soliah or the Harrises in jail. The day-to-day nurturing Patricia received from Al Johnson, who acted as almost a surrogate father, also drove home the lesson that she had to return to the Hearst fold. One could say that the lawyers reverse-brainwashed her, but the truth may be simpler. Patricia was always a rational actor—with the SLA and now with her lawyers. Even in chaotic surroundings, she knew where her best interests lay.

So when Patricia began her secret sessions with the FBI, she buried her former allies with icy specificity. To her lawyers, her interrogators, and her family, she never betrayed the slightest misgiving about turning on Steve Soliah, whom she had, just a few months earlier, professed to love with all her heart. The FBI agents were dazzled by the precision of her memory. Her manner never changed; she still sounded like a lock-jawed aristocrat who always seemed about to roll her eyes at the banality of her inquisitors. But Patricia displayed to the FBI the same quiet intensity that her SLA comrades admired about her. Faced with a task—whether planning a bank robbery or, now, recounting one—Patricia simply completed it.

As March began, Bailey's arrogance once again came to the fore, notwithstanding his rocky performance in the trial. Every day after court for a week, he flew his plane from San Francisco to Las Vegas, where he conducted a paid seminar for trial lawyers. Drink in hand, he lectured for an hour, then returned to the airport to complete the thousand-mile round-trip. Questioned by reporters about this grueling schedule, Bailey said, "It's fun to be a superman," adding, "But that's a fraud. I attribute my appearance here to a very good physician who knew exactly what to prescribe." Bailey had still another iron in the fire. In the middle of the trial, he was negotiating with the publisher G. P. Putnam's Sons to write a book about the case. Bailey lined up his usual ghostwriter, John Greenya, to start work on the book while the trial was under way. To this end, Bailey arranged for the court transcript to be sent to Greenya at his home in Maryland every day, via a brand-new company called Federal Express. Like Steven Weed and Jack Scott, Bailey saw the Hearst case as a vehicle for profit in the then-booming world of publishing. (Weed timed his book, *My Search for Patty Hearst,* to come out during Patricia's trial, further alienating him from his former fiancée and her family.)

As Patricia's lawyer was scurrying back and forth to Las Vegas, her trial turned to a new and stultifying chapter. In legal terms, Bailey's defense was known as physical coercion—that is, that Patricia was forced to commit the bank robbery against her will. This was actually a very narrow defense. It was not, strictly speaking, a defense of brainwashing, which doesn't exist in federal court in the United

States. The defense was simply a claim that the SLA comrades compelled her to participate in the bank robbery through threats of physical force. Under this theory, she should not be convicted because she acted under duress.

To make his case, Bailey wanted to offer testimony from three psychiatrists who had all examined Patricia, each for at least a few hours. Prosecutors objected, saying their testimony was irrelevant, because the doctors could not say whether Patricia was physically compelled to rob the bank. But Judge Carter sided with the defense and allowed the testimony. Browning had anticipated that the judge would rule against him on this issue, so he assigned David Bancroft, one of his assistant U.S. attorneys, to prepare three other psychiatrists to testify for the prosecution in rebuttal. Browning had a fairly cynical view of the whole subject of expert psychiatric testimony. He regarded the experts in terms of quantity, not quality. "If they call two, we'll call two," Browning told his assistant. "If they call three, we'll call three. All I want is a 'wash transaction.'"

So, following Patricia's testimony, the trial bogged down in lengthy and confusing testimony from a series of psychiatrists, who all offered their own jargon-laden analysis of Patricia's state of mind. One phrase that was never uttered during the trial was one that came later to be closely associated with the Hearst case: Stockholm syndrome. The event that gave the syndrome its name took place on August 23, 1973, less than six months before the kidnapping. It took some time for the events in Stockholm to circulate around the world, so it was not a focus of the trial.

Still, then as now, the story of the bank robbery in Stockholm resonated with the Hearst kidnapping. On that summer day in Sweden's biggest city, an escaped prisoner named Jan-Erik Olsson, armed with a submachine gun, walked into the Sveriges Kreditbanken in Norrmalmstorg square. He successfully demanded that the police release his friend Clark Olofsson from prison, and the pair took four hostages into the bank's vault, where they were held for six days. In a series of phone calls from the vault, the hostages made clear their support for their captors, in words that foreshadowed Patricia's own in the communiqués. For example, in a conversation with Prime Minister Olof Palme, one hostage said, "I fully trust Clark and the robber. I am not desperate. They haven't done a thing to us. On the contrary, they have been very nice. But, you know, Olof, what I am scared of is that the police will attack and cause us to die." Another hostage said, "This is our world now, sleeping in this vault to survive. Whoever threatens this world is our enemy." Eventually, the authorities pumped tear gas into the vault, and the captors surrendered. The hostages suffered no serious injuries.

Even though the psychiatrists for the defense did not use the phrase "Stockholm syndrome," their appeals to the jury rested on that rationale. Louis "Jolly" West, the chairman of the Psychiatric Department at UCLA, was Patricia's first witness, but his testimony was as confusing as all that followed. Bailey asked him about brainwashing. "Brainwashing is a term that has become a sort of grab bag to describe any kind of influence exerted by a captor over a captive, but that isn't very accurate from the scientific or medical point of view," West said. Still, he told how in one study of air force pilots captured during the Korean War, in thirty-six of the fifty-nine pilots, "the behaviors desired by the captors was, in fact, acquired." West said Patricia endured a similar experience.

West spent twenty-three hours with Patricia, and he said "as soon as I began to ask her for any information about her previous nineteen months' experience, it became extremely difficult. She would begin to cry." After her kidnapping, "as Cinque repeatedly threatened her with death, she became numb with terror." Later, he said, "Little by little, she was given to understand that to become a member of the group would mean to get out of the closet and to get out of the blindfold and to be relieved of the constant threats of death, at least from them. And since that was the most immediate threat, this was what she was drawn to do. It was a pretty classical example actually of what we would call coercive persuasion." As for the shooting at Mel's Sporting

Goods, West quoted Patricia as saying, "I can't believe I did that. I don't understand why I did it."

In cross-examination, David Bancroft noted first that while the Korean Communists made a specific effort to change the mind-set of their captives, the SLA comrades did no such thing. They were neither organized nor experienced enough to conduct a brainwashing. Rather, her three principal minders—Willy Wolfe, Angela Atwood, and Nancy Ling—simply talked to Patricia, who eventually came around to their way of thinking. Bancroft focused on the period after Patricia came out of the closet, and especially after she hit the road with the Scotts in June 1974. "The defendant was not forthcoming with you with respect to her activities after Los Angeles, that is, after the Mel's store shoot-out until her apprehension," Bancroft said. "She did not give you a full description of the details of what she had been doing for the past year and a half, isn't that correct?"

"That's correct," West said.

Bancroft went on, "In view of the fact that the defendant has taken the Fifth Amendment as to that period, and having in mind, in addition, that she had provided you with only the most sketchy information for that period of time . . . my question to you is how could you tell that the defendant was suffering from a survivor syndrome without knowing in detail what happened to her within the previous year and a half?"

West said the conclusion was his reasonable medical judgment.

Bancroft summed up the prosecution's case in a single question: "Is it your view, Doctor, that a person who was politically embarrassed by their family situation, and had particular, negative feelings with respect to their parents, and whose characteristic mode of expression is deep sarcasm, and if that person—prior to their acquaintance with political matters—in addition felt depressed or trapped, could that person not come to a sudden political expression of their own hostilities?"

West answered maybe, but the point was the question, not the answer. The prosecution was arguing that life with the SLA represented an escape for Patricia. Trapped with Steve and alienated from her family, Patricia found in her captivity a kind of freedom from the pressures of her life.

And so it went, day after day of speculation and psychobabble. Martin Orne, a professor at the University of Pennsylvania, came next, and he too said Patricia had been "quite troubled" by her kidnapping. Speaking in a strong Viennese accent, Orne concluded that Patricia's flat affect as she recounted her kidnapping was proof that she was telling the truth. "Her failure to make it a good story is what I found so impressive," he said. "She had a remarkable resistance to embroidering." In cross-examination, Bancroft had a simple theme: people change. "Let me ask you, Doctor," he said, "people sometimes become involved in political things where they previously have not been, isn't that possible?"

"Of course," said Orne.

"You've heard the expression, 'found religion'?"

Orne had.

"So it's not always the case, then, that looking at a pre-history of non-involvement in something is any good indicator of whether or not one would become subsequently involved in something?"

"That's correct." In other words, people change.

The final defense witness was Yale's Robert Jay Lifton, an expert on the treatment of American prisoners of war by the Chinese and North Koreans. He examined Patricia for seventeen hours. He said his analysis showed that Patricia had been coerced into joining the SLA and robbing the bank. The proof, in his view, was how quickly she switched back to her previous life. "What is impressive to me is the speed with which all of the coercive ideas, that is, the political ideas that were pressed upon her . . . with the exception of what I would call a moderate feminism which came more in relation to Wendy Yoshimura than with the SLA people, how those ideas were no longer present in her so quickly," Lifton said.

Even for a defense witness, Lifton offered an extraordinarily credulous account of Patricia's activities while she was on the run. Bancroft asked him how Patricia described her months with the comrades. "She did tell me about the main activities in that time which were, in my judgment, the military drills, the struggles and criticisms and the physical training activities that she had," Lifton said. Apparently, Patricia did not inform him about the time she spent robbing banks and planning bombings, and the doctor didn't ask about it either.

Joel Fort, the first prosecution psychiatrist, who also had the opportunity to examine the defendant, portrayed an almost entirely different human being from the Patricia Hearst described by the defense. She was, in Fort's view, "extremely independent, strong-willed, rebellious, intelligent, well-educated but not particularly intellectually inclined." She had become sexually active at fifteen and had "a very independent view about sexuality and about rules in general." She was an "amoral person who thought that laws that she didn't agree with should be violated." As a friend of Patricia's told Fort, "She would lie if necessary to get herself out of anything." Fort's Patricia detested nearly everyone in her prior life. Her feelings about her parents ranged "from dislike to hatred." She had had "serious questions" about whether she should go through with her marriage to Steven Weed. Patricia complained about "his expecting her to cook and clean up for him, and to be available for him whenever he wanted sexual relationships, but not responding to her own sexual initiatives when she had those desires. She also found him somewhat boring at times." In her interviews with Fort, she confessed that "in the month prior to the kidnapping, . . . she was having thoughts about suicide."

To Fort, the kidnapping was, perversely, almost a form of liberation for Patricia. He said seven of the eight kidnappers (all except DeFreeze) "were in roughly the same age bracket and the same class background, white middle class, comparable education, either some years of college or graduation from college, coming from business and professional families, doctors, pharmacists, store owners." And five of those seven were women, which Fort found to be "a very important point." He went on, "To put it in kind of cliché of American terms, we could say, how did a nice girl like that or a nice boy like that become an SLA member? . . . None of them, obviously, were born as adherents to an urban guerrilla philosophy or a terrorist kind of ideology. In fact, more specifically, all of them made that evolution within relatively recent years." So, in Fort's view, did Patricia Hearst.

"Something was missing in her life," Fort continued. "She was a strong, willful, independent person, bored, dissatisfied, in poor contact with her family, disliking them to some extent, dissatisfied with Steven Weed, with whom she had been for about three years at the time of kidnapping, and the interaction of that, that kind of vacuum, of something missing, a missing sense of meaning or purpose in life with what seemed on the surface to be offered by the SLAers as she got to know them and as she became impressed, as she describes in the Tania interview, with her commitment, and as she described to me, being impressed with their willingness to die for their beliefs. I think that action was very important to her."

More specifically, Bancroft asked Fort, "Doctor, what can you tell us from a psychiatric standpoint with respect to the claim that she fired the gun at Mel's almost involuntarily or instantaneously?"

"I find it unbelievable," Fort said.

And what about the fact that Patricia had a gun in her purse when she was arrested?

"I thought that was one other additional important piece of evidence, that she was fully aware of what was going on and she was aware that she was a fugitive, that she had a continuing identification as an urban guerrilla."

Bailey was nearly beside himself during much of Fort's testimony, vaulting out of his seat to object, even to demand a mistrial, because the doctor was essentially offering an expert opinion that Patricia was guilty. (Carter denied most of the objections and all of the requests for mistrials.) Bailey spent more than a full day cross-examining Fort, accusing him of exaggerating his credentials and trying to cash in on the notoriety of the Hearst case. Curiously, though, Bailey did little to challenge Fort's conclusions about Patricia.

The next witness, Harry Kozol, a psychiatrist from Boston, backed up Fort's conclusions, saying, "The girl was a rebel. She had gotten into a state where she was ripe for the plucking. . . . She was a rebel in search of a cause." Based on his examination of Patricia and her background, Kozol said, "I think this was all *in* her. In a sense, she was a member of the SLA in spirit, without knowing it, for a long, long time." (Kozol also said Patricia had denied that DeFreeze ever raped her.) Weary of extending the trial, the government never called its third psychiatrist to the stand.

The battle of the psychiatrists echoed a larger debate that was being played out in the country. As the historian Rick Perlstein observed, "The defense psychiatrists offered up what was essentially a left-wing view of the self—as plastic, protean, moldable—and of human beings as the product of their environment, *not quite* responsible for their individual decisions and acts." The prosecution experts, in contrast, reflected a more right-wing view—that individuals were accountable for their own actions and that indulged children, rich or poor, had no right to blame circumstances for their choices in life. This division reflected the earlier debate about Randy Hearst's decision to fund the food giveaway, which was seen by the Left as a humanitarian gesture and by the Right as a concession to terrorists. By the end of the trial, these cultural crosscurrents yielded a paradoxical result—that the Hearst name, which for decades stood for economic royalty and political conservatism, came to represent flabby liberal weakness in the face of adversity.

The battle of experts did have one clear loser: the psychiatric profession itself. Putative leaders in the field reached diametrically opposing conclusions based on the same evidence—that is, the contents of Patricia's head. Psychiatry could scarcely be much of a science, it seemed, if the top doctors could agree on so little. Worse yet, the experts on both sides expressed themselves with a degree of confidence that seemed excessive. How could Orne conclude that Patricia wasn't embroidering? How could Kozol be sure that the pre-kidnapping Patricia was already "in" the SLA? The gladiatorial atmosphere of the courtroom brought out the worst in the doctors, who sacrificed professional humility for a fatuous certainty.

Still, Browning by and large achieved his goal; the muddle of conflicting views neutralized the effect of any single piece of testimony. The doctors' testimony also provided another reason why Bailey had blundered so badly by putting Patricia on the stand. The psychiatrists for the defense testified in detail about the abuse that Patricia recounted. Bailey could have relied on that testimony alone to explain her ordeal to the jury, and he would have spared his client the indignity of taking the Fifth.

Still, at that late date in the trial, there was no way for the lawyers on either side to know how the jurors were leaning. There was ample evidence before them to support a conviction or an acquittal. The prosecutors, who of course bore the burden of proof, were especially worried that a tie would go to the defendant. The central issue in the case remained whether Patricia had made a voluntary decision to join the SLA. On that question, a last-minute discovery transformed the trial—courtesy of the absent, but still somehow ubiquitous, Bill and Emily Harris.

When they were all arrested in September 1975, the Harrises were pretty fond of Patricia. True, they lived in separate apartments by that point, but the couple respected Patricia's political transformation. As Bill told others during the first weeks after their capture, his main issue with Patricia was that she was too reckless and too willing to take chances—that she was *too much* of a revolutionary. He called her his "Ransom of Red Chief problem," a reference to the O. Henry short story. Bill and Patricia had fought a lot during their long months together, he acknowledged, but only because he was trying to keep her tethered to reality. When Bill and Emily saw Patricia's clenched-fist salute and when they heard that she had given her occupation as urban guerrilla, their old disagreements with her faded. Likewise, as a man who appreciated a theatrical gesture, Bill always admired Patricia's mad barrage at Mel's. The woman he called Tania saved him from arrest and might have saved his life.

So when Terence Hallinan came to visit Bill in jail immediately after his arrest—Kayo brought (illegal) Cuban cigars as a gift—Bill said that he and Emily would do what they could to help Patricia. They would testify that she was kidnapped—anything she wanted. But once Hallinan was replaced by Bailey and he cut off Patricia's contacts with Steve Soliah and everyone else in the SLA, Bill and Emily felt the chill. The breach became official when word leaked that Patricia was accusing the SLA comrades of rape. The Harrises vociferously denied that Patricia's relationship with Willy Wolfe was nonconsensual and were adamant that DeFreeze had not had sex with her at all. They insisted that the SLA was dedicated to feminism—and it included more women than men—and they would never have stood for rape among their own.

Shunned now by Patricia, the Harrises set out to defend themselves against daunting legal challenges. They were charged with kidnapping Tom Matthews and were awaiting additional indictments. The specter of charges in connection with Myrna Opsahl's death also haunted the Harrises. What made their legal problems especially vexing was that they were, in fact, guilty of all these crimes. Still, working with skilled lawyers who were experienced in defending radicals, they had some early successes. They succeeded in persuading a judge that the warrantless search of the Precita apartment was unlawful and that the evidence gathered there could not be used against them. But the lawyers were expensive. The Harrises had no money, and robbing any more banks, at least for the time being, was out of the question.

Bill and Emily did have one asset: their story. Jack Scott had persuaded the couple, along with Patricia, to try to write a book as a commercial venture the previous summer, but they found that they had neither the patience nor the aptitude for such an undertaking. Likewise, they had plenty of demands from conventional news outlets—the networks and the big newsmagazines—for interviews, but journalistic rules forbade paying sources. Languishing in jail in Los Angeles, they learned of one possible option. Their lawyer, Leonard Weinglass, approached the journalist Robert Scheer to see if they could work out a deal. Scheer wrote for *New Times,* a new national biweekly that attempted to marry the counterculture sensibility of the underground press with the appearance (and advertising) of a glossy magazine. Unconstrained by the conventional journalistic ethics, *New Times* offered the Harrises $10,000 for an interview.

Scheer and his colleague Susan Lyne wound up spending fourteen hours with Bill and Emily in the Los Angeles county jail. True to their obsessive natures, the Harrises not only gave lengthy interviews but also annotated and expanded the rough transcripts of their sessions. Bill, a disorderly man with meticulous handwriting, wrote in his changes, and Emily used a prison typewriter to produce flawless copy. The *New Times* interview with Bill and Emily appeared in print just before the close of evidence in Patricia's trial.

Carole Westrick was the only woman on the Hearst prosecution trial team. A twenty-three-year-old paralegal, she at first identified more with the defendant in the case than with her colleagues at the counsel table. She was haunted by the thought of Patricia, her near contemporary, confined to a closet. But Westrick's job involved keeping track of the voluminous documents in the case—as well as dealing with the press—and her immersion in the evidence led her to believe that Patricia had made a genuine commitment to the SLA. Still, she worried that her team had never quite made its case about Patricia's state of mind. They needed something more.

The prosecutors passed the Harrises' interview among themselves, reading with half an eye as the psychiatric testimony droned on. The *New Times* reporters had pressed Bill and Emily about their insistence that Patricia, rather than being sexually assaulted by Willy Wolfe, had actually initiated the relationship. Westrick was drawn to one comment in particular from Emily Harris:

> Once Willy gave her a stone relic in the shape of a monkey-face that he had bought when he was in Mexico—he called it an Olmec or something. He had fashioned a macramé chain for it out of some waxed brown string that was lying around the house, sort of a thick thread used for sewing on leather. Anyway, Patty wore it all the time around her neck. After the shootout, she stopped wearing it and carried it in her purse instead, but she always had it with her.

Westrick went to Browning and said she thought this was potentially significant evidence. Browning wasn't sure. What was the big deal? Westrick pointed out that Patricia had claimed that Willy Wolfe raped her. In one of the most dramatic moments of her testimony, she said she "couldn't stand" Wolfe. Westrick passed a note to her boss: "No woman would carry around a memento from a man who raped her and couldn't stand for over a year!" Browning told Westrick to summon the FBI agent who booked Patricia's purse into evidence following her arrest. During a break in the trial, the agent led the lawyers to the FBI evidence room, where he dumped the contents of the purse on a table. There was a smooth black stone charm carved into the shape of a face—the Olmec monkey. Emily Harris was right.

But there was more. Westrick and the lawyers recalled a line from Patricia's "eulogy tape," which had already been played for the jury, with a transcript prepared by the FBI. Originally, the transcript read, "The pigs probably have the little Old McMonkey that Cujo wore around his neck. He gave me the little stone face one night." The passage had never made any sense to the government team. What was an Old McMonkey? But shortly after the tape was played in court, David Kessler, a psychiatrist who was working with the prosecution, happened to ask Bancroft if anyone had ever found the item. No, said

Bancroft, the agents had looked, but they found no Irish or Scottish figurine. Kessler corrected him: Patricia had said "Olmec monkey," not "Old McMonkey." (The FBI transcribers, like many people in law enforcement, were probably Irish Americans.)

Suddenly the evidence for the prosecution looked even more promising. Not only had Patricia saved a gift she had received from Willy Wolfe, but her Olmec monkey might have matched one that Wolfe wore to his death. What a romantic gesture! What proof of her true feelings for Willy! The prosecution moved swiftly to track down the Los Angeles police officers who had sifted the burned-out remains of the house on Fifty-Fourth Street. In short order, they found the LAPD sergeant who had removed the macramé cord and monkey charm from Wolfe's lifeless body. The prosecutors had the evidence shipped to San Francisco. Wolfe's Olmec monkey provided a haunting reminder of how he died. The face of the charm was charred, and the string that held it around his neck was burned.

What made the last-minute discoveries especially sweet was that the prosecutors didn't have to disclose the new evidence to the defense team. Prosecutors have to reveal in advance their initial evidence, known as their case-in-chief, but they don't have to provide notice of evidence they plan to use in rebuttal, after the defense has presented their witnesses. Browning relished the chance to spring a surprise on Bailey. In this, however, he was disappointed. Browning was so excited about the Olmec monkey evidence that he shared his discovery with his fourteen-year-old daughter, who was living with her mother at the time. Evelyn Browning was so impressed that she repeated the tale to a girlfriend who, in turn, told her mother. Unbeknownst to anyone, the mother was following the trial closely and rooting for an acquittal. She tracked down Bailey at his hotel and warned him that the two Olmec monkeys were about to be introduced in the government's rebuttal case.

Bailey prepared for the last-minute evidence as best he could. Patricia told him that she had saved the charm because Wolfe had told her it was twenty-five hundred years old. She cared too much about art history to get rid of it. Affection for Willy had nothing to do with it, she said.

But Bailey didn't think it was worthwhile to return Patricia to the stand to respond, so the defense simply had to endure a procession of government rebuttal witnesses on the subject of the Olmec monkeys. One FBI agent introduced a blowup of the SLA group photograph—showing Patricia's Olmec charm on her necklace. Another agent put the charm taken from her purse into evidence. A third showed the jury the charred remains of the cord and Olmec monkey that had been removed from Wolfe's body. Browning guessed that Bailey might argue that Patricia saved her Olmec monkey out of a concern for the cultural patrimony of Mexico, so he also tracked down an expert in the field.

Clement Meighan was surely the unlikeliest of people to appear as a witness in the trial of Patricia Hearst. A longtime professor at UCLA, he was known as a founding father of modern archaeology, with a special expertise in the history of Mexico.

"Are you generally familiar with the sale of Mexican objects, both authentic and simulated, to tourists in Mexico?" Browning asked him.

"Yes," said Meighan.

"Are figurines from ancient civilizations recovered quite frequently in Mexico?"

"Yes, they are."

Browning showed the professor the two Olmec monkeys, and he played the tape of Patricia saying, "The pigs probably have the little Olmec monkey that Cujo wore around his neck."

Browning asked if Olmec monkeys like the two exhibits at trial were easy to find in Mexico.

"Yes, they are easy to find," Meighan said.

Bailey sneered just a couple of questions on cross-examination. The gist was *You came all the way from Los Angeles for this?*

But the message of Professor Meighan's testimony was clear. There was no reason for anyone to hold on to the Olmec monkey except out of sentiment, or maybe love.

THE VERDICT

Bailey had a final witness. "Now, your honor, we call Mrs. Catherine Hearst," he said.

It was March 17, St. Patrick's Day, and most men in the courtroom contrived to sport green. Al Johnson, though far from his home in Boston, managed to pull together an entire emerald outfit, including suit, shirt, and tie. So, too, did Judge Carter's court clerk, and even Tom Padden, the FBI agent who busted through the back door of Patricia's apartment at 625 Morse Street. Catherine Hearst, in contrast, composed her outfit as she organized her life, with greater restraint. Her brown dress was closely tailored, set off with a pink scarf. She did offer a token nod to the occasion, with a green-enamel shamrock pin.

"Mrs. Hearst, you are the mother of the defendant in this case?" Bailey asked.

"Yes, I am," Catherine said.

"Now, Mrs. Hearst, you have been present throughout the trial, have you not?"

"Yes."

Catherine Hearst was more exhibit than witness. She was the physical manifestation of Patricia's return to the fold—proof, according to Bailey, that the defendant belonged with her family, not with the criminals who had seized her. This wasn't just a show for the jury, either; Patricia's embrace of her Hearst roots was just as real as her mother's love for her.

"Would you tell the jury what kind of girl Patty Hearst was, prior to February 4, 1974?"

"Well, she was a very warm and loving girl," Catherine said, "and she always did things together with the family in groups, and we live a very close family life. And she and I shared a mutual enthusiasm for art, so we always had a great deal in common." There was some poignancy in Catherine's embrace, especially for those who knew how Patricia had spent the last year and a half running down her mother. The reference to art represented a small attempt to mitigate the damage from the Olmec monkey. The implication, if a rather tortured one, was that Patricia kept the charm for the family collection, not as a romantic keepsake.

"Was she," Bailey asked, "sometimes a strong-willed girl?"

"She was," Catherine said with a smile. "I wouldn't want to make anything I say make you think it was an easy job to raise five children, Mr. Bailey."

"Was she also, as has been indicated by several of the witnesses, a bright girl?"

"A very bright girl," her mother said.

It was time to move to closing arguments.

Browning summed up the same way he tried the case, with dogged exactitude and without much flash. It didn't help that he was fighting the flu, too. For the most part, Browning let the evidence speak for itself. He opened with the bank robbery and the security camera photographs, which the jurors had already seen about a dozen times. There was never any dispute that Patricia participated in the bank robbery, but as Browning acknowledged, the key issue in the case was the defendant's state of mind. "In dealing with intent," Browning said, "we can't unscrew the top of a person's head and look in." Intent must be proven by outside factors—by circumstantial evidence.

The most important evidence of Patricia's intent, according to

Browning, was her gunfire at Mel's Sporting Goods. "I suggest it is reasonable to believe that a person who is in fear of being killed by her captors does not, when confronted with an opportunity to escape from the captors, fire weapons in the direction of other persons in order to free the captors and does not fail to try to escape," Browning said.

Browning didn't rev up his rhetoric until the end of his remarks, when he discussed Patricia's turn on the witness stand. "In short, ladies and gentlemen, we ask you to reject the defendant's entire testimony as not credible," he said. "She asks us to believe that she didn't mean what she said on the tapes. She didn't mean what she wrote in the documents. She didn't mean it when she gave this power salute, the clenched-fist salute after her arrest. That was out of fear of the Harrises, she tells us. She didn't mean it when she told the San Mateo County Deputy Sheriff that she was an urban guerrilla, that that was her occupation. She says her statement was simply a sort of shrug-of-the-shoulders type of thing. She says the Tobin conversation [about revolutionary feminism] wasn't the real Patricia Hearst. The Mel's shooting incident was simply a reflex. The untruths in the affidavit [about being drugged] were simply some attorney's idea. She was in such fear that she couldn't escape in nineteen months while crisscrossing the country, or even get word to her parents or someone else. The confession to Matthews was recited out of fear. She couldn't stand Willy Wolfe, yet she carried that stone face with her until the day she was arrested." It is notable that Browning's climax referred to the Olmec monkey, which had just come to his attention a few days earlier.

"It's too big a pill to swallow, ladies and gentlemen," Browning said. "It just does not wash. I ask whether you would accept this incredible story from anyone but Patricia Hearst, and if you wouldn't, don't accept it from her either." Browning spoke for a little more than two hours, and Judge Carter recessed the trial for lunch.

"There are many concepts in the law," Bailey said, reading from a disorderly stack of notes and carrying the microphone like a talk show host working a crowd. "The SLA was so right about so many things that I, as a citizen, am a little bit ashamed that they could predict so well what we would do. But I think an overview of this case is more appropriate than talking just about bank robbery. This is not a case about a bank robbery. The crime could have been any one of a number. It is a case about dying or surviving—that is all Patricia Campbell Hearst thought about. And the question is, what is the right to live? How far can you go to survive . . ."

Bailey gestured with his left hand and knocked over a pitcher of water, which dribbled down the front of his pants.

"A novelist once wrote a most disturbing book—you may have heard about it," Bailey went on. "It was a best seller and a movie. A man who was condemned to hang for killing his wife killed his executioner to survive, and then it was determined that he had not killed his wife. And a judge had to decide whether or not he could be tried for that second killing. Does one have an obligation at some point to die? It was called 'A Covenant with Death,' and we all have a covenant with death. We are all going to die, and we know it. And we're all going to postpone that date as long as we can. And Patty Hearst did that, and that is why she is here and you are here."

Bailey continued in this rambling and at times nearly incomprehensible way for just forty-five minutes, which was mercifully brief considering the circumstances. He barely discussed the evidence at all. He had developed a genuine personal loathing for Joel Fort, one of the prosecution psychiatrists, and he devoted an unseemly amount of time in his brief summation to attacking the doctor—a peripheral figure in the case. ("You may have been puzzled why I was standing here hour after hour letting Dr. Joel Fort shoot his mouth off. Well, I think you found out the answer Tuesday. If you think I was angry, I was.") Bailey only dealt with the subject of the Mel's shooting in a glancing way. ("The charge in this case is the Hibernia bank, not Mel's. You don't have to sort out whether she was right or wrong, or whether she should be punished for Mel's. If I told you if it were not for Mel's, she wouldn't be here, and you wouldn't, either. That is another chapter for another time and for another group.")

Bailey's argument included little about the actual evidence that Browning had discussed in his summation—like the bank security photographs, the communiqués, the Tania interview, the clenched-fist salute, "urban guerrilla," the admission to her friend Trish Tobin that she was a "revolutionary feminist." "Perry Mason brings solutions to all of his cases, in open court usually from the ranks of his opponent's witnesses," Bailey said near the end of his remarks. "Real life doesn't work that way. We can't bring home the bacon. We have given you all we have got. No one is ever going to be sure. They will be talking about the case for longer than I think I am going to have to talk about it, whether it occurs to me, or probably the only people in the courtroom I haven't had to talk about it so far with." On that puzzling note, Bailey concluded.

Judge Carter gave his jury instructions on Friday morning, March 19, and the jurors began deliberating just before lunch. Some lawyers believe that jurors will deliberate one day for each week of evidence. By this standard, the eight weeks of testimony in the Hearst case would have produced eight days of deliberations. As it turned out, this jury took less than one to reach its verdict.

The seven women and five men were a stable, middle-class group. All but one, a flight attendant for United Airlines, were married. Eight had children. All were sequestered, confined to a hotel and cut off from television and newspapers, for the duration of the trial. As a group, they had a great deal of respect for authority, which translated into a clear allegiance to Judge Carter's instructions. Carter had told them, "Coercion or duress may provide a legal excuse for the crime charged in the indictment. In order, however, to provide a legal excuse for any criminal conduct, the compulsion must be present, and immediate, and of such a nature as to induce a well-founded fear of death or serious bodily injury; and there must be no reasonable opportunity to escape the compulsion without committing the crime."

The jurors, led by the former air force colonel and Korean War veteran whom they selected as their foreman, zeroed in on these questions. Was Patricia compelled or coerced to rob the Hibernia Bank? Did she have a well-founded fear of impending death or serious bodily injury if she failed to participate? Did she have a reasonable opportunity to escape? On every issue, they quickly came to consensus in favor of the government. The first vote was 10–2 for conviction, but then one of the dissenters quickly folded. The lone holdout asked to hold the case over Friday night, so he could think further about his vote. On Saturday morning, he quickly joined the others for conviction on both bank robbery and the use of a firearm in the commission of a felony.

Two pieces of evidence mattered the most to the jurors. The first was Patricia's shoot-up at Mel's Sporting Goods. Her action was completely inconsistent with her claims of being under constant duress and unable to escape. The second was the Olmec monkey. The insight by Carole Westrick, the prosecution paralegal, was repeated almost word for word by several jurors. Patricia would not have held on to the little charm if she regarded Willy Wolfe as a rapist, or even if, as she put it, she "couldn't stand" him. And because the jurors believed Patricia was lying about Wolfe, that meant they also thought she was lying about her entire relationship with the comrades. For the jurors, Patricia's decision to take the Fifth, rather than answer questions about her lost year, cast a further shadow over her testimony.

The jury announced that it had reached its verdict in the morning, but it took several hours to gather all the participants, which was especially challenging on a Saturday. No one—not the lawyers, not the court staff, not the journalists—had prepared for such a quick decision. Patricia's coterie surrounded her with words of encouragement. Though she was a jailed criminal defendant, she enjoyed a support network consistent with her status as an heiress. Her parents rarely missed a day in the courtroom, and her sisters and cousin Will rotated in and out as well. On weekends, they visited Patricia in the lockup in jail, and so did friends like Trish Tobin. Bailey was her main lawyer in the courtroom, but Al Johnson served more like a family retainer, sacrificing months of life with his family back in Boston to attend to Patricia's needs. Even Janey Jimenez, the deputy U.S. marshal assigned to Patricia, became more protector than jailer. ("I'll always remember her gallantry as my prisoner, her warming presence as my friend," Jimenez later wrote in a book about their friendship.)

Patricia was uncharacteristically chipper as she moved from the courtroom lockup to the defense table for the reading of the verdict. "What kind of drink are we going to have to celebrate?" Patricia asked Jimenez. "I want a tall Margarita."

"Tequila and tonic for me," the deputy marshal said.

At 4:20 p.m., Judge Carter called for the jury. "Ladies and gentlemen," he said, "have you arrived at a verdict?"

"Yes, sir," Colonel Wright, the foreman, replied with military courtesy.

Wright handed the envelope with the verdict form to the judge, who read it to himself and then turned it over to the clerk. "Ladies and gentlemen of the jury, harken to the verdict as it shall be recorded," the clerk said, using the traditional words. "The United States of America versus Patricia Campbell Hearst, Criminal case 74-364. We the jury find Patricia Campbell Hearst, the defendant at the bar, Guilty as to Count One of the Indictment. Guilty as to Count Two of the Indictment. . . . So say you all."

Patricia took the verdict in silence, without expression. Bailey patted her back. She whispered to him, "I wonder, did I ever have a chance?" She did not look back at her parents, who were in the first row. But when she left the courtroom, Patricia and Janey Jimenez dissolved in tears.

In temperament and personality, Bailey was always a poor fit with the Hearsts. His ego and preening offended Randy and Catherine, who valued and practiced patrician discretion. They were willing to tolerate him as long as they thought he could win their daughter's case. Like most people, Patricia herself was intimidated by Bailey's swagger. For both Patricia and her parents, Al Johnson served as a calming intermediary. But her conviction shattered the alliance between lawyers and client—in subtle ways at first and then with a vengeance.

Bailey, in typical fashion, took the initiative to advance his own interests. Less than forty-eight hours after the verdict, he sent Al Johnson to the San Mateo jail with a letter for Patricia to sign. It read,

March 22, 1976
Putnam/Berkley Publishing Corp.
New York, New York

Gentlemen:

I understand that F. Lee Bailey is writing a book about my trial and life story as it pertains to the trial for which he will contract with you for publication in the United States and Canada.

As an inducement for you to publish this book, I hereby agree not to publish any account of my experiences in book, magazine, or any other form, prior to 18 months from your initial (hardcover) publication of Mr. Bailey's book, and I further agree to cooperate fully and exclusively with Mr. Bailey in his preparation and writing of the book in any manner he requires.

Sincerely,
Patricia Campbell Hearst

It speaks to Bailey's rugged concern for himself that he would confront a client facing thirty-five years in prison (twenty-five years for bank robbery, ten for the weapons charge) with such a document. He later claimed that he had discussed his plans to write a book with both Patricia and Randy. Bailey said they both encouraged him to do so, and his legal fee was calculated with possible book proceeds in mind.

(Randy and Patricia denied any such understanding.) And notwithstanding the first sentence in the letter, Bailey had already signed a contract with Putnam to write a book about the case. In any event, Patricia put her name to the letter. Bailey's incentive for the book deal was clear. His fee to Randy Hearst for his defense of Patricia was $150,000, which he split with Johnson and a handful of other lawyers. His book contract called for a payment of $225,000 and a $40,000 first serial deal with the *Ladies' Home Journal*.

Even though Patricia had been convicted of both charges against her, there was reason to believe that she might fare well in sentencing. Oliver Carter was more casual than most judges about conducting off-the-record conversations with lawyers. Al Johnson, ever amiable, had struck up a friendship of sorts with the judge, and Carter sent the lawyer clear signals that he did not intend to impose a heavy sentence, in the event she was convicted. This hopeful feeling for Patricia's team was reinforced on April 12, the initial date set for sentencing. In an arrangement agreed to by both sides, Carter did not impose an official sentence on that day but rather sent Patricia for a ninety-day psychological examination to determine her fitness to be sentenced. Patricia protested to her lawyers that she didn't want any more doctors probing her mental health, but Johnson assured her that this delay was the best route to a short sentence, maybe even probation. Reluctantly, Patricia agreed.

Then, suddenly, on June 14, Oliver Carter died. And on practically the same day, so, nearly, did Patricia Hearst.

She spent most of the months after the verdict talking—with a rotating cast of FBI agents and other law enforcement officials (often chaperoned by Al Johnson)—about SLA crimes, and, with yet another set of psychiatrists, about her past and present state of mind. After her fourth session with the agents, Patricia returned to her cell in San Mateo feeling unusually tired. She coughed and felt a sharp pain in her chest and then in her arm. Something was wrong. She made her way to the station of the deputy sheriff, who agreed to summon the jail doctor. In the manner of such things in a custodial setting, no one moved very quickly. It was an hour and a half before the physician summoned Patricia to his office.

Patricia thought she had a collapsed lung, but the doctor wasn't sure. In time, though, he agreed that she should be hospitalized, but there were no marshals around to transport her in the proper, secure manner. Patricia's breaths became shorter, and she started to panic. She wanted Al Johnson, but he had headed to the airport after the FBI debriefing. In that pre-cell-phone era, Patricia decided to call her mother to see if she could somehow track Al down at the airport. (She did.) Handcuffed, with a chain around her waist, Patricia was finally taken to Sequoia Hospital, in Redwood City.

The young doctor on duty at the emergency room took a look at an X-ray and determined that Patricia's right lung had collapsed and her heart was in trauma. Her blood pressure was falling, and she was going into shock. The doctor said she needed an operation to put a tube in her chest, and there was no time to move to an operating room. It had to be done in the ER immediately.

"What happens if you don't operate?" Patricia asked him.

"You'll die," the doctor said.

Patricia had the emergency surgery, where her lung was reinflated. She spent ten days in the hospital, where she was also found to be dangerously underweight. While still in delicate health, she was sent on an odyssey around the federal prison system in California, with stops at Pleasanton and San Diego before she returned to San Francisco for sentencing. Her final day in court was delayed, because a new judge had to be assigned to her case.

The new judge was William H. Orrick Jr., a former Justice Department official who had been on the federal bench for less than two years. He had had no previous connection to the case, and he had to learn the facts from the beginning. As it happened, Orrick was assigned to spend much of the summer as the assigned federal judge on Guam, so he took the full trial transcript with him. (It weighed a hundred pounds.) When he returned to San Francisco, he surveyed his fellow judges in the district for their suggestions about Patricia's sentence, which ranged from probation to twenty-five years. In the end, presented with this conflicting advice, Orrick decided to aim for a median sentence—to give Patricia roughly the same sentence as the "average" bank robber in Northern California.

On September 24, 1976, a year plus a few days after her arrest, Patricia stood before Orrick for sentencing. Al Johnson spoke on her behalf, saying she had been "brutalized, vilified, tortured, molested . . . punished, convicted and incarcerated." In other words, she had suffered enough. Browning acknowledged that Patricia had cooperated with the ongoing investigations into her comrades, but he noted too that she had never demonstrated any remorse nor taken any responsibility for her crimes. In imposing the sentence, the judge acknowledged that there appeared to be no need for Patricia to be rehabilitated—she had already turned her life around—but he said he needed to send a message that "violence is unacceptable and cannot be tolerated." In the end, Orrick sentenced Patricia to seven years, which he determined to be the average for bank robbers in the San Francisco courthouse.

The sentence was a bitter disappointment to Patricia, her family, and Al Johnson. In truth, Orrick's sentence was somewhat less draconian than it appeared. Because Patricia had already spent a year in custody, she would probably be eligible for release in one more year or two years at the most. There was an immediate silver lining, too. Orrick indicated he would be receptive to a request from Patricia to be released on bail pending appeal.

To that end, Al Johnson worked out a complicated and onerous bail package. Patricia's parents agreed to post $1 million in security to make sure Patricia made her post-trial appearances in San Francisco, and they put up another $250,000 to guarantee that she would show up for court in Los Angeles as well. (Patricia was also facing charges with the Harrises in connection with her shooting spree at Mel's and the kidnappings that followed.) By mid-1970s standards, these bail amounts were astronomical, and the Hearsts had less available cash than most people thought. Still, as before, the Hearsts found the cash to help their daughter.

But there was an even more unusual, and fateful, bail requirement. Before Judge Orrick would release Patricia, the Hearsts had to agree to provide her with round-the-clock security, consisting of at least four bodyguards at all times. The judge didn't explain how the Hearsts were supposed to go about creating such an elaborate security detail, and there were no agencies that did that sort of thing in the 1970s. So the Hearsts, and Patricia, did what they always did in this period to fix their problems. They asked Al Johnson to take care of them.

"FAVORING THE RICH OVER THE POOR"

A l Johnson worked his way through law school as a cop, and he retained a fondness for the police long into his career as a criminal defense attorney. Bailey found his friend's predilection mystifying at best, but Johnson sought out the cops in any city where he happened to be. Without his family in San Francisco, Johnson befriended many local officers and even went on ride-alongs to help pass the time on long, lonely nights. Suddenly, though, Judge Orrick's order made Johnson's familiarity with the local police a practical asset.

He figured Patricia needed about twelve bodyguards, working in shifts. Moonlighting cops would be ideal, and they would probably welcome the extra income. So Johnson asked for recommendations from the chief of detectives in the San Francisco Police Department, who had become a good friend. The chief said he had just the man to lead the contingent. Bernie Shaw was thirty-one years old and a Vietnam veteran with expertise in hand-to-hand combat. His record as a police officer was exemplary. Even better, he had the kind of stable personal life that would allow him to withstand the attention he might receive from being around the Hearsts. He was married with two young children and had been named the Catholic man of the year in public service by the Archdiocese of San Francisco. When Johnson interviewed Shaw, he was so impressed that he put the officer in charge of hiring the rest of the bodyguards. "You're going to be around a woman who has been through a lot emotionally," Johnson told Shaw. "You have to be very careful around her."

The Hearsts had sold the house in Hillsborough, so Patricia moved into an extra bedroom in the sprawling family apartment on Nob Hill, the most exclusive residential neighborhood in San Francisco. Janey Jimenez, the deputy marshal assigned to Patricia, gave up her career in law enforcement and moved into the apartment too, as a guide and companion. On Patricia's third night at home, Randy and Catherine, as well as Jimenez and Al Johnson, went to the famous bar at the top of the Mark Hopkins hotel to celebrate Patricia's release. The maître d' sent over a bottle of champagne, but the party was cut short when the hotel received a bomb threat, apparently thanks to Patricia's presence.

Still, Patricia started a new life. This chapter was an entirely new one, because even before her time in jail and with the SLA she had been sheltered with Steve Weed for more than a year. Now she was a single woman living in the city and, to put it mildly, she was in an unusual situation; she was world famous, and notorious, and she was facing the prospect of a prison sentence if her appeal failed. But once again, Patricia's strength and adaptability came to the fore. Still in her early twenties, she now embraced another new persona—that of a single and eligible heiress. She wanted to go to parties, and she wanted to date, which she did with her lead bodyguard, Bernie Shaw, seated discreetly at a nearby table.

In the meantime, the legal machinery continued to grind forward. The trial of Steve Soliah, Patricia's former lover, for his role in the Carmichael bank robbery had unfolded at almost the same time as her own in the Hibernia case. During her debriefings, Patricia told the FBI that Soliah had served as a lookout (with Bill Harris) for the invasion team inside the bank. But the prosecutors in Sacramento had already started their case based on the theory that Soliah was one of the robbers *inside*. Because the prosecutors in San Francisco were arguing that Patricia had lied in her own case, the prosecutors in Sacramento decided not to call her as a witness. This proved to be a major tactical error. In a cinematic moment during Soliah's trial, the defense called a customer who had been inside the bank at the time of the robbery. Audience members gasped as the witness walked to the stand, because he looked exactly like Soliah, lending credence to the defense theory of mistaken identity. The defense also called Emily Toback, a sometime girlfriend, who testified that he was with her at the time of the robbery. (Later, Toback was found to have lied about Soliah's alibi; she was visiting an inmate at Folsom State Prison during the robbery.) Still, in light of all the evidence, Soliah was acquitted. The verdict proved to be a godsend for the comrades. Spooked by the jury's decision on Soliah, the authorities all but abandoned the investigation of the robbery leading to Myrna Opsahl's death. It would take many years of effort by her son Jon to revive the investigation.

Patricia and the Harrises were still on the hook in Los Angeles for the shoot-out at Mel's and the kidnappings that followed. Al Johnson, heading into his third year representing Patricia, made several trips to negotiate with lawyers in the local district attorney's office. In the end, Johnson cut a sweet deal for Patricia. The prosecutors in L.A. decided they didn't need to add to the punishment Patricia had received on the federal charges in San Francisco; enough was enough. Patricia agreed to plead no contest (effectively guilty) to charges relating to Mel's, but with a guaranteed sentence of probation. Johnson also went to Sacramento, where the family of Myrna Opsahl was threatening to file a civil suit against Patricia. The Hearsts paid the Opsahls a significant amount of money to forestall a public fight. The two sides promised to keep secret both the existence and the amount of the settlement.

Patricia detested the enforced passivity of waiting around for court decisions, but she received little comfort from her mother, even though, like many women in their twenties, Patricia now had a more sympathetic view of her mother than she did as a teenager. But the strain of the last three years had worn down Catherine, and she had an emotional breakdown after Patricia was released. She withdrew from most activities, including membership in the Board of Regents, which the comrades had found so offensive. Randy had also grieved during his daughter's long absence, but he had grown, too. The kidnapping showed him that his life of hunting lodges and country clubs had been curiously sheltered. When Patricia was gone, a whole new world opened up to Randy. His newly acquired knowledge endeared him further to his daughter, and their bond, always strong, grew even closer.

Knowing his daughter as he did, Randy had a good idea for how Patricia should spend at least some of her time. Like everyone around her, Randy worried about Patricia's security, but he wanted to introduce her to working with something she loved—dogs. Randy gave her a guard dog trained at the Prion Animal Institute. The institute required future owners to spend two weeks on the premises, learning to understand and command the animal. Patricia loved the experience of bonding with Arrow, a two-and-a-half-year-old German shepherd. Unlike every human Patricia encountered, the dog didn't know or care about her history, and the intense activity offered a break from the monotony of awkward dates, FBI debriefings, and legal strategy sessions.

Her relationship with Johnson deteriorated after she got out on bail pending the result of her appeal. During her trial, Johnson operated as her intermediary with the outside world, especially regarding anything related to the multiple legal issues in her life. After Patricia was released, Johnson still tried to play that role, but she soon felt patronized. He had reassured her throughout her trial and sentencing, and both had ended badly. She wondered why she should keep believing anything he said. Still, their bond remained more personal than that between most lawyers and clients. They knew each other well, which was why Johnson was so surprised by a question Patricia asked him out of the blue one day.

"Do you know any divorce lawyers?"

Patricia knew Al Johnson to be a man of starchy rectitude, as well as an observant Catholic. So at first she wouldn't tell him why she was asking. Before too long, though, she confessed that the lawyer was for Bernie Shaw and that they had become a couple.

After Patricia's romance with Shaw became public, the press made much of the unlikelihood of the union between the cop and the heiress. Patricia herself liked to joke that her parents gave them a vacuum cleaner as a wedding present because they were so sure the union wouldn't last. In fact, their relationship, if not their marriage, seemed almost preordained. Like many people, Patricia had a type; she was drawn to men in authority—including a teacher (Steve Weed), kidnapper (Willy Wolfe), protector (Steve Soliah), and, finally, bodyguard (Bernie Shaw). A romance with a cop was also another way for Patricia to repudiate her life with the SLA. Nothing was more central to the worldview of the comrades than the belief that all cops were "pigs"; Patricia (as Tania) always referred to the police that way. Now she had fallen in love with one.

Al Johnson was appalled. He thought Patricia was still too emotionally fragile to engage in a serious relationship, and he felt betrayed by Shaw, whom he had hired in part because he was married. In so many words, Johnson informed Patricia that he thought her bodyguard had his eyes on the Hearst fortune. Understandably, Patricia thought Johnson should mind his own business. All she wanted was the name of a lawyer. Johnson came from Boston, so he didn't know many lawyers in San Francisco, but he told Patricia that he'd met one named George Martinez, and he seemed like a good guy.

Patricia's relationship with Shaw deepened as she awaited word from the court of appeals. Bailey pretty much ceased communicating with her after the verdict (leaving the task to Al Johnson), but Bailey did argue her appeal. Bailey claimed that Judge Carter sandbagged Patricia on the witness stand—that he had issued a ruling barring Browning from asking questions about her other crimes but then changed his mind once she started testifying, leading her to take the Fifth. But in a decision issued on November 2, 1977, a unanimous panel of the Ninth Circuit Court of Appeals upheld Patricia's conviction and sentence. On the sandbagging issue, the judges stated (correctly) that "the record does not show a firm, unequivocal ruling by the trial court" that limited the prosecutor's questions. Bailey asked the Supreme Court to hear Patricia's case, but on April 24, 1978, the justices declined to hear it. Judge Orrick set her return to prison for May 15. Patricia had been out of jail for six months—November 1977 to May 1978.

On the afternoon that she reported back to federal prison in Pleasanton, the scene at the gate was raucous. She arrived in a three-car caravan that included all the main figures from her new life: Bernie Shaw, of course, who was now her fiancé, George Martinez, the lawyer, Janey Jimenez, Trish Tobin, two of Patricia's sisters, and four bodyguards. Journalists, who didn't know the precise date that Patricia was supposed to arrive, had staked out the scene for more than a week, and they stampeded when they saw her get out of her car. Jimenez got a black eye, Tobin cut her leg, and Patricia had to fight her way through the crowd. Later, she observed ruefully that she was one of the few people ever to break *into* prison. This time she brought with her something even more important than her entourage—a plan that would have done her grandfather proud.

In short order, George Martinez went beyond simply representing Bernie Shaw in his divorce to replacing Bailey and Johnson as Patricia's lawyer. Martinez recognized that Patricia's legal options had run out. She could petition Judge Orrick for a reduction in sentence, but that was a long shot. Her only real hope was so audacious that it would not have occurred to most convicted felons—a commutation of her sentence by the president of the United States. But most convicted felons lacked the resources and connections of a Hearst.

Randy and Catherine had formally separated around the time Patricia returned to prison, but they found common cause in the effort to win their daughter a commutation from Jimmy Carter. They formed an organization called the Committee for the Release of Patricia Hearst, under the nominal leadership of the Reverend Ted Dumke, an Episcopal priest whom Patricia had known back in Berkeley. The family did bipartisan political outreach, with Catherine appealing to Republicans and Randy to Democrats. Catherine made the case to Ronald Reagan, her old sponsor, that Patricia was the victim of the evil counterculture; to Democrats like Leo Ryan, the congressman who represented the Hearsts' district, Randy argued that her punishment was excessive. Both ultimately endorsed a commutation. Charlie Bates, chief of the local FBI office, who had kept vigil with the Hearsts in Hillsborough, retired from the bureau and became an outspoken advocate for Patricia's release. Bernie Shaw persuaded dozens of his fellow cops to sign a petition on Patricia's behalf.

The key to the strategy, however, was Patricia herself and the news media. She learned that under the rules of her federal prison, she could give two press interviews a month, and she started filling her quota as soon as she arrived in Pleasanton. Patricia chose her outlets with care, mostly women's magazines and soft-focus columnists. She spoke to *McCall's, Look, Redbook, Ladies' Home Journal*, and several times to Bob Greene, a syndicated columnist who often told stories about strength in the face of adversity. "She is wary of being hurt, and at the same time seems to think that she cannot be hurt any further," Greene wrote. "When it was all happening to me, it was hard for me to accept that there were so many people who didn't care," Patricia told Greene. "I never want to publish a book. I don't ever want to write down what happened to me. I don't even talk to anybody about it anymore." The stories consisted of interviews with Patricia and her family, with few other sources consulted, and the pieces were accordingly highly sympathetic. Many dwelled on her romance with her bodyguard. "Bernie has been visiting her on the average of three times a week," the *Look* story recounted, "and has been writing four to seven letters a week as well, including ones from Arrow, her German shepherd, which he'd had the dog sign with the aid of an ink pad." None of the reporters explored her activities during her year-plus as a fugitive. Neither Mel's Sporting Goods nor Myrna Opsahl was mentioned.

The goal of the media offensive was to turn Patricia's image from convicted felon to wronged victim. But she needed something more than just sympathetic press coverage. So George Martinez convinced her that she had been betrayed by her own lawyers. He took the extraordinary step of filing a motion before Judge Orrick asking that her conviction be overturned because Patricia had received ineffective assistance of counsel from Bailey and Johnson, in violation of the Sixth Amendment. Specifically, Martinez claimed that Bailey had put Patricia on the witness stand with reckless disregard for whether she would have to take the Fifth Amendment in front of the jury. Even worse, he claimed that it was unethical for Bailey to present Patricia the waiver of her right to publish a book just two days after the verdict and, further, that Bailey's interest in writing a book represented a conflict of interest. As Martinez wrote in his motion, "Entering into a literary rights contract created a situation which prevented him from devoting the requisite undivided loyalty and service to his client."

The ineffective assistance motion—against the most famous criminal defense attorney in the United States—was outrageous. It was true that Bailey made a bad gamble in putting Patricia on the stand, but that was the kind of risk that trial lawyers took. It was not the kind of error that merited a new trial. Moreover, Bailey's arrangement for Patricia to cooperate on the Carmichael robbery was a savvy move on his part. His behavior about his book deal, while greedy and insensitive, created no conflict of interest; just the opposite, in fact. The chance for a book deal created an incentive for Bailey to win Patricia's case, not to lose it. That point became clear when Putnam canceled the book contract after Patricia was convicted. The publishing house figured that no one wanted to read a book written by the losing lawyer in what was called the trial of the century.

There was also a measure of poignancy in Patricia's motion based on the alleged incompetence of her lawyers. Bailey was never anything more than a mercenary, and he accepted Patricia's salvo with his customary cynicism. Al Johnson, on the other hand, was heartbroken. He had sacrificed years with his wife and children. He had regarded Patricia as a surrogate daughter, and she, for a time, saw him as a father figure as well. The motion meant that Patricia regarded Johnson as a mere tradesman, and an inept one as well. The attack on Bailey and Johnson represented another declaration of independence by Patricia. In keeping with her return to her family, the motion was also the haughty gesture of an aristocrat who claimed that she was convicted because of a failure by the help—not, certainly, because she was in fact guilty of crimes charged.

Within months of her arrival at the penitentiary, she engineered a successful transformation of the narrative about her case. Public memories of the trial, with its abundant evidence of her guilt, faded, replaced by Patricia's unrefuted account of her travails. The machine-gun-toting Tania was replaced by the innocent-eyed bride-to-be—of a police officer, no less. Her cause had been embraced by Republicans and Democrats, priests and cops. "I just try not to be bitter," Patricia told Bob Greene. "I try to look at the good side of this. A lot of things have happened to me that I don't suppose will ever happen to anyone else. And because of that I've grown. I'm a lot more tolerant of other people." Still and all, the change in imagery didn't change her status. She rose every morning to cook breakfast in forty-gallon steam kettles for her four hundred fellow inmates.

But Patricia's case was about to take a final turn in her favor. At one level, the source of her salvation was bizarre and unpredictable. At another, it was almost fitting that the crucial event was another episode of San Francisco madness—like the ones that led to her kidnapping in the first place. Leo Ryan Jr., her congressman and advocate, had become a pen pal as well. His last letter to Patricia was a short one. "Off to Guyana," he wrote. "See you when I return. Hang in there."

Back in the winter of 1974, the Reverend Jim Jones showed up at the China Basin warehouse and asked to distribute the food. Spooked by Jones's air of menace, the proprietors of the People in Need program declined his services. But Jones's fanatical dedication and that of his followers to a kind of ersatz socialism made them a disciplined and powerful force in San Francisco politics. Jones mobilized the largely African American flock in the Peoples Temple to elect George Moscone mayor of the city in 1975. Then, the following year, Jones was privately courted by Walter Mondale, the Democrats' vice presidential candidate. Rosalynn Carter met with Jones after she became First Lady. At a testimonial dinner, California's governor, Jerry Brown, said Jones "became an inspiration for a whole lot of people. He's done fantastic things."

Still, there were always hints of darker forces at work in the Peoples Temple. Some members died under mysterious circumstances, and others reported that Temple leaders pressured them into sexual relationships. Former followers contacted journalists, who began describing the Temple as a cult. Under new scrutiny, Jones complained about government conspiracies. Press coverage turned more critical in 1977 as members told reporters of kidnappings, extortion, and abuse by church leaders, including Jones himself. Earlier, Jones had rented thirty-eight hundred acres of land in the small South American nation of Guyana for use as an agricultural outpost. As pressure on the church mounted, Jones began demanding that his followers pick up stakes in San Francisco and move there. Hundreds of his acolytes and their families streamed into Guyana, and they founded a rugged community that they called Jonestown.

During this period, reports began filtering back to San Francisco of appalling conditions in Guyana. Jones decreed that his followers were to create a socialist paradise in the jungle, and these former urban dwellers found themselves working long hours for little or no pay, with few opportunities to contact their relatives in California. The reports reached Congressman Leo Ryan, who decided to conduct a fact-finding mission to Jonestown in November 1978. Ryan was also Patricia's leading advocate in Congress, and he jotted her the note just before he left on his mission to Guyana.

Ryan, accompanied by a small group of journalists and aides, made it to Jonestown on November 17. After one of Jones's followers attacked Ryan with a knife, the congressman's group fled to the small local airport. There, the group was set upon by Temple members and Jones's paramilitary force, and Congressman Ryan and four others were shot to death when they boarded their plane. Later that day, Jones and his assistants laced vats of Flavor Aid with cyanide and demanded that his followers commit what he called revolutionary suicide. In all, 909 members of his flock, including 304 children, died in the course of this episode of mass hysteria. The catastrophe generated massive press attention back in the United States, and the fallout from Guyana proved to be strangely helpful for the cause of Patricia Hearst's freedom.

Suddenly all of America was asking what would prompt hundreds of apparently ordinary citizens to take their lives in this manner and kill their own children. What kind of mental coercion would lead to such self-destructive, malevolent behavior? In other words, how could Jim Jones have brainwashed so many people? It was at precisely the time of this debate—late 1978—that Patricia's petition for clemency arrived in Washington, and her supporters made a direct connection between the two cases. John Wayne, the actor, was part of the curiously eclectic pro-Patricia coalition, and he drew the parallel. "It seems quite odd to me that the American people have immediately accepted the fact that one man can brainwash nine hundred human beings into mass suicide but will not accept the fact that a ruthless group, the Symbionese Liberation Army, could brainwash a little girl by torture, degradation, and confinement."

It was against this backdrop that the Justice Department, and then the White House, began to consider her application for a commutation. Browning had left the U.S. Attorney's Office after Patricia's conviction, and his successor, William Hunter, had no investment in the Hearst case. He told the Justice Department's pardon attorney, who reviewed Patricia's claim as an initial matter, that he thought a commutation was "the just and merciful thing to do." Charles Bates also argued in favor of Patricia's release, and his successor as head of the FBI field office in San Francisco offered no objection either. In a memo to the deputy attorney general, the pardon attorney observed, "This is a very unusual and difficult case." Patricia's original status as a kidnap victim rendered her situation unique. He noted further that "the traditional objectives for continued confinement—deterrence, rehabilitation, punishment, retribution, and community risk—have either been fulfilled or are no longer applicable to this case." With credit for time served, Patricia would be eligible for parole in July 1979, but a commutation would mean release in February. In all, the pardon attorney recommended clemency so that Patricia would be released approximately five months before she would likely have been paroled. Benjamin Civiletti, the deputy attorney general (and later the attorney general), ratified the recommendation of the pardon attorney and sent Patricia's file to the White House.

Stuart Eizenstat, Carter's domestic policy adviser, had some misgivings about a commutation. In a handwritten note to Robert Lipshutz, the White House counsel, Eizenstat wrote, "I'm concerned about granting clemency to Patty Hearst. It flies in the face of the President's oft-stated remarks about favoring the rich over the poor." Lipshutz replied, also by hand, that Carter wanted to handle the issue himself, writing to his colleague, "Therefore, it was *not* 'staffed.'" In other words, Lipshutz told Eizenstat to stay out of it. Lipshutz didn't talk to Carter about Hearst either, but he followed White House procedure and prepared a four-page memo for the president about the issue. His summary tracked the Hearsts' description of the underlying events. The Lipshutz memo had a lengthy description of Patricia's kidnapping and purported abuse and only a vague reference to her admission to "involvement in a series of criminal activities with other SLA members." Lipshutz made no reference to Patricia's participation in the Sacramento bank robberies, no mention of her involvement in the bombings in and around San Francisco, and nothing at all about the death of Myrna Opsahl.

Presidents are busy. They make many decisions every day based on some combination of instinct, conscience, and calculation. Presidents also rely on their staffs. The Hearsts knew that Jimmy Carter was a religious man with a deep spiritual investment in the concepts of redemption and forgiveness; he was also a politician heading into an election year. They designed their strategy to allow Carter's head to follow where they thought his heart would lead him. To that end, Carter was presented with a united political front in support of Patricia's release. Ronald Reagan, his likely opponent in the 1980 election, and the U.S. Attorney's Office that had prosecuted her and the FBI agents who pursued her all lent their names petitioning for her release. These negated any political risk to Carter for offering leniency. Reagan could scarcely accuse the president of being soft on crime for taking an action that the challenger himself supported. As Carter weighed his decision—with the airwaves full of talk about brainwashing in Guyana—he heard not a single voice in opposition to clemency.

On January 29, 1979, the president signed a commutation of the remainder of Patricia Hearst's prison sentence. He made no public comment or explanation for his action. Barbara Walters of ABC News reached Patricia in prison, and Patricia said of the president, "I'm really grateful that he was so courageous. It would have been so simple for him to leave everything the way it was. I thought I'd be spending another February 4 in prison." That would be the fifth anniversary of her kidnapping. Instead, she ran through the prison gates into the arms of Bernie Shaw on February 1.

The power and talent of the Hearst family had receded since the beginning of the twentieth century. But the campaign to free Patricia recalled William Randolph Hearst's grandest, and most notorious, crusade. In 1898, relying on his newspaper, his connections, and his will, the Chief tried to hasten the nation into the Spanish-American War. The great publisher understood that the right narrative before the right audience mattered as much as, if not more than, its underlying truth. Eighty years later, his descendants used the same methods to free his granddaughter. On both occasions, the great gift of the Hearsts, including Patricia herself, was to shape the perception of reality, if not reality itself. Everyone from beat cops in San Francisco to the president of the United States found reasons to trust the Hearsts. As before, the Hearsts' tale was believable, if not exactly true.

AFTERMATH

In and around San Francisco, the music stopped when the 1980s arrived. There was, essentially, no more counterculture; the term became obsolete. Radical outlaws like the members of the Symbionese Liberation Army, who even in their heyday were stragglers from the 1960s, virtually disappeared altogether. The FBI finally learned how to identify and prosecute politically engaged criminals, many of whom had turned to conventional crime, like drug dealing. Some were caught; others drifted away. In San Francisco, the AIDS plague arrived, decimating the gay community and sapping, for a time, the political energy of the city. The notion of revolution, which was never appealing to more than a handful of Americans, became absurd. Young people looked for inspiration not to the barrios of Uruguay but to the garages of Silicon Valley, across the bay from Berkeley.

The surviving members of the SLA, and their allies, struggled to find a place in this unwelcoming world. Joe Remiro and Russ Little, who were arrested in Concord the month before Patricia was kidnapped in 1974, were tried together for the murder of Marcus Foster. Without eyewitnesses to the shooting itself (which was done by Donald DeFreeze, Mizmoon Soltysik, and Nancy Ling), the case against Remiro and Little as conspirators was a close one. After lengthy jury deliberations, both men were convicted and then sentenced to life in prison. But an appeals court ordered a new trial for Little on the ground that the judge had coerced the jury into reaching his verdict. In a second trial, Little was acquitted, and he was released in 1981. He spent decades working in information technology for schools. At the age of sixty-nine, Remiro has spent more than forty years as an inmate in the California prison system. The parole board recommended his release in 2015, but as of mid-2016 Remiro remained in custody.

For the most part, the ragtag gang of supporters who sustained Patricia during her months on the lam disappeared. Wendy Yoshimura, who was arrested with Patricia, was convicted of charges relating to the bombing operations of her former boyfriend Willie Brandt. She served less than a year in prison. In subsequent decades, she became a familiar figure in Berkeley as a server at the Juice Bar Collective, a worker-owned organic vegetarian restaurant. She sells her watercolor paintings through a website and at local shows. Jack Scott went on to become a successful physiotherapist for elite athletes. His early work about the commercialization of college sports, and the medical risks to athletes, proved prescient. In 2000, he died of cancer at the age of fifty-seven.

Steve Soliah, Patricia's lover and roommate in the Morse Street apartment, returned to his life as a housepainter following his acquittal in Sacramento for the Carmichael bank robbery. He lived quietly in Berkeley until his death from a stroke at the age of sixty-four, in 2013. Steven Weed, Patricia's former fiancé, gave up his graduate studies in philosophy and became a real estate agent in Palo Alto. He and Patricia never spoke or saw each other after February 4, 1974.

Three of Patricia's associates—Jim Kilgore, Michael Bortin, and Kathy Soliah—became fugitives after the FBI busts in September 1975. Kilgore fled to South Africa, where he spent twenty-seven years as a teacher and anti-apartheid activist. He was extradited to the United States in 2002, where he pleaded guilty to charges relating to explosives and the Carmichael robbery. He was released in 2009, moved to Illinois, and recently published a book called *Understanding Mass Incarceration: A People's Guide to the Key Civil Rights Struggle of Our Time*. Michael Bortin surrendered in 1984, served eighteen months in prison on a parole violation, then moved to Portland, Oregon, where he married Josephine Soliah, Steve and Kathy's younger sister. He runs a business called Zen Hardwood Floors.

Kathy Soliah gave the speech in Ho Chi Minh Park, in 1974, memorializing her friend Angela Atwood, that drew Emily Harris to seek her out. Kathy introduced Bill, Emily, and Patricia to Jack Scott, who took them to the farm in Pennsylvania. When the comrades returned west, Kathy was among the most fanatical of them—a key figure in the Carmichael bank robbery and a zealous advocate and participant in the 1975 bombing campaign. After the arrests in September of that year, Kathy fled to Minnesota, where she had spent part of her childhood. Kathy Soliah started calling herself Sara Jane Olson and she took a job as a cook in a fraternity house. Soon after, she met a medical student named Fred Peterson, whom she married.

Over the next two decades, the couple led a quiet life in St. Paul while raising their three daughters. "Sara Jane" was so comfortable in her new identity that she began performing in amateur theatrical productions in the Twin Cities (like her late friend Angela), and her photograph appeared on posters around town. On May 15, 1999, the syndicated television program *America's Most Wanted* ran a feature on Kathy Soliah focusing on her role in the attempted bombing of the police car in Los Angeles. Afterward, the show received nineteen tips, one of them pointing to a fifty-two-year-old soccer mom and gourmet cook named Sara Jane Olson, who lived in the Highland Park neighborhood of St. Paul. The FBI followed up, compared photographs of Kathy Soliah with those of Sara Jane Olson, and then arrested her on June 16.

Sara Jane, as she preferred to be known, reacted with haughty indignation to her arrest. It was as if the passage of time, plus the stated purity of her intentions, absolved her of any responsibility for her behavior a quarter century earlier. She called her arrest "a witch hunt in the guise of a conspiracy case." Once released on bail, she devoted her energies to producing a cookbook as a fund-raiser for her defense. *Serving Time: America's Most Wanted Recipes* included an essay by Sara Jane, where she said, "The uses and perception of food in various cultures is based on wealth and power." Sara Jane hired Susan Jordan and Stuart Hanlon, two accomplished defense attorneys with long histories of defending radicals, and the case bogged down in procedural squabbling. Delay usually helps the defense in criminal trials, but here the case against Sara Jane was still unresolved when the nation was jolted by the terrorist attacks of September 11, 2001.

In the quarter century after the brief existence of the SLA, the group faded to a historical curiosity. Many of the comrades' activities, like the bumbling food giveaway, took on an almost comic afterlife, and the tale of the Hearst kidnapping lingered as a popular culture reference point, filed in the 1970s pantheon alongside the skyjacking epidemic and disco. After 9/11, though, terrorism—even inept terrorism—wasn't so funny. Around this time, too, prosecutors in Los Angeles began to take note of Jon Opsahl's crusade to hold someone accountable for his mother's death.

The renewed scrutiny put Bill and Emily Harris especially at risk. Following their arrests in 1975, the couple had artfully navigated through a great deal of legal peril. They stretched out both cases against them—for the kidnapping of Patricia and for the kidnapping of Tom Matthews and the others in Los Angeles—until the intense press attention had faded. They pleaded guilty to the Hearst kidnapping and were convicted after a short trial in L.A. Based on the two prosecutions, Bill and Emily served about six years in prison each, from 1977 to 1983.

Most remarkably, perhaps, they stayed married through the years of tumult and the frequent battles between them. Bill remained captivated by Emily's icy intelligence, and Emily loved Bill's antic energy. "My love," Emily wrote to Bill in prison in 1976, "I miss you so much. I have my favorite picture right on the wall at the foot of my bed so I can go to sleep looking at it and wake up the same way. I love you, I love you, I love you." Bill wrote, "Dear beautiful you. I love you Emily. There are so many familiar aspects in you! I know in that literal dungeon we still made life. Do they think they will set the revolution back? No way. Do they think they will intimidate us? Never. I reject this evil, uninformed death-oriented state. Your smile is so beautiful." They exchanged hundreds of ardent, often explicitly sexual letters from prison.

One subject that drew Bill and Emily together was their loathing for Patricia Hearst—or, more specifically, for the post-SLA version of Tania. They both insisted that the SLA had never harmed Patricia and that Tania's embrace of the comrades was voluntary. In a statement accompanying his guilty plea, Bill said, "Patricia Hearst was not tortured, raped, assaulted, brainwashed, denied food or use of a toilet or any form of personal hygiene. . . . Patricia Hearst was not coerced to reject her family and was not forced to stay with us. We encouraged Hearst to return to her family because we all knew that to stay with us she would risk her life and freedom as well as our own." In a letter to Bill around the same time, Emily wrote, "Did you see that horrible bitch on TV with her painted on face saying, 'They were alcoholics, murderers, rapists and they got what they deserved in LA'?"

After their release from prison, though, Bill and Emily got divorced. While in custody, Emily had become a lesbian, and she felt that her life could no longer include a marriage to Bill, even though the two remained close. Emily had studied computers in prison, and after her release she moved to the Los Angeles area and started a successful consulting business, with several major entertainment companies among her clients. She entered into a long-term relationship with a woman and ended all political involvements. She also changed her last name, hoping to avoid any association with her former notoriety.

Bill's first job out of prison was as a receptionist in his lawyer's office in San Francisco. His work there evolved into service as a private investigator. By the late 1990s, Bill had become a well-known PI for a diverse group of clients throughout the Bay Area. Unlike Emily, Bill clung to his ideological passions but now channeled them into more productive directions, like combating prosecutorial overreach. In 1988, Bill married Rebecca Young, a widely respected defense attorney in San Francisco. They bought a house in Oakland and had two boys, to whom Bill became a doting father. Instead of making bombs, he coached peewee soccer.

Then, following 9/11, the District Attorney's Office in Los Angeles wanted to vindicate the Opsahls and close the case of the attempted bombing of the police car, by the International House of Pancakes, in 1975. Mike Bortin, Sara Jane Olson, Bill Harris, and Emily Harris (under her new name), all well along in middle age, faced the prospect of spending the rest of their lives in prison for acts committed twenty-seven years earlier. Each defendant brought his or her own interests, and neuroses, to the question of how to handle the case. Olson preferred to give press interviews about her martyrdom rather than grapple with the overwhelming evidence of her guilt. Bill, encouraged by his wife, thought he could beat the case at trial, based on the age of the evidence against them. (The Carmichael bank building itself, for instance, had been demolished years earlier.) Bill especially relished planning the cross-examination of the expected star witness for the government—Patricia Hearst. Emily, on the other hand, felt genuine remorse about her actions and wanted to put the whole matter behind her by pleading guilty. In the end, they all cut deals, in return for sentences of six years. (Emily got eight years because she had used a firearm.) When Jim Kilgore was captured in South Africa, he took the same deal after he was returned to the United States. The Opsahl family won a small measure of long-delayed vindication.

Bill and Emily served about five years each, starting in 2003, and their second stint in prison proved to be tougher than their first. The rigors of American penal institutions fall heavily on men and women in their fifties. After her release, Emily struggled to restart her business in a fast-changing technology industry. For his part, Bill's marriage suffered during the long separation, as did his relationship with his two sons. Alienated from his family, Bill left Northern California and moved to one of the most remote locations in the United States (near his friend Russ Little). In keeping with his almost supernatural attraction to chaos, Bill moved into a new home that was almost, but not quite, subsumed by the lava from a volcano.

After stepping down as U.S. attorney shortly after Patricia's conviction, Jim Browning ran unsuccessfully for the Republican nomination for California attorney general. He later spent a decade as a superior court judge in San Mateo County, before retiring to Tucson. He died in 2016 at the age of eighty-three.

F. Lee Bailey's career never rebounded after Patricia's conviction. In 1982, Bailey was charged with driving while intoxicated in San Francisco. He was defended by a Los Angeles lawyer named Robert Shapiro (as well as by Al Johnson), and Bailey was acquitted after what was said to be the longest drunk-driving trial in American history. A decade later, Shapiro recruited Bailey to participate in O. J. Simpson's defense on double murder charges in Los Angeles. Starting in 1994, Bailey represented a large-scale marijuana dealer named Claude Duboc in Florida, where the defense lawyer had moved. As part of a plea bargain, Duboc turned over $5.9 million in stock to Bailey, who was supposed to hold the money in trust for later forfeiture to the government. During the pendency of the case, the value of the stock grew to more than $20 million. Bailey proposed to turn over $5.9 million to the government and keep the balance for himself. A federal judge ordered Bailey to turn over the full amount, and he refused. The judge jailed the lawyer for six weeks for contempt of court, and Bailey eventually turned over the full amount to the government. In 2001, the State of Florida disbarred Bailey for his role in the Duboc matter.

In 2010, Bailey moved to Maine and in 2012 passed the bar examination there. The state Board of Bar Examiners voted 5–4 to deny him a law license on the ground that he had failed to prove that he "possesses the requisite honesty and integrity" to practice law. In 2014, the Maine Supreme Court voted 4–2 to affirm the denial of the license to

Bailey. As of 2016, Bailey, at the age of eighty-three, was doing business as a "legal consultant" in a single room above a beauty salon in a resort town in Maine.

Catherine and Randy Hearst's divorce came through in 1982, forty-four years after they were married, but by that point they had already been living separate lives for several years. Catherine moved to Beverly Hills, where she lived a quiet life dedicated to church and family. She died of a stroke in 1998 at the age of eighty-one.

Shortly after the divorce, Randy married an Italian woman named Maria Scruggs, but they divorced after just three years. In 1987, Randy married Veronica DeGruyter Beracasa de Uribe at Wyntoon, the Hearst family estate in Northern California. Veronica was a woman of rather mysterious origin; her mother was said to be a Russian-born princess. Before Randy, her husbands included a Colombian cement magnate. The couple moved to New York City, where they bought a large Fifth Avenue apartment as a wedding gift to themselves. Randy was nominally chairman of the Hearst Corporation but had little to do with management of the company. He still preferred hunting and fishing to office work. Veronica, on the other hand, became an active presence at the company, especially at the magazines *Town & Country* and *Harper's Bazaar,* where she forced out the longtime editor. According to Patricia and her sisters, Veronica also erected barriers between Randy and his daughters. In July 2000, with Randy ill with prostate cancer, he and Veronica paid $30 million for Villa Venezia, a fifty-two-room, twenty-eight-thousand-square-foot mansion in Manalapan, Florida. Randy died on December 18, 2000, at the age of eighty-five.

Randy's career, and those of his brothers, proved the wisdom of their father's decision to leave the management of the Hearst interests to professionals instead of family members. Though many old media companies have withered in recent decades, the Hearst Corporation has thrived, thanks in significant part to an early investment in a company that was first known as the Entertainment and Sports Programming Network. Hearst still owns 20 percent of the company now known as ESPN. The stake in the television sports network is a major reason that Randy died a billionaire.

Patricia Hearst, then twenty-five years old, married Bernie Shaw on April 1, 1979, two months after her release from prison. She had served about twenty-two months. They lived in a modest home south of San Francisco, where Bernie continued working as a police officer. Patricia was still on probation for the next two years, during which she dabbled in one thing or another. She trained beagles to sniff out termites. She did a little fund-raising for a child care center named for Leo Ryan, the congressman who advocated for her release before he was killed in Guyana. She did a lot of horseback riding. She filled out a form every month for her probation officer indicating that she was unemployed. "The form asks why," Patricia told *People,* "and I say, 'Because I don't want to' or 'I don't have to.'" As soon as her probation ended, though, Patricia did go to work—on a book.

While in prison, she often told interviewers that she would never write a memoir, but she quickly changed her mind on the outside. Even after the commutation of her sentence, Patricia remained outraged, in her deadpan way, that she had been convicted at all. She blamed the SLA (and her own lawyers), and she wanted the world to know it. Like her father, Patricia was asset rich and cash poor, to her way of thinking, so the prospect of a book deal was appealing. She received an advance of $600,000, one of the largest ever for a nonfiction book at the time. While nursing her daughter Gillian, born in 1981, she sat with a ghostwriter and told her story.

Every Secret Thing, published in 1982, was an elaboration of her testimony at her trial—a vivid recounting of her ordeal from her kidnapping in 1974 to her release from prison in 1979. In the book, she described herself as a helpless victim for her year and a half with the SLA, living perpetually in fear of Donald DeFreeze and then Bill Harris. She wrote of Willy Wolfe with loathing, Steve Soliah with disdain. She portrayed Jack Scott as a greedy hustler who wanted Patricia and the comrades to sell a book so that he could stash the proceeds in a Liechtenstein corporation. (After publication of the book, Jack Scott sued Patricia for libel; she paid him a $30,000 settlement.) In the book, she did write with some warmth about Lydia Scott, Jack's mother, who became close to Patricia during their cross-country journey. In 1984, Patricia had her second daughter, whom she named Lydia.

Every Secret Thing was a best seller, and Patricia found she enjoyed a return to the limelight. She gave many interviews to friendly and for the most part under-informed journalists. In the mid-1980s, Patricia and her family moved cross-country to the Connecticut suburbs of New York, where Bernie took a job as the head of security for the Hearst Corporation. (Generations of Hearst journalists have cheerful memories of Bernie taking their pictures for their photo IDs.) More settled and relaxed on the East Coast, Patricia let the madcap side of her character show when she agreed to perform cameos in a series of campy movies directed by John Waters. She cowrote *Murder at San Simeon,* a roman à clef mystery based on an actual murder that took place there during her grandfather's lifetime. She also hosted and narrated a documentary about her family's extraordinary estate.

Still, even though Patricia settled into a contented life with a healthy family, she continued to feel wronged by her conviction and her status as a convicted felon. So, in the 1990s, Patricia decided that she wanted a presidential pardon, also known as executive clemency. It is a measure of her sense of grievance, and of entitlement, that she set off on this quest even though no one in modern American history had ever before received a commutation from one president and a pardon from another. Moreover, Justice Department guidelines state that executive clemency is traditionally given only to those defendants who accept responsibility for their actions. "A petitioner should be genuinely desirous of forgiveness rather than vindication," the rules state. But Patricia never acknowledged any wrongdoing on her part. The effect of the pardon would mostly be symbolic—including a restoration of certain rights, such as the right to purchase and possess firearms—but Patricia still ardently sought the relief.

In the late 1990s, toward the end of Bill Clinton's presidency, the reaction in the law enforcement community to Patricia's pardon was very different from what it had been two decades earlier to her commutation. Robert S. Mueller III, then the U.S. attorney in San Francisco (and later director of the FBI), wrote a scathing letter of objection. He said that Patricia was counting on the passage of time to allow her to rewrite history. As for the Hibernia robbery, Mueller wrote, "The record at trial was clear that Hearst's gun was loaded and that she was not only a willing participant in that robbery, but participated with zeal because of her commitment to 'revolutionary' causes. The people who wrote in support of her pardon application obviously know nothing about the bombing of police vehicles by Hearst and her associates or her involvement in the Carmichael robbery and murder. Hearst's claim that she was forcibly raped by William Wolfe and Donald DeFreeze is no more credible now than in 1976." Mueller noted that in later investigations of SLA crimes, Patricia had been singularly unhelpful, pleading a faulty memory and busy schedule. In sum, Mueller said, "Any further grant of executive clemency will be characterized by Hearst and her supporters as vindication and proof of her innocence. The attitude of Hearst has always been that she is a person above the law and that, based on her wealth and social position, she is not accountable for her conduct despite the jury's verdict."

But Patricia had two important allies in her quest for a pardon: Jimmy and Rosalynn Carter. On December 4, 2000, as the recount fight to determine the new president raged, the former president wrote to Clinton. "While I am sure there are a number of meritorious applications pending, there is one in which I have long had a keen interest, and that is the application of Patricia Hearst Shaw," Carter wrote. "The act of pardon, representing the nation's forgiveness of her actions that occurred during her captivity, has enormous significance to her personally. As I understand her desires, she seeks to relate the ultimate meaning and the nation's recognition of those traumatic events 27 years ago, when she was a young woman, to her two now nearly grown daughters." A month later, with just ten days left in Clinton's term in office, the former First Lady faxed a handwritten note to Clinton, which said, "She made a mistake, but she has led an exemplary life for 20 years now. For her sake, and especially for the sake of her daughters, I hope you can find it in your heart to pardon her." On the fax cover sheet to Rosalynn's letter, Clinton wrote in his distinctive left-handed scrawl to Beth Nolan, his White House counsel, "I think I should do this.—BC." On January 20, 2001, Clinton's last day in office, he included a full pardon to Patricia Hearst among the 140 he issued that day.

Patricia Hearst was a woman who, through no fault of her own, fell in with bad people but then did bad things; she committed crimes, lots of them. Patricia participated in three bank robberies, one in which a woman was killed; she fired a machine gun (and another weapon) in the middle of a busy city street to help free one of her partners in crime; she joined in a conspiracy to set off bombs designed to terrorize and kill. To be sure, following her arrest in 1975, she was unlikely to commit these kinds of crimes again. If the United States was a country that routinely forgave the trespasses of such people, there would be little remarkable about the mercy she received following her conviction. But the United States is not such a country; the prisons teem with convicts who were also led astray and who committed lesser crimes than Patricia. These unfortunate souls have no chance at even a single act of clemency, much less an unprecedented two. Rarely have the benefits of wealth, power, and renown been as clear as they were in the aftermath of Patricia's conviction.

Still, at each stage in her life, Patricia used the tools at her disposal. She was a straightforward person, and starting on February 4, 1974, she reacted to her challenges in rational ways. Surrounded by passionate, charismatic outlaws who told her that the police were out to kill them all, Patricia joined with them in a pact of mutual self-defense; when the police did in fact kill nearly all of them, Patricia hit the road with her comrades to try to escape. Little wonder that in such emotionally fraught surroundings a young woman would have fallen in love—twice. But when she and her comrades were caught, Patricia was rational once more. A jail cell, and the prospect of many more years in one, prompted her to make haste to embrace her former life of privilege. A clear thinker, if not a deep one, Patricia understood that for her rich was better than poor and freedom was better than confinement. She chose accordingly.

Bernie Shaw died on December 18, 2013, at sixty-eight, after a long battle with cancer. Patricia herself was just short of sixty at the time, and after losing her husband, she embraced a more fully private life. She rejoiced in her first grandchild. In her dowager years, she found solace in her lifelong love of dogs. In 2015, her shih tzu named Rocket won first place in the toy category at the Westminster Kennel Club dog show. "People move on," she told reporters, smiling at Rocket. "I guess people somehow imagine you don't evolve in your life. I have grown daughters and granddaughters and other things that normal people have." Still, Patricia admitted that her daughters preferred cats. "I don't know what I did wrong," she said, joking. In the end, notwithstanding a surreal detour in the 1970s, Patricia led the life for which she was destined back in Hillsborough. The story of Patricia Hearst, as extraordinary as it once was, had a familiar, even predictable ending. She did not turn into a revolutionary. She turned into her mother.

AUTHOR'S NOTE

Patricia Hearst chose not to cooperate with the publication of this book. I contacted her directly several times, and also through friends, and I regret that she chose not to participate in any way. Because she is the central figure, and because I attribute statements and sentiments to her throughout the text, I think it's appropriate for me to explain how I did the research for *American Heiress*.

As detailed below, I had access to Patricia's perspective from a variety of sources. Her memoir, *Every Secret Thing,* was the starting point. I also read her testimony at her trial and before several grand juries investigating other crimes. I examined dozens of FBI summaries (302s) of her interviews with agents. I reviewed her many press interviews and media appearances over the years. In addition, I interviewed people who knew Patricia and who were with her during the relevant periods. I also reviewed an abundance of documentary and physical evidence about Patricia's conduct, statements, and views. These included her letters, communiqués, and statements to others that they later recounted to investigators, as well as photographs, recordings, and videos.

After Bill Harris was released from prison, he set out to obtain the legal and investigative files from the defense teams in all the prosecutions of SLA figures. He also worked on some of these cases as a private investigator. He collected the files in the cases against himself and Emily Harris, Joe Remiro and Russ Little, Wendy Yoshimura, Steve Soliah, and Kathy Soliah (Sara Jane Olson). When I met Bill, his

plan to sell the collection to the library of a major university had just
fallen through. Instead, I purchased them. The collection consists of
approximately 150 boxes of material, and it served as the most important resource in my research. Following the publication of this book, I
will donate the collection to the library of Harvard Law School, which
has all of my papers.

The collection includes the following:

- the full transcripts, with exhibits, of all the trials
- legal documents, including motion papers and court
  rulings, in the trials
- transcripts of witness testimony before all relevant grand
  juries
- FBI reports (302s) of interviews with hundreds of
  witnesses, including Patricia
- thousands of pages of evidence in the cases, much of
  it obtained by the FBI and produced to the defense in
  discovery, and also evidence generated by the defense's own
  investigations
- research memoranda from private investigators based on
  their interviews with witnesses and examination of evidence
- memoranda from defense attorneys about trial strategy and
  legal issues

Two parts of the collection deserve particular mention. In preparation for the trial of Sara Jane Olson, following her arrest in 1999, two
of her private investigators, Jacqui Tully and Josiah "Tink" Thompson, prepared a narrative history of the SLA from its origins in 1973
to the arrests in September 1975. It is based principally on interviews with Bill and Emily Harris, as well as Russ Little, and it also
relies on the investigators' examinations of FBI interviews, grand jury
transcripts, and other investigatory material. It runs more than sixty
single-spaced pages, and it provides an extremely useful account of
the story from the perspective of the SLA members themselves. The

investigators' narrative includes extensive descriptions of Patricia's behavior, statements, and demeanor from the kidnapping in February 1974 to the period immediately after the arrests in September 1975, as it was described by the SLA comrades.

If Olson had gone to trial, Patricia Hearst would have been the principal witness against her. (Olson pleaded guilty, so there was no trial.) To prepare for Hearst's testimony and ultimately for her cross-examination, Olson's attorneys and investigators attempted to collect all of Patricia's prior statements to law enforcement and the public. This part of the collection alone runs to thousands of pages. It includes transcripts of Patricia's trial and grand jury testimony; the FBI 302s summarizing her interviews; her book, *Every Secret Thing,* as well as rough drafts and outlines; and dozens of media interviews. (The endnotes in my text cite only secondary sources, including *Every Secret Thing,* but for simplicity do not refer to other source material.)

Over the years, the FBI has released thousands of pages of material from its investigation of the Hearst kidnapping (code-named HERNAP) and its aftermath, pursuant to the Freedom of Information Act. There is considerable, but not total, overlap between the FBI material in the Bill Harris collection and that in the public FBI files. My thanks to John Fox, the FBI historian, for guiding me through this material, especially the photographs.

Patricia also spoke for more than twenty hours to Lawrence Grobel for an interview that ran in the March 1982 issue of *Playboy.* The version that ran in the magazine was edited and condensed, but I obtained from Grobel the full transcript of all of his interviews with Patricia.

I also conducted interviews with more than a hundred people connected to the case, including principals, witnesses, government and defense investigators, prosecutors, and defense lawyers. Many of these people recounted their impressions of and conversations with Patricia. These interviews covered the full arc of Patricia's life, from her childhood to the present day.

In short, though I was unable to speak with Patricia, I feel I had ample access to her perspective on the events described. On certain matters, as I describe in the text, the evidence about her behavior and feelings is contradictory. On the central issue in Patricia's case and this book—whether, following her kidnapping, she made a voluntary decision to commit crimes with the SLA—there is conflicting evidence. In sum, I have reviewed as much evidence as I could find about Patricia and made my conclusions in good faith. I trust that readers will do the same.

One of the pleasures of writing a book, and especially of finishing one, is the opportunity to thank the people who helped me along the way. In the Bay Area, I treasure the friendship and guidance of Sydney Goldstein and Chuck Breyer; John and Tina Keker; David Fechheimer; and Tink Thompson. I am also pleased to have the opportunity to thank Howard Cohen; John Q. Barrett; Jane Yeomans; and Madeleine Baverstam. In Sherman, Connecticut, Annie Swanson and Anne Maitland performed, with great skill, the indispensable task of indexing the contents of Bill Harris's many, many boxes of documents.

I am grateful to Jim Browning, the lead prosecutor in Patricia's trial, who shared with me his unpublished memoir about the case. He also allowed me to copy photographs of the Olmec monkeys that belonged to Patricia and Willy Wolfe. I am sorry to report that Jim died suddenly a few weeks after we spoke in early 2016.

I also acknowledge the assistance of my friends at the following collections and libraries: National Archives, Pacific Regional Branch Office, San Francisco/San Bruno, Record Group 118, U.S. Attorney's Files, Case File 810766 (*United States v. Patricia Hearst*); Gustavus Adolphus College Archives (Camilla Hall collection), in St. Peter, Minnesota; San Francisco Public Library; Jimmy Carter Presidential Library, in Atlanta, Georgia; and William J. Clinton Presidential Library, in Little Rock, Arkansas.

I am privileged again to be published by Doubleday, and am happy (again) to thank my editor Bill Thomas, as well as Rose Courteau,

Todd Doughty, Bette Alexander, and Ingrid Sterner. Thanks (again!) to my agent, Esther Newberg, and to my literary *consigliere,* Phyllis Grann.

I remain grateful for the opportunity to work at *The New Yorker* alongside my colleagues and bosses David Remnick, Dorothy Wickenden, and John Bennet. I'm lucky, too, to work with (and for) Jeff Zucker and the team at CNN.

Amy McIntosh and I met some time ago when she edited my copy. I'm delighted that she still does and that she shares her life with me.

NOTES

CHAPTER 1: NERVOUS BREAKDOWN NATION

14 Membership in the Weathermen: Burrough, *Days of Rage,* 218–19.

16 The headlines the next day: Talbot, *Season of the Witch,* 206–18; Howard, *Zebra,* 182–227; *People v. Cooks,* Calif. Ct. Crim. App. (1983), http://law .justia.com/cases/california/court-of-appeal/3d/141/224.html.

CHAPTER 2: FROM INSIDE THE TRUNK

20 George loved to buy land: Nasaw, *Chief,* 11.

21 Hearst, it is often claimed: On the question of whether Hearst actually started the war, see ibid., 130–33.

22 Shortly after their birth: Ibid., 253–57.

23 "The boys, following in": Ibid., 361.

23 There Randy fell: Karen G. Jackovich and Dianna Waggoner, "Patty's Free, but Randolph Left, and Catherine Hearst Wonders What's Next," *People,* April 9, 1979.

24 In 1965, Randy was named: Nasaw, *Chief,* 584–85.

26 "When she did this to me": Hearst, *Every Secret Thing,* 11.

26 "He was everything": Ibid., 15.

28 "She judged things": Weed, *My Search for Patty Hearst,* 33.

28 "If you don't like it": Hearst, *Every Secret Thing,* 24–25.

28 One night at dinner: Weed, *My Search for Patty Hearst,* 37.

29 "Shut your mouth": Hearst, *Every Secret Thing,* 31–32.

CHAPTER 3: THE SLA

31 Cinque M'tume: Cummins, *Rise and Fall of California's Radical Prison Movement,* 240.

31 DeFreeze was thirty: For background on DeFreeze, see McLellan and Avery,

Voices of Guns, 307–21; Bryan, *This Soldier Still at War,* 145–51; Kinney, *American Journey,* 166–68.

34 "It's me they want": Cummins, *Rise and Fall of California's Radical Prison Movement,* 209.

35 Black Cultural Association: McLellan and Avery, *Voices of Guns,* 56–57.

36 On December 11, 1972: Ibid., 87–88.

38 Little, a Floridian: For background on Little, see Kinney, *American Journey,* 149–53; Bryan, *This Soldier Still at War,* 134–45; McLellan and Avery, *Voices of Guns,* 180–83.

39 "I was gung-ho": Bryan, *This Soldier Still at War,* 25.

39 "They go through an area": Ibid., 34.

40 "The revolution don't have nothin'": Ibid., 7.

40 "revolution is horrible": Ibid., 6.

41 Marcus Foster's life: For background on Foster, see John Spencer, *In the Crossfire: Marcus Foster and the Troubled History of American School Reform* (Philadelphia: University of Pennsylvania Press, 2012), 18–25.

42 "Above all, Foster wanted": Ibid., 86–88, 157.

42 "Hey, what are you doing?": Ibid., 172–73. See also Jon S. Birger, "Race, Reaction, and Reform: The Three Rs of Philadelphia School Politics, 1965–1971," *Pennsylvania Magazine of History and Biography,* July 1996, 163–216.

43 Republicans denounced him: Spencer, *In the Crossfire,* 216–18.

44 "We were sitting around": McLellan and Avery, *Voices of Guns,* 111.

44 November 6, 1973: John P. Spencer, *In the Crossfire: Marcus Foster and the Troubled History of American School Reform.* (Philadelphia: University of Pennsylvania Press, 2012), 218–19. On the details of the shooting, see also McLellan and Avery, *Voices of Guns,* 127–29.

CHAPTER 4: THE POINT OF NO RETURN

51 In the course of their brief heyday: Jennifer S. Holmes, *Terrorism and Democratic Stability* (Manchester: Manchester University Press, 2001), 56–57.

51 For some putative victims: Payne, Findley, and Craven, *Life and Death of the SLA,* 186–89; McLellan and Avery, *Voices of Guns,* 152–54.

52 "America suffered more wounds": Perlstein, *Invisible Bridge,* xiii.

54 In the early morning hours: For description of this encounter, see Bryan, *This Soldier Still at War,* 197–203; McLellan and Avery, *Voices of Guns,* 159–64.

56 Keep your hand gun: McLellan and Avery, *Voices of Guns,* 165.

57 "as kids and neighbors": Baker, *Exclusive!,* 47–51.

57 "The house was furnished": McLellan and Avery, *Voices of Guns,* 168. For another description of what was found in the safe house, see Bryan, *This Soldier Still at War,* 205–7.

58 Emily and Mizmoon found: Cumming, "End of an Era," 83–84.

58 The full SLA reassembled: Kinney, *American Journey,* 229.

CHAPTER 5: PRISONER OF WAR

66 Finally, around 9:00 p.m.: Cumming, "End of an Era," 86–88; McLellan and Avery, *Voices of Guns,* 194–96.

71 The second-youngest daughter: McLellan and Avery, *Voices of Guns,* 194–95.

74 "that the FBI's reputation": Weiner, *Enemies,* 311.

76 Her name meant Angel of the Angels: For background on Angela Atwood, see McLellan and Avery, *Voices of Guns,* 80–85; Bryan, *This Soldier Still at War,* 128–31.

77 The two aspiring actresses: Hendry, *Soliah,* 61.

79 "All men must die": Hearst, *Every Secret Thing,* 68.

CHAPTER 6: NOT JUST A BUNCH OF NUTS

88 a former astronaut: Lester, *Girl in a Box,* 70.

88 Swami Number 2: Weed, *My Search for Patty Hearst,* 118–21, 165.

95 "God sent me": Spieler, *Taking Aim at the President,* 80–82.

CHAPTER 7: THREE HUNDRED BALD MEN

99 Mizmoon was white: Soltysik, *In Search of a Sister,* 3, 11, 16.

101 In the joyful first days: Ibid., 35–36; Hanel, "Camilla Hall's Place in the Symbionese Liberation Army," 59.

101 "Revolution has to be social": Hanel, "Camilla Hall's Place in the Symbionese Liberation Army," 60.

102 "But, much as I want": Ibid., 61.

102 Nancy Ling Perry: For background on Perry, see McLellan and Avery, *Voices of Guns,* 174–78; Kinney, *American Journey,* 173–77; Bryan, *This Soldier Still at War,* 118–21.

103 When Ling was hitchhiking: Bryan, *This Soldier Still at War,* 119.

106 Bey also earned a reputation: Chris Thompson, "The Sinister Side of Yusuf Bey's Empire," *East Bay Express,* Nov. 13, 2002.

106 On the morning of February 22: Payne, Findley, and Craven, *Life and Death of the SLA,* 223–25; McLellan and Avery, *Voices of Guns,* 242–44.

110 "Whatever happened": Baker, *Exclusive!,* 21–23; Weed, *My Search for Patty Hearst,* 175–77.

111 "egocentric pain in the ass": Lester, *Girl in a Box,* 73.

CHAPTER 8: "I'M A STRONG WOMAN"

114 "Your mommy and daddy": Kohn and Weir, "Tania's World."

114 "Ajax": Hearst, *Every Secret Thing,* 83.

114 "gesticulating, rolling her eyes": Ibid., 88.

114 "Oh, I wish you could see": Ibid.

116 "I wasn't much of a climber": Kinney, *American Journey*, 176.

118 "I don't like to see": Ibid., 143.

CHAPTER 9: THE BIRTH OF TANIA

126 "We do not comprehend": Burrough, *Days of Rage*, 288–89.

128 "It's just too bad": McLellan and Avery, *Voices of Guns*, 242–43.

132 Patricia's version of her relationship: Hearst, *Every Secret Thing*, 88–90.

135 "Reagan's a jackass": Lester, *Girl in a Box*, 68.

137 "Tiny, you remember": Hearst, *Every Secret Thing*, 96–100.

CHAPTER 10: STAY AND FIGHT

140 Camilla Hall, the one: McLellan and Avery, *Voices of Guns*, 219.

140 The car sat outside: Cumming, "End of an Era," 115–16.

141 She was not impressed: Hearst, *Every Secret Thing*, 105.

143 "They can hide her": Lester, *Girl in a Box*, 66.

144 When Hearst hosted: Talbot, *Season of the Witch*, 186.

144 The next day, however: Lester, *Girl in a Box*, 79.

149 "I think they killed": Ibid., 85.

151 "This is a holdup!": Description of the bank robbery comes from trial testimony, Cumming, "End of an Era," 166–69; Hearst, *Every Secret Thing*, 146–49; McLellan and Avery, *Voices of Guns*, 322–40.

CHAPTER 11: COMMON CRIMINALS

158 "This is for you, Tania": Hearst, *Every Secret Thing*, 153.

160 "The city seemed to crackle": Talbot, *Season of the Witch*, 218.

164 "We need a goddamn South American": Weed, *My Search for Patty Hearst*, 238–39.

168 young woman of the house: Hearst, *Every Secret Thing*, 163–65.

169 They rented a two-bedroom place: McLellan and Avery, *Voices of Guns*, 339–40.

CHAPTER 12: SHOWDOWN AT MEL'S

174 Even by the modest standards: Hearst, *Every Secret Thing*, 195.

174 On one occasion: Ibid., 194.

175 "Gelina would be much better": Ibid., 203.

176 Even through the windshield: The secondary sources consulted for the incident at Mel's include ibid., 203–6; McLellan and Avery, *Voices of Guns*,

341–45. The most detailed account comes from *Symbionese Liberation Army in Los Angeles.*

176 First, they bought: Cumming, "End of an Era," 190.

180 "What did you take?": Hearst, *Every Secret Thing,* 207.

CHAPTER 13: LIVE ON TELEVISION

187 The team included: Domanick, *To Protect and to Serve,* 207.

190 "Tell Bill I understand": Gates, *Chief,* 132.

193 "I saw your lights": The exchange with the women in the house comes from McLellan and Avery, *Voices of Guns,* 349–50.

196 At one point: Ibid., 354–55.

CHAPTER 14: APOCALYPSE ON FIFTY-FOURTH STREET

199 To Patricia Hearst, Disneyland: Hearst, *Every Secret Thing,* 222–24.

201 "What the hell is it": Weed, *My Search for Patty Hearst,* 304, 309.

201 On the afternoon of May 16: Lester, *Girl in a Box.*

205 At that moment, Daryl Gates: Gates, *Chief,* 135.

206 "Don't leave my dogs behind!": McLellan and Avery, *Voices of Guns,* 359.

208 "Look!" said Bill Harris: Hearst, *Every Secret Thing,* 222–26.

209 "I was a soldier": Ibid., 226.

210 "Tania's found": Weed, *My Search for Patty Hearst,* 321.

210 "I should go down there": Lester, *Girl in a Box,* 171.

CHAPTER 15: "THE GENTLEST, MOST BEAUTIFUL MAN"

217 Then, with their finances: Hearst, *Every Secret Thing,* 233–36.

219 "I was being left alone": Ibid., 240–41.

219 Rejected sexually by Emily: Ibid., 240.

221 The front of the small: Hendry, *Soliah,* 113–17.

223 Emily still had Kathy Soliah's address: Hearst, *Every Secret Thing,* 243–45.

CHAPTER 16: JACK SCOTT MAKES AN OFFER

232 All three were in full battle dress: Hearst, *Every Secret Thing,* 262–66.

CHAPTER 17: ROAD TRIP

239 Among other topics: Hearst, *Every Secret Thing,* 271.

243 "Within a few minutes": Ibid., 272–73.

244 "For the first time in months": Ibid., 276.

246 On March 30, 1972: McLellan and Avery, *Voices of Guns,* 389–90.

247 When Bill arrived, he disrupted: Hearst, *Every Secret Thing,* 278–79.

250 "She was calm and friendly": Ibid., 275.

250 "I hope you'll have a chance": Quoted in McLellan and Avery, *Voices of Guns,* 399.

255 "I went out for a jog": Hearst, *Every Secret Thing,* 288.

CHAPTER 18: THE STREETS OF SACRAMENTO

259 "I had to do everything": Hearst, *Every Secret Thing,* 298.

261 "an easygoing young man": Ibid., 325.

268 The Harrises drew up: McLellan and Avery, *Voices of Guns,* 431–32.

CHAPTER 19: DEATH OF A "BOURGEOIS PIG"

274 Family and church dominated: Hendry, *Soliah,* 140.

274 On that Monday: McLellan and Avery, *Voices of Guns,* 444–45.

280 "We had developed our own": Hearst, *Every Secret Thing,* 339.

280 "Our position on equality": Ibid., 340–41.

CHAPTER 20: FEMINIST BOMB-MAKING

282 "The components were easily purchased": Hearst, *Every Secret Thing,* 345.

283 She envisioned simple pipe bombs: Ibid., 345–46.

283 According to Patricia: Ibid., 346.

285 Indeed, as Patricia heard the story: Ibid., 353.

287 "We began to destroy": Quoted in McLellan and Avery, *Voices of Guns,* 455, 456.

289 Between bombings: Hearst, *Every Secret Thing,* 344–45.

CHAPTER 21: FREEZE!

292 In the middle of the search: Alexander, *Anyone's Daughter,* 341.

292 In any event, at around two: McLellan and Avery, *Voices of Guns,* 435–37.

297 "I was a pretty fair athlete": Kohn and Weir, "Tania's World."

300 Still, he cooperated: McLellan and Avery, *Voices of Guns,* 469–70.

301 "Daddy! How could you": Ibid., 476.

303 The agents decided: Ibid., 487–90.

305 When Patricia stood up: Hearst, *Every Secret Thing,* 359–61.

CHAPTER 22: "THERE WILL BE A REVOLUTION IN AMERIKKKA AND WE'LL BE HELPING TO MAKE IT"

309 "Never sign anything": Hearst, *Every Secret Thing,* 362.

CHAPTER 24: MORE EXCITED THAN SCARED

334 A former newspaperman: Tim Weiner, "Remembering Brainwashing," *New York Times,* July 6, 2008.

341 "Right now we are brainwashing": Alexander, *Anyone's Daughter,* 211.

343 He was smoking at least two packs: Ibid., 170.

CHAPTER 25: THE SEARCH FOR OLD McMONKEY

352 "It's fun to be a superman": Alexander, *Anyone's Daughter,* 321.

353 Stockholm syndrome: The most extensive modern description of Stockholm syndrome can be found in Nicola Tufton and Elizabeth L. Sampson, " 'Stockholm Syndrome': Psychiatric Diagnosis or Urban Myth?," *Acta Psychiatrica Scandinavica,* Feb. 2008. For an account of the underlying bank robbery, see Daniel Lang, "A Reporter at Large: The Bank Drama," *The New Yorker,* Nov. 25, 1974, 56.

359 "The defense psychiatrists offered up": Perlstein, *Invisible Bridge,* 618.

CHAPTER 26: THE VERDICT

366 a green-enamel shamrock pin: Alexander, *Anyone's Daughter,* 447.

372 "I'll always remember": Jimenez and Berkman, *My Prisoner,* 190.

372 "What kind of drink": Ibid., 84.

375 Patricia thought she had: Hearst, *Every Secret Thing,* 414–17.

CHAPTER 27: "FAVORING THE RICH OVER THE POOR"

383 Later, she observed ruefully: Hearst, *Every Secret Thing,* 433–34.

AFTERMATH

395 Afterward, the show received: Hendry, *Soliah,* 227–29.

400 In 1987, Randy married Veronica: Vicky Ward, "The Mansion Trap," *Vanity Fair,* Nov. 2008.

401 "The form asks why": Nancy Faber, "Patty Hearst Has Found Sanctuary in Her Year-Old Marriage to Bernard Shaw," *People,* March 31, 1980.

SELECTED BIBLIOGRAPHY

Alexander, Shana. *Anyone's Daughter: The Times and Trials of Patty Hearst*. New York: Viking Press, 1979.

Anspacher, Carolyn, and Jack Lucey. *The Trial of Patty Hearst*. San Francisco: Great Fidelity Press, 1976.

Austin, Curtis J. *Up Against the Wall: Violence in the Making and Unmaking of the Black Panther Party*. Fayetteville: University of Arkansas Press, 2006.

Bailey, F. Lee. *For the Defense*. With John Greenya. New York: New American Library, 1976.

Baker, Marilyn. *Exclusive! The Inside Story of Patricia Hearst and the SLA*. With Sally Brompton. New York: Macmillan, 1974.

Belcher, Jerry, and Don West. *Patty/Tania*. New York: Pyramid Books, 1975.

Berger, Dan. *Captive Nation: Black Prison Organizing in the Civil Rights Era*. Chapel Hill: University of North Carolina Press, 2014.

———. *Outlaws of America: The Weather Underground and the Politics of Solidarity*. Oakland, Calif.: AK Press, 2006.

Boulton, David. *The Making of Tania Hearst*. New York: W. W. Norton, 1974.

Bryan, John. *This Soldier Still at War*. New York: Harcourt Brace Jovanovich, 1975.

Burrough, Bryan. *Days of Rage: America's Radical Underground, the FBI, and the Forgotten Age of Revolutionary Violence*. New York: Penguin Press, 2015.

Castiglia, Christopher. *Bound and Determined: Captivity, Culture-Crossing, and White Womanhood from Mary Rowlandson to Patty Hearst*. Chicago: University of Chicago Press, 1996.

Choi, Susan. *American Woman*. New York: Perennial, 2003.

Collier, Peter, and David Horowitz. *Destructive Generation: Second Thoughts About the '60s*. New York: Summit Books, 1989.

Coyote, Peter. *Sleeping Where I Fall: A Chronicle*. Berkeley, Calif.: Counterpoint, 1998.

Cumming, Gregory Garth. "The End of an Era: The Rise of the Symbionese Liberation Army and the Fall of the New Left." Ph.D. diss., University of California, Riverside, 2010. http://escholarship.org/uc/item/8tw2935x.

Cummins, Eric. *The Rise and Fall of California's Radical Prison Movement*. Stanford, Calif.: Stanford University Press, 1994.

Daugherty, Tracy. *The Last Love Song: A Biography of Joan Didion*. New York: St. Martin's Press, 2015.

Davis, Brian Joseph. *I, Tania*. Toronto: ECW Press, 2007.

Debray, Régis. *Revolution in the Revolution?* New York: Grove Press, 1967.

Dershowitz, Alan M. *The Best Defense*. New York: Vintage Books, 1983.

Didion, Joan. *After Henry*. New York: Vintage International, 1992.

Domanick, Joe. *To Protect and to Serve: The LAPD's Century of War in the City of Dreams*. New York: Pocket Books, 1995.

Durden-Smith, Jo. *Who Killed George Jackson?* New York: Alfred A. Knopf, 1976.

Echols, Alice. *Daring to Be Bad: Radical Feminism in America, 1967–1975*. Minneapolis: University of Minnesota Press, 1989.

Ellis, Richard J. *The Dark Side of the Left: Illegal Egalitarianism in America*. Lawrence: University Press of Kansas, 1998.

Franklin, H. Bruce. *Back Where You Came From: One Life in the Death of the Empire*. New York: Harper's Magazine Press, 1975.

Gates, Daryl F. *Chief: My Life in the LAPD*. With Diane K. Shah. New York: Bantam Books, 1992.

Gitlin, Todd. *The Sixties: Years of Hope, Days of Rage*. New York: Bantam Books, 1993.

———. *The Whole World Is Watching: Mass Media and the Unmaking of the New Left*. Berkeley: University of California Press, 2003.

Graebner, William. *Patty's Got a Gun: Patricia Hearst in 1970s America*. Chicago: University of Chicago Press, 2008.

Grobel, Lawrence. "The Playboy Interview: Patricia Hearst." *Playboy,* Aug. 1982, 69.

Hanel, Rachael. "Camilla Hall's Place in the Symbionese Liberation Army." Master's thesis, Minnesota State University, Mankato, 2004.

Hayden, Tom. *Reunion: A Memoir*. New York: Random House, 1988.

Hearst, Patricia Campbell. *Every Secret Thing*. With Alvin Moscow. New York: Doubleday, 1982.

Hendry, Sharon Darby. *Soliah: The Sara Jane Story*. Bloomington, Minn.: Cable, 2002.

Herman, Judith. *Trauma and Recovery*. New York: Basic Books, 1997.

Horowitz, David. *Radical Son: A Generational Odyssey*. New York: Touchstone, 1997.

Howard, Clark. *Zebra: The True Account of the 179 Days of Terror in San Francisco*. New York: Richard Marek, 1979.

Isenberg, Nancy. "Not Anyone's Daughter: Patty Hearst and the Postmodern Legal Subject." *American Quarterly* 52 (Dec. 2000): 639–81.

Jackson, George L. *Blood in My Eye*. Baltimore: Black Classic Press, 1990.

————. *Soledad Brother: The Prison Letters of George Jackson*. Chicago: Lawrence Hill Books, 1994.

Jacobs, Ron. *The Way the Wind Blew: A History of the Weather Underground*. New York: Verso, 1997.

Jenkins, Philip. *Decade of Nightmares: The End of the Sixties and the Making of Eighties America*. New York: Oxford University Press, 2006.

Jimenez, Janey, and Ted Berkman. *My Prisoner*. Kansas City, Kans.: Sheed Andrews and McMeel, 1977.

Joseph, Peniel E. *Waiting 'til the Midnight Hour: A Narrative History of Black Power in America*. New York: Henry Holt, 2006.

————, ed. *The Black Power Movement: Rethinking the Civil Rights–Black Power Era*. New York: Routledge, 2006.

Kilgore, James. *Understanding Mass Incarceration*. New York: New Press, 2015.

Kinney, Jean. *An American Journey: The Short Life of Willy Wolfe*. New York: Simon & Schuster, 1979.

Koerner, Brendan I. *The Skies Belong to Us: Love and Terror in the Golden Age of Hijacking*. New York: Broadway Books, 2013.

Kohn, Howard, and David Weir. "Tania's World: The Inside Story of the Patty Hearst Kidnapping, Part Two: People in Need." *Rolling Stone,* Oct. 23, 1975.

Lester, John A. *Girl in a Box: The Untold Story of the Patricia Hearst Kidnap*. San Jose, Calif.: Shoestring, 2004.

Lunde, Donald T. *Hearst to Hughes: Memoir of a Forensic Psychiatrist*. Bloomington, Ind.: AuthorHouse, 2007.

Lyne, Susan, and Robert Scheer. "The Story of the SLA: How and Why the Group Kidnapped Patty Hearst and Came to Be Urban Guerrillas." *New Times,* April 16, 1976, 26–36.

————. "Twenty Months with Patty/Tania." *New Times,* March 5, 1976, 18–36.

McLellan, Vin, and Paul Avery. *The Voices of Guns*. New York: G. P. Putnam's Sons, 1977.

Miller, James Andrew, and Tom Shales. *Those Guys Have All the Fun: Inside the World of ESPN*. Boston: Little, Brown, 2011.

Nasaw, David. *The Chief: The Life of William Randolph Hearst*. New York: Houghton Mifflin, 2000.

Pascal, John, and Francine Pascal. *The Strange Case of Patty Hearst*. New York: New American Library, 1974.

Payne, Les, Tim Findley, and Carolyn Craven. *The Life and Death of the SLA*. New York: Ballantine Books, 1976.

Pearsall, Richard Brainard, ed. *The Symbionese Liberation Army: Documents and Communications*. Amsterdam: Rodopi N.V., 1974.

Pearson, Hugh. *The Shadow of the Panther*. Cambridge, Mass.: Perseus Books, 1996.

Perlstein, Rick. *The Invisible Bridge: The Fall of Nixon and the Rise of Reagan*. New York: Simon & Schuster, 2014.

Rosenfeld, Seth. *Subversives: The FBI's War on Student Radicals, and Reagan's Rise to Power*. New York: Picador, 2013.

Sale, Kirkpatrick. *SDS*. New York: Random House, 1973.

Sanders, Prentice Earl, and Bennett Cohen. *The Zebra Murders: A Season of Killing, Racial Madness, and Civil Rights*. New York: Arcade, 2006.

Scott, Jack. *Bill Walton: On the Road with the Portland Trail Blazers*. New York: Crowell, 1976.

Soltysik, Fred. *In Search of a Sister*. New York: Bantam Books, 1976.

Sorrentino, Christopher. *Trance*. New York: Farrar, Straus and Giroux, 2005.

Spieler, Geri. *Taking Aim at the President: The Remarkable Story of the Woman Who Shot at Gerald Ford*. New York: Palgrave Macmillan, 2009.

Stone, Robert, producer and director. *Guerrilla: The Taking of Patty Hearst*. Magnolia Pictures, 2003.

Swanberg, W. A. *Citizen Hearst*. New York: Galahad Books, 1961.

The Symbionese Liberation Army in Los Angeles. A report published by the Los Angeles Board of Police Commissioners, July 19, 1974.

Talbot, David. *Season of the Witch*. New York: Free Press, 2012.

The Trial of Patty Hearst (transcript). San Francisco: Great Fidelity Press, 1976.

U.S. Congress, Committee on Internal Security. The Symbionese Liberation Army. 93rd Cong., 1974.

Van Deburg, William L. *New Day in Babylon: The Black Power Movement and American Culture, 1965–1975*. Chicago: University of Chicago Press, 1995.

Varon, Jeremy. *Bringing the War Home: The Weather Underground, the Red Army Faction, and Revolutionary Violence in the Sixties and Seventies*. Berkeley: University of California Press, 2004.

Walton, Bill. *Nothing but Net*. With Gene Wojciechowski. New York: Hyperion, 1994.

Weed, Steven. *My Search for Patty Hearst*. With Scott Swanton. New York: Warner Books, 1976.

Weiner, Tim. *Enemies: A History of the FBI*. New York: Random House, 2013.

Wilson, Major Carlos. *The Tupamaros: The Unmentionables*. Boston: Braden Press, 1974.

PHOTO CREDITS

Grateful acknowledgment is given to the following for permission to reprint the photos in this book:

Insert 1

Page 1: Corbis

Page 2, bottom: Corbis

Page 3, top: Corbis

Page 3, bottom: Associated Press

Page 4, top: Corbis

Page 4, bottom: Corbis

Page 5: Polaris

Page 6, top: Polaris

Page 6, bottom: Getty

Page 7, top: Peter Breinig/*San Francisco Chronicle*/Polaris

Page 7, bottom: Los Angeles Times Photographic Archive, Library Special Collections, Charles E. Young Research Library, UCLA

Page 8, top: Associated Press

Page 8, middle: Corbis

Page 8, bottom: Art Rogers/*Los Angeles Times*/Polaris

Insert 2

Page 1, bottom: Associated Press

Page 2, top: Getty

Page 2, middle: Associated Press

Page 2, bottom: Corbis

Page 3, top right: Corbis

Page 3, bottom: Corbis

Page 5, middle: Getty

Page 5, bottom: Getty

Page 7: Associated Press

Page 8: Associated Press

Page 8, inset: Associated Press

INDEX